Social Media Security

Leveraging Social Networking While Mitigating Risk

Social Media Security
Leveraging Social Networking
While Mitigating Risk

Michael Cross

Technical Editor
Rob Shimonski

AMSTERDAM • BOSTON • HEIDELBERG • LONDON
NEW YORK • OXFORD • PARIS • SAN DIEGO
SAN FRANCISCO • SINGAPORE • SYDNEY • TOKYO
Syngress is an imprint of Elsevier

SYNGRESS

Acquiring Editor: *Chris Katsaropoulos*
Editorial Project Manager: *Benjamin Rearick*
Project Manager: *Malathi Samayan*
Designer: *Matthew Limbert*

Syngress is an imprint of Elsevier
225 Wyman Street, Waltham, MA 02451, USA

Notices
Knowledge and best practice in this field are constantly changing. As new research and experience broaden our understanding, changes in research methods or professional practices, may become necessary. Practitioners and researchers must always rely on their own experience and knowledge in evaluating and using any information or methods described here in. In using such information or methods they should be mindful of their own safety and the safety of others, including parties for whom they have a professional responsibility.

To the fullest extent of the law, neither the Publisher nor the authors, contributors, or editors, assume any liability for any injury and/or damage to persons or property as a matter of products liability, negligence or otherwise, or from any use or operation of any methods, products, instructions, or ideas contained in the material herein.

Library of Congress Cataloging-in-Publication Data
Cross, Michael, 1965-
 Social media security: leveraging social networking while mitigating risk / Michael Cross.
   pages cm
 Includes bibliographical references and index.
 ISBN 978-1-59749-986-6 (pbk.)
 1. Social media--Security measures. 2. Online social networks--Security measures.
3. Risk management--Social aspects. 4. Computer security. I. Title.
 HM742.C77 2013
 005.8--dc23

                                                                                    2013036147

British Library Cataloguing-in-Publication Data
A catalogue record for this book is available from the British Library

For information on all Syngress publications,
visit our website at store.elsevier.com/Syngress

ISBN: 978-1-59749-986-6

Printed and bound in the United States of America
14 15 16   13 12 11 10 9 8 7 6 5 4 3 2 1

Contents

Acknowledgements xiii
About the Author..xv
About the Technical Editor xvii

CHAPTER 1 What is Social Media?..1
What is social media? 1
Understanding social media..1
Different types and classifications 2
    Collaboration 3
    Blogs 4
    Content communities 5
    Social networking sites 6
    Virtual worlds 7
    Sites that fall under multiple classifications 8
The value of social media 8
    Value can be found in the potential...11
    Mobile social media...11
Cutting edge versus bleeding edge 13
    Dealing with the "is it a fad?" question 13
    Brief history of social networking 14
The problems that come with social media 16
Is security really an issue? 17
Taking the good with the bad...18
Bibliography 19

CHAPTER 2 Opportunities of Social Media.......................................21
Opportunities of social media..21
New methods of marketing to customers 22
    Branding 24
Building social authority...26
Engaging customers..27
    FOMO 29
Sharing information 30
    Knowing what NOT to say 32
Getting the word out 34
    COBRAs...35
    eWOM 36
    Hashtags..38
    Missing the mark ... mistakes in responding to people............39

Taking advantage of collective intelligence 41

Bibliography 42

CHAPTER 3   **Employment and Social Media** **45**

Employment and social media 45

Using social media to find employees 45

Candidate screening 47

     Asking for a prospective or current employee's password 48

     Legal issues 50

Using social media to find employment 51

     Getting referrals 52

     Branding yourself 53

     LinkedIn 55

Limiting personal information 59

     Adding too much additional information 59

     Public profiles 61

     Passwords 63

     Securing other settings on LinkedIn 65

Employees using social media 66

Allowing social media in the workplace 68

Bibliography 69

CHAPTER 4   **Considerations for setting up Social Media** **71**

Considerations for setting up social media 71

Why are we doing this? 72

     Requirements gathering 72

What is the place of social media in your organization? 73

     Is it really needed? 74

     How will it be used? 75

     How will it not be used? 77

Identifying your audience 78

     Younger audiences 79

Internet versus intranet 80

What's being said about your brand? 82

     Monitoring conversations 83

Making the right decisions early 85

     Setting corporate goals 86

     Getting the right people together 86

     Remembering technology in the equation 87

Identifying how you'll represent yourself on the Internet 91

Approved representatives 92

     Preexisting accounts 92

Privacy 92

    Some privacy concerns in using social media 93

Training and policy 94

Bibliography 95

CHAPTER 5   **Being Bold Versus being Overlooked** **97**

Being bold versus being overlooked.. 97

Good social media campaigns 98

Bad social media campaigns... 99

Sometimes it's better to be overlooked...................................... 100

Social media hoaxes.. 104

The human factor.. 106

    The oops factor 106

    Acronyms and abbreviations in messaging............................ 107

    Netiquette.. 108

    Don't feed the trolls 109

Content management 110

    Stale and outdated content 111

    Linking content across different sites 113

    Censorship 118

Promotion of social media... 121

    Contests... 122

    Directories... 122

    Not everyone is on the internet 122

Bibliography 123

CHAPTER 6   **Risks of Social Media**....................................**127**

Risks of social media... 127

    Sources of risk 127

Public embarrassment.. 128

    The content you post can and will be held against you 129

    Removing videos from YouTube 131

    Removing photos and tags that others post on Facebook....... 132

    Removing posts on Facebook 132

    Reporting abuse 133

Once it's out there, it's out there... 134

False information 135

    Misrepresenting yourself 137

    Misrepresenting your business.. 137

    False information isn't necessarily bad 138

Information leakage 139

    Be clear about what's private... 139

Providing too much information...140

WikiLeaks...140

Corporate espionage 142

Retention and archiving content 143

eDiscovery 143

Backing up social media..144

Archive Facebook 145

Archive Twitter 146

Multisite third-party tools 147

Other tools for individual sites..147

Loss of data/equipment...148

Selling and recycling equipment..149

Lost or stolen phone/tablet...150

Backup and restore 152

Personal data or equipment...156

Bibliography 158

CHAPTER 7   The Dark Side..**161**

The dark side of social media 161

Cybercrime 161

Scams...162

Cyberstalking..164

Cyberbullying...166

Cybersex and other intimate issues...167

Predators 175

Social engineering 177

Dumpster diving 180

Phishing 180

Fake sites...181

Hacked accounts 186

An example of how hacking works 187

Protecting yourself...188

Defaced sites...188

Keeping track of who's logged on 189

Trusted contacts 190

Bibliography 191

CHAPTER 8   Risk Management..**193**

Risk management..193

Assessing risks..193

Sources of risk revisited...195

Laws and regulations 196
  Privacy policies and terms of service.............................. 197
  Sarbanes–Oxley Act.. 197
  Health Insurance Portability and Accountability Act 198
  Fair information practice principles.................................... 198
  Payment card industry data security standard....................... 199
  Digital Millenium Copyright Act.. 199
  Intellectual property and trademark infringement 200
  Discrimination 201
  Defamation 202
  Harassment 202
Insurance... 203
Forensics 203
  Digital forensic software.. 204
  Don't delete messages 205
  Acquiring information from social media sites 206
Police use of social media.. 207
  Incriminating yourself 207
  Defending yourself online 208
  Outdated content... 208
  Direct use of social media to solve crimes 209
Malware, viruses, and explcit distribution............................ 210
  Scareware/ransomware 211
  Baiting... 212
  Browser hijacking 212
  Protecting yourself from backdoors and exploits 213
  Protecting yourself from viruses and malware 214
Bibliography 216

CHAPTER 9   Policies and Privacy 217
Policies... 217
  Pros and cons 217
  Creating a policy.. 218
  Enforcing policies... 220
  Getting people to read it 221
  Policies affected by social media.. 222
  How not to report a violation... 227
Privacy 228
  Your own worst enemy 229
  What friends say about you 230
  Using Facebook lists... 230

Restricting who can see your Facebook posts 232
Restricting who can see your friends and who you follow 234
Protecting your tweets 235
Checking the risk of a site 235
Blocking users 238
Blocking users on Facebook 238
Blocking users on Twitter 240
Blocking users on YouTube 241
Blacklisting users on WordPress 241
Controlling app privacy 242
Managing apps on Facebook 242
Checking the privacy of apps before you install 244
Removing apps 244
Blocking apps in Facebook 245
Location awareness 246
Being aware of your location and situation 246
Location-based social networks 247
Removing location information from Facebook 248
Removing location information from Twitter 248
Hiding events 249
Privacy of photos 249
Bibliography 251

CHAPTER 10 Security **253**
Security 253
Keeping track of accounts 254
Security reviews 254
Security strategies 255
Fake accounts 257
Brandjacking 258
Defensive profiles to prevent impersonation 259
Reporting fake accounts on Facebook 261
Reporting inappropriate profiles on LinkedIn 262
Passwords 262
Bad passwords 263
Good passwords 264
Hacking 101 266
Verification for password resets 267
Protecting your account with two-step verification 267
Privacy and information sharing 268
Locking down personal information 269
Doxxing 273
The Human Flesh Search Engine 275

Facebook graph search.... 276
Controlling exposure to search in Facebook...........................277
Content security 277
Preapproving or turning cff comments................................278
Stop people from posting on your timeline 279
Hiding sections of a timeline 281
Seeing through the eyes cf others 281
Bibliography 282

CHAPTER 11 Where do We go from Here? **285**
Where do we go from here?...285
The pitch, the promise, and the reality 285
Who's in charge here?...287
Accountability...288
Governance 289
Clear and understandable roles 291
Crisis management...293
Continuity planning 295
Monitor social media 295
Reading is fundamental 295
Notifications..296
Keeping track of "likes" 298
Keeping track of dislikes 299
Monitoring hashtags 299
TweetDeck 300
Using tools on blog sites...300
Facebook Insights 301
Google Analytics 301
Monitoring multiple social media sites................................302
Keeping it fresh.._.............................303
Deciding what's working and lessons learned......................306
Creating Facebook pages 306
Dialing it back and retaking control 310
Reviewing social media 311
Getting rid of accounts, pages, and sites..............................311
Friends versus followers 314
Removing friends and who you're following 315
Additional administrators 315
Ongoing training.............. 317
Bibliography 317

Index 319

Acknowledgements

This book is gratefully dedicated to my wife and children, who were unbelievably supportive and helpful in making this possible. As I completed the chapters, my wife read them and provided the perspective of a reader who wants to know how to use social media effectively and securely. At the time this book comes out, my wife Jennifer and I will have been together 20 years. I love her as much today as when we first got together, and anyone who knows her can understand why.

We have three children that are full of ideas and dreams, and have no reservations in sharing them. Throughout this book, each of them showed their interests and individuality, and contributed their own suggestions. Sara at age 10 showed her compassion for others, offered insights into the concerns children have about cyberbullying and online harassment, and took interest reading the sections on those topics. Jason at age 8 showed his love of technology and how things work, but still managed to surprise me when he offered suggestions about adding information on hacking. Emily at age 7 shared her independence and thoughts on protecting others, proposing I add information on blocking users and sites. Rather than being upset about how little they saw me as I worked on the book, they found their own ways to become a part of it.

About the Author

Michael Cross is a SharePoint Administrator and Developer, and has worked in the areas of software development, Web design, hardware installation/repairs, database administration, graphic design, and network administration. Working for law enforcement, he is part of an Information Technology team that provides support to over 1000 civilian and uniformed users. His theory is that when the users carry guns, you tend to be more motivated in solving their problems.

Michael has a diverse background in technology. He was the first computer forensic analyst for a local police service, and performed digital forensic examinations on computers involved in criminal investigations. Over five years, he recovered and examined evidence involved in a wide range of crimes, inclusive to homicides, fraud, and possession of child pornography. In addition to this, he successfully tracked numerous individuals electronically, as in cases involving threatening email. He has consulted and assisted in numerous cases dealing with computer-related/Internet crimes and served as an expert witness on computers for criminal trials. In 2007, he was awarded a Police Commendation for the work he did in developing a system to track local high-risk offenders and sexual offenders.

With extensive experience in Web design and Internet-related technologies, Michael has created and maintained numerous Web sites and implementations of Microsoft SharePoint. This has included public Web sites, private ones on corporate intranets, and solutions that integrate them. In doing so, he has incorporated and promoted social networking features, created software to publish press releases online, and developed a wide variety of solutions that make it easier to get work done.

Michael has been a freelance writer and technical editor on over four dozen IT-related books, as well as writing material for other genres. He previously taught as an instructor and has written courseware for IT training courses. He has also made presentations on Internet safety, SharePoint, and other topics related to computers and the Internet. Despite his experience as a speaker, he still finds his wife won't listen to him.

Over the years, Michael has acquired a number of certifications from Microsoft, Novell, and CompTIA, including MCSE, MCP + I, CNA, and Network +. When he isn't writing or otherwise attached to a computer, he spends as much time as possible with the joys of his life: his lovely wife Jennifer, darling daughter Sara, adorable daughter Emily, and charming son Jason.

For the latest information on him, his projects, and a variety of other topics, you can follow him on Twitter @mybinarydreams, visit his Facebook page at www.facebook.com/mybinarydreams, follow him on LinkedIn at www.linkedin.com/in/mcross1, or read his blog at http://mybinarydreams.wordpress.com.

About the Technical Editor

Rob Shimonski (www.shimonski.com) is a security expert specializing in penetration testing, ethical hacking, and security engineering and design. Having been involved in Social Media since its inception, Rob has deep knowledge on its use, benefits, and flaws. He has over 20 years experience working with security and technology.

Rob is also a best-selling author and editor with over 15 years experience developing, producing, and distributing print media in the form of books, magazines, and periodicals. To date, Rob has successfully created over 100 books that are currently in circulation. Rob has worked for countless companies including CompTIA, Entrepreneur Magazine, Microsoft, McGraw Hill Education, Cisco, the National Security Agency, and Digidesign.

What is Social Media?

INFORMATION IN THIS CHAPTER:

- What is Social Media?
- Understanding Social Media
- Different Types and Classifications
- The Value of Social Media
- Cutting Edge Versus Bleeding Edge
- The Problems That Come With Social Media
- Is Security Really an Issue?
- Taking the Good With the Bad

What is social media?

Technology has become less about connecting computers and more about connecting people. A major reason for this evolution is that the use of social media has exploded in the last few years, making it easier for individuals and businesses to contact others and get their messages across to large audiences. According to a July 2012 study by the McKinsey Global Institute, there are 1.5 billion people using social networking throughout the world, with 80% of them interacting regularly with other social media users. Its popularity and the drive to reach to customers has led to 70% of companies using social media. Social technology has become a way of life in how we socialize and do business.

However, while social media is a powerful tool for interacting with others, many people and organizations have jumped into using it without considering the risks. The threats you face can affect your safety, job, and business. In this book, we'll show you how to deal with the potential dangers, but before that, let's start by understanding what social media is and how it's evolved.

Understanding social media

When you think of social media, you probably think of sites like Facebook, Twitter, and LinkedIn. After all, it's common to go to a company's site and see graphic links that take you to the company's presence on these other sites. In making this connection, you're not wrong. The same way that you associate traditional media with newspapers, TV stations, and other methods of publishing professional content, you can understand social media by looking at how information is being communicated. Social media is defined by how it's used and the technology that supports its features.

Social media takes traditional forms of media to a whole new level. It is different from a news article or billboard that has information professionally created, polished, vetted through people who check and sign off on the content, and sent out as a one-way message to an audience. With social media, the information is generated by a user or brand, generally isn't intensely scrutinized before being sent out, and transmitted in a way that allows two-way communication with people. Also, while it is often costly to get a message out using traditional media, using social media is relatively inexpensive or free.

One of the major features of social media is of course its social aspect. Traditional media tells a person what the message is and doesn't interact with the consumer. Features of social media provide the ability for users to comment on what's being said. If a columnist posts an article on a blog, a person can respond to it immediately by adding his or her own remarks. The columnist could then reply to these comments, creating a conversation. Rather than telling people what they should think, social media changes the information into an informal exchange of views. Even better, anyone can join in on sites that are accessible to others with no real technical experience. The readers can even go and create their own blogs, allowing them to write about any topic they want or share a free flow of ideas. Unlike traditional mediums, boundaries are broken down; the reader can become the writer any time he or she wants.

By looking at these functions and features, we can see that social media is a term that describes various technologies being used to engage people in collaboration, the exchange of information, and interactivity with Web-based content. Because the Internet is always evolving, the technologies and features available to users are always changing. This makes social media more of a hypernym (or blanket term) than a specific reference to any particular use or design.

Different types and classifications

As soon as you begin looking at social media, you quickly realize there are significant differences in the purpose and functionality of different sites. Twitter may be great for sending out short messages to an audience but useless for cooperating with others on writing a long article. Similarly, if you were posting a video instead of text, you would probably use a site like YouTube. Because there are hundreds of social media sites and applications, it is important to differentiate between them. By narrowing them down into specific groups, it's easier to understand the types of social media available to you and which you should use for a specific purpose.

In a 2010 article published in Business Horizons, Andreas Kaplan and Michael Haenlein created a classification scheme for different types of social media. Through the use of existing theories in the fields of media research and social processes, they identified six categories:

1. Collaborative projects
2. Blogs
3. Content communities
4. Social networking sites
5. Virtual game worlds
6. Virtual social worlds

Collaboration

Collaboration sites allow multiple users to generate content and contribute to a final product, making the content produce a community or group effort. The most popular example of this would be *wiki's*, which are Web sites that allow individual users to add and edit content. On a wiki, I write something, you add to it, and perhaps someone else edits what we wrote. Because peers with different experience and knowledge are reviewing the content, inaccuracies are eventually discovered and corrected. By everyone working together, the content builds.

The term "wiki" comes from the Hawaiian word for "fast," which was used by Ward Cunningham in naming the first such site in 1995 called WikiWikiWeb (http://c2.com/cgi/wiki?FrontPage). Undeniably, the most popular wiki today would be Wikipedia (www.wikipedia.org), which has been edited over 1 billion times and has (at the time of this writing) over 4,179,670 articles. As you can see by this, the amount of information produced can be significant when people jointly create and work together.

In organizations, wikis and other collaboration tools can be extremely useful for communicating information and allowing members of a team to contribute to what's being said. As with many types of social media, collaboration sites can be either on the Internet where they are accessible to the public or select groups of people, or on a company's intranet where it is only accessible to those with secure network access. Organizations like Disney, Cingular Wireless, British Telecommunications, and CERN (the European Organization for Nuclear Research) have all used wikis for projects with great success. Users of the wiki require little to no assistance from the IT department, decreasing the need for administrative effort. Added to this, collaboration sites can serve as a repository of information on a project, centralizing information that was previously scattered in documents, presentations, and other files across the corporate network.

The *collaboration project* classification also includes social bookmarking sites, such as reddit (www.reddit.com) and Delicious (www.delicious.com). A *bookmark* is a shortcut to a location on the Internet. As seen in Figure 1.1, these sites are used to post links to content on other sites, such as Web pages, videos, and images, and associate keywords called *tags* that are used to categorize each link and make them easier to find. Other people search the site, view these links, and can add them to their own bookmarks with additional tags. Sites like reddit will even allow you to

FIGURE 1.1

Delicious is a social bookmarking site.

vote on them as part of a rating system. Similar to Facebook, users can request to be added as a friend, thereby creating a network of people with similar interests. Not only is this useful for organizing your favorite links to content on the Internet, but it allows you to view what others have shared as their favorite bookmarked pages.

Blogs

Blogs allow a person or group to post content on a Web page as a series of submissions. What a person writes about on a blog is only limited by their imagination, but it works similar to a diary or log. Each entry is stamped with the date and time and is displayed in reverse chronological order. They are used for such purposes as personal diaries, to express commentaries and to communicate information as a series of entries. Blogs may also allow others to comment on the author's initial entries, allowing interaction with the writer.

Originally called a "weblog," the term was shortened when Peter Merholz posted on www.peterme.com "For What It's Worth … I've decided to pronounce the word "weblog" as wee'-blog. Or "blog" for short." As the shortened name gained popularity, this led to people writing blogs to be called *bloggers*.

While blogs are Web pages, a variant is a microblog, which allows people to post short messages that can be read by others. The most popular example of this is Twitter (https://twitter.com), which allows users to send and read text messages (called "tweets") that are up to 140 characters in length.

While blogs and microblogs are traditionally text, most sites will also allow you to post other types of content such as links, images, music, and video. In addition to this, video blogging has become a popular method of exchanging information, in which a person records themselves and posts the video content on the blog as the message.

Blogging and microblogging can be extremely useful in companies. Blogs can be used as part of a communication strategy on intranet and public sites, sharing information that the company wants people to know about. An example of this is when

Netflix US ✓
@netflix

We're sorry for the Christmas Eve outage.
Terrible timing! Engineers are working on it
now. Stay tuned to @Netflixhelps for
updates.

← Reply   ⇄ Retweet   ★ Favorite   ••• More

2,526   **210**
RETWEETS   FAVORITES

8:25 PM - 24 Dec 12

FIGURE 1.2

Netflix tweet about service outage.

Netflix experienced problems with streaming content on Christmas Eve 2012 due to an issue with Amazon Web Services. Netflix immediately responded to the issue on their technical blog and Twitter, providing status updates to customers (Figure 1.2). Not only was the technology used to keep in touch with customers but also using it in this way can decrease the number of upset customers calling their support number. After all, why would you need to call if they're sharing information online?

Content communities

Content communities are sites that allow users to share multimedia content. These communities include sites like YouTube (www.youtube.com), Daily Motion (www.dailymotion.com), Imagr (http://imgur.com), Tumblr (www.tumblr.com), and FlickR (www.flickr.com). People will upload images, video, music, or other content and provide a description, which other users can then search for and view. A common feature of these sites allows for comments to be added to a page displaying the content and to share links to the multimedia on other social media sites like Twitter and Facebook.

Businesses can benefit from content communities by sharing multimedia that promotes their products or brand, or to exchange information with customers or interested parties. For example, let's say you worked for a hospital and had a great PowerPoint presentation on preventing diseases. By uploading the slides to a site like Slideshow (www.slideshow.net), you can use the site as a repository for your information, which people can then view when searching for this topic or through links on other sites. The same can be done by setting up a channel on YouTube to host videos that your company produces, such as new commercials or video of a corporate event.

Podcasts are audio or video that are streamed, and often episodes or series that share a common theme. The term comes from the words iPod (an Apple device on which podcasts are often viewed on) and broadcast. People may create podcasts to disseminate information as when an instructor might want to share a series of lectures, advertising, recorded interviews, and even as a form of video blogging. Sites like iTunes (www.apple.com/itunes/podcasts/) allow you to search through thousands of podcasts and subscribe to them, while other sites like filmmaker Kevin Smith's Smodcast (www.smodcast.com) are specific to weekly episodes related to his projects, interests, and interviews with other people.

In addition to the communication benefits of content communities, organizations can find it useful and profitable in having online content stored on these sites. Content communities can be used as centralized storage for multimedia being used by your Web site and social media sites. Video files, presentations, and other multimedia take up space on a server's hard drive. As Internet Service Providers (ISPs) hosting a Web site will charge for additional space, keeping multimedia on such sites can lower the costs of having an online presence. However, in doing this, you should remember that you don't want to use this as the only storage location for your media, as you should always keep a copy of these files on a network server that's regularly backed up. After all, if your social media content were ever deleted, corrupted, or vandalized, you would want to upload another copy to the site as soon as possible.

In using content communities, it's always important to review the sites Terms of Service and identify who ultimately owns the content you upload. Some sites may state that by uploading the content to your site, you give up any rights you had to it. In doing so, the content may now be owned by the site to use as they wish, or considered *public domain*, where the content is no longer subject to copyright and available for public use.

Social networking sites

Social networking sites enable people to connect or network with one another through the use of profile pages. As seen in Figure 1.3, profile pages allow you to provide a summary of yourself or business, photos, contact information, interests, or other facts that define who you are. On these pages, you may post additional content such as video, audio files, or links to other content. Using this information, others with similar interests can search for you or your business' page, request to add you as a "friend" or contact, and/or follow posts on your page.

There are a number of different social networking sites on the Internet. The most popular social networking site is Facebook (www.facebook.com), which boasts 1.06 billion active users monthly, but it is by far not the only one. There are other general social networking sites like Google+ (http://plus.google.com) and Myspace (www.myspace.com), as well as those focusing on more specific audiences like LinkedIn (www.linkedin.com) for businesses and professionals and Classmates.com (www.classmates.com) for people wanting to reconnect with school, work, and military friends.

Businesses can benefit from social networking in a number of ways. By having a presence on sites like Facebook, you have the potential to reach a large number of people. This allows you to promote your brand and share information with those who follow your posts. In addition to this, social networking sites that are more audience

FIGURE 1.3

Facebook profile page.

or topic specific can assist with business needs. For example, a site like LinkedIn can provide an alternate method of finding employees or finding a new employer.

Virtual worlds

A more media-rich form of social media are virtual worlds. In these worlds, a user can interact with others using an avatar, which is an animated character that he or she controls. In a *virtual game world*, a person performs specific missions, quests, or tasks but can also communicate and work with others to achieve goals. *Virtual social worlds* are somewhat different from the games, as they are more social in the purpose of allowing a person to connect with others through their avatars as if it were the real world.

Virtual game worlds that allow large numbers of people to interact with one another are referred to as Massively Multiplayer Online Role Playing Games. The most popular of these include World of Warcraft and Everquest. In these games, a person takes on the role of a character that they create and can do such things as fight, complete quests, or explore and interact with others.

While online game worlds have typically been accessed through a computer connected to the Internet, home video game systems like Playstation 3 and X-box have games that allow players to connect with one another through a network. If the system is connected to the Internet, a game may allow the player to talk or text with others, allowing multiple people to act together as a team. For example, a combat game might allow you to be part of a military unit with other players, whom you can speak with as you're playing.

Social worlds also allow people to play in a virtual environment but are designed with social aspects as a primary focus. The most popular example of this is Second Life (www.secondlife.com). In a 3D environment, you use an avatar to function in a way similar to real life or perhaps how they wish your life was. After creating your character, you can meet and talk to others, attend events, and purchase items or services with virtual money.

For organizations, virtual worlds can be beneficial for marketing to large groups. As the environment mimics a landscape, such as the real world or a specific setting, a business could advertise in it through product placement. An avatar could have the opportunity to drive a new car your company is promoting, or your business could have a billboard advertising your services on the side of a building. Even though it isn't in the real world, it is still reaching real potential customers. An example of how virtual money can translate to the real thing is "Relay for Life of Second Life," in which proceeds raised go to the American Cancer Society. Fund-raising and events in Second Life raised $375,000 in 2012 and over $1.5 million to date.

Sites that fall under multiple classifications

While the categories we've discussed do well to separate different types of social media into recognizable groups, you'll often find that a social media site or an application doesn't easily fall into a single category. Many sites offer numerous features to users making a single classification difficult or impossible.

If you were to look at Twitter, the main function they're known for is microblogging, where you create short messages for others to read. However, they also allow you to create profile pages, on which you can add a summary of yourself and photos. By looking at the profiles of others, you can then choose to follow what they have to say and they can follow you. These features also make it a social networking site. Even more difficult to classify are platforms like Microsoft SharePoint that provide a wide variety of features, allowing for collaboration, social networking, and the ability to store images, video, and other files in libraries. As you can see by this, the versatility of social media sites and applications can make them challenging to categorize.

However, classifying social media into groups doesn't consist of hard and fast rules that pigeonhole a site or an application into a single group. This applies to any kind of classification. For example, you could be classified by race, gender, age group, and other factors. The categories help to understand the features and qualities of what's being discussed.

The value of social media

Throughout this chapter, we've discussed some of the benefits that different types of social media can bring to you personally and as an organization. However, the value you find in using social media is dependent on how it's used. The choices you make will effect whether you find social media beneficial or detrimental to your personal or corporate presence.

While it's common for people and businesses to use social media, they aren't necessarily using it the same way. There are many different sites to choose from, with the most popular ones embraced by small and large companies alike. As shown in Figure 1.4, a 2013 study of Fortune 500 companies by University of Massachusetts Dartmouth found increased usage of social media by big business. The study found that 73% of the 2012 Fortune 500 primary companies have corporate Twitter accounts, 66% (332) have corporate Facebook pages, and 62% (309) are using YouTube. The adoption of social media by large companies has surged over the years and become a common feature of major corporations.

What's surprising about business usage of social media is that large and small companies don't necessarily find the same sites useful. While larger companies have found Twitter and Facebook to be the sites that are most useful to their organization, smaller businesses may not find the same results. In 2013, a survey by the Wall Street Journal and Vistage International found that 30% of small business owners used LinkedIn regularly and 41% said it had the most potential for helping their business. As shown in Figure 1.5, the other sites were used less and seen as less beneficial.

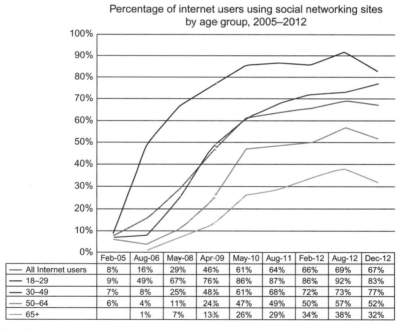

Percentage of internet users using social networking sites by age group, 2005–2012

	Feb-05	Aug-06	May-08	Apr-09	May-10	Aug-11	Feb-12	Aug-12	Dec-12
All Internet users	8%	16%	29%	46%	61%	64%	66%	69%	67%
18–29	9%	49%	67%	76%	86%	87%	86%	92%	83%
30–49	7%	8%	25%	48%	61%	68%	72%	73%	77%
50–64	6%	4%	11%	24%	47%	49%	50%	57%	52%
65+		1%	7%	13%	26%	29%	34%	38%	32%

FIGURE 1.4

Fortune 500 Business use of social media sites.

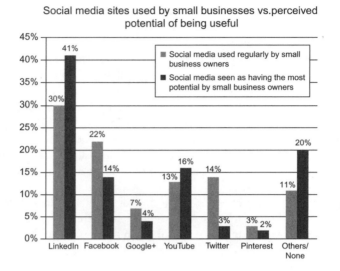

Social media sites used by small businesses vs. perceived potential of being useful

FIGURE 1.5

Social media sites used by small businesses versus their perceived potential of being useful.

A reason why small businesses don't get as much out of using these sites is that they don't have the resources that larger corporations have. A larger company will hire knowledgeable people who can use social media to their advantage and budget money and time to these sites as they would other aspects of their business like advertising or customer service. The survey found that only 4 out of 10 smaller businesses had an employee that was dedicated to handling the company's social media, with almost half spending only 1–5 hours a week on it and one-third spending no time at all.

If you're worried about foraying into social media or already done so and not getting the most out of it, you're not alone. Harvard Business Review Analytics Services reported that while 79% of the 2100 businesses surveyed were using or planning to use social media, only 12% felt they were effective at it. This small group of successful companies established a presence on multiple social media channels where they learned about their customers, established user groups, researched and educated people about new products, and followed best practices to meet their goals. As we'll see throughout this book, being successful in social media involves having a strategy that includes planning, creating policies and guidelines, training, implementation, and monitoring.

In going by these statistics, if you're part of the majority who feel they aren't getting all that they hoped from social media, don't worry. This doesn't mean you should give up and throw the baby out with the bathwater. Tossing away the good with the bad is never a sound decision, and you'd be better off trying to determine what's working and what isn't. In doing so, you can roll things back and focus on creating a new strategy that incorporates best practices.

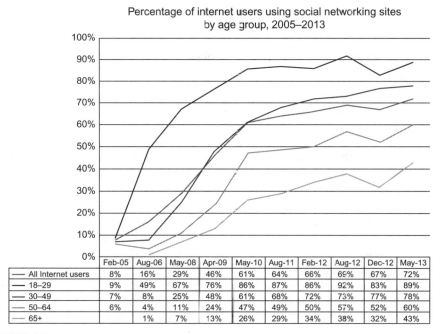

	Feb-05	Aug-06	May-08	Apr-09	May-10	Aug-11	Feb-12	Aug-12	Dec-12	May-13
—— All Internet users	8%	16%	29%	46%	61%	64%	66%	69%	67%	72%
—— 18–29	9%	49%	67%	76%	86%	87%	86%	92%	83%	89%
—— 30–49	7%	8%	25%	48%	61%	68%	72%	73%	77%	78%
—— 50–64	6%	4%	11%	24%	47%	49%	50%	57%	52%	60%
—— 65+		1%	7%	13%	26%	29%	34%	38%	32%	43%

FIGURE 1.6

Percentage of Internet users who use social networking, by age group.

Value can be found in the potential

While a primary feature of social media is the user-centric ability to publish your own content, the goal is community orientated in having people pay attention to what you have to say. Is there a potential audience? The answer is most definitely yes. Social media has the potential to reach a large segment of the online population and members of every age group. According to Pew Internet & American Life Project, 72% of adults on the Internet use social networking sites. As seen in Figure 1.6, the number of people using these sites has dramatically increased since 2005 across all age demographics.

Once you've tapped into the customers available on the Internet, statistics have shown that social media can result in tangible results. In a survey conducted for the 2012 Social Media Marketing Industry Report, 58% of marketers using social media for over 3 years reported increased sales. Other benefits include increased exposure for a brand, new business partnerships, new customers, and reduced marketing expenses.

Mobile social media

In developing social media strategies, it's important to recognize how social media will be accessed. Mobile phones, tablets, and other devices are commonly used to connect to social media channels. According to Pew Internet & American Life

Project, 40% of people with mobile phones access social networking sites on their phones and 28% do so everyday. Furthermore, Cisco reports that people are using mobile devices at a continually increased rate. In 2012, data traffic from mobile devices increased 70%, and average Smartphone usage increased 81%. They predict that by the end of 2013, there will be more mobile-connected devices than there will be people on Earth, and that this number will increase to over 10 billion devices by 2017. These staggering numbers show that mobile devices are an important part of how you incorporate social media into a business.

Many social media sites offer mobile apps, which users can download from an App Store or Web site. Once the application is installed on your mobile device, you have a quick and easy interface to using features of the site. For example, the Facebook app allows you to do such things as view profile page and update your status and information, while the Twitter app enables you to tweet from a mobile device. Content from the sites is displayed on the device in a format specifically for mobile users, making it easier to use.

Being aware of how mobile devices are used can help in creating a social media campaign that boosts sales and raises awareness of your brand. There are apps available for mobile devices that will help customers to search for products and businesses, such as finding a type of restaurant within your area. Mobile tagging can be used so that the device can read a two-dimensional barcode through a camera on the phone that takes the person to a Web site that displays additional information about a product or service. These tags can also display digital coupons that are instantly redeemed in the store. According to eMarketer, although most promotions are in print publications, an estimated 92.5 million Americans redeemed a digital coupon in 2012. They also predict that by 2014, 100 million people will use digital coupons. Beyond this, simple tweets or updates promoting sales or events can reach a consumer while they're on the road or possibly in your store. When considering this, the benefits of including mobile users in social media campaigns become clear.

Unfortunately, mobile users can also be a source of problems for organizations. Usage of mobile devices within an organization should always be a security concern. Even if your company has blocked all social media sites through a firewall, this only means that an employee can't access social media through a networked computer or other device. It doesn't stop a person from visiting Facebook, Twitter, or other sites through his or her personal mobile phone or tablet. This means that there is the inherent security risk that they could leak information, upload data, or breach security in some other way by using the mobile device at work. While sitting in front of their computer, a disgruntled employee or someone involved in corporate espionage could take a picture of sensitive information displayed on their monitor and then upload it to a content community. A more innocuous breach of security would be a person getting excited over a new product or direction the company was taking and tweeting about it or posting information on a social networking site. While later chapters will discuss these issues in greater detail, policies and training are important methods of deterring and detecting such problems.

Cutting edge versus bleeding edge

The attitude of decision makers can have a significant impact on how an organization uses technology and addresses security. On one extreme, social media may be treated as a cutting edge approach to publishing information and communicating with people. In such a case, they may dive into using it without forethought or proper risk assessment. On the other end of the spectrum, it may be treated as bleeding edge technology that is largely untried, untested, and/or poses a substantial threat. When an organization views social media as this, they may decide to completely block users from accessing social media sites and vehemently oppose using social media for their own potential benefit. As we'll see later in this section, social media is neither a new concept nor one that's untried.

In any project, you need to have decision makers and members of the team implementing the project to become evangelists for it. If they don't believe in it, then others won't. However, a balanced approach is needed. You don't want to create an atmosphere of "yes men" who see nothing but good and don't address the potential problems. An example of this was one project I was involved in where I was chastised for being negative by pointing out security issues. Just because you're addressing risks does not mean you're undermining the project; quite the opposite in fact. Your goal should be to have an end product that is both secure and enthusiastically utilized by the organization. In other words, you want to stay on the cutting edge without getting cut.

Dealing with the "is it a fad?" question

Being that the term "social media" has become a household word for anyone with an Internet connection, you might think that people would assume it is here to stay. However, a survey by Harvard Business Review Analytics Services found that 11% of the companies felt that social media for business purposes was a passing fad. This should not be unexpected. Anytime there is a new way of doing business, it takes time to get everyone on board.

There will always be some who won't accept a new method or technology until they've been left behind. An example I always think of is an experience my wife had when attending college. An older instructor had always used traditional methods for doing graphic arts and believed this would never change. He said that "computers are a passing fad." Obviously, he was wrong.

Deciding on whether your organization will use social media requires more than an off-the-cuff dismissal of it. An educated decision requires looking at what's available, how others are using it, what benefits can be achieved, and what problems can be avoided. Without doing the work to find these answers, you can easily find yourself being left behind, while your competitors reap the rewards.

Earlier in this chapter, we mentioned how Harvard Business Review Analytics Services found that 79% of businesses were using or planning to use social media. Of these, 58% were already using social media and 21% were planning to use it.

This means that there is a good chance that your competitors are already using or planning to use social media even if you haven't. It also means that you can learn from the mistakes and successes of others in generating your social media strategy.

Social media has become entrenched in the business world to the point where professions have extended from it. Positions like *Chief Digital Officer* and *Social Media Officer* are being used in business to focus on the strategy needed to pull together social media for organizational gain. If a company doesn't wish to handle their own social media, firms have grown to fill this need so that businesses can outsource the work to professionals.

Having a successful social media strategy requires getting everyone on board. It requires creating a solid communication plan that will address the concerns of others and will answer the questions they have. By showing that social media is a proven method of business that's being used by others, you can answer the question of whether it's a fad and worth pursuing.

Brief history of social networking

While the term "social media" is relatively new, the concept of it is not. For decades, computers have been used by people to connect with others, share information and data, play games, work together on projects, and use software and systems for social interaction. While the technology has changed, the basic premise of its use hasn't.

In 1978, Ward Christensen and Randy Suess launched the first Bulletin Board System (BBS), which allowed people to connect to their system of phone lines. BBSs became a hobby for numerous people, and many organizations came to use them for a variety of purposes. For example, a number of libraries used BBSs so that people could view available books and reserve them. From personal experience, my own board called Dark Knight BBS ran for a number of years, allowing computers to use a dial-up connection to access the system via a modem. On the BBS, a person would use features that were essentially precursors to types of social media. A person could upload and download images, software, and other files (similar to a content community); read textual commentary (which was essentially a blog); and play games. There were hidden areas for those who worked on the BBS with me, allowing us to collaborate on changes made to the system. A major feature of BBSs was that people could post messages to communicate with others. In some cases, the message boards were networked with other BBSs, thereby allowing people to interact with others they wouldn't normally meet. For example, my board in North America would make a long distance each night to Arkham BBS in England (run by Nigel Hardy) and transfer messages between the systems. This allowed a community of computer users to socialize overseas as well as with people within their own areas. Other message networks also allowed communication with people throughout the world.

BBSs were widely used until the Internet became popular in the mid-1990s. While the Internet had been available to government, Universities, and military, it wasn't until this time that private ISPs provided the ability for everyone to use the Internet. In 1994, Geocities was started by Beverly Hills Internet and allowed users to create their own sites. Users had control over their content, and until it was purchased by Yahoo! and shut down for American users in 2009, it had approximately 38 million user-created Web pages. Other ISPs like America Online (AOL) allowed people to create searchable profile pages. An initial competitor to AOL that later became a subsidiary of the company is CompuServe, which was founded in 1969 as a computer time-sharing service and was the first to offer electronic mail services.

Connecting with other people was an important part of the early Internet. Usenet was a discussion board that had similarities to the message networks on earlier BBSs. People could post to newsgroups, and the messages were distributed across servers across the world, and share files like images and audio. In recent years, usage of Usenet has declined, as people have shifted to using content communities, blogs, and social networks to exchange information and files.

Social networking sites first rose to popularity in the mid-1990s with sites like Classmates.com and Six Degrees (www.sixdegress.com). Classmates.com started in 1995 as a way to reconnect with old friends and colleagues from school, work, and the military but includes online copies of old yearbooks, video, and images. Six Degrees was based on the concept that everyone was connected to each other by six people or less and allowed people to create profile pages, search others, link friends, and create groups. The site failed in 2001 but is now open to previous members. Another site that followed the same concept of six degrees of separation was Friendster (www.friendster.com), which later displayed the connections between users as a "circle of friends." Some of its features in making connections were akin to online dating sites, but its social networking features made it popular at the time. Although popularity declined in North America, it remained so in Asia and has since relaunched in 2011 as a platform to play online games.

As the mid-2000s approached, more major social media sites appeared. In 2001, Wikipedia was launched, growing to become the largest wiki in the world. In 2003, Second Life, MySpace, and LinkedIn went online, each with different target audiences. LinkedIn focused their attention on business professionals, Second Life launched to provide a virtual social world, and while MySpace offered itself up as a generalized social network. For a time, MySpace was the most popular social network, but this popularity has declined in English speaking countries in favor of Facebook. Facebook launched in 2004 by Mark Zuckerberg and his roommates as a social networking site at Harvard University but became available to the public in 2006. Between this in 2005, YouTube was launched as media sharing site and allowing people to upload and view videos and other multimedia. The same year Facebook went public; Twitter was launched and quickly became the premier microblogging site. In addition to these other sites, there have been a considerable number of other social media sites, each of which has experienced varying levels of success. This trend continues, with new sites appearing, such as when Google ventured into the realm of social networking sites, launching Google +.

Whereas the World Wide Web was pioneered in 1989 with Tim Berners-Lee creating the HTML, the creation of Web pages largely required professionals with technical knowledge to generate the pages. Over time, the desire for users to generate their own content became a fundamental part of social media sites, as did technologies to make the experience more dynamic. This concept and the technologies that enable users to generate their own content led to the concept of Web 2.0. The term was coined in 1999 by Darcy DiNucci to describe shift from static Web pages to the Web of tomorrow and became popularized to describe the latest technologies being used in the creation of social media.

The concept of Web 2.0 was used in the creation of one of the common definitions of social media. In a 2010 article published in Business Horizons, Andreas Kaplan and Michael Haenlein formalized a definition of social media, saying: "Social Media is a group of Internet-based applications that build on the ideological and technological foundations of Web 2.0, and that allow the creation and exchange of User Generated Content." However, Tim Berners-Lee has said "I think Web 2.0 is, of course, a piece of jargon, nobody even knows what it means. If Web 2.0 for you is blogs and wikis, then that is people to people. But that was what the Web was supposed to be all along."

In looking at what social media is and how it has evolved, a better definition might come from an originator of the term. In 1997, an executive at AOL named Ted Leonsis was largely credited as coining the term *social media* when talking about the need to offer users "social media, places where they can be entertained, communicate, and participate in a social environment." As you can see by looking at the history of the Internet and social media, Leonsis describes the basic model of how social media has been used from the beginning.

The problems that come with social media

While there are many benefits to using social media in an organization, it follows that there are numerous risks to using the technology to share information. All too often, people and companies will use social media without making proper decisions on security, what type of social media to use for a specific purpose, or how to use existing sites and tools.

Even if an organization decides against implementing their own social media strategy, others may decide to post their own information about a company. When this happens, you may find what you thought was secret is now available for everyone to read, or that inaccurate claims have been made. This is why it's not only important to monitor what's being released by your employees but also what others are saying on the Internet.

A major issue related to wikis is that information posted on a wiki may not necessarily be true, and that many people reading these mistakes, hoaxes, or outright lies will accept it as the truth. John Seigenthaler experienced this when his biography on Wikipedia was modified to state he'd been a suspect in the assassination of John F Kennedy and Robert Kennedy. Although false, the information appeared on Wikipedia for a considerable amount of time. It was more than 100 days before the inaccurate information was identified and removed. Unfortunately, when looking at the damage that can be done to a reputation, it's important to remember that it doesn't matter whether it's true, but whether people believe that it's true.

In June 2005, the *Los Angeles Times* decided to try something new on their public Web site and created a wiki that featured an editorial called "War and Consequences." Calling it a *wikitorial*, the newspaper invited people to contribute and edit this opinion piece. It didn't take long before things got out of hand, and it soon became filled with pornography and profanity. After a few days of trying to maintain this experiment in opinion journalism, the *Los Angeles Times* ultimately gave up and took it down.

In looking at this example, you can see that it may have been better to have used a blog where people could post comments, rather than a wiki that allowed Internet users to modify the article itself. Another alternative could have involved preventing the content from being published immediately by using moderators to review the changes prior to them appearing to the majority of readers. By using the approval processes available in collaboration sites, you prevent misleading, inaccurate, or inappropriate information from being seen on your Internet or intranet site.

As you'd expect, problems can also extend to other kinds of social media. A number of companies have encouraged employees to run blogs, including Microsoft who makes broad use of employee blogging. These blogs are useful for marketing, putting a face to the company, providing useful information and tips to customers, and sharing expertise. However, they can also cause some headaches to a corporation. Robert Scoble is an example of this. While working at Microsoft, he had a blog that promoted his company's products but also had a recurring tendency to criticize his employer and praise what competitors were doing. While applauded by a fan following, Scoble's example does lend to the argument that a company may want to make some clear guidelines on what an employee should and should not do on their blogs.

Protecting your interests and assets is an important part of social networking. In terms of the content, the copyright material you post online can be shared, making it ambiguous to users as to whether it's public domain or intellectual property. When posting multimedia on content communities, you run the risk that images, audio, and video may be shared, reused, and even posted on sites you didn't intend for them to appear on. For example, if you work for a computer company, I may see a copyright photo of your latest laptop and share it in a tweet or on my blog. You didn't authorize me to use it, and since I found it on FlickR or some other site, I thought it was okay to use for my purposes. However, is this is such a bad thing? In such cases, you need to weigh the loss of control against the benefits of it possibly increasing interest in your product or brand.

Is security really an issue?

When looking at the problems that can occur when using social media, it should come as no surprise that security is an issue. Many people using social networking sites, blogs, and other social media may have already exposed themselves to risk without even realizing it. As it is being used at greater levels by organizations and individuals, the exposure to these risks has also grown.

Some of the security issues that you should be aware of and which will be discussed in future chapters include:

- Having your network or devices exposed to malicious code
- Employees falling prey to social engineering tactics or scams
- Having sites or accounts hijacked or vandalized
- Having sensitive, embarrassing, or false information communicated to the public
- Making yourself vulnerable to criminal acts
- Having information that was for internal use made available to competitors
- Having content on Internet servers that may be accessible to others, as opposed to your own internal network servers
- Providing too much personal information on blogs and social networking sites
- Liability issues related to searching for employees on the Internet
- Infringements of existing legislation or regulations

While by no means a complete list of things you should be aware of, it does show that even a small list contains a large number of possible problems. Taking security seriously does not mean cracking down on employees, taking away access, and limiting their ability to do things. The basic tenet of computer security is to give people the access they need to do their jobs. While social media may extend what people are doing, it does not mean that security concerns will prevent them from using it.

In discussing security throughout this book and applying the knowledge to your organization, you should always remember and communicate to employees that it is for everyone's best interest. Imposing changes can be met with resistance, but when people recognize why security is in place and that it protects them, it is generally accepted. It's when people don't understand that they try and find ways around the precautions you put in place.

Taking the good with the bad

Using social media can be incredibly easy, but it doesn't come without its share of problems. That's just the way it is with most things worth pursuing in life. You need to take the good with the bad.

Millions of people go on social media sites everyday for work and fun. Their actions have moved beyond being what could be considered a hobby and become a normal part of their day-to-day lives. Using social media, they can share photos and video, read news, be part of events, play games, look for jobs, discover new things, find old and new friends, and many other activities. In using it, social media has become a platform on which people's personal and professional lives are built. Unfortunately, many people use it blindly, unaware that they're putting themselves at risk with the information they reveal, the sites they visit, the items they download, and the links they click.

Many organizations have seen the vast, untapped potential of social media and invested an increasing percentage of their resources into making it work for them. It provides new ways of advertising, making sales, building partnerships, and reaching customers. If your business is thinking of using social media or already using it but having trouble tapping its full potential, the promise of a large customer base and audience is already there. There is also the risk of impersonation, scams, security breaches, and other problems.

Unless you're a hermit living in a cave, you already have experience with these kinds of opportunities and problems. Businesses open in locations where they can build a customer base and make the most money, and people move to where they have the best prospects. However, as you move into the bigger areas, you also have to be aware of hazards. The bigger the population, the greater the chance you'll have to take precautions against con artists, vandals, and other criminals, and you already know that the Internet has the biggest population of all.

As we move into the next chapters, we'll help you make social media work best for you, as a safer, richer experience. You'll see that risks can be reduced by following the best practices that have proven successful for others. This includes making educated choices, setting up proper policies and guidelines, getting people to follow good security practices in their personal and professional social networking, using preemptive measures to avoid problems, using technology to your benefit, and monitoring what's being said. By taking the right steps, you'll be taking control of the social media being used.

Bibliography

Barnes, N. G., Lescault, A. M., & Wright, S. (2013). *2013 Fortune 500 are bullish on social media: Big companies get excited about Google +, Instagram, Foursquare and Pinterest.* Retrieved August 10, 2013, from University of Massachusetts Dartmouth: <http://www.umassd.edu/cmr/socialmediaresearch/2013fortune500/>.

Bercovici, J. (2010, December 9). *Who coined 'social media'? Web pioneers compete for credit.* Retrieved March 11, 2013, from Forbes: <http://www.forbes.com/sites/jeffbercovici/2010/12/09/who-coined-social-media-web-pioneers-compete-for-credit/>.

Brenner, J. (2013, February 14). *Pew Internet: Social networking (full detail).* Retrieved March 10, 2012, from Pew Internet & American Life Project: <http://pewinternet.org/Commentary/2012/March/Pew-Internet-Social-Networking-full-detail.aspx>.

Chui, M., Manyika, J., Bughin, J., Dobbs, R., Roxburgh, C., & Sarrazin, H., et al. (2012, July). *The social economy: Unlocking values and productivity through social technologies.* Retrieved August 10, 2013, from McKinsey & Company: <http://www.mckinsey.com/~/media/mckinsey/dotcom/insights%20and%20pubs/mgi/research/technology%20and%20innovation/the%20social%20economy/mgi_the_social_economy_full_report.ashx>.

Cisco visual networking index: *Global mobile data traffic forecast update, 2012–2017.* (2013, February 6). Retrieved March 10, 2013, from Cisco: <http://www.cisco.com/en/US/solutions/collateral/ns341/ns525/ns537/ns705/ns827/white_paper_c11-520862.html>.

Harvard Business Review Analytic Services. (2010). The New Conversation: Taking Social Media From Talk to Action. *Harvard Business Review*.

Kaplan, A. M., & Haenlein, (2010).M. (2010). Users of the world, unite! The challenges and opportunities of social media. *Business Horizons, 53*(1), 59–68.

Laningham, S. (2006, August 22). *Developerworks interviews: Tim Berners-Lee*. Retrieved March 11, 2013, from IBM: <http://www.ibm.com/developerworks/podcast/dwi/cm-int082206txt.html>.

Maltby, E., & Ovide, S. (2013, January 31). *The Wall Street Journal*. Retrieved August 8, 2013, from Small Firms Say LinkedIn Works, Twitter Doesn't: <http://online.wsj.com/article/SB10001424127887323926104578273683427129660.html>.

Mobile Spurs Digital Coupon User Growth. (2013, January 13). Retrieved March 10, 2013, from eMarketer: <http://www.emarketer.com/Article/Mobile-Spurs-Digital-Coupon-User-Growth/1009639#VtDzxL6QcVIG76xo.99>.

Stelzner, M. A. (2012). 2012 Social Media Marketing Industry Report. *Social Media Examiner*.

Opportunities of Social Media

INFORMATION IN THIS CHAPTER:

- Opportunities of Social Media
- New Methods of Marketing to Customers
- Building Social Authority
- Engaging Customers
- Sharing Information
- Getting The Word Out
- Taking Advantage of Collective Intelligence

Opportunities of social media

Social media offers individuals and businesses a lot of opportunities that didn't previously exist. It provides new and interesting ways for people to connect with others and the ability to create your own content and configure security on what people can see. A simple comment can be posted and read by large groups, allowing you to stay in touch with people in a simple, efficient manner, and you can advertise an event and get RSVPs without ever sending an invitation. Social media enables you to achieve the goals you want without any significant technical skills.

Some of the benefits in using social media can be major, while others enhance a person's life in small ways. As an example, we can look at Disney's PhotoPass (www.disneyphotopass.com) site. Disney has professional photographers throughout the parks, who can take your photo and have it automatically added to an account on the PhotoPass site. Going to the site, you can review and edit the photos and share albums of pictures on Facebook. If shared, a Facebook friend can click a link on their activity feed or your profile page and view the photos. As you're walking around the park having new photos taken, a friend or relative could see the photos before you even did, allowing them to join in your experience as its happening. For Disney, it's one more way of making their parks more enjoyable, improve customer relations, and promote the parks to others.

For businesses, social media offers organizations the ability to reach customers in new ways. In using it to promote products and raise corporate awareness, an organization may coax a target audience to purchase their products. It is also a way to engage consumers, providing a way to interact with them and improve customer service. Still others find its primary usefulness in sharing information, allowing people to view videos, images and read about a brand, social issue, or an event. If any goal of your business involves interaction between people, social media may provide the results you need.

In this chapter, we'll look at some of the major opportunities social media offers and discuss problems you may encounter. As we discussed in the previous chapter, there are many different types of social media, and not all of them may be ones you want to utilize. Of those you decide to use, there are common mistakes that are made that could make your organization vulnerable to risk. By understanding these pitfalls, you'll have a better chance of avoiding them.

New methods of marketing to customers

If your business has used traditional forms of media to market to customers, you're probably used to paying to reach thousands of readers with local newspaper advertisements, and somewhat more people with a local radio or television commercial. What you're trying to do is market your product to as many potential customers as possible, but more and more people today aren't reading newspapers, listening to radio, or watching TV stations. They're accessing entertainment and information over the Internet, using computers, mobile phones, tablets, and other devices. This means that if you want to get the most from your marketing efforts, you need to use new methods of reaching consumers. With the changing landscape of how people are accessing information, social media is capable of reaching more people with little to no cost.

The decrease in people using traditional media isn't lost on news outlets. A 2012 report by Pew Research Center found that since the year 2000, people who read news in newspapers has dropped by 47% and magazines by 29%. For adults under the age of 30, it was found that about the same amount of people got their news from social networking sites (33%) and television (34%). Since 2010, the number of people who get their news from social networking sites has doubled. If there is a growing trend for people to get information from social media, then this should factor into how you're reaching customers.

Does this mean that you should give up on traditional media altogether? Not at all. Traditional media reaches large numbers of people, but you should incorporate social media into existing campaigns and marketing strategies. Some of the most successful campaigns use a blend of social and traditional media.

Social media can have a significant impact on marketing a brand or an ideas. An example of this was Barack Obama's 2008 presidential election campaign, which incorporated Facebook, MySpace, Twitter, podcasting, and YouTube with more traditional advertising. His strategy of using social media has been considered to be a tipping point of that election, and comparative to how Franklin D. Roosevelt used radio extensively in the 1932 election, and how effective use of television in the 1960 election helped John F. Kennedy. While there is no way of knowing exactly how many new votes Obama attracted, it reached out to younger voters by using new technology and helped to substantiate a platform that promoted change. While he used @BarackObama for election campaigns, he continues to use @WhiteHouse for presidential purposes with 3,758,589 followers at the time of this writing.

Incorporating social media into existing campaigns can be done with less effort than you might think. Many large and small businesses will mention on posters, newsletters, business cards, email, commercials, and other advertisements that the business can be followed on Twitter, Facebook, or other sites. The corporate Web site will include links to social media. As we'll discuss later in this chapter, hashtags for Twitter can also be used as a focal point of some campaigns, getting people to join in the discussion of a product.

Social media also provides the ability to immediately identify whether a campaign is working or not. Facebook provides users with links to "Like" a post and show their approval and another to share the post with others. The number of people who have liked and shared the post is visible to everyone. Similarly, Twitter allows people to retweet your message, so that their followers also see what you said. In addition to this, comments are available on sites like Facebook and YouTube, which allow people to remark on content you posted. This provides you with input that was previously obtained by using focus groups or other methods that took considerable time to return results. Because they are valuable in finding what your customers think, it's important to monitor them regularly.

Polls and surveys are also available on social media sites. LinkedIn allows you to create polls, which can be used by employers to identify current trends, qualifications, interests, and so on. For example, if a hiring recruiter was curious about whether a pay scale, benefits, or some other element of a job was most important to potential applicants, you could find the answer using the online poll. Similarly, Facebook allows you to create surveys, which could be used to gather feedback about your brand. For example, a survey could be used to find whether people like a current campaign or would like a limited time product to become permanently offered.

Social media sites also offer an opportunity for a new location for advertising. Product placement could be used in virtual social worlds like Second Life or virtual game worlds like World of Warcraft. There are a large number of popular games available through social networking sites, where advertising could be used. For example, in 2013 a popular game by Zynga called CoasterVille was used by Progressive Insurance for advertising, displaying their logo in the game on merry-go-round, and having a quest featuring their fictional spokesperson "Flo". 7–11 stores and YoVille (another Zynga game) had a successful cross-promotion in 2010, where people buying a Slurpee in a special cup would get a code they could enter in the game to get a special prize. Virtual advertising can result in real-world purchases.

Another area where social media can help with sales or make it easier for people using your services is mobile apps. These are applications that run on mobile devices like tablets or cell phones. There are apps that can be tied to the location feature in your phone, which uses GPS technology to show you the closest store to your location or even where a product may be located in a store. Disney provides a free app that provides the latest information on wait times of rides, making it easier for people to enjoy their vacation and spend less time waiting in line. One of the commonly used apps for social media are ones that provide an interface to your social networking accounts, allowing you to easily use sites like Twitter and Facebook on a mobile device.

Foursquare (www.foursquare.com) is a popular application and site, which uses location awareness to provide you with information on restaurants, stores, and other venues close to your physical location. You can also view comments about a business and use a "check-in" feature to show that you visited it. Checking into a location also gives you points in Foursquare that allow you to achieve certain levels similar to a game, which can be used in getting discounts or offers at certain businesses. Many businesses also offer discounts through Foursquare by simply visiting the store checking in through the app.

Social media provides many opportunities for marketing to new and existing customers, allowing you to interact with them, meet their needs, and promote your products with greater efficiency. Before making any great strides into marketing a product or an idea with social media, you should first make yourself identifiable and define your brand.

Branding

A *brand* is an identifying image or imagery that belongs to a business or an individual and used so that people associate it with the brand's owner. To understand the term, think of some of the old cowboy movies where you saw a hot branding iron used to burn a pattern into cattle. People would see the design and knew who the cattle belonged to. In terms of marketing, branding refers to making a logo, name, slogan, or an idea recognizable to consumers. When people see or think of a brand, they relate the owner's product with a designed perception of how the owner wants it to be viewed. If a manufacturer promotes its truck as tough, when people see the advertised logo they associate it to the truck and think of strength. If you then buy the truck, you become associated with the perception of strength and think yourself as tough by proxy. Building brand recognition is important because it makes people create an association between the brand's owner and the image they are trying to present.

An important part of branding is consistency, as a brand needs to be identifiable across any form of media. This includes print and other traditional media, as well as social media. An example of this is the discount retailer Target, which always uses the same red and white color scheme and bull's-eye trademark. If a brand isn't consistent then people won't be able to easily recognize it.

It's a simple fact that people are comfortable with familiarity, and this inspires confidence and a sense of reliability. To illustrate this, let's say you see an advertisement for a company and notice the logo. If someone came door-to-door saying he worked for the company, but had a similar but different logo on his business card, it would raise a red flag to you. You might wonder whether it's a con artist posing as a representative of the company. When it comes to branding on the Internet, the same holds true.

Inconsistency in branding on the Internet can indicate that the site you wanted to go to is the wrong one. If you regularly checked your bank account online, and one day visited the site to see that the fonts and design were somehow different, you would be right in suspecting that something may be amiss. After all, how do you know that you weren't redirected to a hoax site that was trying to look like the official one? In such a case, a hacker may have created the site to fool you into entering your username, password, or bank information.

Another issue is when fake logos are used. For example, Pale Moon is a browser based on Mozilla Firefox, and their site has reported that fake versions of the software may be infected with viruses or malware. Their Web site at www.palemoon. org/warning-fakes.shtml provides information that one way to identify you're downloading from a bogus source is if the site is using unofficial logos for download links. Since there are such threats on the Internet, people should have a healthy suspicion when faced with something out of the ordinary.

Unfortunately, it's common for organizations to make their own sites look foreign from one another. The company's intranet may be maintained by an IT department, their Web site may be designed and hosted elsewhere, and their social media sites may be created by someone else in the company. In such a case, the sites may use disparate fonts, styles, colors, and other design differences. The person creating a new social media site may even decide to spiff up a logo by changing its colors to match other elements of the site or use a 3D version that looks dissimilar to the official version. When people search for the company on Facebook, Twitter, or other social media sites, they are left wondering whether this is the official page or something another person created.

To avoid such issues, companies should develop design documents that outline the branding of the site. At a minimum, these documents should contain:

- Information on the brand's official color scheme or pallet.
- The typefaces or fonts to be used.
- How the business or product name is to be spelled (I kid you not). Sometimes organizations will spell or abbreviate the name of their business or products in several different ways. In addition, there may be specific ways the letters should be in upper and lower case.
- Logo to be used and color specifications. It may also be advisable to include information on its recommended placement. For example, if a slogan or tagline is to appear near it, or the logo should appear in the upper left corner whenever possible.
- Design, illustration, and photographic styles, so that the visual representation remains consistent.

By creating a reference source of how things are to appear, anyone creating a new site, video, brochure, document, business card, or other electronic or printed material can understand how to present the brand in a consistent way. In doing so, it helps to maintain an expectation of how the brand is presented and maintained. Anything that veers away from the design will appear unprofessional and possibly illegitimate.

Building social authority

To effectively present yourself or your organization online, you need to build your reputation. Because tweeting a message or posting a comment can result in lots of people responding and creating a conversation, you can't completely control what's being said. Social interaction is part of the fundamental framework of social media, so the only way to shape or influence these conversations is by building your social authority.

Social authority is a term that's used to describe a person or organization's expertise and how influential they are on topics. In other words, you're seen as an authority in a particular area, so people are more willing to listen to what you have to say. This is done by driving conversations and contributing valuable insight into discussions. In building social authority, you are establishing yourself as a leader in an area.

The factors that determine your social authority are based on who you know, what you know, and what they know. An easy way of figuring out your social authority is to look at:

1. The number of friends or followers you have
2. The importance of those friends and followers

At first glance, these things may seem somewhat petty, but it starts to make sense when you think about it. If I follow more people on Twitter than are following me, others are influencing me, but I'm reaching very few people with my opinion. I've essentially become the lone voice in the wild, because no one is really listening to what I have to say. If I have a lot of friends and followers, then I reach a larger audience, which means I have the opportunity to influence a great deal of people. If some of those people are leaders in their fields, then this gives what I have to say even more merit. After all, if Bill Gates retweeted a comment someone made about computers, you would think that this is valuable information. The social authority of a friend or follower is important, because it authenticates you within a certain field or professional community.

In looking at this, you may be mentally calculating whether your personal Twitter account has the right balance of followers to those you're following, or if your Facebook friend list needs to be trimmed down because there aren't enough important people. Don't be overly concerned about this. You follow people on Twitter because you find what they have to say interesting, so don't stop following people because of vanity over having a high social authority rank. If people don't have anything of value to say anymore, then trim them out. Social authority will build organically by offering interesting, valuable comments that people want to share.

For businesses, the same holds true in many ways. By consistently offering authentic and beneficial content, an organization will entice people to share their post, link to it, or retweet what was said. By staying true to the image you've developed for your brand and offering content that people want to read and talk about, you generate interest in your organization and its products. Once you've captured the interest of an audience, you'll find that your social authority will begin to grow.

While social authority is important to the image of your company, another reason it's important to an organization is because it can affect search engine optimization rankings. Search engines like Google and Bing look at links in social media sites as part of how a site is ranked in search results. Remember that search engines use robots that look at content on Web sites, and this includes social bookmarks, user-generated content, and links, shares, and tweets from sites like Twitter, Facebook, LinkedIn, Google+, Pinterest, Tumblr, Instagram, YouTube, and so on. Basically, if it finds links to you, then the search engine figures that you must be more important than someone that no one's talking about, so you move higher in the search rankings. However, not all links are weighted equally. You've probably already had a passing thought that if you put links to your blog everywhere, then it will be high in the rankings. Search engines use algorithms that take such sneaky moves into account by weighting a link with the social authority of the person who made it. Links from people with a high social authority are given more importance, because they are essentially acknowledging your authority.

By using an honest and a genuine approach, you can increase your social authority and attract more people to your social media sites. If you present yourself with authentic information, people will be influenced by what you have to say and want to share that information with others. Over time and with work, your brand will be seen as a leader that others want to follow.

Engaging customers

Many organizations who use social media forget the key point that it's social. It's not about pushing sales; it's about being genuine and interacting with people. If you want to do direct marketing and make hard sells, that's what infomercials and phone solicitors are for. Social media marketing is more subtle and involves gaining the respect and interest of people, so they follow what you're saying and share it with others. Once people are interested in what you're sharing, they'll become interested in what you're selling.

Engaging customers involves making them feel a part of what you're offering, so they feel like part of a group or movement. If your organization is involved with a charity or cause that's important to your target demographic, let people know about it. If you want to be seen as affable, then show fun aspects of your business. For example, if you owned a restaurant, you might post photos of your friendly staff with amusing remarks or feature pictures of a sports team you sponsor.

FIGURE 2.1

Infographics provide information in an attractive format.

By using content that is interesting and entertaining to the viewer, it can make a connection with potential customers.

Capturing the imagination or attention of a person is important. One method of doing this is through infographics, which is an image that mixes facts and graphics together into a visual representation of a topic. The image might incorporate cartoon like images, graphics, maps, charts, and text to convey your message. There are a number of tools for creating infographics, such as Infogram (http://infogr. am) and Visual.ly (http://visual.ly), and if you have a graphics program like Adobe Photoshop, you can create one yourself. Figure 2.1 shows part of an infographic about my personal Facebook account, which I created within seconds using the online tools at Visually. While making custom infographics are considerably more work, they offer the reward of providing complex information in an easy-to-read format. Such graphics are attractive and share information in a way that is more likely to be shared by others.

Because infographics contain facts about a topic, you need to gather this information prior to creating it. If you were providing information about your organization, you would probably have this information at hand. If you need additional statistics or other facts, there are a number of free tools available online, such as:

- Google Public Data (www.google.com/publicdata), which allows you to explore public-interest datasets and create graphics, link to information, or embed the information on pages.
- Gapminder (www.gapminder.org), which allows you to search and view statistics in a variety of formats, including text, charts, and maps.
- Daytum (www.daytum.com), which allows you to collect information related to yourself or your organization to generate statistics you can share.

If your goal is increasing sales and getting new customers, remember you don't have to be obvious about it. Many of the best campaigns have involved generating interest without making a pitch. An example of this is Converse sneaker's use of their Web site (www.converse.com) and Facebook page (www.facebook.com/converse) to promote events that were sponsored by the company. By posting videos, photos, and information about music performances, basketball games, skateboard

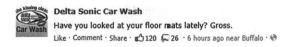

Delta Sonic Car Wash
Have you looked at your floor mats lately? Gross.
Like · Comment · Share · 👍120 💬26 · 6 hours ago near Buffalo · 🌐

FIGURE 2.2

Update posted on Facebook.

competitions, and other events, they attracted interest from people within a target age group. The result was people equating Converse with events where people would wear their line of shoes.

In posting content on a social networking site, you'll quickly realize whether or not a particular post or campaign is working or not. As we mentioned, on Facebook users can indicate their approval by clicking a "Like" link, click "Share" to have it appear on their own page, or click "Comment" to offer a few words of their own. An example of this is seen in Figure 2.2.

In looking at the content of this message, you'll notice it doesn't specifically sell anything. The car wash business posted it as winter was ending, and simply mentioned about how gross my floor mats might be, which got me thinking about how I should go to them and pay for an interior cleaning. It was short and to the point and got people thinking. You'll also notice that within 6 hours, the post had generated 120 "Likes" and inspired 26 people to comment.

If you're unsure whether you're on the right track, remember that there's no harm in asking whether people are enjoying the conversations you've offered or would like to see anything different. In doing so, you're drawing them into the conversation and making them feel that they're a part of what's happening.

FOMO

FOMO is an acronym that stands for "Fear of Missing Out" and refers to people's apprehension of missing social interactions or events. You may have met someone or had the experience of getting a phone call while talking to someone else and paused the conversation to talk to the other person. You'll take the other call, even though you may not know who it is. It is the fear of missing something more important that compels a person to temporarily halt one activity, because the next may be better. Ironically, in trying to connect with one person, you're disconnecting from another.

In social media, FOMO is common and can be a serious issue. In 2010, a survey by Retrevo Gadgetology found that 48% of people checked or updated their Facebook or Twitter accounts during the night or as soon as they woke up, with 56% needing to check Facebook at least once a day. Those under the age of 25 were more likely to do this, with 18% doing so before even getting out of bed.

For those with a social media presence, people experiencing FOMO will have an effect on the activity of a page, blog, or discussion in Twitter. These people will help to drive conversations, sometimes at a relentless pace. It can also be an issue when you consider the lengths people will go to stay in touch online at the risk of losing touch with real-world relationships.

For businesses, FOMO can be a problem because employees using social media will use it at the expense of other work. Of those surveyed 11% of people over the age of 25, and 22% of those under 25, didn't mind being interrupted during a meeting to respond to a message. Such activity shows how social media can negatively affect workplace productivity.

FOMO becomes a serious problem when your online social life affects your real personal life. Of those surveyed, 12% of those over the age of 25, and 24% of those under 25, didn't mind being interrupted while going to the bathroom. A greater number of people gave the electronic messages they received priority over those they were dining with, as 32% didn't mind being interrupted during a meal. Most disturbing was the fact that 7% of people said they would stop during sex to check a message. Needless to say, if your social media use becomes an obsession, having a negative impact on your life, cut back on your use and consider getting help.

Sharing information

Social media provides many different ways to share information with people. Most of the content you'll create will probably be textual, but as you write blogs, tweet messages, and post comments, you might also consider including images and video on a routine basis. While you won't do this every time, providing visual content makes it more appealing.

Many people and companies upload pictures to Tumblr or Instagram and then share them on social networking sites like Facebook or Twitter. Doing so allows the photos to be viewed on multiple sites, reaching more people, and promoting your presence on the other sites. Even if you don't use photo-sharing sites, you can still upload pictures to Facebook or Twitter and have them attached to your messages.

There are many different reasons for sharing information with social media. Many schools have started taking advantage of social media by using Twitter or Facebook to provide emergency notifications. Important information like school closures due to intermittent weather, outbreaks of serious viruses like H1N1, and other important information can easily be disseminated through such media. Because many younger people will check messaging and social networking sites before their email or phone messages, it also has a better chance of reaching its audience faster.

Since social media tries to engage people in a conversational tone, your messages will usually be more genuine and less professional than other types of writing. However, this isn't a constant, and you should gauge your tone and messages to suit the situation. In 2012, the Gap and American Apparel both tried to use Hurricane Sandy as a sales ploy. The Gap tweeted to stay safe and how "We'll be doing lots of Gap.com shopping today. How about you?" American Apparel however was more offensive, sending out emails that advertised: "In case you're bored during the storm … 20% off everything for next 36 hours." Bored was not the word for it, as the storm ultimately cost an estimated $75 billion in damages, with

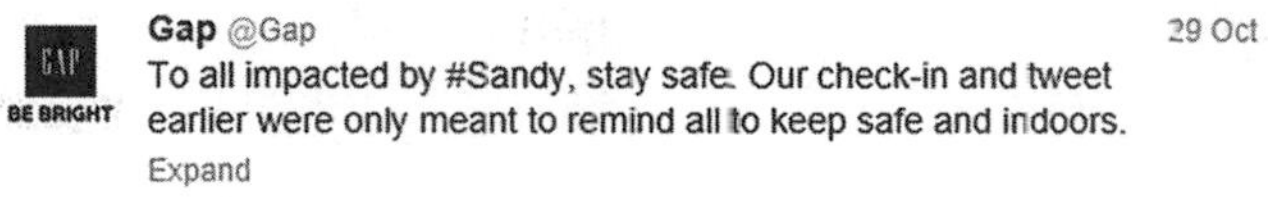

Gap @Gap   29 Oct
To all impacted by #Sandy, stay safe. Our check-in and tweet
earlier were only meant to remind all to keep safe and indoors.
Expand

FIGURE 2.3

Gap tweet apologizing for a previous flippant tweet

168 people dead or missing. As seen in Figure 2.3, the Gap apologized on Twitter, but no apology can be found on American Apparel's Twitter or Facebook sites. What can be found on Twitter are endless angry tweets that include people threatening to boycott American Apparel and saying things that couldn't be repeated here. Obviously, this is not how to engage potential customers.

Many times, simple tweets and posts are fairly straightforward, but it can be more complicated during times of crisis, a large campaign, or when making a major announcement. An easy way to approach writing such messages is to first gather information using the 5 Ws, which is a memory tool you may have learned in school to remember the questions that must be answered when writing a report. Answering *who?*, *what?*, *why?*, *where?*, and *when?* gives you an understanding of how you'll communicate and what needs to be said.

Who will be releasing information is vital in situations where multiple people may be providing content. Some campaigns may involve advertisers releasing material in print or television; technical support staff may be posting information to a blog and so on. Knowing who is involved will define the level of coordination needed between each person and group.

It's also important to know who you're writing for, so you understand your target audience. If you were promoting an event and didn't know it was for families and children, you wouldn't want to mistakenly say it's a great place to go for a date. Similarly, if a new product was designed for older customers, you wouldn't want to attach a photo of the latest teenage boy band posing with the product. By knowing who your demographic is, you can post appropriate content.

What you're publishing on social media sites also has some considerations. You may find that your employer wants graphics, an electronic poster, specifications of a product, video, links to a special Web site, or some other content included with the social media campaign. There may also be certain information that must be included in the message. Since Twitter allows you a limited number of characters, a longer message may need to be posted on Facebook, with the Twitter message referring to it. If it's a long document, then you'll be creating a link to a PDF, chart, or some other material that's saved on your company's Web site.

Knowing what kind of material is involved in a social media campaign will also help you decide *where* to put it. Where content is saved can be important, as the company may have policies that dictate certain data must reside on their own servers. Even if this isn't the case, you may find it beneficial to upload images to content communities like Instagram and share the photos to other sites or have videos posted to a YouTube channel where Twitter, Facebook, and blogs can link to it.

Because the messages you create can start a discussion, you'll want to know *why* you're posting the information. After all, if you post on Facebook that the company is sponsoring a special event, people will ask follow-up questions. Knowing why a comment is being made prepares you for the follow-up questions. Maybe the reason why an event is sponsored is that your company partners with a charity or cause, or perhaps it's to launch a new product. By having as much information available before you create a discussion, you'll have a firm understanding of what you'll say and what you shouldn't mention.

Finally, you'll want to know *when* to share information. Apple has had a number of issues over the years, where information or pictures of new products were leaked prior to being officially announced. In fact, there's been so many that there's been speculation on whether some were planned. The leaks have ranged from Apple's own Web site releasing specifications for a new computer prior to its unveiling, photos and information on unreleased features, parts or products appearing on sites, to an iPhone prototype being lost in a San Francisco bar. Some of these could have been avoided by properly managing when and how information is shared with the public.

Some information is sensitive to when it's released and shouldn't be revealed until a specific date and time. For example, if you know your boss is going to do a major unveiling of a new product on the 23rd of this month at 3 p.m., then you don't want a word of it to leak out before that time. Since there may be multiple people involved in publishing the information, this could require coordinating the release of content. A publicist may need to know when to send out a media release, the Webmaster would need to understand when to update a page on the Web site, and your social media person will need to know when to start tweeting and posting updates on social networking sites. If anyone sent out the information too early, then the secret's exposed, and the initial presentation of the product will lose its impact. By keeping information on a need-to-know basis, and making sure that the scheduled times for publishing it are clearly understood, problems can be avoided.

Knowing what NOT to say

Even though most posts and tweets will be informal, quick, and genuine messages, it's always a good idea to take a moment to think about what you're going to say so you make a clear and concise statement. It's equally important to consider what not to mention. Saying too much or saying the wrong thing can be embarrassing, make the organization vulnerable to legal action, and even be a security issue.

Some organizations have strict regulations, legislation, or policies that restrict certain kinds of information from becoming public. Hospitals and doctors are required to keep a current or former patient's medical information private. A simple tweet saying that a celebrity was just in for a procedure or has a medical condition could result in a lawsuit, especially if it caused public embarrassment. Similarly, there are laws to prevent publishing a person's name in connection to a crime if that person is under a certain age. If the police, a prosecuting attorney or some other authority posted information about a case in a tweet or on Facebook, mentioning a young offender's name in relation to the crime would violate the young person's rights. To protect yourself and your company from criminal or civil litigation, you need to ensure that you're staying within the parameters of what's allowed to be said.

The same level of care also needs to be taken when using your personal accounts to share information. If your company has an employee confidentiality agreement, you may be restricted from releasing any information about the company. These exist for good reasons. For example, you might be excited that you're working on a particular project and mention it on Facebook or add it to your experience on LinkedIn. However, making such a statement could reveal classified information related to the company, letting competitors know that your organization is working on a particular product or service. To avoid problems, you should be aware of any policies that could affect you. Even if you're authorized to handle the social media for your organization, you may be limited in what you can mention on your personal accounts.

While we'll discuss privacy and information sharing settings in Chapter 10, you should be aware of what people can see on your profile pages. When you create a page on Twitter, LinkedIn, Facebook, and other sites, there are fields that allow you to provide contact information. There may also be other areas on the page like a summary box, where you can include a blurb about yourself. If you included information like your address, phone number, and other personal data on your profile page, it may be visible to anyone who views the page. You might think this is rare, but I've lost count of the number of emails I've sent to friends and strangers informing them that everyone can see their cell phone number or something else that should be private on the page. To avoid problems, you should leave these fields blank, configure settings to limit its visibility, or only include information that you want everyone to see.

If you have a Facebook account, you've almost certainly used the field at the top of your profile page to update your status. In it, you've probably posted all sorts of information about events in your life, such as your relationship, birthday, birth of a child, new project, or any number of other things. However, it is wise to pay particular attention to what you're saying before you click the "Post" button and publish it to the world. Depending on your security settings, not only will your friends see the post, but all of the people those people have added as friends. The basic rule is read it before your release it.

As an example, let's look at Angelique Sobschak, a wedding planner from the TV show *Rich Bride, Poor Bride*. As an early adopter of social media, she's used it to connect with fans, potential customers, and members of the public. However, mistakes happen. As seen in Figure 2.4, one of her posts revealed:

- Her approximate age. While not a major faux pas, it could possibly cause problems of age discrimination. Also, as we'll see in Chapter 7, this could be combined with other information for social engineering purposes or identity theft.

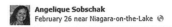

Angelique Sobschak
February 26 near Niagara-on-the-Lake

I am leaving for Jamaica in four days and I get to spend my
4???? birthday at Runaway Bay....Iree Mon,

FIGURE 2.4

Facebook post containing possible security issues.

- She was going to be out of the country after March 2. If a burglar read this, it would be the same as putting a sign on your front lawn saying "the house is empty. We're out of town."
- She was going to be at Runaway Bay, Jamaica. If a potential stalker read this, you can imagine the problems that could ensue.

By being aware of the information you're publishing on social media sites, you can reduce the chances of posting something embarrassing or that will impact your safety. While security is often associated with the settings you configure on a site or program, it also relates to taking defensive precautions on the information you share with others. Because of this, knowing what not to say can help protect you and your organization.

Getting the word out

The opportunities social media provides for a business can be quite broad, but its core advantage is the ability to reach people. For businesses, it provides new ways of marketing to people and allows you to promote your business, advertising, sales, events, products, and services you offer. Using it as a tool for sharing content, you can reach a wide audience, which can reach even more people if you use different types of social media together.

Although it doesn't require professionally created content, you can mix the quick, authentic information that's user-generated with professional graphics or ads. Don't feel that you should segregate traditional media from social media campaigns. After all, if you've got the resources available to you, use them.

Creating user-generated content is pointless if no one reads it, so you've got to let people know that it's out there. If I don't know you're on Facebook, then I may not look for you there. Mentioning your social media presence in other advertising will attract people, as will cross-promotions where you mention partnerships and they do the same. Beyond anything though, remember to post links to your social media sites on your company's Web site. The first place people will generally go to find your business is your official Web site, so it's always a good idea to include links to follow you on Twitter or find you on Facebook.

As we've mentioned, when you use social media to get word out, you also get word back. This can be through comments, tweets, posts, and Likes but also through the content they post about your product. The customers viewing your social media content will have access to their own Facebook pages, Twitter accounts, YouTube channels, and other sites that allow them to voice an opinion. They also have the ability to share what you post, so that it reaches a broader audience. Because of this, you need to monitor what's being said and be prepared to lose a certain amount of control. After all, not everyone will have something nice to say.

COBRAs

When a business uses social media, it's important that they make people feel involved. One method of doing this is through COBRAs. *COBRA* is an acronym for *Consumer's Online Brand Related Activity* and involves promoting products by getting customers to show their use and popularity. To do this, a business invites visitors to their social networking site to post a video or photo that includes the product.

A good example of how COBRAs can engage customers to show activities related to a brand is Converse sneakers. As seen in Figure 2.5, Converse posted

FIGURE 2.5

Converse post asking people to add the photo of their Converse sneakers to their Facebook wall.

a message asking people to upload photos of their Converse sneakers on their Facebook wall. The request turned into an ongoing campaign where people were asked to upload photos of their shoes, which were highlighted on the page and added to albums. The photos are also available on other sites. For example, if you go to Photobucket (www.photobucket.com/images/converse/), you'll find over 54,000 photos related to people wearing Converse shoes. These and other campaigns resulted in over 35,797,238 people liking their Facebook page and following what they have to say.

There are many other COBRA campaigns that have garnered attention from customers. Tim Hortons coffee shops invited Facebook users to send photos that include the brand's coffee, which were featured on www.facebook.com/TimHortons. Photos included people across different countries drinking Tim Hortons coffee, creative photos of their cups, and even funny pictures modified with PhotoShop. Anyone who liked the Tim Hortons page would see the pictures on their activity feed. In doing so, subtle advertising was reaching customers, even though it wasn't obviously recognized as such.

Another interesting way of using COBRAs was done by Sharpie, a company that makes markers and pens. In addition to using different backgrounds drawn with Sharpie products on their sites, the company also encouraged customers to upload pictures of artwork they'd created. People could view the images on their Facebook site, Instagram, and Sharpie's blog which challenged people to try and top what other's had done. They would do features on some of these customers, showcasing some of the more creative uses of Sharpie's products. Not only did this show how the products could be used, but improved customer loyalty by recognizing their abilities.

In using COBRAs, you're fostering an online relationship between the customer and the business. The reward for the business is that the customers themselves are promoting the product and providing feedback that can be used for future campaigns and business use. The reward for the customer who uploads a video or photo is a sense of involvement and recognition from a brand they love. Because the business shows customer appreciation by featuring a photo or video you created, it gives you an even greater positive feeling about the brand. This is extended to other customers who join in through comments and Likes. In the end, COBRAs have the potential to create a good relationship between a business and its customers and give consumers the feeling that they're part of what makes it successful.

eWOM

Any organization can tell you that word of mouth is one of the most important things for how a business is promoted. If people say positive things to others, then the word of mouth advertising can generate new business. This is especially true when people know one another, so the recommendation is coming from a trusted source. In social networking, people have the ability to provide such recommendations through *eWOM*, which is *electronic word of mouth.*

Everyone has an opinion, and social media gives them a forum to share it. If a person has something to say about your business, they can post it on Facebook, tweet it on Twitter, or use any number of other sites to share what needs to be said. If that opinion is positive, it can entice a lot of interest in your brand, bringing in new customers. Unfortunately though, not all opinions are positive ones.

Many customers who have a problem will never tell the business directly. They will however tell their friends. The old theory was that one upset customer will tell 9 other people, meaning that you didn't lose one customer from a bad experience, you actually lost 10. However, a person can easily share a bad experience with considerably more people using social media. According to Pew Internet & American Life Project, the average Facebook user has 245 friends. If the user allows friends of friends to view what's on their page or the post is shared by those reading it, the eWOM will reach even more people. This is especially true when you consider that people tend to be friends with people more popular than they are. Pew Internet & American Life Project reports that the average friend on Facebook has 359 friends. A person complaining to 9 people about your business is nothing when you consider that they can now reach thousands.

A common place where consumers will interact with other consumers is on review sites. These sites allow customers to voice their experiences with a business or product, rate quality of service and other elements of a company, and endorse or recommend against using the brand. For example, TripAdvisor (www.tripadvisor.com) allows people to write reviews on hotels, flights, vacation rentals, and restaurants. Others reading the review can then click a button indicating whether the review was helpful, similar to the like button used on Facebook. Prior to visiting a location and purchasing a product or service, you can see details people have provided about it, average costs, and read reviews to identify common problems or benefits. If you want additional information on a particular brand, you have the option of sending a message to the reviewer through the site.

Just because someone has a negative experience doesn't mean you as a business owner can't respond to it. Sites like TripAdvisor do allow owners to register and respond to reviews made on their site. Similarly, if someone writes about your organization on a blog, there's nothing stopping you from making a comment. In doing so however, you should be careful as to what you say. Viewers will scroll down a page reading the reviews and your responses, so it will stand out if you're only responding to positive reviews and ignoring the negative ones. Similarly, it will also be obvious to viewers if you suddenly stop responding to reviews, such as when a scandal, lawsuit, or health risk is being reported in the media. While companies used to be able to ignore a scandal until it was no longer news worthy, something posted on the Internet will not go away.

Prior to addressing comments, an organization should have a general idea of how they'll be addressed. The person responsible for social media should understand customer relations and how to handle eWOM complaints. In developing policies and procedures, this person must also understand what to do beyond making a quick response to poor service, such as during publicly embarrassing situations like lawsuits. This might include waiting for a statement from a lawyer or public relations representative to be posted to a Web site, so that the social media person can refer people to new and updated official statements. As we'll see in Chapter 9 when we discuss policies, the more you prepare, the less likely you'll inflame a situation by saying or doing the wrong thing.

Hashtags

Hashtags are a great way of getting other people to view what you've said on a subject and for grouping tweets together as part of a campaign. A *hashtag* is created by putting a number sign or pound symbol (#) in front of a keyword in the tweet. This makes it work like a link, as anyone clicking on the word is shown other tweets containing the same hashtag. For example, if you saw the hashtag #socialmedia in a tweet, you would click on it to see other social media–related tweets. Hashtags can be a powerful tool in getting people to view what you have to say on a subject. Since people click hashtags because they're interested in that topic, it follows suit that they have the same interests as you and would be more likely to retweet your message or follow you.

As seen by the success of Domino's Pizza in the United Kingdom, campaigns involving hashtags are popular and can generate a lot of interest. On March 5, 2012, they promoted on Twitter and their Facebook page (www.facebook.com/DominosPizza) that for every person that included #letsdolunch in a tweet between 9 a.m. and 11 a.m., the price of a pizza would drop by one pence. It was done to get more people ordering lunch from Domino's and the discount was available from 11 a.m. to 3 p.m. that day. After 85,000 tweets, the price dropped from £15.99 to £7.74.

CBS Broadcasting Inc. also uses hashtags on Twitter accounts. Some of their Twitter accounts using hashtags are #BigBangTheory for the TV program The Big Bang Theory (@BigBang_CBS) and #Survivor is used by the show Survivor (@Survivor_Tweet). Using these accounts allows them to share information about the show and generates interest by allowing fans to share in discussions.

Existing hashtags allow you to interact with others on a common interest, but if you're creating a campaign, you'll probably want to create an original hashtag. After all, you don't want to advertise that people should use a hashtag to tweet about your product, only to find that someone else is using it for theirs. There are a number of ways to find out what hashtags are currently being used. The easiest way is to go on Twitter or Google, enter the hashtag you're thinking of using, and see if any results show up in your search. There are also other sites that provide data on hashtag like www.hashtags.org, which uses Twitter's streaming API to show activity related to a hashtag for the last 24 hours. Another site that lets you quickly view information is Hashtagify.me (www.hashtagify.me). As seen in Figure 2.6, using this tool, you're provided with animated graphical displays of information,

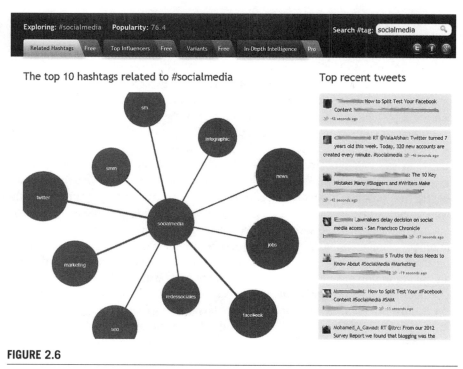

FIGURE 2.6

Hashify.me provides information on hashtags.

including variant spellings of the one you entered, top influencers, tweets, and other tags related to the one you entered.

Missing the mark ... mistakes in responding to people

There are many times when you'll want to respond to a comment someone made on a social media site. Someone may have posted or tweeted something that requires a direct answer or says something that you want to endorse. Maybe they have a question you want to answer or provided a great suggestion and want to give them credit. Conversely, maybe they made a negative or incorrect statement about a service you provide. While you could send them a direct message in Twitter or email them through a link on their blog or Facebook page, this would be private and hidden from others. If others had the same question, then they'd never see it; and if you're responding to a negative remark, it looks like you had no comment on the matter. In situations where you want to address the person and make a public response, other tactics are needed.

On Facebook, people can comment on posts that others make. If you want to address a person who makes a comment, it's common practice to mention their name at the beginning of what you have to say. However, sometimes less is more.

There are times when you'll want to avoid people making rebuttals to your comment and possibly turning it into a long, drawn out argument for all to see. If you agree with the person, you can click on the thumbs-up icon below his or her comment, indicating you like it.

Just as you'll want to address someone making a comment on Facebook, sometimes you'll want to address what someone said in a tweet. You may want to mention a particular username at the beginning of the tweet, such as when you're responding to something they tweeted to you. For example, let's say that @mybinarydreams complained about the service of your Main Street store, and you wanted to say "@mybinarydreams you're thinking of our competition. We don't have a Main Street store." While it's great that you're responding to the person directly, the problem is that by specifying the username at the beginning of the tweet, it will only appear to those following both you and the person you mentioned. For the reply to be visible to everyone (e.g., those just following you and not the other person), you want to add a period before the name. Another way to mention the person is to use the username within the other text, such as after the first word or so. In doing so, it's still personalized but will be available for all to see.

Sometimes the best way of handling a situation is to do nothing. On Twitter you have followers, on Facebook you have friends, and on other sites there are people who are following what you have to offer because they like it. In other words, you're not alone. If someone makes an inaccurate or improper remark, you'll often see other people jump to the defense and address the matter. After all, if you were a fan of a person or an organization and someone posted negative or aggressive comments, you might take it personally since they're insinuating you're wrong for liking the person, business or product. The comments other people make will often deflate an argument and carry more weight than anything a representative of the brand has to say.

If you do need to interact with the person, remember that the methods you use in dealing with an upset customer is similar to how you'd deal with them in person:

1. *Allow them to vent*. The first thing an upset person wants to do is get the problem off his or her chest and complain about it. The blood pressure is up, and they're agitated. While it's visible when you're looking at a person, you might think that it wouldn't be obvious online, but you'll often notice that the comment seems quickly composed and may have spelling mistakes. Of benefit to you is that you'll be able to see the time and date of the comment, and they may have calmed down by the time you respond.

2. *Be empathetic*. Understand that they have a point to make, so respect that. People want others to take them seriously, especially when there's a problem. If you show that you're willing to help and work with them, it will go a long way. Being that it is online and may have had time to calm down by the time you respond, you might combine this with the next step.

3. *Propose a way to resolve the issue*. People don't want lip service but want closure. If they have a problem with service, they want to hear that you understand

that there was a problem and you'll take steps to ensure it doesn't happen again. If they have a broken product, they want to know you're willing to replace it. By offering to make things better, it will show that you care about the customer and can turn the bad situation into one that promotes your brand.

In dealing with customers through social media, you shouldn't feel the need to immediately respond. The person is not in front of you, so it doesn't require an automatic response. This is especially true if the comment irritates you and you've taken it personally. It would be better taking a moment to formulate a response. After all, you're reacting to it after just reading it, but the author may have calmed down after writing it awhile ago. Writing an angry retort to a comment you've just seen could inflame the situation, even though it had settled down before you reacted.

Taking advantage of collective intelligence

Collective intelligence is a sociological concept that describes how a group intellect begins to form when people work together. By interacting and even competing with one another, the group shares information and collectively solves problems, giving them a greater chance to find answers than they would have on their own. The reason this works is because the crowd achieves wisdom by finding a consensus in correct answers and dismissing or discarding incorrect or deviant ideas.

To make this a little easier to understand, let's look at the 1947 Jimmy Stewart movie *Magic Town*. In the film, Stewart goes to the small town of Grandview to conduct opinion polls and finds that the opinions of its citizens exactly match national polls. Statistically, Grandview is a microcosm of the United States, which is why their collective viewpoint is a duplicate of the entire country. Although individually each person has diverse knowledge or differing beliefs, their collective intelligence provides accurate data.

Collective intelligence can be harnessed from social media through a variety of means and can be beneficial to your organization. Surveys and polls are available on sites like Facebook and LinkedIn, allowing you to identify trends and patterns in people's opinions. By monitoring the Likes, shares, and comments on social networking sites, you will eventually see certain patterns arise in people's viewpoints that show the popularity of one opinion over another. To give an example, let's say that you owned a shoe company and wanted to identify which product line would sell the most. By uploading photos to a social bookmarking site like Pinterest (www.pinterest.com), people can click a link indicating they like the product or *pin* (i.e., repost) photos they really like to their personal page called a *pinboard.* These photos can be shared with others on other social networking sites like Facebook, increasing exposure to the product. By monitoring the reactions of people, you'll see trends where a majority of people liked one shoe over another, and thereby predict that it will sell better than others. While the results might not have a guarantee, they would tend to be more accurate than the opinion of a single or small group of decision makers.

Crowdsourcing is another term related to these collective and collaborative efforts. Each person in a larger group (i.e., crowd) provides input and\or performs small tasks that together achieve an end result. When many people think of crowdsourcing, Wikipedia comes to mind as articles are submitted by individuals and reviewed by others with inaccurate information ultimately edited out. Because so many people have knowledge or expertise in so many areas, they are collectively able to establish the truth and eventually weed out any falsehoods from the article. Another example of crowdsourcing would be the International Bar Database (www.bardb.net), where you can add information on drinks, prices, and other facts about a bar you visited into the database. In doing so, a collaborative effort results in developing a final product that many others can use.

Public sites that allow people to work with others in collaborative efforts like wikis can provide a useful resource tool in finding information, but it is important to validate whether the information is legitimate. Within the business itself, there are tools that allow you to benefit from the same methods without having it accessible to the public. As we'll discuss further in Chapter 4, collaborative features on platforms like Microsoft SharePoint or sites like Yammer (www.yammer.com) can also be incredibly useful for your company. Microsoft SharePoint has social networking features and is installed on your corporate network servers or in the cloud (i.e., hosted on the Internet), while Yammer is an Internet social networking site for businesses that were purchased by Microsoft in 2012. Both allow you to share files and collaborate on projects within your organization without having to email documents, so you avoid multiple versions of the same document being worked on by different people. Also, by creating new sites in SharePoint, you can have internal wikis that allow members of your organization to create knowledgebases of information. Because people can collaborate on the same documents, communicate with others within the organization and extended groups like partners and vendors, it provides the ability for a group to collectively solve problems and complete projects.

As you can see by this, the act of sharing information and working with others provides tangible results. Interaction, networking, and collaboration allow you to be part of a larger, more complex entity, where the combined knowledge, experience, and efforts of the group help to find answers, complete projects, and predict trends. Through crowdsourcing, individual actions collectively shape the project and help to complete a final goal.

Bibliography

Brenner, J. (2013, February 14). *Pew Internet: social networking (full detail)*. Retrieved March 10, 2012, from Pew Internet & American Life Project: <http://pewinternet.org/Commentary/2012/March/Pew-Internet-Social-Networking-full-detail.aspx>.

Cisco visual networking index: Global mobile data traffic forecast update, 2012–2017. (2013, February 6). Retrieved March 10, 2013, from Cisco: <http://www.cisco.com/en/US/solutions/collateral/ns341/ns525/ns537/ns705/ns827/white_paper_c11-520862.html>.

Eisner, A. (2010, March 15). *Is social media a new addiction?*. Retrieved August 5, 2013, from Retrevo: <http://www.retrevo.com/content/node/1324>.

Facebook for developers. (n.d.). Retrieved August 1, 2012, from Facebook: <https://developers.facebook.com>.

Harvard Business Review Analytic Services. (2010). The new conversation: Taking social media from talk to action. *Harvard Business Review*.

Ho, E. (2012, October 31). *Sandy fail: American apparel's hurricane sale doesn't go over well*. Retrieved March 26, 2013, from Time Newsfeed: <http://newsfeed.time.com/2012/10/31/a-little-bored-american-apparels-hurricane-sandy-sale-doesnt-go-over-well/>.

Mobile spurs digital coupon user growth. (2013, January 13). Retrieved March 10, 2013, from eMarketer: <http://www.emarketer.com/Article/Mobile-Spurs-Digital-Coupon-User-Growth/1009639#VtDzxL6QcVIG76xo.99>.

Pew Research Center for the People & the Press. (2012, September 27). *In changing news landscape, even television is vulnerable*. Retrieved March 25, 2013, from Pew Research Center for the People & the Press: <http://www.people-press.org/2012/09/27/in-changing-news-landscape-even-television-is-vulnerable/>.

Stelzner, M. A. (2012). 2012 Social media marketing industry report. *Social Media Examiner*.

Tsukayama, H. (2012, February 3). *Your Facebook friends have more friends than you*. Retrieved March 24, 2013, from Pew Internet & American Life Project: <http://www.pewinternet.org/Media-Mentions/2012/Your-Facebook-friends-have-more-friends-than-you.aspx>.

Twitter Developers. (n.d.). Retrieved 08 01, 2012, from Twitter: <https://dev.twitter.com/>.

Employment and Social Media

INFORMATION IN THIS CHAPTER:

- Employment and Social Media
- Using Social Media to Find Employees
- Candidate Screening
- Using Social Media to Find Employment
- Limiting Personal Information
- Employees Using Social Media
- Allowing Social Media in the Workplace

Employment and social media

If you've looked in the want ads of your local newspaper, you might notice fewer jobs being advertised. While times are tough during an economic downturn, this doesn't mean there aren't any jobs. You may just be looking in the wrong places. According to a survey by Pew Internet & American Life Project, as of May 2013, 72% of adults on the Internet use social networking sites, so it should come as no surprise that this has also become the new landscape of a job hunt. Human resource professionals and hiring managers are looking for quality applicants online, where many candidates are finding success in locating available positions in their fields.

As we saw in the last chapter, the number of people using traditional news sources is declining, while the number of people using social media for information is increasing. More and more, businesses are tapping into using social networking and other online resources to advertise positions. Positions may be advertised on corporate Web sites, online databases called job banks, and online communities for posting classifieds like Kijii (www.kijii.ca, www.kijii.it, etc.), eBay Classifieds (www.ebayclassifieds.com), and Craigslist (www.craigslist.org). They may also be found using any number of social media sites like Twitter, Facebook, and LinkedIn.

Using social media to find employees

Looking for employees online has become a common process for many companies. If you're looking for people with a specific skill set, experience, or education, it's as easy to search for that person as it is to shop for anything else online. Not only does it allow employers to find new talent, but it gives them the ability to view information on a person prior to contacting them with a job offer.

In 2012, Jobvite (www.jobvite.com) conducted a survey of professionals in Human Resources and recruiting and found that 92% of American companies are using social media to find potential employees. When asking them which social networks are being used to find employees, they found:

- 93% used LinkedIn (www.linkedin.com)
- 66% used Facebook (www.facebook.com)
- 54% used Twitter (www.twitter.com)

The fact these three sites are primarily used should come as no surprise. As LinkedIn is used for business social networking and allows users to post information as an online resume, it has the perfect design for finding the candidate you want. The survey found that almost half of employers using social media to find candidates found more people to choose from than traditional methods, and that the quality of those candidates were an improvement. When fishing for talent, you want a big pool, and these three are currently the major sites people use for social media.

Using social media to find employees has a good record of achieving results. The survey found that 73% of employers were successful in hiring someone through social media. Of those hired, 89% were found on LinkedIn, 25% through Facebook, and 15% on Twitter. Being that so many organizations successfully use social media, it's in your company's best interest to pursue this as a method of finding employees.

There are a number of ways to find potential employees using social media. LinkedIn Recruiter (http://talent.linkedin.com/Recruiter) is a tool that is specifically designed for finding candidates who have setup a profile on LinkedIn's site. The tool allows you or your Human Resources department to find candidates on LinkedIn. This means you don't necessarily need to hire an outside headhunting firm to find potential employees on your behalf.

Even if you don't use the tool, LinkedIn allows you to search people's profiles. If you go to LinkedIn and type keywords describing a position you're looking to fill into the search field, the results returned will be a listing of people with those attributes mentioned in their profiles. If you want to narrow down your search even further, click on the *Advanced* link beside the search field, and you can search for people by a combination of criteria like location, industry, title, company and other criteria.

LinkedIn allows organizations to create their own company pages, and gives them the opportunity to post job openings. These available positions will then be suggested to people who have skills related to your advertised job. In seeing these available jobs, even if a person isn't looking they may be intrigued by an opening with your company.

One of the simplest ways of finding candidates is to create a page on your existing Web site, and then advertise the position on social media. The Web page describes the details of the job, but you advertise by tweeting the link to it on Twitter, and posting comments on Facebook and LinkedIn. You should also take advantage of your employees' social networking and encourage them to advertise a link to the job, as this can reach an even greater number of potential applicants.

Another method of using social media to attract candidates is to create a video that promotes your company and tells people why they would want to work there. By uploading the video to YouTube, it can reach a wide audience, and you can reach even more people by posting links to it on LinkedIn, Facebook, and Twitter. To make a job ad more interactive then a textual advertisement, you could also create a video that tells people about important job openings in your organization.

While advertising an existing job can attract people who are actively seeking employment, you should also try and find passive candidates. A passive candidate is someone who isn't aggressively looking for another job, but might consider it if he or she were asked. If you find someone who peaks your interest, offer the job. You may be pleasantly surprised.

Candidate screening

The percentage of businesses that screen candidates and do background checks through social networking is a minority, but it is debatable whether this will increase or decrease in the years to come. As we'll see in this section, existing and new legislation, potential lawsuits, lack of verifiable data, and privacy concerns have caused hiring managers and Human Resource professionals to stop using social media to screen applicants. However, although a minority, there are still a large number of employers who research a potential employee's social media activity to determine whether he or she matches what a business is looking for in an employee.

According to a 2012 survey conducted by Harris Interactive for CareerBuilder (www.careerbuilder.com), 37% of hiring managers and Human Resource professionals used social media to research job candidates, and of those who didn't 11% were planning to. In screening candidates this way, there were a number of things employers were looking for when doing their research:

- 65% were looking to see if a person conducted himself or herself professionally
- 51% were trying to determine if the person was a good fit for the company
- 45% were doing research on the person's qualifications
- 35% were looking to see if the person was well rounded
- 12% were looking for reasons not to hire the person

Acquiring this information through social networking sites may be done in a variety of ways. A simple method involves using search engines like Google, or (as we'll discuss later in this chapter and Chapter 10) those that do deep Web searches that search public records not normally indexed by standard search engines. Using these tools, you can find a considerable amount of information including that found on social networking sites. Of course, the easiest way is to visit social media sites and view the person's profile pages and posts. If a candidate hasn't set his or her privacy settings to limit access to information, then everyone can see it.

When screening a candidate you don't know, mistakes can be made. It's important to remember that there is a lot of false information on the Internet, so you can be mislead by what you read. Also, if the applicant has never had an interview, then the employer would never know what he or she looks like. As such, they wouldn't be able to recognize any photos on the site, and could easily mistake another person with the same name for the applicant.

The 2012 survey, CareerBuilder found that 15% of the companies didn't research candidates using social media because their organization prohibited it. They have this policy for good reasons. A 2011 survey by the Society for Human Resource Management provided a breakdown of the rationale of companies who don't use social media for screening, and included the following reasons:

- 66% were concerned about legal risks related to finding information about a protected status
- 48% were concerned about the ability to verify the information found on a person's social networking page
- 45% were concerned that information about the candidate might not be relevant to the person's potential or performance on the job
- 34% recognized that all of the candidates might not have information on these sites
- 33% were concerned that information they found about a candidate might not be relevant as to whether they were a good fit for the company
- 33% were concerned about invading the candidate's privacy

Screening applicants with social media could make a company vulnerable to lawsuits. If a site showed a candidates race, religion, gender, sexual orientation, disability, or something else protected by existing legislation, it's possible that the organization could be sued for discrimination when not offering employment. The company would then need to prove that the information didn't influence their decision not to hire the person. On the other hand, if there was something on a site indicating a propensity for violence or some other criminal behavior, you could be at risk of a negligent hiring lawsuit since the information was available but you did nothing. A good way to avoid this problem is to hire a third party to do the screening, specifying that you want to receive only the information that you indicate.

Asking for a prospective or current employee's password

Over the past few years, there has been a growing trend for employers to demand the usernames and passwords for any social media sites their employees belong to, and for candidates to provide these credentials as a condition of employment. It has even extended to universities and colleges demanding this information from current students, and those applying to the schools. The demand to violate their privacy is simple: if you want to be here, we want to see what's on your social media sites.

One highly publicized case is that of Kimberly Hester, a teacher's aide from Frank Squires Elementary School in Cassopolis, Michigan. A parent complained to the school about a photo on Hester's Facebook account, which showed a pair of jeans bunched around her coworker's ankles. It showed no nudity, and only showed the jeans around the ankles. Hester and the coworker were called into separate meetings with the school principal, Peter Bennett, and the school's district superintendent, Robert Colby. During the meeting with Hester, the two men produced 32 pages of comments her coworker had made with Facebook friends and family, and had circled comments they felt were inappropriate.

The hysteria of the traveling pants did not end there. They wanted Hester's username and password, so they could review her account. Hester refused, and she and the coworker (who eventually resigned) was given a five-day suspension. Hester fought the action, and was assigned as an aide to a class run by Colby's wife, told to do 47 online courses dealing with topics like fire extinguisher safety, and prohibited from talking to coworkers or to bring her cell phone on school grounds. Ultimately, she was put on unpaid leave as the union and school district argued her case. Once an arbitration process is completed, a lawyer provided by the union has plans to take the case to Federal court.

Unfortunately, there are reports throughout the world of employers demanding such information from their employees, and candidates who are hoping to gain employment. As many people are fearful of losing their job in a recession or desperately want to get a job, many of those asked will begrudging provide the information, even though it means violating the terms of service most social media sites have. Many sites including Facebook have a security rule about not sharing your password with others, meaning that the employer is forcing the person to break these rules.

If you're concerned about your employer asking you to reveal a username and password to a personal social media site, you would do well to review any existing corporate policies involving password security. Many organizations have policies related to technology. These are often created by an IT department, and specify that you are not allowed to share passwords with other people. The rule exists to keep passwords secure, so employees don't share accounts with coworkers, and (as we'll discuss in Chapter 7) to prevent social engineering. If your company has such a policy, then it probably isn't specific as to what passwords are okay to share, and which ones aren't. As such, you could try refusing to provide the password on the basis that it violates an existing corporate policy of not sharing passwords.

For employers thinking of requesting this information, you should be concerned about violating an employee's privacy. Such demands have an effect on morale, and will probably damage any positive relationship a manager has with his or her employees. Also, it may have an impact on security of internal passwords. After all, if an employer doesn't care about an employee's personal password security, the employee may feel the same about the corporate passwords he or she uses.

Of utmost importance however, employers should also be concerned whether existing laws or pending legislation will make your demands for a social media user's credentials illegal.

Legal issues

If you're lucky, you may live in an area where there is legislation protecting your rights to privacy, so you're not required to provide your password to an employer. In California, Assembly Bill 1844 prohibits employers from requiring employees and job candidates to disclose their login credentials to social media sites, demand access to personal social media in the employer's presence, or provide any information on personal social media content. If you refuse an employer's demands under this bill, you cannot be disciplined or fired.

Another piece of legislation to protect social media users in California is Senate Bill 1349, which protects students and prospective students. Those enrolled or applying to postsecondary institutions can't be asked to provide their usernames, passwords, and other information related to social media. In doing so, colleges and universities can't demand that applicants and current students provide access to social networking accounts as a condition of being a student.

However, while this directly addresses demands to provide your user credentials, it does not address other methods of accessing data. There are a number of tools available on the Internet that can be used to perform background checks of people by searching publicly available information and public records. One such tool is BeenVerified (www.beenverified.com), which enables you to perform online background checks, and also offers an app for iPhone. In using this tool, it will look up information collected from thousands of public records and other sources available to the public, and allow you to view links to sites where the target of your search is mentioned. The results that are displayed can include information from social networking sites, photos, property records, criminal records, and personal information like current and previous addresses, phone numbers, and so on. The results may require some analysis, as more than one person with the same name may be returned.

Such tools and services that provide background checks have come under the scrutiny of the Federal Trade Commission (FTC), which enforces the Federal Credit Reporting Act (FCRA). This Act regulates how consumer information is collected, disseminated, and used. Under the Act, any company that provides a service of assembling and evaluating consumer report information for third parties is considered *consumer reporting agency*. Businesses that use reports by these agencies for such things as employment, credit, insurance, tenant screening, and checking qualifications for scholarships or educational programs are subject to the terms of the FCRA. For these reasons, the FTC has charged a number of companies for violating the FCRA, including those that offer apps or services for performing background checks and screening.

Complaints have been made against BeenVerified, and similar sites. In 2012, an online privacy service named Albine (www.albine.com) complained to the FTC that

BeenVerified did not remove information when requested. Like many online sites that could be used for background checks, BeenVerified has an option to opt-out of information appearing through the searches. While it was initially removed, Albine found that it later appeared in searches. Albine itself provides a subscription service to have information removed from searches on such sites.

In June 2012, another site that collects and sells personal data to employers and recruiters was fined by the FTC. The FTC alleged that Spokeo (www.spokeo.com) posted fake endorsements for their services that were created by their own employees, and didn't follow the steps required to protect consumers under the FCRA. The case was settled with Spokeo agreeing to pay $800,000.

Under the FCRA, consumers have the right to dispute inaccurate or incomplete information. As such, when requested, the provider of the information has to show you what information they have on you and give you the opportunity to dispute it. If there is any information that is inaccurate, incomplete or unverifiable, the agency who obtained the information has to correct it. Such agencies also can't report on outdated information that's negative. For example, if you went bankrupt, after 10 years the company could not disclose any information regarding the bankruptcy. In cases of credit reports, the act allows you the right to know your credit score.

Another important feature of the Act is that if the employer is running a background check on you, they must get your permission prior to doing so. This is needed when background checks are done for any employment decisions, including hiring, retention, promotion, or reassignment. The employer must tell you that the information from the consumer report may affect decisions made about the person's employment, and has to be provided in writing. If the report may be used throughout the person's employment, the employer must clearly provide this fact to the employee or candidate. The applicant or employee must then provide written permission for the check to be done. Upon getting this information, the employer needs to inform the consumer reporting agency that they have complied with the FCRA requirements, notified the candidate or employee being checked, and will not discriminate against them or misuse the information.

Using social media to find employment

Seeking employment can be more work than the actual job you find. It's frustrating, time consuming, and occasionally disheartening. A problem people face when looking for a work is that they're used to the traditional process of looking in the want ads of a newspaper, but the Internet has changed all that. As we've mentioned, today those jobs may be posted on Web sites, searchable in databases, or advertised through social media. However, social media isn't just for employers to find candidates. You can harness the same tools to find employment regardless of whether you're actively seeking work or waiting for an offer to come to you.

As with many things, the importance of being noticed is location, location, location. You want to be where the recruiters are looking, so you should start by having accounts on the major social media sites. As we discussed earlier, recruiters seek employees on LinkedIn, Facebook, and Twitter. While we'll discuss LinkedIn in greater detail later in this chapter, for now remember that these will be your focal points in social media. They will provide connections to other people who can let you know of jobs that are available, promote yourself to potential employers, and enable you to be noticed by recruiters.

As we've seen from the previous sections, thinking that the first impression you make on an employer is during an interview may be wrong. In the age of social media, an employer can form an opinion by looking at a person's online activities. They could be looking at how you're presenting yourself, the photos you're putting up, and the comments you're making. As such, when posting content, you will want to keep this in mind and conduct yourself accordingly.

You should also consider other ways to get yourself noticed, and showcase your abilities. For example, writing a blog allows potential employers to see your communication skills, interests, knowledge of topics related to your field, and makes you memorable. Another way to advertise your skills and interest in a job is by posting a video on YouTube. The video could simply be a short clip of yourself talking about the type of job you're looking for, and why someone should hire you. It will allow employers to put a face to your name, and give you the opportunity to sell yourself. With any content outside of your social networks, you should publish links to the video and new blog entries so more people will have a chance to view them.

In using social media to promote yourself and find work, don't feel that you have to spread yourself thin. You don't need to setup accounts on every social networking site you hear about. It's better to have a few good profile pages, than try and use an overabundance of social media poorly.

As we'll discuss later in this chapter, sites like LinkedIn allow you to search for jobs on their site, allowing you to find positions you're interested in within a specified area. If there's a particular company you're interested in, you can also search for that business and view information about it and any advertised positions they may have available. Without using social media in your job search, you're missing out on these potential sources of employment.

Getting referrals

You've probably heard the adage about how "it's not what you know, it's who you know" that gets you a job. Although we've all worked with a few people that may give the first part some credence, it's the later part that's a proven fact. Having someone referring you to an employer is a major asset to getting a job. If someone within the company can suggest you for a job, it can increase your chances of getting offered a job and being hired.

Since there are so many adults who use social networking, it's fairly easy to find people in the same industry as you or employed where you'd like to work. By adding them as a connection in LinkedIn, following them on Twitter, and making friends with them on Facebook, you improve your chances of hearing when a job's available or having them recommend you. In saying this, I am not recommending a sleazy tactic where you fake interest in people. What I am suggesting is rather than limiting yourself to having Facebook "friends" you met socially or to play games, make more career-related contacts. If I'm in the same industry as you, and we have similar interests, it makes sense to make you part of my network. If I like your previous tweets, I should follow you on Twitter. After all, if you talk about things I should know, it's to my benefit to listen. Also, getting to know people at a company you *think* you want to work at may provide you with information that shows you really don't want to work there.

Subscribing to blogs, following tweets, and listening to what's being said by the corporate and personal accounts of a business and its employees is beneficial in other ways. During an interview, you'll have better insight into the business, its products, and the direction it's taking with various projects. Reviewing what a company is talking about gives you the ability to reiterate this information during the interview process, showing that you're a knowledgeable candidate with great interest in the company.

Even though you're the one looking for work, making these connections can also be of benefit to the other person. In fact, it can be money in their pocket. Because candidates who are vetted through existing employees have been found to be high-quality ones after being hired, many companies offer referral bonuses to employees. According to the Jobvite survey, 65% of companies encourage employees to refer potential candidates, with one-third of them offering a bonus of over $1000.

Branding yourself

In the previous chapter, we discussed the importance of branding. When it comes to finding employment, it's important to remember that you are the brand being marketed. How you present yourself in different social media will have an impact on how potential employers will see you.

When looking at online profiles, a potential employer will look for things that make you shine in a positive light, and stand out from others who applied. Just as when branding a company, you want to brand yourself to inspire trust, reliability and instill confidence. The 2012 CareerBuilder survey found that 29% of employers found something on a candidate's online profile that caused them to hire the person. There are a number of things employers look for in a good candidate:

- 58% felt they got a good feel for the person's personality through the profile
- 55% found the person put across a professional image
- 54% found the person's background information supported their professional qualifications
- 51% felt the person was well rounded and showed a range of interests
- 49% found the person had great communication skills
- 44% felt the person was creative
- 34% found great references had been posted about the person by other people

When looking for employment, you are marketing yourself, so you should design your online profiles to match how you want employers to perceive you. In crafting your profile pages, you're trying to make employers remember you and want to interact with you. In saying this, it doesn't mean to create a false persona. After all, if you're trying to portray yourself as something you're not, eventually the real you will come out and people will see behind the facade. You also don't want to create a false representation of yourself because you want to work with people who like you for you. Much of your life will be spent with the people you work with, so you want them to accept you for who you are. In branding yourself, you want to show the best parts of yourself.

Although the belief of anonymity on the Internet is fading slightly, many people tend to lack self-censorship on their profiles and posts. Something they might not say in real life somehow manages to get tweeted or blurted into comment. These are things that can be held against you when looking for work. In the previously mentioned survey by CareerBuilder, 34% of the managers and Human Resource professionals researching candidates found reasons not to hire a person. These reasons included:

- 49% found photos and information that was provocative or inappropriate
- 45% found comments or photos that dealt with the candidate drinking or using drugs
- 35% found the person had poor communication skills
- 33% found the person had bad-mouthed previous employers
- 28% made comments against a race, gender, religion, or something else that could be considered discriminatory
- 22% found the person lied about their qualifications

If an employer screened you by looking at your social networking sites and didn't like what they found, chances are you'd never know. In the 2011 survey by the Society for Human Resource Management, 73% of the companies who used social media to screen job applications never gave the candidate a chance to explain any questionable material. Because of this, you should check whether there's any questionable material on your sites before they do.

At this point, you may be thinking of all the possible places you or someone else may have posted the wrong thing. After all, there's probably a silly photo or two, but this isn't the kind of things most employers or someone thinking of recommending you for a job would be concerned about. What would be a problem would be things like vulgar jokes, photos from parties where you appear drunk, or angry comments you made about the boss or a bad day at work. If there is anything like that on your profile pages, then it's time for damage control.

Since the Internet is decidedly very big, the first thing is to decide where you'll focus your efforts. The surveys we discussed help with this. The 2012 Jobvite survey showed that recruiters are primarily using LinkedIn, followed respectively by Facebook and Twitter when searching for new talent. The 2012 CareerBuilder site showed 65% of employers use Facebook, 63% use LinkedIn, and 16% use Twitter when researching a person for a job. These are the major social networking sites, so you should focus your efforts on cleaning up anything of concern.

What you need to do next is decide what you want on your pages. The comments and other content should be things you'd feel comfortable having a future employer or coworkers seeing. A good piece of advice is never have anything on your profile pages that you wouldn't want your mother to look at. If you'd be embarrassed by it, then you should edit and delete. Another good method is to look at the photo or comment, and imagine it on a billboard at the side of a highway. Is it something you wouldn't want to be seen in public? If so, get rid of it.

How you convey and type a message is also important. Employers look for good communication skills, and your abilities will be seen with every post and tweet. In the 2012 Jobvite survey, it was found that 54% of recruiters had a negative reaction to grammar and spelling mistakes, and 61% disliked profanity. Cleaning up what you say is important to how employers perceive you.

In pruning anything damaging from your profiles, you should put it into the context of the organizations to which you're applying. For example, there's nothing wrong with saying that you think a particular soft drink is the best you'd ever tasted, unless you're applying to their competitor. It is a bad idea to make comments or jokes that place one company over another in the industry you're seeking employment. Similarly, you want to make sure that you don't go against the basic philosophies of an organization you're applying to. If you're applying to oil companies, tweeting that you're against fossil fuels may not be your best move. Most importantly, remember there are comments no employer wants to see. As mentioned earlier, you want to avoid bashing your boss online, since possible future employers will wonder if you'll do the same to them. When in doubt, try and look at your profile objectively, and ask "Would I recommend this person?"

LinkedIn

By this point, you've probably realized that LinkedIn can be an essential resource for seeking employment. According to Pew Internet & American Life Project, as of August 2012, 20% of adults on the Internet say they use LinkedIn, which accounts for why a majority of recruiters use it as a primary social media resource for finding candidates who are actively and passively seeking employment.

After creating an account, you can create a profile page that lists the features of yourself that make you marketable. This includes:

- Contact information, inclusive to a Twitter account, Web site, Facebook page, email, blog, etc.
- Work and volunteer experience
- Skills and expertise, where people can endorse you as having proficiency
- Certifications and education
- Other information, such as publications, awards, and so on

In completing these sections, it's important to be honest. Aside from ethical reasons, lying can get you in serious trouble later. If you were hired by a company and they later discovered you'd falsified your qualifications, you could (and probably would) be fired.

Completing the jobs sections on your profile is important, because not only do employers use it to review your skills, but LinkedIn will use it to suggest available jobs. After logging into LinkedIn, you'll see a section on the right-hand side of the home page listing jobs you might be interested in, and you'll receive a summary of them sent to you via email. A complete profile will provide you with more potential job opportunities.

By complete, I also mean to fill out the summary field that's located at the bottom of your profile page. While you could enter any information you wanted, the box is generally used to provide a brief summary of yourself and goals you might have. If you're fresh out of school or changing fields, you may not have anything in your job history related to a new profession. Using the summary box, you could include this information by writing a concise overview of your new or transferable skills.

Because the people you add as contacts will be used to suggest jobs within your social network, it is a good idea to extend this network by joining groups. LinkedIn groups connect you to a wider scope of people, allowing more people to know of you, which results in increased traffic to your profile. To find groups related to your job interests and skills, you can use the Groups menu at the top of LinkedIn's pages to view suggested groups related to your information, view groups you belong to, browse a directory of groups, or even create a new one.

To search for jobs, you can click on the Jobs menu at the top of the page, and a page will appear providing a longer listing of available jobs related to your skills, those found within the network of people you've added as contacts, and a search feature. By entering titles, skills or companies of interest into the search field, a list of potential employers is returned. By clicking the "Advanced Search" link, it will expand to show additional criteria for your search, allowing you to narrow it down by country, zip code, industry, job functions, and (if you have a premium account) salary range. As seen in Figure 3.1, clicking the link for more options provides even more criteria to narrow your search results.

Using the search features may require some playing around. Depending on the criteria you enter, you may see a flood of results or filter out a lot of possible jobs. For example, if you selected only jobs posted in the last day, you will miss any opportunities posted 2 days ago. Because of the different methods available to find opportunities, the more you work with LinkedIn's features, the better chance you'll find your dream job.

Endorsements and recommendations

After entering your skills and experience into a profile, you can acquire endorsements from connections to verify that you have expertise in those areas. For example, if you said you were skilled at speaking another language, a connection who knew you were fluent could then provide an endorsement. As seen in Figure 3.2,

FIGURE 3.1

LinkedIn search.

 SKILLS & EXPERTISE

Most endorsed for...

FIGURE 3.2

LinkedIn endorsements.

your contacts can quickly endorse your expertise by simply clicking the plus sign beside a skill you've added.

When adding any items in the Skills & Expertise section, it doesn't matter if they're mentioned in other areas (such as education or work experience). People who are searching for these skills may find your profile page in their results, and can instantly see that other LinkedIn members have confirmed your skill set.

Getting endorsements can be done by connections who visit your profile, or by requesting your contacts to endorse you. Another method is to endorse others. People you endorse will get a notification, and many will reciprocate.

Another way that your contacts can confirm you're a good job candidate is through recommendations. By hovering your mouse over the *Profile* tab on the top navigation bar and clicking *Recommendations*, a page will appear that lists your work and educational experience, and has an "Ask to be recommended" link beneath each entry. Clicking the link allows you to send an email to contacts asking them to recommend you. If they choose to recommend you, they can essentially write a short reference letter, showing their approval of you.

Creating a custom URL on LinkedIn

When you create a LinkedIn profile, the URL automatically associated with your page can be a complex and difficult to remember. For example, when initially creating my LinkedIn profile, it was given the URL of https://ca.linkedin.com/pub/michael-cross/31/746/b21. Not exactly the user-friendly address I'd want to include on a resume or link. To remedy this, LinkedIn allows you to create a custom URL for your profile. To illustrate the results, rather than being stuck with the mishmash of letters and numbers I'd been given, I changed mine to www.linkedin.com/in/mcross1.

Making such a change not only makes your profile more recognizable and in line with your personal branding, but can help optimizing how a search engine indexes a link to your page. If you include your business or name in the URL, there is a greater chance that it will rank higher in the results when someone searches for those words. To change your URL, log onto LinkedIn and do the following:

1. Hover your mouse over your name at the top right of the screen. When the menu appears, click *Settings*.
2. Click on the *Profile* tab, at the bottom left of the screen. By default, this will already be selected.
3. Click on the link labeled *Edit Your Public Profile*.
4. Scroll down until you see a box labeled *Your public profile URL*. Click on the link that says *Customize your public profile URL*.
5. When the screen appears, you'll see the base URL of www.linkedin.com followed by a box. In the box, type in the end portion of the URL you want.
6. Click the *Set Custom URL* button.

A common problem is finding that the name you want may have already been taken, and you'll need to select something a little different. However, regardless of what you choose, it should be an improvement. With some effort, you should find something close to your name, or something that relates to how you want to present yourself to potential employers or colleagues.

Getting the word out

Because there are many possible ways on LinkedIn to find or be offered a job, it can be easy to miss the obvious step of telling people you're looking for work. Let your LinkedIn contacts, Facebook friends, and Twitter followers know about your job search. In doing so, you may find that they know about a job opening and may even recommend you for it.

If you do let people know you're looking for work through social media, be aware of who will view any announcements that you're seeking employment. If you're current employer doesn't know you're looking for another job, the two of you may get a shock if you've forgotten the boss or coworkers are your Facebook friends and LinkedIn contacts. Trust me when I say, this has happened more than once to people.

Limiting personal information

When you first setup your account in LinkedIn, the information you enter on your profile page is public by default. In other words, if I stumbled across your profile page using Google, I could view everything on your profile even if I wasn't logged onto LinkedIn. If a criminal were to view this information, they could see where you worked, schools you attended, and anything else you entered into sections of the page. This can be useful in the wrong hands to steal your identity, so you should always limit the amount of personal information showing to others.

There are many different areas in LinkedIn where you can add, remove and configure information that's displayed to others. As potential employers and contacts will use the information that's visible on the page to search and review your experience, there will be some areas that you'll want everyone to see, some that you'll only want your contacts to see, and other facts you may want to leave completely blank.

Adding too much additional information

The profile page itself contains several areas that should be of concern. As seen in Figure 3.3, the *Additional Info* section contains fields where you can show your interests, birthday, marital status, and advice to contact you. Your birthday and marital status shouldn't be included, as it could be used to discriminate you from being offered a position. If you do enter a birthday, avoid entering the year.

To remove personal details from showing in *Additional Info* area of your profile:

1. After you've logged on, hover your mouse over the *Profile* menu item on the navigation bar at the top of the screen, and click *Edit Profile*.
2. Scroll down to the section called *Additional Info*.

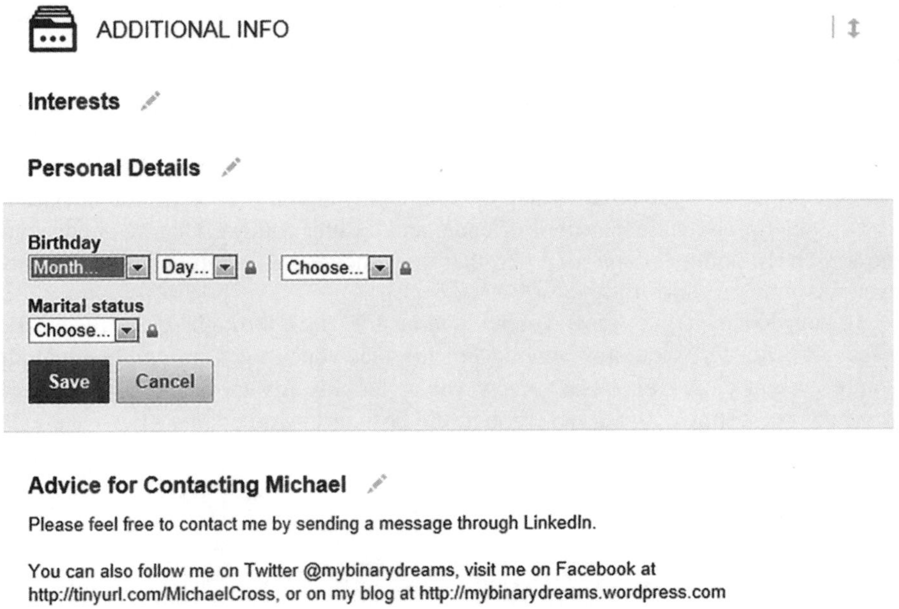

ADDITIONAL INFO | ↕

Interests ✎

Personal Details ✎

Birthday
Month... ▼ | Day... ▼ 🔒 | Choose... ▼ 🔒
Marital status
Choose... ▼ 🔒

Save | Cancel

Advice for Contacting Michael ✎

Please feel free to contact me by sending a message through LinkedIn.

You can also follow me on Twitter @mybinarydreams, visit me on Facebook at
http://tinyurl.com/MichaelCross, or on my blog at http://mybinarydreams.wordpress.com

FIGURE 3.3

Additional Info section of LinkedIn profile page.

3. Click on the pencil icon beside *Personal Details* to edit that area.
4. Set the dropdown lists so they don't show a birthday or marital status.
5. Click the Save button.

You should also be careful what you put in the *Advice for Contacting* you box, as you don't want to include addresses, phone numbers, or other personal information that can lead to problems. LinkedIn allows members to send messages through the site; so many people invite others to use that.

As you'd imagine, you'll find people have put some odd things that could raise eyebrows in the *Interests* section, so you'll want to be careful what you add here. It's always good to include interests that are relative to employment. Saying you have a love of eating, wine and spirits may be good if you're a chef, but may go against you if you're a diet consultant. Since recruiters look for well-rounded people (and in saying that, I'm not continuing the eating-related example), adding your more socially acceptable interests could also help you.

Another section to review when you edit your LinkedIn profile is the *Summary* section we mentioned earlier, which is found at the top of the page. The summary can be used to provide a brief description of your abilities, goals, education, and experience, but some people use this to enter contact information. You should never include your address, phone, email address, or other information in this section.

While you're essentially creating an online resume by filling out the fields on your profile page, you should remember that people can contact you by sending messages in LinkedIn. Since this is how people can contact you, you don't need to provide anything else.

Public profiles

Your public profile is information that can appear to everyone, including those searching for you in search engines like Google or Bing. If I'm not a contact of yours or even a member on LinkedIn, I will still be able to view what you've allowed me to see on your public profile. As mentioned, when you first create the account, everything on the profile is public. Because it's initially blank, this isn't a problem, but it creates a growing risk as you fill up the profile with more and more information.

It's up to you to limit what can be seen. Deciding what to include can be a precarious decision, because you want employers to see enough to offer you a job, but not anything that could allow someone to do such things as impersonate you, steal your identity, or apply for credit cards using the information on your page. In some cases, you may also want to limit exposure to information on your page because of the industry or position you work in. For example, you might want to prevent competitors from seeing a project you worked on, or your current position might require anonymity (as in the case of an undercover police officer). While much of what you publicize is a personal decision, there are some areas where you'll want to limit access.

You should always make careful decisions when considering what information people are able to review browsing your public profile. To change what people are allowed to see, consider doing the following:

1. Hover your mouse over your name at the top right of the screen.
2. Click *Settings* on the menu that appears.
3. Click the *Profile* tab in the bottom-left corner of the screen.
4. Click on *Change Public Profile*.

As seen in Figure 3.4, when the screen appears, there is a list of options at the right of the screen. By unchecking any boxes in the list, those areas of your profile won't be visible to the public. At a bare minimum, you should consider unchecking the *Show Details* boxes under Current Positions, Past Positions, and Education. In doing so, people will be able to see jobs you've held and schools you've attended, but won't be able to view any specifics related to them. Preventing these details from being viewed not only defends you, but may also protect your current and previous employers. The details provide information on the work you performed, and may include information on projects, procedures included in your duties, and systems used by an organization. For example, if you worked in IT, a hacker viewing the details of your job would probably see the types of servers, routers, and

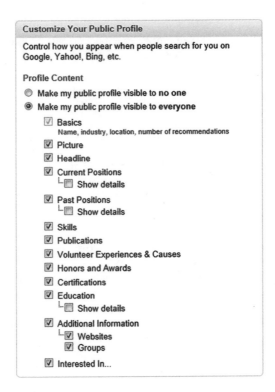

FIGURE 3.4

Customize your personal profile in LinkedIn.

other systems that you have experience with and used by the employer. This could be very helpful in finding ways to compromise security.

In looking at the options available in the *Customize Your Profile* section, you'll notice that the top one is *Make my public profile visible to no one*. Choosing this is the most secure, but will prevent anyone other than your connections from seeing your profile. If you're actively or passively looking for work, then you would not choose this option. It is however useful if you're not interested in a job and only using LinkedIn to connect with colleagues, access groups, or review information available through the site.

As you check and uncheck the boxes in this section, you'll notice that your profile to the left of the box will change. The information appearing on the left side of the screen is a preview of your public profile, and allows you to see how things will appear to others as changes are made. Because changes are saved as you modify the checkboxes, you don't need to click a "Save" button when you're satisfied with how it looks.

TOOLS & TIPS...

Email accounts for social media

You may want to consider creating a special email account for social media usage. On sites like LinkedIn, your primary email account is visible to your direct contacts, so they could use lookup tools on the Internet to find additional information about you. There are a number of free email services online, and this will allow you to read messages from people without having them contact any email accounts you use day to day. It can also reduce any SPAM messages that are disseminated through social media sites, and allow you to dispose of the account easily if you encounter problems with people. In some cases, a new account may already be created for you when you setup your social networking site. When you use Google+, you setup a Google account that includes Gmail. For Facebook, an email address based on your profile name is automatically created, and any email sent to it automatically appears in your Facebook messages. While social media is about interacting with people, it does not mean sacrificing security.

Passwords

While we'll discuss passwords in greater detail in Chapter 10, it is important to look at how passwords can be changed on sites like LinkedIn, and security issues that seem common among social media sites. Logging into LinkedIn requires two things:

1. Your email address
2. Password

For your email address, you should never post it so that others can see it on your profile page. If you do, a hacker will have half of what's needed to logon. You should also consider creating a separate email account for social media sites, which are used for logging on and receiving email from the sites. If you have an email address displayed on social networking sites, consider creating an Outlook (https://login.live.com) or Gmail (www.gmail.com) account and displaying that on your pages.

The second part of your login is what most people associate with security, and make little effort in making secure. As we'll discuss in Chapter 10, there are a number of tips that will reduce your chances of having an insecure password that is easily hacked. Some of these tips include changing it regularly every few months, and try and make it different from the previous version. When you do so, don't make it easy to guess. For sites like LinkedIn, you should be aware of how to change the password:

1. After you've logged on, hover your mouse over your name at the top right of the screen. Click *Settings* on the menu that appears.
2. When the settings page appears, click on the Password Change link.
3. Change your password on the screen that appears.

Your password may have already been compromised

On June 6, 2012, it was reported that a hacker had acquired and published the passwords of LinkedIn members on the Internet. Later that day, LinkedIn responded with an update on a blog confirming that "some of the passwords that were compromised correspond to LinkedIn accounts." This was an understatement. The hacker had uploaded 6.5 million LinkedIn passwords and 1.5 million eHarmony passwords to a Russian hacking site.

The security breach resulted in a $5 million class-action lawsuit that was started by two LinkedIn users. The case was dismissed before going to trial, with the Judge declaring that the plaintiffs hadn't shown they'd suffered any actual harm from the security breach. The judge further pointed out that even though they had paid for premium accounts, this was to acquire additional services and not additional security.

If you are a member of LinkedIn and have concern that your password may have been compromised, you can check by using a tool at https://lastpass.com/linkedin to determine if it was on the known list of passwords that were posted online. eHarmony users can also check using a similar tool at https://lastpass.com/eharmony. As seen in Figure 3.5, by entering your password and clicking the button, it will show you whether your password was one of the one's compromised.

Hacking 101

In the case of LinkedIn and eHarmony's security breach, the data the hacker uploaded was actually a list of hashed passwords. When sites and applications store your password, they generally don't save it as the text you enter (called clear text or plaintext). Instead, an algorithm is used to encrypt the password and store it as what's called a *hash*. In the case of LinkedIn, they used an outdated SHA-1 algorithm that left them vulnerable to decryption. For example, if your password was "password", it would be saved as the following (without quotes): "5baa61e4c9b-93f3f0682250b6cf8331b7ee68fd8". While this looks pretty secure to you and I, the problem is that there are password cracking programs that use files called *rainbow tables*. Without diving too far into cryptographic analysis, a rainbow table is basically a list of pre-computed hashes that are used to recover the text password

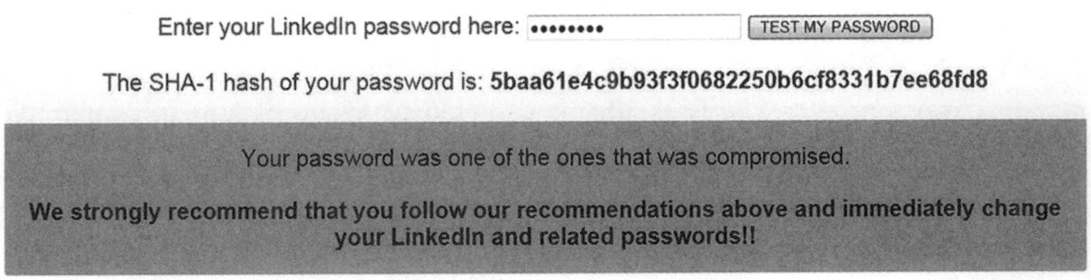

Enter your LinkedIn password here: ••••••• [TEST MY PASSWORD]

The SHA-1 hash of your password is: **5baa61e4c9b93f3f0682250b6cf8331b7ee68fd8**

Your password was one of the ones that was compromised.

We strongly recommend that you follow our recommendations above and immediately change your LinkedIn and related passwords!!

FIGURE 3.5

LinkedIn Password Checker at LastPass.

from a hash. Using these, the hashed passwords can be converted to text relatively quickly, allowing you to use the password to hack someone's account.

Still sounds difficult? Let's make it easier. Let's say you've acquired a password database from the aforementioned Russian hacking site. After all, the site is easy to find since the media publicized that the passwords were uploaded there. You could then use programs like Ophcrack (http://ophcrack.sourceforge.net) that use rainbow files to quickly convert the hashes to text passwords. If you didn't want to download the software, you could also go online and use a hash calculator like that found at http://www.xorbin.com/tools/sha1-hash-calculator, which will convert text to a hash, and vice versa. Once you've converted the password to text, you're now able to go to the site, type in the text password, and logon to that person's account.

Securing other settings on LinkedIn

While there are a wide variety of settings in LinkedIn, there are some other settings that you may want to configure. For the ones we'll discuss here, all of them can be accessed through the Accounts & Settings page, by doing the following:

1. Hover your mouse over your name at the top right of the screen.
2. Click *Settings* on the menu that appears.

LinkedIn can show your name, location, and industry on profile pages. This may not be an issue for some people, but others may not want this information publicized on the Internet. As seen in Figure 3.6, the Basic Information page has a *Display Name* option, which allows you to select whether your full name is shown, or just your first name and last initial. The page also has a *Location & Industry* section, which LinkedIn uses to suggest jobs related to your field and location. If you don't want people to see this information, you have a couple of options. First, you can set the *Location Name* option to show your city, or a larger general area. As you can see in Figure 3.6, based on my zip code of 90210 (and no, unfortunately that's not real), I have the option of choosing "Beverly Hills, California" or "Greater Los Angeles Area." Another option is to enter zeros in the zip code field, so that only your country is used.

To modify the settings for your name, location and industry, follow these steps:

1. Click the *Profile* tab in the bottom-left corner of the screen.
2. Click on *Edit your name, location & industry*.
3. When the screen appears, click the appropriate option to set whether your full name or just you first name and last initial appears as the name on your profile page.
4. In the *Location & Industry* section, click the appropriate option to set whether your *Location Name* will show your city or a greater geographic area.

If you travel or work from multiple computers, the information you send and receive may go over insecure or public networks. If you use LinkedIn on public computers (such as Internet café's or business centers in hotels), or use shared

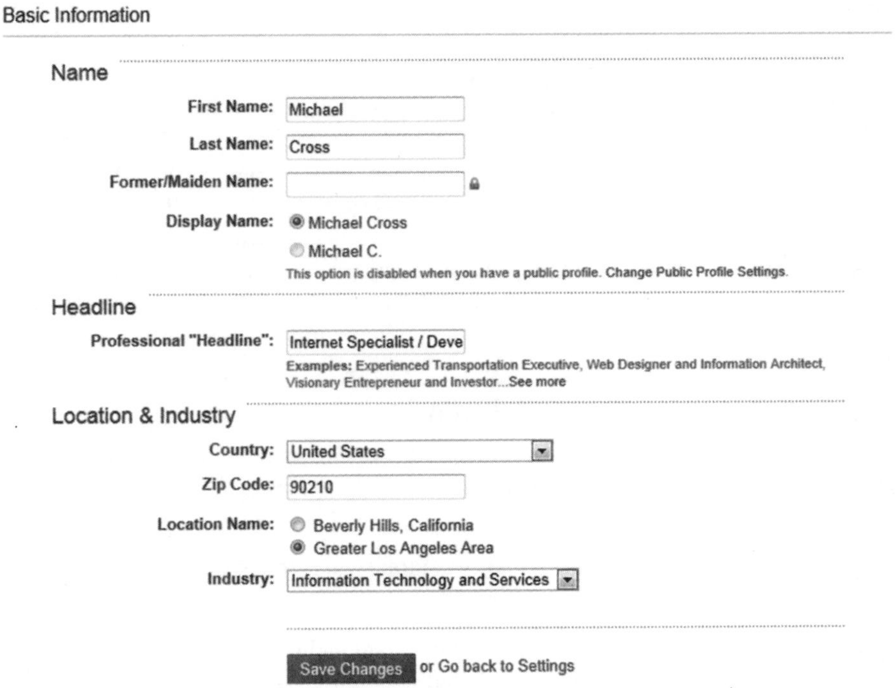

Basic Information

Name

First Name:	Michael
Last Name:	Cross
Former/Maiden Name:	🔒
Display Name:	◉ Michael Cross
	○ Michael C.

This option is disabled when you have a public profile. Change Public Profile Settings.

Headline

Professional "Headline": Internet Specialist / Deve

Examples: Experienced Transportation Executive, Web Designer and Information Architect, Visionary Entrepreneur and Investor...See more

Location & Industry

Country:	United States ▼
Zip Code:	90210
Location Name:	○ Beverly Hills, California
	◉ Greater Los Angeles Area
Industry:	Information Technology and Services ▼

Save Changes or Go back to Settings

FIGURE 3.6

Name, Location & Industry information in LinkedIn.

Wi-Fi connections (such as in airports, restaurants, and so on), you should set LinkedIn to use secure browsing mode. When this feature is activated, your browser will use Hypertext Transfer Protocol Secure (HTTPS) when browsing LinkedIn, which provides encrypted communication and secure identification of a network's Web servers. To modify your security settings, you should:

1. Click the *Account* tab in the bottom-left corner of the screen.
2. Click on *Manage Security Settings*.
3. When the screen appears, check the box that says *When possible, use a secure connection (https) to browse LinkedIn* and then click *Save Changes*.

Employees using social media

As you can see from the previous sections, there are a lot of different security configurations that can be made for a LinkedIn account, and chances are many of your employees and coworkers haven't used them. Many people accept default settings, meaning that anything typed into LinkedIn and other social networking sites may be available for the entire world to see. This can create a large number of security risks for individuals and your organization.

Security is a major issue for employees using social media, and a reason why many companies haven't allowed it in the workplace. Network administrators and IT staff will go through great efforts to protect a network by configuring computers, devices and software, and implementing security measures to prevent the outside world from seeing corporate data. However, there's nothing they can do about an employee's failure to properly set security on a personal social media site. Even if the business uses social media, it generally isn't an IT person who handles the Twitter, Facebook, and other accounts, so they have no control over how the accounts are configured and reconfigured. Instead of taking a proactive approach to network security, the business is suddenly forced to react to security breaches from social media.

The employee's control over security settings on so many different social media sites creates a shift in how a company needs to address security. Rather than focusing only on the organization's network security, the IT staff is placed in a role of having to become educators. They need to directly share recommendations on how to properly configure these accounts, or share that information with other people in the organization that train staff. Rather than manage the security of a network, computers, and other devices through configuration and software, there's suddenly an increased need to manage it through policy.

However, the need for education goes beyond the configuration of accounts, as there's a need for employees to know how to control information and conduct oneself online. Many organizations worry that employees could mention the company in an embarrassing way, or release internal information. It's a valid concern, but employees aren't the only ones working for you. Companies should also be concerned whether contractors, vendors, partners, and others related to the organization are leaking information and making embarrassing comments. After all, some vendors or contract workers may have more sensitive information than some of the people working for you, and can embarrass you just as easily.

A fine example of this is seen in an infamous mistake that was made on Twitter. James Andrews was then the Vice President of Ketchum, a public relations firm, and traveled to Memphis to do a presentation. After arriving, he tweeted the following: "True confession but i'm in one of those towns where I scratch my head and say 'I would die if I had to live here!'." Andrews' presentation was to FedEx, a major client of the firm, whose headquarters is proudly located in Memphis. A FedEx employee followed Andrews on Twitter, and passed the tweet to others in the company. Ironically, Andrews was there to talk about social media, but it was FedEx who instructed him. While chastising him in their response, they informed him that a "hazard of social networking is people will read what you write." FedEx ended their email paraphrasing the original post, by saying: "true confession: many of my peers and I don't see much relevance between your presentation this morning and the work we do in Employee Communications."

While the incident between Andrews and FedEx occurred in 2009, it attracted international attention and continues to be talked about years later. A company may have concerns about its own employees using social media properly, but there is no guarantee that others you do business with won't create problems. A lapse in judgment can have far-reaching implications, involve more than just the business you're working for, and linger for years. Although a mistake may be forgotten, mistakes in social media may never go away.

Allowing social media in the workplace

There are many good reasons why organizations haven't allowed social media in the workplace. However, many of the arguments against social media in the workplace are the same ones that were used against allowing employees any kind of Internet access:

- It lowers productivity. After all, I don't want my employees looking for other jobs, playing games or updating their status during company time.
- It could create a hostile work environment. If a colleague viewed or posted something offensive, it could result in harassment or workplace bullying complaints or lawsuits.
- Information could be leaked. A person could send confidential information to another person, or cause embarrassment with comments they make.
- It's a security risk. There are all sorts of malicious programs and viruses that could infect our network.

Issues are issues regardless of the medium. Employee productivity can be lowered by goofing around on Twitter or any other Web site, just as it can by wasting time by chatting around the water cooler. If I sit at my desk for a half hour looking for another job on LinkedIn, is it any more of a waste of company time than reading want ads in a newspaper? Regardless of how it happens, employee productivity can be controlled through proper management. The same applies to many other issues. If someone is looking at porn on an adult Web site, a magazine, or by browsing Twitter accounts, the issue is that they're violating corporate policy and conduct. Regardless of how it's done, the fact is that they're breaking the rules.

For other arguments dealing with technology, they are equally valid but need the same measure of unbiased consideration. There is a distinct risk that someone could leak information. However, this was just as valid a concern when email was new in the workplace, and most employees have proven they're responsible. While problems do exist with workers sending sensitive data, making inappropriate comments, or inadvertently leaking classified information, the real problem is that it's happening. It's not the forum that's an issue; it's what's being said.

Arguments related to the security of a network, computer, or other devices can be more complex. Computers on a network should be protected by antivirus software, and firewalls that prevent access to known security risks, such as sites known to disseminate malware and those used for social engineering (phishing). However, social media isn't always accessed from a network computer. People will use social networks and other sites from home computers, smartphones, and other devices that aren't constantly connected to a corporate network. Any devices owned by the company could be locked down using group policies or configurations that prevent installing software, but there's no protection for an employee's home computer. If possible, a company can offer an employee program that allows them to borrow and install a licensed copy of antivirus software or purchase software at a reduced price. They should at a minimum educate employees by raising awareness of common threats, make recommendations on installing the latest updates to software, suggest customized settings for social networking sites, and other information that will enhance security.

Because so many different kinds of content can be accessed with social media, the performance of a network can be bogged down by people watching videos or accessing other large files. Remember that social media is user-generated, so you're not always dealing with content that's been optimized for the Web, and made into a smaller size. A blog may have an incredibly large photo, or huge videos may be available to view. If a number of employees view such files, it can slow down the network. If the infrastructure of a network can't handle so much bandwidth being used, there is always the option to block access to social networking sites during peak hours. For example, a network administrator could configure a gateway to block types of social media during work hours, but allow people to visit YouTube or others sites during lunch hours.

While many organizations have resisted social media, there is no escaping it. Employees are already using social media in their personal and professional lives, and will continue using it even if the organization they work for has no social media presence. Just because your company doesn't allow access to social networking sites on a workstation, it doesn't mean that you can't tweet on your personal mobile phone or use Facebook when you get home. In other words, it's already too late. Even if you don't allow it in the workplace, social media is already accessible to employees.

Bibliography

Brenner, J. (2013, February 14). *Pew Internet: Social networking (full detail)*. Retrieved March 10, 2012, from Pew Internet & American Life Project: <http://pewinternet.org/Commentary/2012/March/Pew-Internet-Social-Networking-full-detail.aspx >.

Bureau of Consumer Protection Business Center. (2012, January). *Using consumer reports: What employers need to know*. Retrieved March 17, 2013, from Bureau of Consumer Protection Business Center: <http://business.ftc.gov/documents/bus08-using-consumer-reports-what-employers-need-know >.

CareerBuilder. (2012, April 18). *Thirty-seven percent of companies use social networks to research potential job candidates, according to new CareerBuilder Survey*. Retrieved March 17, 2013, from CareerBuilder: <http://www.careerbuilder.ca/share/aboutus/press-releasesdetail.aspx?id=pr691&sd=4%2F18%2F2012&ed=4%2F18%2F2099 >.

Downey, S. (2012, May 4). *Why DeleteMe is a subscription service and not a 1-time thing*. Retrieved March 17, 2013, from Abine: <http://www.abine.com/blog/2012/why-deleteme-is-a-subscription-service-and-not-a-1-time-thing/ >.

Edwards, J. (2009, January 20). *Worst Twitter post ever: Ketchum exec insults fedex client on mini-blog*. Retrieved April 1, 2013, from CBS Money Watch: <http://www.cbsnews.com/8301-505123_162-42740256/worst-twitter-post-ever-ketchum-exec-insults-fedex-client-on-mini-blog/ >.

Federal Trade Commission. (n.d.). *A summary of your rights under the Fair Credit Reporting Act*. Retrieved March 17, 2013, from Federal Trade Commission Consumer Information: <http://www.consumer.ftc.gov/articles/pdf-0096-fair-credit-reporting-act.pdf >.

Jobvite. (2012, July 9). *Jobvite social recruiting survey finds over 90% of employers will use social recruiting in 2012*. Retrieved March 18, 2013, from Jobvite: <http://recruiting.jobvite.com/company/press-releases/2012/jobvite-social-recruiting-survey-2012/ >.

Office of Governor Edmund G. Brown Jr. (2012, September 27). *Governor Brown signs laws to protect privacy for social media users*. Retrieved March 17, 2013, from Office of Governor Edmund G. Brown Jr.: <http://gov.ca.gov/news.php?id=17759 >.

Silveira, V. (2012, June 6). *An update on LinkedIn member passwords compromised*. Retrieved March 12, 2013, from LinkedIn: <http://blog.linkedin.com/2012/06/06/linkedin-member-passwords-compromised/ >.

Society for Human Resource Management. (2011, August 25). *The use of social networking websites and online search engines in screening job candidates survey findings*. Retrieved March 15, 2013, from Society for Human Resource Management: <http://www.shrm.org/Research/SurveyFindings/Articles/Pages/TheUseofSocialNetworkingWebsitesandOnlineSearchEnginesinScreeningJobCandidates.aspx >.

Taylor, L. C. (2012, April 5). *Suspension over Facebook photo by U.S. teacher's aide becomes a right-to-privacy lawsuit*. Retrieved March 17, 2013, from thestar.com: <http://www.thestar.com/news/world/2012/04/05/suspension_over_facebook_photo_by_us_teachers_aide_becomes_a_righttoprivacy_lawsuit.html >.

Vallone, J. (2012, July 11). *People search online big business, but FTC watching*. Retrieved March 17, 2013, from <http://news.investors.com/technology/071112-617755-websites-gather-tons-on-people.htm?p=full >.

Considerations for setting up Social Media

INFORMATION IN THIS CHAPTER:

- Considerations for Setting Up Social Media
- Why are We Doing This?
- Identifying How Social Media Will be Used in Your Organization
- Identifying Your Audience
- Internet Versus Intranet
- What's Being Said About Your Brand?
- Making the Right Decisions Early
- Identifying How You'll Represent Yourself on the Internet
- Approved Representatives
- Privacy
- Training and Policy

Considerations for setting up social media

Many people and organizations jump into using social media without giving any consideration as to why they're really doing it, what they're hoping to achieve, and whether they've considered all their options. While using social media, because so many others are, is certainly a motivating factor, just because someone else is doing something doesn't necessarily mean you should follow their example. That's the logic of lemmings, and you certainly don't want to follow someone over a cliff.

Even if an organization is in the same industry as another company, there are often differences between them. Although they could be very much alike, each company has unique needs and slight differences. In some cases, those differences can be quite distinct. If you looked at two department stores, you might find that one is a discount chain and the other serves higher-end products. They probably wouldn't carry the same products and would have different clientele who might even frequent different social media sites. Even the tone of how they address customers through social media might be different, with one appealing to a sense of humor and the other to a sense of decadence. While it could be beneficial for each company to see how the other is using such sites, you can see that how they utilize them would be very different.

Before creating a social media presence, there are many considerations that should be made that are specific to your needs. You should define clear goals, identify how it will be used, understand the audience you're trying to reach, and decide how you'll represent yourself. These are components of creating a strategy that will guide how social media will be used to your advantage.

While much of this chapter will focus on the business use of social media, this isn't to say we've forgotten individuals using social sites. After all, an organization's employees will use these sites, either on behalf of the company or on their own time. In using them, you should understand how companies target you in social media, possible security risks, and how inappropriate use can impact your employer and employment.

Why are we doing this?

In the excitement of any new endeavor, you'd be surprised how many people forget to ask the simple question "why are we doing this?" If you ask a key player, you'll find that some will be defensive and others will parrot back something they heard in a sales pitch or seminar. For those who have thought out why they're using social media, they can generally explain what the organization is hoping to achieve, how they're working toward those goals, and perhaps even tell you some indicators being used to measure success.

An organization may have many reasons why a social media presence is necessary, because different departments may want to use it for different purposes. Sales staff may see it as a way to raise product awareness and lead customers to the company's Web site to place orders. Customer service may want to decrease the number of support calls and use these sites to provide information on service outages and answers to common questions. HR may see it as a way of hiring employees and interacting with other professionals. Developers may want to create blogs providing technical support and inform customers about software upgrades and new versions of products. As you can see by this, different people will have different ideas on how the company should use social media.

Requirements gathering

Gathering the requirements of an organization is an important step in determining how those needs will be met. Never assume that you know what people want. Using surveys and interviewing department managers can provide important insight into how social media can solve problems and improve how things are currently done. If you're unsure about what they want, go back and get them to clarify it so you have a firm understanding. You may have started by looking at how social media could be used for one purpose, only to find that there are a number of ways it can provide solutions.

When asking about requirements, you'll want to initially keep things simple and avoid making too many references to specific technology or solutions. Remember that you're the expert, and many will be learning as they go. Just because you know the difference between a content community and a social network, the people you're talking to may not. Because of this, you may get inaccurate answers if they don't comprehend what you're saying. For example, one time I asked a person whether he wanted a blog on his new site and he said yes. When I later noticed it wasn't being used, I realized he didn't know what a blog was and had been too embarrassed to ask. Once you know what a group requires, you'll be able to discuss ways to meet those needs and introduce new terms, processes, and sites as part of educating them about social media.

By gathering requirements that are specific, realistic, and measurable, you'll find that you're getting information that will be used throughout your social media project. To avoid any disputes, you should create a requirements document that outlines the needs and specifications in a clear and thorough manner. The document can then be reviewed by those you've interviewed, who can correct mistakes or agree that you understood each need.

In talking with managers and coworkers, you'll often find that people have resources you were unaware of. Perhaps, the HR department is already using a social network like hr.com and has access to information on how others achieved success using social media. They would also have insight regarding rules and regulations related to their particular field of expertise. As an added benefit, you may find people who are enthusiastic and want to play a bigger part in helping you to achieve success.

If your organization is already using social media, then it's not too late to go back and gather requirements for your organization. In fact, it's a good idea to do so every so often. Doing so will help you build on what you've already achieved, identify mistakes that need to be fixed, and discover things that have changed. You may find new goals or that previous ones need to be refined.

When setting goals, you should establish how you'll know if they've been met. Indicators of success do not need to be overly complicated. For example, if your HR department wanted to use social media to hire people, the indicators of success might be setting up a page on LinkedIn, posting jobs, searching for active and passive candidates, and (of course) hiring people found on that site. By setting goals and having clear indicators and milestones for success, you will be able to show whether social media is working for the organization as intended. It will also help to guide you in its use, the types of social media involved, and the role it plays within the organization.

What is the place of social media in your organization?

By learning what's needed in your business, you'll begin to understand how social media will be used. You'll often find that different departments will have common needs, such as wanting to communicate information more efficiently, and others that are unique to a specific group. These needs can be matched with features on various social media sites, equipment they'll need to purchase, and so on, so that they're able to perform the tasks they need to achieve results.

When a business looks at using social media, they'll also need to decide how it will physically be used. Many departments may only want employees to access it from computers on their network. However, some departments may want to post and access content on the go, which means the company will need to purchase smartphones, tablets, or other devices so employees can use social media on the road. Not only does this need to be identified so the business includes the necessary equipment in their budget, but it may also lead to questions about whether the devices are configured to broadcast its physical location, which is used by social media sites like Foursquare.

Is it really needed?

You've probably heard the adage "If dreams were horses, then beggars would ride." Not everything someone identifies as desirable or necessary for social media may be a priority or even possible. Just because everyone wants brand-new tablets to access social media doesn't mean the business can afford it. Similarly, they may want to see information about each person who visits their page on a social site, only to find out that the feature doesn't exist. As the requirements mount, you'll find that there are varying degrees of what's needed and realistic.

The MoSCoW principle is a technique that helps to prioritize requirements, so that everyone involved understands the importance of a particular need or desire. The word *MoSCoW* comes from the first letter of Must have, Should have, Could have, and Won't. In using it with a list of requirements, you associate a requested item with one of the following categories to set its priority:

- *Must*, which is something that has to be included in a project. If the requirement isn't met, then this could cause your social media project to fail. For example, if the primary reason for starting the project was to have updates about media releases posted on Twitter, then a Twitter account would be a must.
- *Should*, which is a requirement that is a higher priority and should be included if possible. For example, the social media person would probably need a smartphone or tablet to post and access content on social media sites at any time. This should be included, but if you couldn't afford it, the person could use the laptop he or she already has to do the work.
- *Could*, which is a requirement that may be desirable but isn't really needed. If there's time and available resources it may be included. For example, graphics can enhance a site and help to increase interest in your brand. Paying for an account on an infographics site would help with this, but it wouldn't prevent you from being successful.
- *Won't*, which is something that won't be included in the current project. It may be included in the future, but it isn't needed now.

As you determine what will and won't be included, the shape of how social media is used and the business' presence on these sites will begin to take form.

You'll be able to associate the necessary functionality with the features offered by various sites and platforms. Key players will be established, and you'll begin to see who will be using it and how it will be used. While there will still be questions that need to be answered, many of them will be resolved through the information you've compiled.

How will it be used?

Prior to looking into the prospect of using social media, you probably had a number of core reasons, which were expanded on as you gathered the requirements of others in your company. In looking through this information, you'll find that how social media will be used falls into three basic categories:

1. An Internet-based social media presence for you and\or your organization. These would include Twitter, Facebook, and other publicly accessible sites.
2. Internal social media. As we'll see later in this chapter, there are platforms that run on an *intranet*, which are private networks that use Internet-based technologies. These are used to provide sites and services that are accessible to people on your corporate network, such as Microsoft SharePoint. There are also sites on the Internet that limit access to members of an organization, such as Yammer.
3. Internet sites that members of your organization can use and\or join, such as we mentioned earlier in the example of your HR department using a site like hr.com.

A presence on the Internet is what most people think of when an organization looks at using social media, and what we focus on in this book. However, it isn't the only possible solution for your social media needs. If you're trying to reach the public, then you would want to create an Internet presence. If you wanted to provide social networking between members of your staff or give them the ability to interact with others in their profession, then you might want to look at creating your own internal social networking platform or use existing sites.

As we'll discuss in greater detail later in this chapter, software platforms like Microsoft SharePoint can be installed on corporate network servers or accessed via the Internet to provide social networking and collaboration features to users. SharePoint allows you to create sites that provide blogs, wikis, profile pages, and many other features. Because you control security, individual SharePoint sites can only be accessed by those you designate. This can be very useful as a replacement for a corporate intranet Web site, as it allows members of your organization to collaborate with one another, share documents and it also provides a platform for Web-based applications and communication.

Although there are resources to create individual sites for groups in your company, don't feel that you need to reinvent the wheel and create something that already exists. This is especially true when there's a need to interact with others in the same profession who work outside of your organization. There are hundreds of social media sites available on the Internet. Some of these are used by the general public, but there are many that are specific to certain groups of professionals. If you search Google, and enter your profession followed by the word "social network," you'll probably be surprised that a social network or community exists. For example, if your IT staff wanted a social network for developers, you'd find sites like:

- *Stack overflow* (www.stackoverflow.com), which is a great source for posting problems with code, chat about development issues, getting answers to questions, and so on. Badges are earned as you assist others by answering questions.
- *Reddit—programming* (www.reddit.com/r/programming), which provides voting on news related to programming topics, resources, and news.

Depending on how social media will be used in your organization, you may find that some of these resources are available or already being used. In creating a social media strategy for your business, you should identify such things as:

- Do key members of the organization already have Twitter or LinkedIn accounts? You may find that a number of individuals have accounts of their own, which may mean that you don't need to create new ones for them. If you decide to use corporate Twitter accounts for each of these members (such as one for the CEO, social media representatives, so on, regardless of who they are), then you may need to clarify that one is for business and theirs is only for personal use.
- Has a member of staff may have previously created an organization page on Facebook or added information about the organization to Wikipedia? Before going too far, you should search major social media sites and any additional ones you're planning to use to determine whether a page or an account already exists.
- Do we have access to any of the accounts previously created for the organization? It's possible someone created a Facebook page or Twitter account, but it has remained dormant. You may need to find who created it, what the password is, or if you need to report the page so that the social media site can delete it.
- Are the existing accounts and pages legitimate? If you find pages and accounts related to you or your organization and it wasn't created by you or someone in your company, someone may be impersonating you and you'll need to take action, as we'll discuss in Chapter 10.

You should also investigate what your intranet is using for its Web site. If your intranet is running SharePoint, it may not be obvious. In branding the site, the business may have added your business logo, personalized it with a unique name, added custom navigation and page designs, or have other elements that make it indistinguishable from SharePoint sites that don't have any customization. In such a case, you may think your intranet is a standard Web site, especially if many of the social networking features are not currently being used.

As you discover what's already being used, decisions may need to be made as to what will be replaced. While many businesses use social media as an extension of their existing Web site, some may see a social media presence as a replacement.

A small business that doesn't get much benefit from paying hosting fees, domain name registration, and paying to have static Web pages professionally modified may decide that a page on Facebook is all they need. Similarly, if the company decides to use SharePoint or some other collaboration site, they may decide that the current intranet Web site is no longer needed.

There may also be internal processes that will be replaced by your social media presence. For example, let's say that when your company posts a new press release on its Web site, you email every news outlet that the media release is available on your site. This requires administration, because you need to maintain a distribution list of email addresses. If you decided to use Twitter, this process might be changed. Anyone following you would be notified about the new press release in your tweets and be able to click a link to open it directly. By this one simple change, there is zero administration for maintaining an email distribution list and the email account used specifically to send out press updates is no longer needed. Depending on your organization, you may find a number of changes can occur as social media sites are used.

How will it not be used?

A message conveyed once can be read many times. When thinking of social media, people tend to gravitate toward it, being content created by the user, and can overlook the perspective of the reader. As you start to use social media in your organization, it's important to remember that there are more people who will read content than write it. While your organization may have a few people who will post a message or write a blog, there are many more who use social media sites as a source of information.

In gathering requirements, you may find a number of departments who have no use for social media. In saying that, they may mean creating content. They may find it very beneficial to read information on wikis and blogs or find out the latest information from a vendor's social networking page or tweets. This is an important requirement to identify, as it may require accounts to be setup, policies to change, changes to firewall settings, and so on.

You will also find that there are people in your organization who have no use whatsoever for social media. This shouldn't discourage you in trying to get people to adopt social media. Some departments and positions may simply not have a use for it. For example, the payroll department may care less about a public social media presence, because any of their information would be sent internally to employees. Others may not see a need to communicate any information. It's a simple fact of life that not everything is for everyone. If you encounter this, just let them know that the business is implementing it and you're available if they change their minds and you can help in the future.

You also shouldn't feel that you need to be on all of the social media sites or use ones that aren't of benefit to you. It's better to have a good presence on a few sites than to have a poor one on many sites. Choosing the ones that will be of most advantage and keeping them updated with fresh content will attract and keep people following what you have to say.

Even though you don't use all of the sites, you will want to create accounts on the most popular social media sites as a defensive measure against impersonation. As we'll discuss in Chapter 10, if you create LinkedIn and Twitter accounts for senior members of your staff, it can aid against others pretending to be that person. Setting up such accounts will also reserve the account names for your use, so they're not taken by others. This is something that actor Leonard Nimoy experienced when he tried to register as LeonardNimoy, only to find someone else had taken the name. As a result, he was left using the Twitter account @TheRealNimoy.

Identifying your audience

Knowing who your audience will be is important for any business. If you're creating a social media presence, you'll want to know who will be viewing your pages and tweets so that you can create appropriate content for them. You'll also want to know this so that you create accounts on sites they're using. By understanding who you'll be talking to, you'll know how to talk to them.

While social media sites are used by millions of people, some are more popular than others. According to Pew Internet & American Life Project, as of December 2012, the following percentage of adults said they visited these sites:

- 67% use Facebook
- 16% use Twitter
- 15% use Pinterest
- 13% use Instagram
- 6% use Tumblr

Also, as we mentioned in Chapter 3, as of August 2012, 20% of adults use LinkedIn. While this gives us an understanding of which sites adults are using the most, the demographics of your target audience may also consist of specific genders, ages, races, and so on.

Since 2009, women are more likely than men to use social networking sites. As of December 2012, 71% of women as opposed to 62% of men used these sites. This however is not the case when you look at certain sites on the Internet (and no, I don't mean *those* sites). In visiting www.socialstatistics.com, you'll find that the male\female ratio is reversed on Google+. At the time of this writing, the site showed (based on a sample set of 183,464 profiles) that 69.4% of men and 29.2% women used Google+.

The Pew Internet & American Life Project's *State of Social Media Users* study also found that specific groups of people tend to use other popular sites more than others. The number of Twitter users doubled since 2010, with more men using it than women. It has a higher usage among people who are black than Latino or white Internet users and has most used by people between the ages of 18–29 and those who live in urban areas.

Facebook is by far the most popular social media site looked at in the survey and is more popular among women than men. While a high number of people in all groups use the site, it is most popular among people of age 18–29 and those with some college. While the household income of those using Facebook is fairly evenly spread, most of those using the site had higher incomes of over $50,000/year and lived in urban areas.

Pinterest is especially popular among women with five times more female Internet users than men using it. The highest groups of people on Pinterest are those with college or higher education and those making higher incomes. It also appeals more to white people, those under the age of 50 and people living in rural or suburban areas.

Instagram is also more popular among women than men and those who are under the age of 50. In terms of race, more black Internet users are on Instagram, followed by Latino, and then white users. It is also more popular among people with some college, and those with lower household incomes, with Internet users making less than $30,000/year being its highest group. Instagram is also more popular in urban areas than those in suburban or rural areas.

Although fewer Internet users are on Tumblr than the other social media sites included in the survey, it appeals equally male and female Internet users. It was slightly more popular among Latino users than white or black users. Most of those using Tumblr were found to be in the age range of 18–29% and were mostly living in urban areas.

Younger audiences

While the survey only focused on groups who were 18 years or older, don't think that children aren't major users of social media. Even though the terms of using social media sites often have an age requirement, children will enter an age that will allow them to access. In a 2011 survey, Consumer Reports found that of 20 million Facebook users who were minors, 7.5 million of them were under the age of 13 and 5 million were 10 and under. Even though Facebook's terms of use states "You will not use Facebook if you are under 13," this should come as no surprise. There are a considerable number of games available on Facebook, and many that are designed to appeal to younger audiences.

Other sites may also have restrictions that may or may not be adhered to in real life. For example, Twitter's Terms of Service doesn't specify a specific age, but states that you can only use it "if you can form a binding contract with Twitter and are not a person barred from receiving services under the laws of the United States or other applicable jurisdiction." While the legal age you can enter into a contract can vary from state to state and country to country, the common age in most parts of the United States, Canada, and the United Kingdom is 18. However, a person may enter into a legally binding agreement under certain conditions, such as when the person is under the age of 18 but has parental consent. Despite this, there is no real control on social media sites for preventing a minor from using the service, as it's essentially an honor system that trusts a person is honest about their age when creating an account.

In 2010, Pew Internet & American Life Project reported that 73% of Internet users between the ages of 12 and 17 used social networks. Of those who were 14–17 years old, 82% of them reported using social media, while 55% of those aged 12–13 admitted to using these sites. Of course, being that they aren't allowed to use such sites under the terms of use, one can assume the actual number is higher as a number of kids would be resistant to admitting the truth.

The types of sites frequented by younger Internet users differ from those used by adults. A September 2009 survey by Pew Internet & American Life Project found that only 8% of Internet users aged 12–17 use Twitter. It also found that 8% of online teens use virtual worlds like Second Life, with younger users aged 12–13 using these sites more than older teens. In addition to the previously mentioned popularity of Facebook, they are also more prone than adults to use sites that allow them to create and share content.

Internet versus intranet

Social networking isn't only used for reaching people on the Internet. Many companies use products with social networking features to share information with employees. These software platforms and sites allow employees to create profile pages, chat with coworkers, assign tasks, share documents, create their own pages, blogs and wikis, and other features that enable user-generated content and collaboration. Such products are increasingly common on corporate intranets. In fact, they may be used as a company's internal Web site, which only employees have access to, or as an extension of an existing internal or public site to allow employees, partners, vendors, and others to collaborate on projects.

Collaboration is a major factor in using such products, as these features provide an opportunity for employees to use technology for sharing information and working as teams. Common features of collaboration include shared calendars, discussion boards, task management, file sharing, and storage. Using such features, you can have multiple people working on documents, so that multiple versions of the same document aren't being created and passed between people via email or as files in various directories. As documents are changed, versions of the file can be created so that you can revert to a previous version if needed. You can also add many of the features available on your primary site to smaller collaboration sites, allowing you to create wikis, blogs, and other features that are only available to members of your team.

Microsoft SharePoint is a popular platform that provides the features we mentioned. Figure 4.1 shows a team site created in SharePoint 2010, which allows specific members of a team to generate their own content and collaborate on projects together. Using SharePoint, users of an organization can publish their own content, creating Web pages, organizing files into searchable libraries, and perform other tasks that previously required the intervention of IT staff. It also provides records and content management features to manage documents and assign a life cycle to

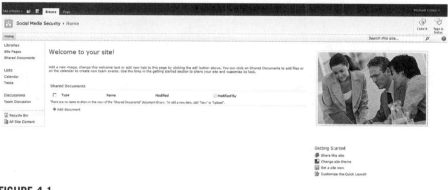

FIGURE 4.1

SharePoint 2010 team site.

content, so that it is archived or deleted when it is no longer relevant. Groups created in SharePoint allow you to control who can view, contribute, and approve content, ensuring that only those with the correct permissions can access information. If you need additional functionality, components that can be added to your pages called *Web parts* can be purchased or developed, allowing you to run other applications or content within the environment.

There are a large number of organizations who use SharePoint for their corporate intranet. In 2011, Microsoft's market research reported that 78% of Fortune 500 companies use SharePoint. However, while it is a powerful platform, it does involve certain overhead of having the infrastructure to support it, inclusive to servers to host the Web frontend and SQL Server backend, as well as having IT staff to provide technical support. Because smaller to medium companies may find this cost prohibitive, Microsoft has a cloud-based version available called SharePoint Online that doesn't require a stand-alone version running on corporate servers. SharePoint Online provides the features of the stand-alone platform but has the site hosted on Internet servers.

Creating a corporate social network on the Internet may not be an option for many companies. Your organization may have policies or regulations that require any data to be stored on internal servers and would not allow using a multitenant server for business purposes. For example, the European Union has strict privacy laws that protect data on citizens. If data stored on the cloud resided on servers in the United States, US law enforcement and Intelligence agencies could potentially access a company's data under the Patriot Act. Similar concerns may exist for storing data on servers in other countries with antiterrorism or other legislation that allows them broad powers over accessing information.

If you're not prevented from hosting a social network for your business on the Internet, SharePoint is not the only option for businesses. Huddle (www.huddle.com) and Yammer (www.yammer.com) are social networks for businesses that also provide collaboration features. Both of these have integrated support for SharePoint and

FIGURE 4.2

A site created on Yammer.

Office 365. For example, in Office 365, you can replace the SharePoint newsfeed with one from Yammer or embed the Yammer newsfeed into a SharePoint site. In doing so, Yammer appears as part of the existing SharePoint or Office environment.

As seen in Figure 4.2, without any changes in branding the site so that it has a different look and feel, Yammer has an appearance and functionality similar to Facebook. It allows you to provide status updates, post events, create polls that others can answer, and share images, videos, and documents. For communicating with others, you can send and receive email within Yammer or chat with others who are online. It also allows you to create groups and invite users, so that they can join you in a project and work with you as a team. If someone does especially well, there is a feature that allows you to praise the person, giving them the recognition they deserve.

Once you've created a new social network on Yammer, you can invite other people in your company. When logging in, access is determined by the domain of your email address, ensuring that only those with a corporate email account can log on to the network. Administrative features allow you to invite, remove, or block users who have joined.

Yammer is available free of charge, but fees are applied if you want more advanced features. As is the case with SharePoint Online, pricing is done through subscription or can also be combined with Office 365. Other sites like Huddle provide a free trial, but charge after the trial period has expired.

What's being said about your brand?

It's always good to know what people are saying before you enter a conversation. Before and after implementing social media for your business, you should review mentions of your business so you can gauge how people view your organization, track trends and activity, and identify issues you may encounter. By understanding the perspective of those you're engaging, you won't be caught off-guard and will be able to plan how your campaigns will create a positive opinion of your brand.

Before you begin using tools to monitor social media, you should create a list of what you're going to monitor. Any sites or apps you use will require you to provide sites or keywords that will be used to search for conversations and other activity related to that criteria. Some of the things you may decide to monitor include:

- Names of people and accounts. You will want to watch for instances where your name or the names of key people in your organization are mentioned, as well as any accounts they have. This could include email addresses and usernames, like those used on Twitter.
- The name of your organization or brand name. Depending on the size of your business, this might also include any subsidiaries your company owns.
- The names of your products and any related project names. Some industries will try and conceal the real name of a product being developed by using codenames prior to their release. For example, Windows 7 was referred to as *Blackcomb* and *Vienna* prior to its final release, while movie makers tried to hide the filming of the movie *The Dark Knight* under the secret identity of "Rory's First Kiss."
- The URLs of your corporate Web site and any social media sites being used.

While monitoring mentions of your own brand, you should also consider monitoring those of competitors. In doing so, you'll see what's working for them, what's unpopular, and gain insights into how you'll create future campaigns and conversations. The information you acquire from these trends and conversations can also be useful in advertising, sales, and other areas of your business.

Monitoring conversations

There are many different ways to monitor social media. While we'll discuss a number of tools in Chapters 5 and 11, you don't necessarily need to purchase additional software or subscriptions to online services prior to starting a presence. There are ways you can investigate what's being said, what people are interested in, and who's linking to your site. Some of these are offered by social media sites themselves, while others are available through mobile apps and third party Web sites.

Google Alerts (www.google.com/alerts) allows you to get updates on results found by the search engine, which can be emailed to you immediately, daily, or once a week. Going to this Web site, a "Search query" box allows you to enter the terms you want to be updated on. These terms could be a name, organization, Twitter username, URL, or anything else you wanted to be notified about as Google finds it. This provides an easy way of following what's being said by yourself and others on specific topics, people, or other entities related to your business.

Search engines can also be useful to monitor what's being said and get an overview of how your brand is perceived and where it's mentioned. By typing your Twitter username into a search engine like Google, you'll see results of tweets you've made and others that include your Twitter name. Searching for your name,

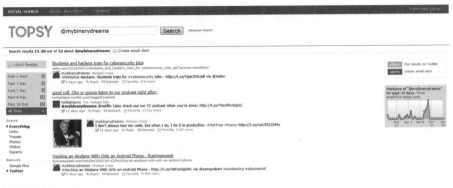

FIGURE 4.3

Topsy.

business name, site, products, and other keywords related to you can return results that will let you know what's being said about your brand and on what sites. If you're searching for a name with spaces in it, you should include them in quotation marks to search for that exact phrase. If you want to limit the results to searching a particular site, include the word "site:" followed by the domain name of the Web site you're searching, for example "*BusinessName* site:facebook.com." Alternatively, you can use the Advanced Search features to get the results you want.

As we'll discuss in Chapter 11, online monitoring tools often have free features or a trial period where you can evaluate its full functionality. These provide a better way of searching for social media content and monitoring conversations. For example, Topsy (www.topsy.com) provides a search engine that returns the most recent and relevant results based on the calculated social influence of a conversation. As seen in Figure 4.3, by typing in your Twitter username, business name, Web site URL, or other search criteria, it will return results of where you were mentioned and allow you to see which posts and tweets link back to your site. It also provides free analytics, where you can search and compare mentions within Twitter that have been retweeted or contain links. This lets you to compare mentions of your organization's name, domain name, Twitter account, or other terms you're interested in.

As we've mentioned in previous chapters, hashtags are words used in twitter that start with a number sign (#). Clicking one in Twitter allows you to see any other tweets using the same hashtag, allowing you to follow the conversation. By searching for ones created for a campaign, you can follow their usage. If several are being used by a campaign, you can use tools like Topsy to see which is the most popular.

Such sites can also be useful in following trends and seeing what people are talking about. Tools like Topsy allow you to view the latest trends in conversations and search for topics to see what people currently find interesting. Of course, in looking at what people want to know about your business, you shouldn't ignore the tools already available to you.

Your corporate Web site can also give you clues as to what interests' people. You should look at which pages are most viewed on your site. If people are visiting pages with press releases, product support, or other areas of interest, then consider including updates about this information on your social media sites. If your site has search features, you can look at the queries people are making when searching your site and identify trends in topics that are currently of interest. In gathering this information from the IT staff or Webmaster of your Web site, you may find valuable insight into what topics will engage people through your tweets and posts.

As you create your social media presence, you'll also find that the sites themselves provide monitoring tools. Twitter provides a couple of ways to search for what's being said. By clicking on @*Connect* on the top navigation bar and then clicking the *Mentions* tab on the left side of the screen, you'll see a list of anything containing your username. This includes any mention of your username in tweets, as well as replies. You can also enter a name or username in the search field at the top of the screen to search for any mentions of an account or a name.

Twitter also provides an advanced search feature at www.twitter.com/search-advanced, where you can search for words, phrases, and hashtags. You can limit results on the basis of tweets to and from specific accounts, mentions of a username in tweets, and those that originated near a location. You can also limit results to positive and/or negative tweets, questions, and whether to include retweets.

Facebook also provides ways to follow conversations and view information related to your page. By clicking on the Notifications icon in the upper left hand corner of the screen, a dropdown menu will appear showing who's Liked or commented on one of your posts. Clicking on the notification takes you to the post, allowing you to view the comments.

Facebook pages also provide basic information about new and total likes to your page, but as the number of users who like your page increases, you gain access to Insights. As we'll discuss in Chapter 11, Facebook Insights is an analytics platform that allows you to view user statistics like daily and monthly active users, new users, daily comments, and so on. These provide a benchmark for determining the quality of what's posted on your pages, allowing you to see whether new content has generated conversations and impacted users through Likes and comments.

Blog sites like WordPress (www.wordpress.com) also provide important information that should be monitored. After logging into your blog, you can review the comment people have made, statistics on the number of people who have visited and where they're from, top searches, and the number of followers and shares to the blog. Such information helps to keep a pulse on what people find most interesting about your site, and what kinds of information you should provide more of to generate conversation and interest.

Making the right decisions early

The earlier you make decisions about your social media presence, the fewer problems you'll have later. The worst approach is winging it, without any forethought about what you hope to achieve or how you or your business will manage the sites and accounts. As we've seen throughout this chapter, there are many questions that need to be answered, and many decisions that need to be made by the right people in an organization.

Setting corporate goals

Before implementing social media, you should identify what you want to achieve from it. Many businesses make the mistake of jumping into the social media pool, simply because that's what everyone else is doing. However, unless you have an understanding of what the business hopes to get out of its investment, you'll never really know whether you're succeeding or not. Clearly defining goals will help to guide you in how you'll handle your social media presence, the type of posts and tweets you make, and identify the markers that show whether you're successful.

First, you should set some high-level objectives, which will be the primary goals for what you want to achieve. These could include:

- Increasing visits to your corporate Web site or an ecommerce site, resulting in higher sales
- Engage the consumer and build customer relations
- Raise awareness or change the perception of your organization or a product
- Generate conversations about products in an effort to advertise
- Decrease the number of support calls (e.g., people phoning a call center) by providing online support
- Increase the number of shares, Likes, or people following what your business has to say
- Increase entries into a contest

Without setting objectives, you won't know what to measure as success factors and whether your strategy is working. You might consider social media a success because you have a certain number of Likes on a Facebook page, but you'd be unpleasantly surprised if your boss was doing this to increase sales.

You should also set secondary goals, which can be used as milestones related to the primary ones you've set. For example, you might set a goal of acquiring a certain number of subscriptions to a blog, comments on Facebook, or followers on Twitter by a certain date. You may want to see an increase in sales or a decrease in advertising costs over a specified period. As you reach these targets, you can see that you're getting closer to achieving the big goals.

Getting the right people together

Unless you have a smaller business, creating a social media presence generally isn't a one person job. No matter how smart you are, chances are you don't have all the answers to questions that need to be asked. To do it properly, you need to bring key players and specialists within your business together early in the process.

Forming a governance committee for social media can be a big advantage for organizations. As we'll discuss in Chapter 11, such committees can be extremely useful in formulating policy, training, monitoring, crisis management, and establishing guidelines and procedures. Members can be from different areas of your organization but should include people who can answer common questions and identify risks. This might include a representative of the IT department, legal department, public relations, training, and other members of your organization who can help ask the right questions and give the right answers.

By creating a governance committee, you're surrounding yourself with people who can make effective decisions and recommendations. This group can help define the roles and procedures that will be used in social media and help you to understand who to contact for guidance in specific situations.

Remembering technology in the equation

Because setting up social media accounts is so easy, it's easy to forget concerns related to the technology being used. There may be new email accounts that need to be set up, existing IT-related policies that need to be adhered to or modified, concerns about devices, and firewall rules that may need to be changed. If you're planning on certain devices like smartphones or tablets to be used, then these may need to be purchased and configured by the business prior to the organization's social media launch. While the account may be simple to set up, other elements related to technology may require considerable thought and work.

If a business plans to use social media, then they will probably want computers or devices on the network to access those sites. Firewall rules may exist that will block social networking and other sites, preventing a person from visiting Facebook, LinkedIn, Twitter, and so on. It could be somewhat embarrassing if you announced your business' new social media presence, only for employees to find that the organization didn't trust the site and still blocked computers from accessing it. Even worse, if you needed to send an important tweet, you might find that your tablet or smartphone couldn't do it due to such restrictions. To avoid these problems, you'll need to notify your IT department as to what social media sites employees are allowed to visit. If employees in general aren't allowed to use social media, then you'll need to notify them as to what network accounts, computer names or devices should have access.

Just because social media sites are easy to use, remember that setting up social media for a business goes beyond the actual account creation. By working with your IT department, you'll be able to identify where changes need to be made, and what restrictions need to be in place to keep the business and its employees safe.

Nonwork computers

There are many potential threats on the Internet, and people using social media will access it from work and home. Antivirus software may protect computers on a corporate network, but how would you know if an employee's personal devices are protected? A home computer might be used to click a link that installs malicious software (i.e., malware) or exposes a machine to code that exploits vulnerabilities.

In such a case, passwords used to access a business' social media accounts, and other sensitive information could be compromised. To avoid such problems, you might consider offering an employee program where antivirus software is offered to employees at a discounted price. Depending on the software license agreement your company has with Symantec, McAffee, or other vendors, you may be able to offer active employees free home use of the antivirus product.

Since browsers can save a password for a site, it's also possible an unauthorized person can access the account. Internet Explorer, Chrome, and other browsers will give the option of saving the password for a site, so you don't have to type the password the next time you visit. However, if the social media accounts were saved on a nonwork computer or device, it could be disastrous. Imagine how embarrassing it would be if a tweet was sent by a child using an employee's family computer, or the chaos that could result if a person in an Internet café used a computer after you accessed the company's social media site. To prevent this, you need to be aware of such problems and implement policies to prohibit saving passwords or accessing accounts from certain locations.

Shortened URLs and related risks

URLs (Uniform Resource Locators) are the Web site addresses you enter into the address bar of your browser. They contain the domain name of a site (such as facebook.com) and any directories and files that you're trying to open. An example of a URL would be Microsoft's page on family safety when using social media, which is http://www.microsoft.com/security/family-safety/kids-social.aspx. As you can see from this, some URLs can be quite long and cumbersome. It also may be a concern when you're making a tweet that allows a limited number of characters in the message. In the example just given, the URL is 118 characters long, but you're only allowed to have 140 characters in a tweet. This would be a dilemma if it wasn't for shortened URLs.

Shortened URL services take a long URL like the one mentioned and converts it to a smaller Web address. Two of the most popular services are TinyURL (www.tinyurl.com) and Bitly (www.bitly.com). When you go to either of these sites, you're presented with a field where you can enter the full URL, click a button, and be presented with a small URL. For example, when I entered the Microsoft social media page mentioned into TinyURL, it provided the URL http://tinyurl.com/4jahns7. If you want a more user friendly URL, you can optionally create a custom URL like http://tinyurl.com/kidssocial. If you entered these shortened URLs into the address bar of your browser, a request would be made to tinyurl.com to resolve the address to the full URL and redirect your browser to the correct site.

Twitter also offers its own service, using a t.co domain that will automatically shorten any link in your tweet to 20 characters. A problem with the Twitter shortened URL is that it is only available for tweets, so this won't necessarily help you if you want to shorten a URL for use on other social media sites. However, since it does decrease the characters automatically in the URL, it means you can send longer tweets without first converting links with Bitly or TinyURL.

Examine suspicious URLs

If you're using social media, then you won't just be creating shortened URLs, you'll also probably click on links from other people. Before you open a shortened URL, it is often wise you examine it. While we'll discuss security related to hijacked accounts in Chapter 7, you should look at the message to see if there's anything odd about it. As with email, you may get strange tweets from people you're following, but with messages offering tips to lose weight or get rich quick schemes with a link for additional information. If you receive a direct message in Twitter from your boss saying "LOL, funny pic of you" with a link, and you know the person shouldn't have photos of you, chances are it's not from that person. These days, you need to be as wary of posts on social networking sites and tweets as you do with email. It may be SPAM sent from a hijacked account, and clicking the link may compromise your account or computer.

Even though a shortened URL may hide the original address, it doesn't mean that you can't check the URL and determine its origin. Using a site like unshort. me or LongURL (www.longurl.org), you see where the link will lead you without going to the actual site. To illustrate how to do this:

1. In your browser, go to www.unshort.me.
2. In the box on the main page, type in the following URL (which I've created and points to my blog): http://bit.ly/10TjJ3v.
3. Click the button labeled "unshorten."

After clicking the button, you'll see a new screen appear with the full resolved URL. If you recognize the site, you could click on the link and go to it. If you don't recognize it, you should reconsider visiting it or find out more information about it.

When in doubt, if you know and trust a person sending a link, you can of course send a message to the person and ask if they sent the link. However, if the account was hijacked, the person responding may not be the actually owner of the account. Another problem is that many of the people you follow on Twitter (or who follow you) may not be people you actually know. Similarly, Facebook friends may be added for games or LinkedIn contacts because they're in the same industry as you. In such cases, you couldn't be certain about the legitimacy of the link.

At this point, if you're really curious about the link, you could use any number of sites to see if they're listed as a problem. There are numerous sites that allow you to compare a Web site to information in Web site reputation engines, domain blacklists, and other sources that will determine if it's possibly dangerous. Some of these sites include:

- URLVoid (www.urlvoid.com)
- McAfee SiteAdvisor (www.siteadvisor.com)
- Malware Domain List (www.malwaredomainlist.com)

While these methods require you to manually check the links, there are also software solutions that will examine suspicious URLs for you. As we'll discuss in Chapter 7, firewalls may be configured to check a URL against known malware sites, and apps like Norton Safe Web may be used to scan your newsfeed for unsafe links. Being aware that a link may be dangerous and taking steps to insure its safe will go a long way in protecting yourself from malicious software being installed on your computer.

Using centralized corporate accounts and email

In setting up accounts for social media, it's important to consider the email address you'll use. When you set up a new account on social networking sites, you provide an email address in its creation. For businesses, corporate email addresses should be used, so the account is associated with the company and accessible when needed. If an employee uses a personal email account or creates an account solely controlled by that person, it can lead to a number of problems.

Any account can be compromised. If it happens, you would need to access the account's settings to change the password and verify that a hacker hasn't made changes or posed as you by sending messages or posting content. If you don't have the correct password for a social media account or access to the email account used to create it, it will be more difficult regaining control. Until then, a hacker could send SPAM, post bogus information, or cause any number of other problems.

If a business allows employees to create corporate social media accounts using personal email, and he or she is the only person who knows the password, it creates a single point of failure. If the employee was unavailable or unwilling to provide the password (as in the cases of vacations, termination of employment, accident, injury, death, etc.), then it could be some time before you regain control. Without access to the person's email account, you would never see notifications about how a password or an email address associated with a social media account was changed or see any verification emails when new accounts are created. By using corporate email accounts, other employees can monitor the email when your social media person is unavailable, and your IT staff could reset the password and regain control if it's compromised. Any social media accounts setup created with the email could then be taken over by requesting a password change from the site.

As we'll discuss in Chapter 9, policies and procedures can save considerable problems for an organization. However, when considering how you'll set up a social media presence, you'll need to make decisions that will affect what those policies will be. One item to consider is whether accounts will be created for roles in a company or if individuals will own their own accounts. For example, while you may create a Twitter account for the business itself, you may decide to create one for the CEO, public relations person, and so on. By naming the Twitter username after a business role, it won't be tied to a particular person's name. If you look at the Vatican's Twitter account for the pope, it is called @Pontifex and doesn't reflect any particular person. As one person steps out of that role, the Twitter username doesn't need to be changed, which saves them from having to update Web pages, printed material, and anything else asking people to follow that account.

If you haven't already, you may want to consider creating email accounts for authorized positions representing the company in social media. For example, if you had a public relations representative, you might create an email account named pub licrelations@*yourdomainname*. In creating a Twitter account with this email and naming it after the position, it truly represents the company and not a person in it. In doing so, you're laying claim to business ownership of the account.

Ownership of a social media account is important. If you imagine a salesperson in your company having a Twitter account with lots of followers, you could lose those customers and potential clients if the person left your company, changed the account password and settings, and retained control of it. It's important for businesses to set up email and social media accounts properly, as it will allow them to keep control of the accounts and avoid possible lawsuits over who owns the account.

Identifying how you'll represent yourself on the Internet

The impression you make on social media sites can have a lasting effect, especially if it doesn't match the image you want to convey. The way you present your brand to the public should be consistent regardless of who's making a post or tweet. Early in developing social media, there should be a clear understanding of how the business is to be portrayed, so that you can keep to that image.

While social media is generally seen as informal, this isn't always the case. If you work in an organization that needs to present itself in a serious and professional manner, the tone and level of professionalism might be higher than other businesses. For example, people wouldn't appreciate a mortician being insensitive about his work. The tone of your message needs to match the seriousness of a situation and the professionalism of your work. While it seems like common sense, there are many cases where you don't see the image of a profession or business matching the expected public perception.

This not only applies to organizations as a whole but also to how employees use social media. In 2008, a photo of a nurse showing off her bra appeared on Facebook. The photo was taken on a ward at Northampton General Hospital in Britain and showed patients in the background. Although later reinstated, the hospital fired her and blocked access to social networking sites in the hospital. In 2009, photos of nurses having a food fight on a ward at Stafford Hospital in Britain appeared on Facebook. The photos were taken at a time when the hospital was trying to improve standards and work conditions, after a report found up to 1200 patients died as a result of poor nursing care, neglect, and being short staffed. Needless to say, neither of these incidents helped to convey a level of professionalism expected from health care professionals.

While these are extreme examples, they do show how the image of your company and its employees are an important part of how the public sees you. Employees are seen as representatives of a company, whether they are responsible for their own social network activities or act as social media officers for the business. Before content goes public, you should identify how you want to be represented and identify whether your organization has an existing code of conduct that employees are to follow.

Approved representatives

As your business establishes a social media presence, chances are you don't want everyone to have access to the accounts and publishing content on behalf of the organization. After all, the more people representing an organization through social media, the more difficult it is to control. Centralizing responsibility for social media minimizes numerous risks by having a single person or group of people acting as a spokesperson for the company.

Policies should be created specifying which positions in the company are authorized to speak on behalf of the organization as an official source. For example, the public relations expert, CEO, social media person, or other officials within the organization may be allowed to post information through social media and other sources, but others may be restricted from doing so. Confidentiality agreements should also be created and signed by employees, so they know that they are not to divulge classified, sensitive, or other internal information to the public without authorization.

Preexisting accounts

While businesses are taking social media more seriously, individuals have been using it for years. It's not uncommon for a member of an organization to be gung-ho and set up a social media presence with his or her own email. Unfortunately, this can be a major problem. The person may lose interest in a site or an account after moving on with his or her career, leaving it dormant. When the business discovers this problem, they may not know who created it or how to take it over. Prior to venturing into creating a social media presence, you should identify whether such accounts already exist and shut down any you find by notifying the site.

Privacy

In terms of information, *privacy* relates to data that's collected and stored, and its availability for others to view. The degree of privacy desired or required by a person or business can vary, although there are often some consistencies. You don't want data available to those you don't know and trust, which could be used to cause embarrassment, financial loss, or potentially victimize you. Organizations may also have unique requirements for privacy and need to limit what's shared about employees, clients, and business partners. Prior to using social media, you should address privacy concerns and identify what kinds of information must be kept private.

Depending on the industry and location of a business, there may be strict regulations and legislation controlling whether certain data can be shared and even restricting who views it within the organization. There are many sources of information that are protected by legislation, and either cannot be disseminated to the public or can only be shared under certain conditions. These include:

- Medical records, which are protected in many countries by doctor–patient confidentiality and by legislation, such as the Health Insurance Portability and Accountability Act (HIPPA) and Health Information Technology for Economic and Clinical Health Act (HITECH) in the United States.
- Criminal records, which may include protected details of ongoing investigations or legal cases. Even when information can be released to the public, specific information may still be protected. An example of this is the Youth Criminal Justice Act in Canada, which bans publishing the identity of young persons under the age of 18 who have committed a crime.
- Financial records, including transactions, which are protected in the United States under such legislation as the Right to Financial Privacy Act (RFPA).

The confidentiality of information is important, not only to the security of a customer or client but also to the reputation and integrity of your organization. Even if your business doesn't fall under such regulations, people will often have an expectation that information will be kept private. If people don't feel that personal or sensitive information is safe, they won't use your services. Because of its importance, your company may have internal policies that control information.

Some privacy concerns in using social media

Privacy should be an immediate concern when you sign up to use a social media site. When you create an account, you're required to enter information to identify yourself. For example, when you create a Facebook account, you enter your name, email address, birthday, gender, and then go on to upload a profile picture, cover photo, and add additional facts about yourself. If security settings aren't configured to restrict certain information, then this may be available for anyone to view. Even if security is set, certain information is considered public. To allow others to find and add you as a friend, your name, username, profile picture, cover photo, gender, and networks (which may identify your city or other revealing facts) are treated as public information.

Even if you're diligent, others may not be. People you add as friends may identify you by tagging you in photos, status updates, locations, or reveal other information about you. Social networking sites often provide tools to find friends and contacts, which may require them gaining access to your email account. Sites like Facebook make this feature immediately available when you create an account, inviting you to give Facebook access to the contact list of an email account. If you allow this, contact information from the list is uploaded to the site, so the app can compare email addresses in your contact list to those of existing Facebook users. While the point of this is to help you find friends, it is done so by allowing a site access to your email account and the contact information of coworkers, business contacts, friends, family, and others who may have never intended their information to be uploaded to a social networking site. If permission is given to access an email account issued by an employer, this can also raise additional security issues.

Even if one site you use is protective of your data, others may not be. User data on social networking sites are packaged into databases and may be shared with third parties. Personal and private information like your name, age, gender, location, interests, hobbies, photographs, activities, and so on may be combined with other information on the Internet to create a comprehensive profile on you. The data gathered about you may be used by direct marketers, advertisers, data brokers, and others who may find the information beneficial or sell it others. By amassing information about what's liked and followed, advertisers gain a real-time understanding on preferences and predictions about your interests and activities.

Data compiled from social media and other public sources can be searched online, revealing a considerable amount of information about you. For example, People Search sites like Spokeo (www.spokeo.com) and PeekYou (www.peekyou.com) allow you to search aggregated data sources to see a person's usernames, work, schools, social media activity, public records, relatives, and so on. Depending on who's conducting the search and what's found, such information could be used to track your activities and location, impersonate you, or cause other problems which affect your employment or ability to rent an apartment.

Prior to creating a social media account, you should identify what kinds of information you're willing to share. In doing so, you'll have a better idea of what data you'll enter when setting up your social media accounts. If the company has multiple locations or phone numbers, you should decide what address and number will be displayed on pages. For personal or business use, you may want to create a new email account for social media accounts, as this will decrease the amount of SPAM and notifications going to the email you use for day-to-day use. For personal accounts, limit the amount of information related to your employment and location and avoid filling out your address, phone, or anything else that enables others to contact you directly. If these are required fields when creating the account, then make sure the information isn't visible afterward. Remove anything you're not comfortable sharing from your profile pages and adjust privacy settings on the account. You don't want a person you barely know or who's seen the information online visiting your work or home.

Training and policy

As we've mentioned through this chapter, if you're creating a social media presence for an organization, it's good to see what's already available to you. Your organization may already have policies related to areas of concern with social media. These may include confidentiality agreements that have to be signed by employees, policies on acceptable use of technology, and so on. There may also be policies that outline how to use email, which can be modified to address social media usage.

While we'll discuss policies in greater detail in Chapter 9, you should see what policies already exist and can be modified to meet your needs.

Another area worth examining is training. If you work for a larger organization, you may have staff that train employees or create training material for your company. By talking with them, you may find that they're already taught about online privacy or security, customer relations, dealing with classified information, or other topics related to social media. You may also find that there are videos or sites that you want to refer that provide this information. By addressing concerns and discovering the resources already available to you, you can save yourself a lot of work later and avoid unforeseen problems.

Bibliography

Brenner, J. (2013, February 14). *Pew internet: Social networking (full detail)*. Retrieved March 10, 2012, from Pew Internet & American Life Project: <http://pewinternet.org/Commentary/2012/March/Pew-Internet-Social-Networking-full-detail.aspx>.

Consumer Reports. (2011, May 10). *CR survey: 7.5 million Facebook users are under the age of 13, violating the site's terms*. Retrieved April 12, 2013, from Consumer Reports: <http://pressroom.consumerreports.org/pressroom/2011/05/cr-survey-75-million-facebook-users-are-under-the-age-of-13-violating-the-sites-terms-.html>.

Dolan, A. (2010, April 22). *Captured on Facebook, the food-fighting nurses at hospital where 1,200 died*. Retrieved April 22, 2013, from Mail Online: <http://www.dailymail.co.uk/news/article-1267800/Captured-Facebook-Nurses-food-fight-Stafford-hospital-1-200-died.html?ITO=1490>.

Duggan, M., & Brenner, J. (2013, February 14). *The demographics of social media users—2012*. Retrieved April 12, 2013, from Pew Internet & American Life Project: <http://pewinternet.org/Reports/2013/Social-media-users/The-State-of-Social-Media-Users.aspx>.

Facebook. (2012, December 11). *Terms*. Retrieved April 12, 2013, from Facebook: <www.facebook.com/legal/terms>.

Facebook. (2013). *Data use policy—information we receive about you*. Retrieved April 29, 2013, from Facebook: <https://www.facebook.com/about/privacy/your-info>.

Lenhart, A., Purcell, K., Smith, A., & Zickuhr, K. (2010, February 3). *Social media and young adults*. Retrieved April 12, 2013, from Pew Internet & American Life Project: <http://www.pewinternet.org/Reports/2010/Social-Media-and-Young-Adults.aspx>.

Low, L. (2011, April). *Sharepoint 2010: The first 10 years*. Retrieved April 02, 2013, from Technet Magazine: <http://technet.microsoft.com/en-us/magazine/gg981684.aspx>.

Nursing Standard, (2008, October 8). Nurse who showed bra on Facebook reinstated. *Nursing Standard, 23*(5), 9.

Twitter. (2012, June 25). *Terms of service*. Retrieved April 12, 2013, from Twitter: <https://twitter.com/tos>.

Van Hoboken, J., Arnbak, A., & Van Eijk, N (2012, November 27). *Cloud computing in higher education and research institutions and the USA Patriot Act*. Retrieved April 12, 2013, from Social Science Research Network: <http://papers.ssrn.com/sol3/papers.cfm?abstract_id=2181534>.

Being Bold Versus being Overlooked

INFORMATION IN THIS CHAPTER:

- Being bold versus being overlooked
- Good social media campaigns
- Bad social media campaigns
- Sometimes it's better to be overlooked
- Social media hoaxes
- The human factor
- Content management
- Promotion of social media

Being bold versus being overlooked

Many businesses and individuals compete for the attention of social media users, wanting to get their message across to as broad an audience as possible. A person may want more followers and friends for a number of reasons. They may want to connect to people with similar interests, gain benefits in games by getting additional neighbors or allies, or gratify their vanity or competitive spirit by having more friends than their peers. For businesses, the number of followers is important, as it helps them reach more existing and potential customers. The goal of social media campaigns is to get noticed. You want the campaign to be bold enough to be shared, discussed, and make social media users feel involved. You want to attract positive attention and not be overlooked.

While there's no formula on how to have a successful social media campaign, there are many good and bad examples to learn from. In this chapter, we'll look at a number of campaigns and elements that can make or break your social media presence. We'll see how you can get the most out of social media by engaging people in a positive way and how to avoid common pitfalls that can expose you and your organization to potential problems.

Good social media campaigns

One of the best examples of a company shifting away from old advertising techniques and taking full advantage of social media is *Nike*. For years, Nike's advertising showed top sports figures succeeding by wearing Nike products, while telling customers to do the same with the command "Just Do It." While their hero worship campaign did undeniably well, a different approach was needed for a social media campaign. Rather than say what to do, they made people a part of what was happening.

In 2013, a new campaign called #MAKEITCOUNT started which focuses on motivating people to achieve goals they set. Nike promoted a three-part process of picking people you know on Twitter and Facebook who will encourage you achieve what you want, choosing a goal (such as working out at the gym, basketball), and then using what Nike offers to help you succeed. In getting people to encourage you, you send a tweet to your friends with the hashtag #MAKEITCOUNT. A hashtag is created, i.e., the # is put in front of a keyword in the tweet, so that when someone clicks on the word, any other tweets containing the same hashtag are displayed. By clicking #MAKEITCOUNT, you see tweets from others who are taking action on trying to achieve their goals.

Advertising includes videos on YouTube and their site, but the core campaign involves Twitter. The video on their site is interactive, including boxes that pop up in the video reflecting a goal you might set. It uses words like *we* and *I* to make it personal and features motivational phrases about how in 2013 *we* will #MAKEITCOUNT. The boxes that pop up in the video are also motivational with phrases like "I will train 1 hour a day" and "I will #MAKEITCOUNT one training at a time." By clicking on one of these pop-up boxes, the video stops and you have the option of tweeting about how you're setting this as a goal. Another video created for the Nike Fuelband (which tracks your activity) shows a film director and his friend breaking the rules, taking Nike's money for a commercial, and traveling around the world. The video went viral and (at the time of this writing) has been seen over eight and a half million times on YouTube. It shows how a different approach to advertising, where a product isn't directly pitched, can work.

In addition to the advertising, Nike offers a number of apps for your phone and new products. One app works as a personal trainer, while another uses GPS (Global Positioning System) to track information as you run and lets you to hear feedback and cheers from your friends. Another app syncs with sensors in the soles of Nike basketball shoes and provides information about how you're playing. As you can see, by using social media to its fullest, you not only engage customers, but can draw in new ones and have new products created and promoted.

Another great example of using social media to promote products and generate interest in a brand occurred in 2009, when *Burger King* started a campaign called the *Whopper Sacrifice*. The premise poked fun at the Facebook fixation over how many friends a person had and got them to decide whether they'd choose a hamburger over a fair-weather Internet friendship. After installing an app on your Facebook account, if you removed 10 people as friends, you could print out a coupon for a free Whopper.

The tongue in cheek campaign of sacrificing friendship for food was hilarious, and people saw the benefit. It rewarded them by cleaning up any unwanted friends from their account, which decreased the number of status updates, ads related to Likes, etc., that appeared on their feeds, and ultimately made the accounts more secure. If you didn't have any unwanted friends, there was nothing stopping you from deleting and friending them again. Best of all, there was the physical reward of free food. The campaign was successful, with 82,000 people using the app to delete over 200,000 friends in a week.

Unfortunately, the campaign was quickly shut down by Facebook. Facebook wanted Burger King to change the app, as it violated their privacy policy. Normally, when you unfriend someone, it is done quietly and no one is notified. Before removing the friend, a feed story was posted about how the friend was sacrificed for a Whopper. While not said, by decreasing the number of friends a person had, the functionality of the app would have an impact on the reach of banner ads that generated income for Facebook.

Bad social media campaigns

Not all social media campaigns go as planned or accepted in a way you intended. There are many examples of campaigns that have gone wrong, sometimes with funny or almost tragic results. Looking at them provides valuable insight into why they failed and what not to do.

Hashtag campaigns can often go awry because you have little control over them. People can write whatever they want, and with a 140-character limit, so the tweets can be fast and furious. Because they're not posted to a page you have control over, you don't have the option or deleting particularly offensive ones. Unfortunately, while you like your product, others may feel differently. It doesn't take long for a hashtag to become a bashtag.

While the humorous *Whopper Sacrifice* campaign did well for Burger King, their competitors have not fared so well in social media campaigns. The fast food chain *Wendy's* attempted to play on their successful 1980s advertising campaign of *Where's the beef?* In October 2011, they tweeted about launching their thickest burger ever and decided to use the hashtag #HeresTheBeef. Unfortunately, they apparently didn't check whether it was already being used. Prior tweets using the hashtag related to comments about men's bodies, and also used by people voicing their complaints (i.e., beefs) about various issues. Wendy's also apparently didn't consider the sexual innuendo of the hashtag, which was not lost on Twitter users. Mixed into the conversation were negative tweets about Wendy's, including one from People for the Ethical Treatment of Animals (PETA) about the suffering of cows. The campaign failed miserably and became a footnote as to why you should be thoughtful and choose good names for hashtag campaigns.

In January 2012, *McDonalds* also made an attempt at using a hashtag campaign to promote their products, starting with the tweet shown in Figure 5.1. Things quickly

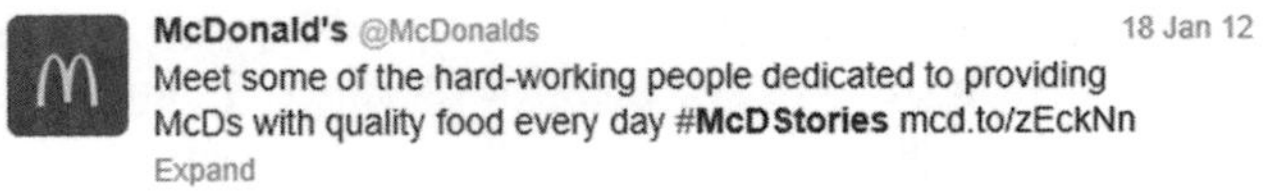

> **McDonald's** @McDonalds   18 Jan 12
> Meet some of the hard-working people dedicated to providing
> McDs with quality food every day **#McDStories** mcd.to/zEckNn
> Expand

FIGURE 5.1

Tweet from McDonalds starting the #McDStories campaign.

spiraled out of control. People began using the hastag #McDStories to tell horror stories about the food. These included tweets about get physically ill, things found in food, and the quality of the products. Links to videos, photos, and wild accusations about the brand abounded. Even celebrities and organizations joined in. Actress Alicia Silverstone tweeted against the company, saying "turns out I'm not the only one displeased with @McDonalds #McDStories." PETA also got into the mix on this one, alleging that mechanically separated chicken was used in nuggets, to which McDonalds corrected by stating it was USDA-inspected white meat. While the back and forth was funny to followers, the campaign was obviously a dismal failure.

Sometimes it's better to be overlooked

In making a decision between being bold versus being overlooked, sometimes it's better to be overlooked. Public attention isn't always positive, and not all publicity is good publicity. At times, you may need to do damage control and deal with issues related to you or your business. While it may be important to address a problem by commenting on a person's post or releasing a prepared statement, you don't want to dwell on it and certainly don't want to provoke additional responses that will make you the focal point of attention.

A case in point is Amy's Baking Company of Scottsdale, Arizona. In May 2013, the restaurant was featured in an episode of *Kitchen Nightmares*, a reality show in which Chef Gordon Ramsay spends a week with a struggling or failing restaurant, attempting to revive the business. The show was disastrous for owner's Amy and Samy Bouzaglo, with Amy claiming the source of their problems was due to online bullies and bloggers. She proceeded to insult them and referred to them as "haters." They also stated that they had gone through a few hundred employees, characterizing them as dirty and lazy. This was not a good approach. You want to promote your employees and business as professional and competent. If you're concerned about how you're represented in social media, you don't want to insult people who review your business online.

The issue the owners spoke of related to an incident that occurred years before, in which Joel LaTondress left a 1-star review on Yelp. The critical review spoke about how he'd visited the restaurant's patio, received bad service, and experienced a defensive reaction when he told Samy that he didn't like the pizza. Instead of ignoring the online comments, apologizing, or making a humble comment to invite the customer back, Amy Bouzaglo did the opposite. She responded by insulting him and accusing him of being sent by a competitor. She wrote "unless you have been living on another PLANET it is summertime in ARIZONA MORON!!! Only TRAMPS and LOSERS want to sit outside" and suggested him "Do US a favor and keep your ugly face and you ugly opinions to yourself." The exchange inspired negative comments from others on Yelp and the Chow Bella blog of the Phoenix NewsTimes site and even attracted a local television station to do a news piece on the story.

The appearance on *Kitchen Nightmares* did not help their reputation. They were caught on camera showing contempt for employees and patrons alike. They are shown physically and verbally assaulting customers, keeping tips left for their servers, threatening to burn food that was returned, unable to take criticism, and firing an employee who asked a question. Ramsay decided he was unable to help them, and Amy's Baking Company became the first establishment in the show's history that Ramsay walked away from. While the show made them internationally infamous, what happened next made them an Internet phenomenon.

A post on the company's Facebook page (www.facebook.com/amysbakingco) addressed their appearance on the episode. This was good. It showed transparency and mentioned how they paid their employees a good wage. Unfortunately for them, it also included a comment that they didn't steal tips. Since Samy was shown on video taking the tips of a server and admitting to it being common practice, this obviously contradicted their side of the story. It angered people and cast doubt on anything else they had to say. At the time of this writing, it led to 9544 comments on this post alone, few of which could be called flattering.

What followed was a tirade of posts that has been called the most epic meltdown ever to occur on Facebook. It started with a comment of how the owners would "not bend to the will of these haters and sinners" and followed with rants that included:

- "I AM NOT STUPID ALL OF YOU ARE. YOU JUST DO NOT KNOW GOOD FOOD …"
- "TO REDDIT. I FORBID YOU FROM SPREADING YOUR HATE ON THAT SITE. THIS IS MY FACEBOOK, AND I AM NOT ALLOWING YOU TO USE MY COMPANY ON YOUR HATE FILLED PAGE."
- "This is Samy. I am keeping note of all names here. We will be pursing action against you legally, and against reddit and yelp, for this plot you have come together on. you are all just punks."

The posts from the owner's account continued, firing a stream of insults, with each post invoking hundreds of comments. Needless to say, this is not how you want to generate conversations about your brand. People responded by mocking them, inclusive to voicing outrage about the episode, pointing out how the posts didn't follow the basic rules of netiquette (which we'll discuss later in this chapter), and attacking the business and owners directly. Entertained, many Facebook users began liking the page so they could follow new posts on their feed, with over 94,000 Likes at the time of this writing. It became the topic of articles, televised news, blogs, and discussions across social media sites.

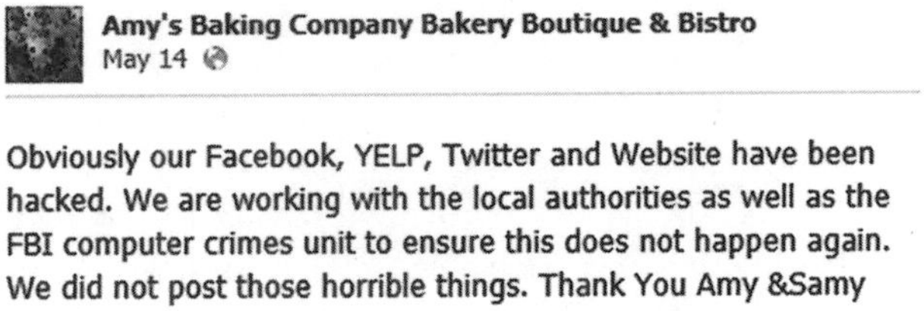

 Amy's Baking Company Bakery Boutique & Bistro
May 14

Obviously our Facebook, YELP, Twitter and Website have been hacked. We are working with the local authorities as well as the FBI computer crimes unit to ensure this does not happen again. We did not post those horrible things. Thank You Amy &Samy

FIGURE 5.2

Post from Amy's Baking Company's Facebook page.

On May 14, 2013, the story took a new twist, with the post shown in Figure 5.2 appearing on the company's Facebook page. It claimed that the couple's Facebook, Yelp, and Twitter accounts were hacked and that they didn't actually make the offensive posts that had caused so much attention. Of the 2267 comments on the post, there were many that disbelieved the claim and thought it unlikely (to put it mildly) that the Scottsdale Police and FBI were investigating. In trying to determine the validity of this, the Scottsdale Police provided me confirmation that they took a report regarding Computer Tampering from that address.

While the owners deleted the offensive posts added after the show, they didn't disappear from the Internet. Screenshots of the posts appeared on Web sites, and the Twitter account for Amy's Baking Company (@bouzagloabc) showed tweets originating from the Facebook page. As we'll discuss later in this chapter, you can set up social media accounts to automatically publish content across multiple sites. In doing so, making a post on Facebook also goes out as a tweet. However, if you set up an account this way, anything you want removed must be deleted from each site. This wasn't done (at the time of this writing), so they were visible and retweeted. Many comments and tweets from people concluded that the owners were unstable, and a hashtag called #crazyamy was created to facilitate conversations on Twitter. A number of parody Twitter accounts were also created, with people posing as the restaurant owners. It showed how social media could be used to retaliate against a disliked person or business.

People doubted that the couple's social media accounts were hacked, because the messages seemed consistent to previous posts. As seen in Figure 5.3, prior to the alleged hacking attempt and appearance on *Kitchen Nightmares*, there were posts containing profanity and insults. In doing so, they poorly represented the business and creating animosity between themselves, potential customers, and the people they were trying to reach through social media.

Because the show caught the owner on camera taking the server's tips, a petition was started on Change.org. The petition was to the US Department of Labor, The Wage and Hour Division, and Tom Horne, Arizona Attorney General, requesting that they investigate the couple for stealing tips. At the time of this writing, there were 32,737 supporters of the petition.

To make things worse, the couple's criminal pasts fell into focus. When a court document appeared on the Internet, it showed that in August 2001 Amanda Bossingham (now Amanda Bouzaglo) applied to M&I Bank for a line of credit

Amy's Baking Company Bakery Boutique & Bistro
October 3, 2012

We like to call them the "Camel Toe Mafia" just a bunch Pussies
hiding behind a computer screen. Or working for YELP

Like · Comment · Share   218   812   106

FIGURE 5.3

Post from Amy's Baking Company's Facebook page.

using another person's Social Security Number and was approved for a $15,000
line of credit. On June 15, 2004, she was sentenced to 14 months in prison, 36
months of supervised release, and ordered to pay $36,294.95 in restitution. Because
Amy Bouzaglo was part of the Amy's Baking Company brand, this reflected badly
on the business. After all, a customer paying the bill might think twice about giving
a credit card to someone convicted of Identity Theft. Although the court document
stated that she has turned her life around and supported a number of charitable
events, the positive aspects are often the least reported. It was yet another strike
against the business.

If you're going to promote yourself as part of the brand, you need to be aware
that skeletons in your closet could come back to haunt you. There are many examples of people attempting to deny an embarrassing past, including Bill Clinton's
famous quotes of "I didn't inhale" and "I did not have sexual relations with that
woman." When such moments come to light, it is generally better to be open and
honest. If you are concerned about something in your past, it may also be wise to
separate your identity from the identity of the business. In other words, don't be
the face of your business, if your face is in a mugshot somewhere. If an issue isn't
common knowledge, you should be preemptive and strategize how you're going to
address the public relations issues relating from things you've done in the past.

In trying to promote and defend their business, Amy's Baking Company has
become a case study in what not to do with social media. Ironically, while claiming their business was failing due to negative online reviews and cyberbullying, the actions of Amy and Samy Bouzaglo attracted what they were fighting
against. Regardless of your feelings about the business or its owners, the backlash
against them became a feeding frenzy of negative attention. While some responses
on Facebook, Twitter, and other social media sites were valid, others simply vented
anger or attacked the couple as a form of entertainment. Negative restaurant reviews
appeared on sites like Yelp from people who had never visited the restaurant, simply containing insults or comments about the show. In addition to this, there were
"flamers" or "trolls," which are Internet terms for people who will post inflammatory
comments until they receive a reaction. As we'll discuss later in this chapter, responding to them and showing they've rattled you is like adding fuel to the fire, which is
exactly what the restaurant owners did.

Social media hoaxes

Sometimes, the things you read online may not be true. Hoaxes and urban legends have been spread through email, message boards, and other methods of communication since the early days of the Internet, so it should come as no surprise that they're now shared on social media sites. There are many different kinds of hoaxes, including bogus stories, manipulated images, outdated information, and cruel pranks. As we'll see in Chapter 7, there are also scams designed to get your money or personal information. For all of them, they enforce the rule: don't believe everything you see on the Internet.

Reports of missing persons or requests to assist law enforcement are often retweeted and shared on social networking sites. They allow information to be shared with a larger audience in the hopes that someone may have valuable knowledge about a case. Unfortunately, an email, a post or tweet like this can be passed around long after a case is solved. Such is the case of Laura Clark who briefly went missing for just over 24 hours in February 2013. A photo, description, and information about her disappearance were quickly published online and still shared on social media sites. A Facebook page called "Help Find Laura Clark, Missing on 26th Feb 2013" continues to exist, without any update that the person was found. Although West Midlands Police issued a press release on their Web site and informed people via Twitter that the teenager was found, it hasn't stopped the posts and tweets about her being missing.

While some alerts about missing children are simply outdated, some fake ones are about people who were never missing or don't exist. As seen in Figure 5.4, one such alert deals with a child being abducted by someone with the license plate 72B 381. If you search for this license plate on Google or Bing, you'll actually find several variations of the hoax, with various boys and girls being abducted in different locations. It's completely untrue.

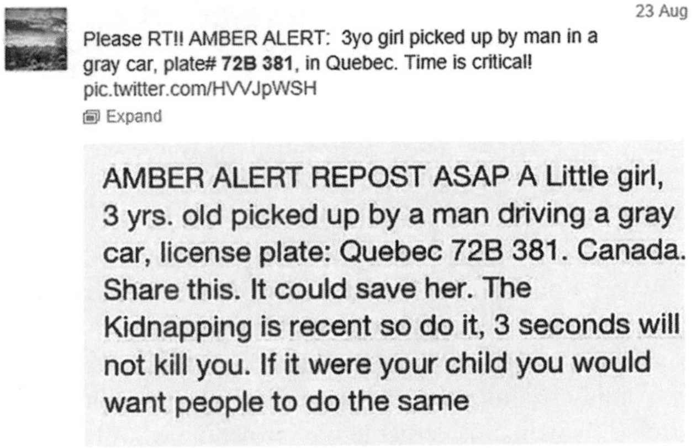

23 Aug

Please RT!! AMBER ALERT: 3yo girl picked up by man in a gray car, plate# **72B 381**, in Quebec. Time is critical!
pic.twitter.com/HVVJpWSH

Expand

> AMBER ALERT REPOST ASAP A Little girl, 3 yrs. old picked up by a man driving a gray car, license plate: Quebec 72B 381. Canada. Share this. It could save her. The Kidnapping is recent so do it, 3 seconds will not kill you. If it were your child you would want people to do the same

FIGURE 5.4

Missing person Tweet is a hoax.

Before sharing such pleas for help, you should verify that it's a legitimate request. An AMBER Alert is a notification through a bulletin system, which originated in the United States but implemented in 15 other countries. Active AMBER Alerts in the United States, and information on International alert systems, can be found on the National Center for Missing and Exploited Children's page at http://www.missingkids.com/Amber. Requests for information on a criminal case may also be verified through the law enforcement agency by visiting their site.

Sometimes a hoax can go viral, being shared by large groups of people within a very short time. In 2012, Nolan Daniels posted a photo of him holding a Powerball ticket with the winning numbers of a $588 million jackpot. He offered to give one million dollars to a random person who shared the picture, and within a few days the photo had been shared two million times and had 27,000 comments. Alas, the photo had been doctored, and no one walked away as a random millionaire. When people realized the most shared photo on Facebook was a hoax, Daniels was left fielding angry retorts and media attention.

Another common type of hoax found on social media sites deal with people who have been erroneously reported as deceased. Some like Morgan Freeman have experienced a virtual afterlife more than once. In 2012, a fake memorial page named "RIP Morgan Freeman" was created on Facebook, starting a rumor that the actor had died. Less than 2 months later, a tweet fraudulently claimed that CNN reported the actor had passed away. The actor responded on his Facebook page (www.facebook.com/MorganFreeman) stating "Like Mark Twain, I keep reading that I have died. I hope those stories are not true… But if they are, I'm happy to report that my afterlife seems identical to my life when I was alive."

Not all social media sites have policies or procedures on what happens to the accounts of deceased users. Generally, they will follow the requests of the family reporting that a user has died. In the case of Facebook, an account may be deactivated with the profile removed or memorialized. Another user (such as a family member) can use an online form to request what happens to the account. If they choose to have the profile memorialized, it remains accessible with sensitive information like contact information removed, and security settings are changed so that only friends can post to the wall. This allows mourners to post messages of condolence and remembrance. While the online form requires some proof of death, such as a link to an obituary or news report, some pranksters have taken advantage of Facebook and changed the statuses of accounts.

On June 25, 2009, a story was tweeted of actor Jeff Goldblum's untimely death, in which he died in a way that falsely claimed the lives of other actors. The tweets told the chilling tale of how the actor fell from a cliff while filming a movie in New Zealand. Unfortunately, it's probably not the last time we'll see a post or tweet of an actor reported dying this way, complete with a link to an "official" news article. Using sites like swellserver.com, you can add a name into the URL to have it automatically create a news story with that name. For example, http://michael.cross.swellserver.com/news/top_stories/actor_new_zealand.php automatically creates an article that I have died filming a movie.

When using social media, you want to ensure that the information you share with others is authentic. If you're sharing fake stories, it can undermine your credibility. In some cases like outdated missing person stories, it can cost law enforcement time and resources in addressing tips and requests for information on cases that are long solved. While there are too many hoaxes to list here, there are a number of sites that provide information on various hoaxes and urban legends. Snopes (www.snopes.com) and Hoax-Slayer (www.hoax-slayer.com) are two sites that can be useful in checking the validity of a story before you decide to share or retweet it to others.

The human factor

Even in the most secure environments, the element that makes an organization vulnerable and causes unexpected problems is people. Mistakes happen, especially when dealing with content that is user generated and informal. A person may post information that shouldn't be released, provide updates that compromise security, type things incorrectly, or make comments that are taken the wrong way. With a little awareness, you can avoid common mistakes that can cause a great deal of embarrassment or make you vulnerable to risk.

The oops factor

When handling social media for an organization, you may use several different accounts. In addition to corporate accounts, you may have your own accounts for social media sites. If you're using a family computer or sharing a workstation, several people may use the machine and have access to social networks. This leads to the obvious risk that a person could mistakenly use the wrong account to make a tweet or post a comment. Over the years, there have been a few incidents where people think they're making a personal tweet, but actually sent an unauthorized one with the company account.

In 2012, there was an issue where an apparent employee of the ticket sales company *StubHub* thought they were using a personal account, but sent out a tweet using the business' @StubHub Twitter account. The tweet (with its expletive edited here) stated: "Thank f*** it's Friday! Can't wait to get out of this stubsucking hell hole." StubHub deleted the tweet shortly afterward and took responsibility by apologizing for the inappropriate language.

Also in 2012, KitchenAid's Twitter account (@KitchenAidUSA) was used to send out an insulting tweet against President Barack Obama during a presidential debate and included an insensitive reference to his late grandmother. It stated: "Obamas gma even knew it was going 2 b bad! 'She died 3 days b4 he became president.'" The tweet got extra attention, because it included the #nbcpolitics hashtag. KitchenAid quickly took responsibility, deleted the errant tweet and responding to it. They suggested that the person who made the tweet would be fired, stating: "It was carelessly sent in error by a member of our Twitter team who, needless to say, won't be tweeting for us anymore."

Both of these incidents show the need to be especially careful that you're using the correct account to make tweets or post comments. Many sites provide the ability to keep you logged onto a site after closing the browser or logging off the machine. For example, Twitter has a checkbox on their logon page that says "Remember me," and when you log on to Facebook, there is a checkbox to "Keep me logged in." By checking the box, a cookie is stored on your computer and used the next time you visit the site. If you don't want to automatically log on to that account, ensure such checkboxes aren't checked. It's also important to get in the habit of properly logging off a social media site when you're done using it. In doing so, you'll need to log on with a username and password next time you visit.

You should also consider deleting cookies from your browser. On Internet Explorer, you would do the following:

1. Click on the *Tools* menu in your browser, and then click the *Internet Options* menu item.
2. When the *Internet Options* dialog box appears, click on the *General* tab.
3. In the *Browsing History* section, click the *Delete* button.
4. When the *Delete Browsing History* dialog box appears, ensure the *Cookies* checkbox is checked. Check any other boxes for items you want deleted.
5. Click the *Delete* button.
6. When you return to the *Internet Options* dialog box, you can optional check the *Delete browsing history on exit* checkbox. In doing so, your history of sites visited and any other settings made on the *Delete Browsing History* dialog will be deleted each time you close the browser.
7. Click *OK*.

Firefox also provides the ability to delete cookies from the sites that you visit. To remove them, you would do the following:

1. Click on the Firefox button at the top left-hand corner of the browser.
2. Select the *History* menu, and then click *Clear Recent History*.
3. When the *Clear Recent History* dialog appears, click on the *Time Range to Clear* drop-down menu and select *Everything*.
4. In the list of items, ensure the checkbox labeled *Cookies* is checked.
5. Click *Clear Now*.

Acronyms and abbreviations in messaging

Acronyms are words that have been shortened by using the first letter of each word, while *abbreviations* are shortened versions of a word. They've been commonly used in electronic messages even before the Internet became popular, but achieved increased popularity with texting, chats, and tweets as it saves having to type out common phrases. For example, rather than typing out "be right back," you would type "BRB." Similarly, you might type "You hate text messages from people" as "u h8 txt msgs from ppl." While handy for shortening messages, you should avoid them professionally and for business use.

In many cases, shortening a message appears less professional and can be more confusing. If you're responding to a potential employer on LinkedIn, you want to appear as a good candidate and not someone texting his or her buddy. A few extra characters will go a long way in showing your ability to communicate. Also, if readers are unfamiliar with a shortened word, they won't know what you're saying. This can detract from your message, leaving a reader to either ignore your point or try to interpret it. People shouldn't need to translate a simple message and search Google for terms.

If used incorrectly, they can also cause problems. An acronym that's been misused by many people over the years is *LOL*, which is short for "Laughing Out Loud." Unfortunately, you'll see people mistakenly believe it stands for other phrases like "Lots Of Love" or "Lots of Luck." The last thing you want to do is tweet something like "Sorry about the death of your family, LOL." If you're not positive about its meaning, don't use it.

It's also important to realize that some acronyms contain profanity, which can contradict your branding or the beliefs you're trying to convey. For example, someone responding to a funny message or typing something humorous might end it with ROFLMFAO, or attempt to convey their disbelief by typing WTF. Because it's used so often, you might not even realize ROFLMFAO stands for "Rolling On the Floor Laughing My F***ing Ass Off" and WTF is "What The F***." Obviously, this might offend more than a few people reading your message.

It may be common sense, you should always understand what you're saying in a post, tweet, or an email. For personal use, if you're unfamiliar with a shortened term, either avoid using it or look it up. There are countless abbreviations and acronyms, so don't feel that you're out of the loop. Sites like gaarde.org (www.gaarde.org/acronyms) provide explanations, and can help you understand the meaning of an acronym or abbreviation and whether it's appropriate to use.

Aside from Internet acronyms, an organization may also use industry-specific abbreviations, acronyms, and jargon. Unless you're specifically addressing an audience that will understand its meaning, or it's become a household word, you should avoid using them. You want your messages to be clear and not confuse people. Don't detract from the importance of a message by inspiring an unrelated conversation about an acronym or a term you've used.

Netiquette

Netiquette is short for network etiquette and refers to the proper behavior when writing content and using technology. Just as the rules of etiquette teach you how to act in society, netiquette shows you how to conduct yourself in social media. By following good behavior, you can avoid a number of problems with social interaction and know the best way of handling yourself online. In addition to some tips already discussed in this chapter, the rules of netiquette include:

- Follow the Golden Rule. Treat others as you want to be treated, and the respect will generally be returned to you.

- Use appropriate language. Inappropriate comments or swearing will generally have a backlash effect and may violate the site's Terms of Service.
- Don't be abusive. Name calling, personal attacks, and intentionally verbally abusing someone won't win you too many friends and may get you in trouble. If it violates the Terms of Service, you may find yourself kicked off of a site, and in some cases could make you vulnerable to litigation (e.g., slander, defamation of character).
- Honesty is the best policy. If you're caught lying, pretending to be someone else, using fake accounts, or providing false statistics and other information, no one will trust you. Be honest … especially if you've already been caught making a mistake.
- Avoid using the caps lock. Writing words in capital letters can be used for emphasis in messages, but writing everything in capitals represents shouting at a person. For example, you might write "I really NEED a break" to emphasize your feelings. However, writing everything in upper case might offend some people. Unless you want to yell at your followers, don't write every word in capitals.
- Don't be lazy with your typing. If you ignore basic grammar and don't type in mixed case (i.e., a combination of upper and lowercase), it will be more difficult to read. While there are exceptions like chat rooms or texting with friends, it doesn't apply to writing blogs or status updates on social networking sites like LinkedIn. It just makes you look lazy and unintelligent.

Don't feed the trolls

As mentioned earlier in this chapter, there are times when you'll experience people who will try to antagonize you. *Trolls* and *flamers* are people who make inflammatory comments. They will often pick apart everything you say and even make personal attacks. They can be infuriating, but that's what they're trying to do.

Initially, you should try and assume a person is acting in good faith. If you're in a sensitive mood, it's easy to misread someone. Maybe they made a joke or comment that was taken the wrong way or struck a nerve. They may have a valid opinion or complaint, or one that they feel is legitimate. You need to determine if this is the case. You can't presume people are troublemakers until you've dealt with them.

If you need to respond to something that angers you, wait before doing so. Counting to 10, taking a quick breather, or even waiting overnight before responding can help you calm down before responding. After calming down and rereading their comment, don't defeat yourself by getting worked up again.

Once it becomes apparent that a person is trying to antagonize you and others, you should change your approach. Remember that their goal is to make you flustered and mad. If you show this, they've won. Don't let them achieve what they wanted and show emotion. Rather than falling into an argument, replying with a professional or even complimentary tone can throw them off.

If it's your page, remember that you have some control over the content. If offensive language is used, delete their comments. If they complain, give a brief, professional response that offensive content will be deleted from your page or site. You don't want others feeling uncomfortable reading visiting your blog or Facebook page. If it's pointless for them to post antagonizing and offensive remarks, they will eventually move on and bother someone else.

Don't feel you're alone. Unless you're dealing with a public relations crisis and large groups of people are mad at you, you can assume other people are annoyed by the inflammatory comments and behavior. If there's no lynch mob, then you can often count on some support. Other people may turn on the person, making them unwelcome. In most cases, trolls are annoying to everyone.

In all cases, don't respond to personal attacks. If it gets to be too much, you should try and contact the site for action or referral. You can report a post as abusive or contact the site administration to complain about harassing behavior. In doing so, the person may be warned or even have their account suspended or deleted. While they may be able to get back on using another account, you've inconvenienced them. If it's difficult or uneventful trying to antagonize you, they won't want to deal with you.

In all cases, if threats are made, you should consider contacting the police. Making threats online is no different from a person making them face-to-face with you. A person may be trying to intimidate you or may be promising that they'll hurt you in some way. Since you could never be completely certain whether a threat was idle, it's best to take them seriously and report the person.

Content management

Regardless of the medium or content being published, some management is required. You shouldn't consider social media as a fire-and-forget technology, where information is posted to a site and forgotten. Some content will become outdated and may need to be removed from a site, with fresh content taking its place.

Content management is the process of collecting, managing, and publishing digital content throughout its life cycle. The life cycle of data used in social media consists of different stages, starting with it being produced and ending with it no longer being relevant:

1. *Creation*, in which you research and write text and generate other content like images or video.
2. *Editing*, in which the content is reviewed and possibly revised. For example, sites with collaboration features like SharePoint or Yammer enable multiple users to work on the same document, while others like Wikipedia rely on crowd-sourcing, in which users will review and edit incorrect information.
3. *Publishing*, in which the content now becomes available for others to view online.
4. *Monitoring*, in which conversations and comments on your material are observed and possibly responded to, and updates or new versions of content are generated.
5. *Removal*, in which old and possibly outdated information is archived or deleted.

What happens to the content when it is no longer relevant may depend on your organization's policies, regulations, or the site you're using. For example, as we'll discuss in Chapter 6, your business may be required to archive old data for a specific period of time before its deleted. For personal use, your decision may depend on the limitations imposed by the site. For example, if you had a blog that provided a limited amount of storage space, you might want to delete old content so you had more free storage space for publishing new content.

Stale and outdated content

One of the most difficult things about maintaining a site is keeping the content fresh. If there's nothing new, the draw to follow you or visit a page simply won't be there. You can manually tweet and publish new information, but there are times when this is difficult or even impossible. Maybe you're on vacation or it's outside of business hours, or you're busy with some crisis or event. There may also be times, such as during a press conference, when you'd like the information to go out at a scheduled time. This is where automatically posting content can help.

There are a number of tools that can help with managing content. One such online tool is HootSuite, which allows you to monitor and manage your accounts on a number of different social media sites, including Twitter, Facebook, LinkedIn, Google+, MySpace, Foursquare, WordPress, and mixi. If you have additional accounts on other sites, you can add various apps to Hootsuite, which allow you to manage content and monitor sites like YouTube, Reddit, Yammer, and others. You choose which of your social media sites you want to monitor and add them to a dashboard. This allows you to oversee what's happening on different sites from a central source and add new content as you see fit.

A feature of HootSuite is the ability to schedule when content is to be published. As seen in Figure 5.5, by clicking on the Publisher icon on the left side of the screen, a calendar interface appears. This allows you to view, edit, add, and delete any items you've scheduled to have published. To schedule new content to be published, click on a date and time in the calendar.

By clicking on a particular date and time, a screen similar to the one shown in Figure 5.6 appears. In the left pane, you click on the accounts you've set up to monitor in HootSuite. You can select multiple sites or use the calendar in Figure 5.5 to schedule different posts to be published on different sites at the same time. Once you've selected where the content should be published, you can use the text box in the right pane to type your tweet or post. Below this, you select the date and time that HootSuite is to publish the content. If you want to be emailed when the content has been published, click the *Email me when message is sent* checkbox. Once you're finished, click the *Schedule* button to save and schedule the item.

In scheduling content this way, you still need to be aware of what's being published. Organizations have automatically scheduled tweets, only to find that other events occurring in the world have made their statements insensitive. An example of this occurred in 2013, when *American Rifle*, a journal affiliated with the National

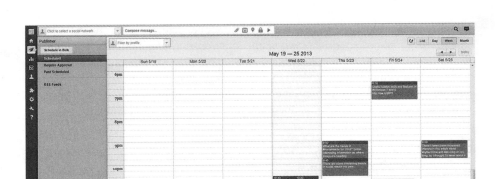

FIGURE 5.5

HootSuite publisher allows you to schedule when content is automatically published.

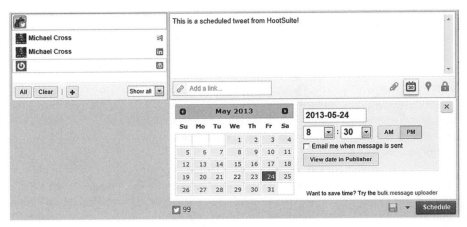

FIGURE 5.6

Scheduling content to be published automatically.

Rifle Association, had a tweet automatically sent through HootSuite. The tweet went on @NRA_Rifleman on the same day a gunman shot moviegoers at an Aurora, Colorado theater during a screening of *The Dark Knight Rises*, killing 12 people. The tweet, which was later deleted, read: "Good morning, shooters. Happy Friday! Weekend plans?"

Following trends

Topics or content that are especially popular on a social media site are said to be *trending*. For example, a trend may be a word, phrase, or hashtag on Twitter that many people are using, or content like videos that are being viewed on YouTube. By following trends, you can see what people are most interested in on a social media site.

On Twitter, you can view a list of trending topics by looking at the *Trends* pane next to your timeline. By default, you see hashtags and keywords that are based on the people you follow and your location. To change the location, you can click on the link in this pane entitled *Change* to display a dialog box. If you click the *Change* button, you can select a different location and get a new list of trends for that locale.

You can also view, register, and provide descriptions for hashtags and words that are trending using sites like What The Trend (www.whatthetrend.com). Using this site, you can view a list of the most popular trends right now or the past 24 hours. You can view and provide descriptions, which indicate why a topic is trending. The site also provides reports on the top trends for the past 30 days, when the hashtag or word first appeared, how long it was in the top 10, the most active trends, and those that have been recently marked as SPAM. Using this site, you can get a better idea of which trends you want to follow or be a part of.

When following trends, you need to be careful as to which ones you use. The same day that the Aurora, Colorado shooting previously mentioned occurred, an online store called Celeb Boutique sent out a tweet using their @celebboutique account. They noticed that the #Aurora hashtag was trending, but never bothered to look at why there was a trend. They decided to capitalize on it, and sent out the following tweet: "#Aurora is trending, clearly about our Kim K inspired #Aurora dress;)." The distasteful tweet inspired backlash from Twitter users, and the company apologized for their ignorance a short time later.

The popularity of a tweet or trend may be skewed by whether it was promoted. By advertising on Twitter, you can have a trend promoted so that it appears on the list of trending topics beside a user's timeline. Even though the promoted trend is marked as being promoted, it allows any hashtags or keywords related to a social media campaign to get extra attention.

Twitter isn't the only social media site that uses trends. For example, YouTube provides a dashboard (www.youtube.com/trendsdashboard) that allows you to view and compare the most visited and shared videos by gender, age, and location. It also provides a map (www.youtube.com/trendsmap) that displays this information to show the geographic location of the most popular videos, which can also filter results by the same criteria. Using this information, you're able to see what content is most popular in specific demographics.

Linking content across different sites

If you're managing social media on multiple sites, it can become cumbersome posting the same content several times over. In such a case, you may want to post to one site and have it automatically appear on others. For example, when you post a status update on Facebook, you may want it to automatically go out as a tweet. While you can post to multiple sites using tools like Hootsuite, there are other alternatives. Many social media sites provide *apps*, *plug-ins*, or *widgets*, which are programmed components that perform a specific function or service.

Cross-posting to different sites often requires some investigation of what plug-ins or widgets are available. Let's say you have a blog on WordPress (www.word-press.com), and you wanted mention of new blog entries to appear on Facebook. In doing so, the status update advertises your blog, attracting more people to read it. To find a plug-in that provides this functionality, you'd visit Facebook's App Store (https://apps.facebook.com) and look at what's available. You might use the one at https://apps.facebook.com/wordpressdotcom/ and add the app to your Facebook account by clicking on the *Start sharing ...* button on this page. Setting up such functionality is essentially the same as adding any other app to Facebook where you give permission to post updates. Once you're done, any new blog entries you publish will also create a Facebook post about it.

Having your content posted to several places does pose some risks. First of all, the visibility of content will not be the same across all sites. You may have config-ured settings on Facebook so that posts are only visible to Friends, but those set-tings don't apply to other sites. A post that's automatically tweeted will appear on Twitter and may appear in search engine results. This could be bad if you've made an unkind comment about someone (e.g., your boss), thinking they'll never see it because the person isn't a Facebook Friend. You shouldn't trust that you'll remem-ber how something's set up months or years down the road, so occasionally review these and other social media settings.

It's also a good idea to document how things are set up for future reference. You'll want to keep track of which social media accounts are configured to auto-matically post to other sites. If you tweet something, you'll want to know where that comment has gone. Is it only on Twitter or is it now appearing on Facebook and LinkedIn? By documenting how you've configured cross-posting information, you'll know where you need to go to delete something that went out by mistake.

Remember that deleting something from one site will not remove it from others. Widgets will have privileges to post content on one site, but don't have privileges to delete content on others. In other words, you'll need to manually log on to each site and delete your unwanted post from each one.

Automatically cross-posting information does pose some risk, but it can also increase the efficiency of publishing content. By properly managing your social media and knowing how such automated features are configured, you'll spend less time publishing the same content to different sites. As we'll see in the following sections, by following a few steps it's relatively easy to set up.

Linking twitter to linkedin

LinkedIn provides the ability to show a link with your Twitter account's name, allow-ing people to click it, view your tweets, and follow you on Twitter. You can also set up LinkedIn so that tweets appear as status updates in your activity. To configure this:

1. Log on to LinkedIn (www.linkedin.com).
2. Go to https://www.linkedin.com/static?key=twitter.
3. Click the *Get Started* button.

4. Twitter will open in your browser, asking if you want to authorize the app. Click *Authorize App* and you'll be redirected back to LinkedIn.
5. On the screen that appears, select whether the Twitter account is visible to *Everyone* or *Do not display my Twitter identity on my profile*.
6. Below the previous option, select whether tweets will be shared in your LinkedIn status. The options are *All tweets* or *Only tweets the contain #in*.
7. Click the *Save Settings* button.

You may run some risk if you allow all tweets to appear in your status. There is always the possibility you'll tweet something that you wouldn't want a potential employer or colleague seeing, or could be taken the wrong way. To avoid this, it's always a good idea to select the option of only sharing tweets that contain the #in hashtag. If you tweeted something like "Working on a new infographic about productivity #in," it would appear in your LinkedIn status. If you tweeted the same thing without #in hashtag, it would not appear on LinkedIn. The option gives you more control and only displays the tweets you want on LinkedIn.

After you've linked Twitter to LinkedIn, you can change settings, add additional Twitter accounts, or remove Twitter through your LinkedIn settings.

1. After logging into LinkedIn, move your mouse over your name in the upper right-hand corner of the page. A drop-down menu will appear.
2. Click on *Settings*.
3. Click on the *Profile* tab located toward the bottom of the page. By default this should already be selected and showing the available options.
4. Click on the *Manage Your Twitter Settings* link, and a dialog box will appear.
5. To remove your existing Twitter account click on the *Remove* link below the accounts name.
6. To make the account invisible to others, uncheck the box labeled *Display your Twitter account on your LinkedIn profile*.
7. To add additional Twitter accounts, click on *Add Your Twitter Account* link. Twitter will open in your browser, asking if you want to authorize the app. Click *Authorize App* and you'll be redirected back to LinkedIn.
8. On the dialog box, click *Save Settings*.

Linking your twitter account to facebook

Twitter provides the ability to publish tweets to your Facebook profile and any pages you administer through the Profile Settings page of your account. To post tweets to Facebook, follow these steps:

1. Log on to Twitter (www.twitter.com).
2. Click on the gear-shaped icon in the upper right-hand corner, and then click *Settings* from the drop-down menu that appears. Alternatively, you can also go to https://twitter.com/settings/account.
3. On the left-hand side of the screen, click on the *Profile* tab.
4. Toward the bottom of the page, click on the *Login to Facebook* button.

5. Enter your username and password on the screen that appears.

6. When prompted, click *Okay* to accept the permissions.

7. Once Twitter has finished connecting to Facebook, several options will appear on the Facebook section of the page. Click on appropriate checkboxes to specify whether Twitter should *post retweets to Facebook* and/or *post to my Facebook profile*.

8. To have Twitter post tweets to a page you own or administer, click on the *Allow posting to one of your pages* link below these options.

9. When prompted, click *Okay* to accept the permissions.

10. Once Twitter has finished connecting to Facebook, a new option entitled *post to my Facebook page will appear*, with a drop-down box below it. Click on the drop-down box and select the page you want tweets to be posted to.

To change your settings you can return to the Profile Settings in Twitter. To prevent tweets from appearing on your Facebook profile or pages, ensure that the appropriate checkbox is unchecked. To disable Twitter from posting to Facebook, click on the *Disconnect it* link in the Facebook section of your Profile Settings.

Linking your facebook page to twitter

Just as you can post from Twitter to Facebook, you can also do the reverse. In configuring this, content you add to Facebook will also be sent out as tweets. Given that tweets can only contain 140 characters, you might wonder what happens when you post information that's longer than the limit. If the text in a Facebook post is particularly long, only part of it will be tweeted with a link to the full post on Facebook. This allows Twitter users to follow your tweet back to Facebook. To link a Facebook page to Twitter, do the following:

1. Log on to Facebook (www.facebook.com).

2. Go to www.facebook.com/twitter/.

3. If you wanted to link your profile to Twitter, you could click on the button labeled *Link My Profile to Twitter*. However, if you just want to link posts on a page to Twitter, click on the link below it labeled *Link a Page to Twitter*. This link is the one we'll use for the rest of the steps.

4. When a listing of pages appears, click the *Link to Twitter* button beside the page you want to link.

5. Twitter will open in your browser, asking if you want to authorize the app. Click *Authorize App* and you'll be redirected back to Facebook.

6. On the page you were previously, you have the option of choosing what kind of new Facebook content will also be tweeted on Twitter. As seen in Figure 5.7, click on the items you also want to appear on Twitter, and then click *Save Changes*.

To change what you've done, simply revisit www.facebook.com/twitter page again. You'll now see a list of your pages, with mention of which ones are linked to Twitter. To change your settings, you would click the *Edit Settings* link to see the list of checkboxes in Figure 5.7. To unlink a page, click on the *Unlink from Twitter* link.

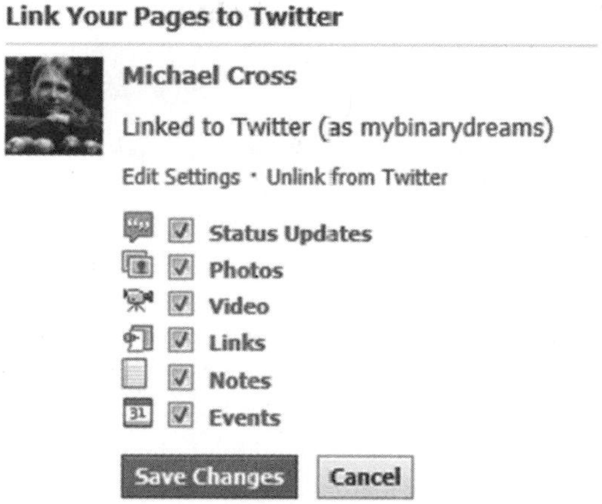

Link Your Pages to Twitter

Michael Cross

Linked to Twitter (as mybinarydreams)

Edit Settings · Unlink from Twitter

- ☑ **Status Updates**
- ☑ **Photos**
- ☑ **Video**
- ☑ **Links**
- ☑ **Notes**
- ☑ **Events**

[Save Changes] [Cancel]

FIGURE 5.7

Change Settings to post Facebook content on Twitter.

Adding internet social media content to a web page

A major reason for having an intranet site is to provide Web-based services and content to your employees. You may want to post announcements informing them of changes, provide a calendar of events, or offer easy access to policies, procedures, or other documents. To provide additional content to employees on the internal network, you can also add feeds to social media that's available to the public. In doing so, content posted on public social media sites become available on your intranet, providing it with fresh content.

Many social media sites provide tools to display content and/or interact with an organization's social media presence. Content from your social media sites can be viewed on your corporate Web site or an intranet site that's only available to employees. Using widgets, plug-ins, and controls, visitors to your Web sites can view tweets and posts without having to log on to sites like Twitter and Facebook.

Twitter provides the ability to create various widgets that can be used to show a timeline, favorites, list or to search for a user account on a Web page. To add a Twitter feed for your account on a Web page, you would do the following:

1. Log on to your Twitter account.
2. Click on the gear-shaped icon in the top right of the navigation bar (or go to https://twitter.com/settings/account).
3. Click on the *Widgets* tab located on the left side of the page.
4. When the *Widgets* page displays, click the *Create new* button.
5. As seen in Figure 5.8, fill out the fields to configure your widget. You can specify the username of the Twitter account you'd like to display, the height of the control, theme, and link colors. If you do not want replies to tweets showing in the display, then ensure the *No replies* checkbox is checked. As you make changes in these fields, the preview of your widget will change on the right-hand side.

6. Click the *Create widget* button.
7. Copy the code that appears in the box below your preview and paste it into the HTML of the Web page where you want the widget to appear.

Facebook also has a number of plug-ins that can be added to a Web site, which are available at https://developers.facebook.com/docs/plugins. Social plug-ins allow you to add various features to a Web page to interact with your Facebook page. For example, by going to this site and going to the *Like Box* link, a tool is displayed that allows you to create the necessary code to display how many users like the page, recent posts, and a link to like the page without having visited it.

Censorship

When creating user-generated content and accessing information on the Internet, you probably never considered that you were exercising a human right. Article 19 of the Universal Declaration of Human Rights states that everyone "has the right to freedom of opinion and expression; this right includes freedom to hold opinions without interference and to seek, receive and impart information and ideas through any media and regardless of frontiers." Even though the Act was adopted by the United Nations in 1948, the fact that it applies to "any media" makes it applicable to the Internet. This right is not without limits or necessarily followed by some countries. The ability to access content on the Internet may be restricted by governments and businesses.

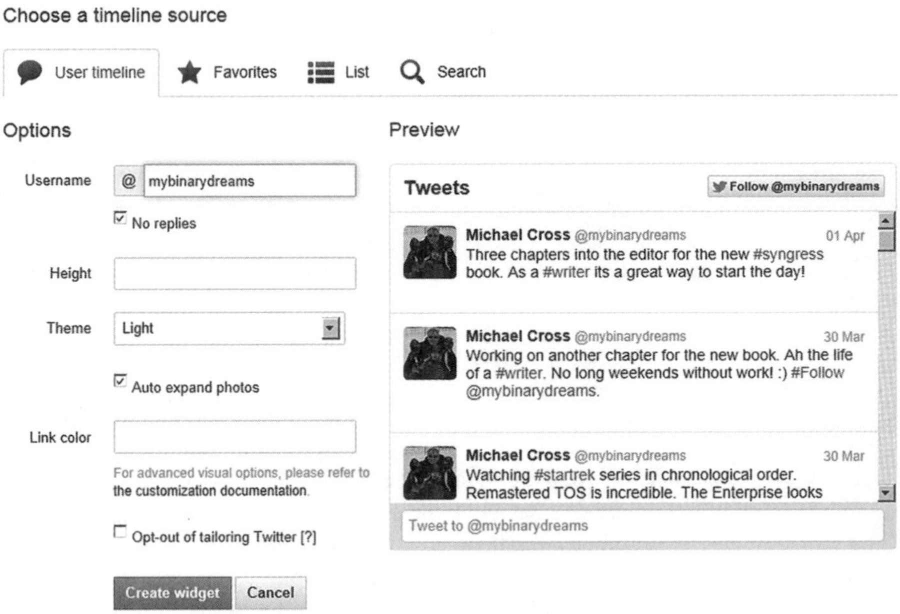

FIGURE 5.8

Create a Twitter feed widget.

Censorship is the practice or system of suppressing ideas, opinions, and information that may be deemed objectionable or dangerous, and/or limiting access to that material. While you might consider censorship a bad thing, in some cases it's not. In the same way that yelling "fire" in a crowded movie theater isn't protected as freedom of speech, you can't commit libel (i.e., false statements that damage a person's reputation) when expressing your opinions on the Internet. Keith Smith versus Williams is a British libel case in which Tracy Williams falsely accused Michael Keith Smith of being a sexual offender and bigot in a Yahoo discussion group that had 100 members. The court ordered her pay £10,000 plus costs.

Social media sites may also impose limitations on what is available on their sites. For example, Facebook's Terms of Service limits posting content that "is threatening or pornographic, incites violence, or contains nudity or graphic or gratuitous violence." Twitter guidelines are different, prohibiting the use of obscene or pornographic images in a profile or header photo or as the background of your profile page. As you can see, the use of certain content differs between sites. Before including certain content on a page or as part of a social media campaign, it's important to review the Terms of Service for the sites you use to identify what is and isn't allowed.

Censorship by country

Even if something is acceptable in your country, it may be deemed offensive or dangerous in other countries. Countries may block or partially restrict access to sites or content, such as specific pages or videos. The OpenNet Initiative (www.opennet.net) provides information and interactive maps that allow you to view which counties filter access to sites and view detailed profiles of each country. As seen in Table 5.1, censorship of social media sites occurs to varying degrees in a number of different countries.

Table 5.1 Social Media Sites Blocked by Country

Social Media Site	Countries Frequently Blocking Site	Countries Intermittently or Partially Blocking Site
Facebook	China, Libya, North Korea, Vietnam	Algeria, Bangladesh, Belarus, Burma (Myanmar), Egypt, Indonesia, Iran, Pakistan, Saudi Arabia, Syria, Tunisia, Uzbekistan
Flickr	North Korea	China, Germany, Iran, Mexico, Pakistan, Saudi Arabia
Orkut (social networking site developed by Google)	Iran, North Korea, Saudi Arabia	India
Twitter	China, North Korea	Algeria, Belarus, Cameroon, Egypt, Iran, Malawi, Pakistan, South Korea
YouTube	China, North Korea, Tunisia, Turkey	Bangladesh, Eritrea, Indonesia, Iran, Mexico, Pakistan, Philippines, United Arab Emirates

Even though sites and content may be blocked or restricted in certain countries, this isn't to say that social media is nonexistent. As we'll discuss in Chapter 10, sites have been used as a crowd-sourcing tool for Internet vigilantism in China, allowing people to research and share information on crimes and other censored incidents. As sensitive content is often suppressed, citizens who don't trust state-run media outlets will collaborate online to find additional facts and share it on blogs, discussion boards, and other sites. In doing so, a person or group involved in criminal or socially unacceptable behavior is exposed to public humiliation.

Lacking faith in the Chinese judicial system, those who seek vigilante justice may also target a person with coordinated cyber-attacks, hate email, and so on. To suppress information online, the Chinese government tries to make it inaccessible. If a case involves a politician or others the state wants to protect, then sites and keywords may be blocked so that information on a person can't be searched. For example, on the Chinese microblogging site *Sina Weibo* (www.weibo.com), the name of Chinese leader Xi Jinping is blocked as a search word. Similarly, when another political leader's son was involved in a high-speed car accident involving a Ferrari, the keyword "Ferrari" was blocked from online searches.

Self-censorship

Organizations and individuals may also censor the Internet by controlling what's accessible. An employer may have firewall rules configured to block all social networking sites or limit access to only certain ones. For example, the organization may allow access to Facebook so that employees can visit the company's page, but block other social networking sites (e.g., Reddit, LinkedIn) where they don't have a corporate presence. Similarly, as we'll discuss in Chapter 9, a business or an individual may configure browser settings or use parental control software to block certain sites.

The content an organization blocks may be unique to the corporate policies, industry regulations, or legislation. For example, even if the organization is fairly permissive in what they allow employees to access, they would probably block content communities or sites that specialize in pornographic content. If you were visiting such a site and a fellow employee saw it, you and your business could be vulnerable to sexual harassment complaints and/or a law suit. To minimize this risk, your organization should block access to these types of sites.

Censoring your pages and blogs

There may be times when you'll want to censor certain content or comments on your pages or blog. Perhaps profanity isn't something you want appearing on your pages and blogs, or the content isn't suitable for certain ages or geographic regions. To limit what's visible or published on these sites, you can take advantage of settings with censorship features.

As we'll show you in Chapter 11, there are a number of settings that control who can view a Facebook page and restrict inappropriate comments. Using these, you can have the page only visible to people in certain countries or prevent people in those countries from seeing it. You can also set age restrictions on the page, so it isn't visible to people under a certain age. There are also page moderation settings and profanity filters that prevent people from making posts or comments that contain vulgarity or keywords that you specify.

Similar features may also be found on the blog site you're using. In Chapter 9, we'll show you how you can blacklist certain words on WordPress blogs, so that any comments containing certain words will be flagged as SPAM and not posted. In using it, you can block people from using profanity on your site.

You can also install plug-ins on your blog that will take care of censoring inappropriate words for you. For example, Filtration (http://wordpress.org/plugins/filtration/) is a plug-in for WordPress blogs that filters out keywords you specify and removes or overwrites unwanted text in titles, content, and comments. For example, if you wanted to filter the word "bleep," it would be removed any time it's used. If you wanted it replaced with a character, such as an asterisk, it would appear as "*****."

Humor

Humor and sarcasm don't always translate well and may be considered offensive by some. When speaking, a person can hear the tone and inflection in your voice and know that you're joking. A person reading a remark may think you're being serious or insulting them in some way. Also, humor isn't universal. What one person finds funny may not go over well with everyone. You need to understand your audience and try and avoid humor that may be offensive or not in line with your brand.

When you do use humor, keep it PG-13. You never know the age and sensitivity of someone reading it, especially when you consider that the text you post could appear in search engine results. You may also wind up limiting access to your page. A page containing adult humor could be blocked by firewalls and browser parental controls for swearing or having adult content.

Promotion of social media

If you're starting a social media campaign, you want to reach as many people as possible. With that comes some impatience. While friends and followers will come in time, there are some things you can do to promote yourself. As we discussed in Chapter 2, the trick is to generate interest and inform people about your brand and social media presence.

Advertising on sites can increase the number of people who visit your page or follow you. Social media sites make money through advertising, which is why sites like Facebook display ads on pages. In clicking an ad, you visit a page or Web site. Similarly, Twitter will promote the tweets or trends created by advertising partners, so they appear high on the list of trends and tweets. In advertising on social media sites, you're getting word out to other users who may be interested in following your brand.

Contests

Contests are a great way of getting people to visit your sites and follow on Twitter, Facebook, and other social media sites. After setting general rules for the contest, you specify a prize that limits the winners to people who have posted on your site or follow you. One example of this would be a restaurant that gives a gift card for the 100th person that comments on your Facebook page. Another example is one I experienced at a conference, which offered a prize to a random person who tweeted to the conference's Twitter account. Not only will you promote your brand by offering prizes associated with it, but you'll generate a lot of interest in your social media sites.

In promoting your social media presence, it's important that you review the Terms of Service for each site. Social networking sites like Facebook have rules on how contests and other promotions are run. As we saw earlier in this chapter when discussing the *Whopper Sacrifice*, you don't want your campaign shut down by breaking the rules.

Directories

There are a number of directories on the Internet that list users of Twitter, Instagram, and other social media under specific categories. Browsing these directories, you can find others with specific interests or expertise and begin to follow their activities. The result is more people with interest in your brand following what you have to say. Some of the directories available include Twiends (www.twiends.com), WeFollow (www.wefollow.com), Twellow (www.twellow.com), and Blogarama (www.blogarama.com).

Not everyone is on the internet

It's easy to forget that not everyone uses social media or even has Internet access. According to a 2013 report by the International Telecommunication Union, only 39% of the world's population is online. Most of those without access are in developing countries, but even if we look at those in the developed world, 33% don't have Internet access. As seen in Figure 5.9, your ability to reach people using social media may be diminished by the area of the world targeted by your campaign.

Depending on the region you're targeting in a social media campaign, the results may vary. However, as Internet access has steadily increased over the past decade, don't feel that a social media presence isn't worth pursuing. It will simply make you an early adopter for that area. It will however mean that you may need to combine traditional and social media in your advertising, which isn't a bad thing.

Don't feel that you're limited to promoting your social media presence through the Internet. In looking at some of the more successful campaigns, like those at the beginning of this chapter, you'll notice that they incorporated different kinds of media to promote their campaign. You may have posters in your store inviting people to join in a hashtag campaign on Twitter, or you might provide the URL to your Facebook

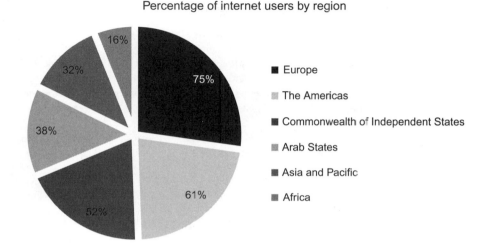

FIGURE 5.9

Percentage of Internet users in the world by region.

page on a business card. If your business advertises in newspapers, TV, or radio, you can attract people to your site by mentioning it in advertisements or sending out a press release to media outlets. Mentioning your social media presence where you can attract more potential customers and people interested in your brand. The trick is to be creative, get people to visit your page, and become involved in your conversations.

Bibliography

Amy's Baking Company Bakery Boutique & Bistro. (2010, May 10). Retrieved May 13, 2013, from Facebook: <www.facebook.com/amysbakingco>.

Amy's Baking Company. (2013, May 10). *Kitchen Nightmares*. Fox Network.

Bray, A. (n.d.). *The US Department of Labor and the Wage and Hour Division (WHD): Investigate Amy's Baking Company Bakery Boutique & Bistro in Scottsdale, AZ.* Retrieved May 19, 2013, from Change.org: <http://www.change.org/petitions/the-us-department-of-labor-and-the-wage-and-hour-division-whd-investigate-amy-s-baking-company-bakery-boutique-bistro-in-scottsdale-az>.

CaseCheck. (2006, March 21). *Michael Keith Smith v Tracy Williams, HC (QBD), 21/03/06.* Retrieved May 29, 2013, from CaseCheck: <http://www.casecheck.co.uk/CaseLaw.aspx?EntryID=12855>.

Cavaliere, V. (2012, July 20). *'Dark Knight Rises' shooting: Twitter outrage as clothing store tries to capitalize on 'Aurora' dress in wake of Colorado tragedy.* Retrieved May 22, 2013, from New York Daily News: <http://www.nydailynews.com/news/national/twitter-outrage-clothing-boutique-capitalize-aurora-article-1.1118731>.

Facebook. (2012, December 11). *Statement of rights and responsibilities.* Retrieved April 12, 2013, from Facebook: <www.facebook.com/legal/terms>.

Facebook. (2012, December 11). *Terms*. Retrieved April 12, 2013, from Facebook: <www.facebook.com/legal/terms>.

Facebook. (2013). *Data use policy—information we receive about you.* Retrieved April 29, 2013, from Facebook: <https://www.facebook.com/about/privacy/your-info>.

Facebook. (n.d.). *Memorialization request.* Retrieved May 24, 2013, from Facebook: <https://www.facebook.com/help/contact/?id=305593649477238>.

Gross, D. (2012, December 3). *Fake lottery winner may be Facebook's most shared image.* Retrieved August 08, 2013, from CNN: <http://www.cnn.com/2012/12/03/tech/innovation/fake-facebook-lottery-winner>.

Help Find Laura Clark*, Missing on 26th Feb 2013.* (2013, February 27). Retrieved May 27, 2013, from Facebook: <https://www.facebook.com/pages/Help-Find-Laura-Clark-Missing-on-26th-Feb-2013/336618656450564>.

Henochowicz, A. (2013, April 1). *Sensitive words: Xi Jinping on Facebook.* Retrieved May 29, 2013, from China Digital Times: <http://chinadigitaltimes.net/2013/04/sensitive-words-xi-jinping-on-facebook/>.

International Telecommunication Union. (2013, February). *The world in 2013: ICT facts and figures.* Retrieved May 30, 2013, from International Telecommunication Union: <http://www.itu.int/en/ITU-D/Statistics/Documents/facts/ICTFactsFigures2013.pdf>.

Jill, J. (2012, October 23). *Morgan Freeman mocks Twitter death hoax: 'I hope those stories are not true'.* Retrieved 25.05.13, from examiner.com: <http://www.examiner.com/article/morgan-freeman-mocks-twitter-death-hoax-i-hope-those-stories-are-not-true>.

Johnson, J. (2012, October 6). *StubHub Twitter account posts vulgar tweet.* Retrieved May 22, 2013, from Social News Daily: <http://socialnewsdaily.com/2774/stubhub-twitter-account-posts-vulgar-tweet/>.

KitchenAid. (2012, October 3). *KitchenAid.* Retrieved May 22, 2013, from Twitter: <https://twitter.com/KitchenAidUSA/status/253708391124459520>.

LaTondress, J. (2010, August 1). *Amy's Baking Company.* Retrieved May 19, 2013, from Yelp: <http://www.yelp.com/biz/amys-baking-company-scottsdale?sort_by=rating_asc>.

Laudig, M. (2010, August 2). *Ouch! Today's hard lesson on Yelp.* Retrieved May 19, 2013, from Chow Bella (Phoenix NewsTimes Blogs): <http://blogs.phoenixnewtimes.com/bella/2010/08/ouch_todays_hard_lesson_on_yel.php>.

McDonalds. (2012, January 20). *McDonalds.* Retrieved May 20, 2013, from Twitter: <https://twitter.com/McDonalds/status/160494703018651648>.

OpenNet Initiative. (n.d.). *Social media filtering map.* Retrieved May 29, 2013, from OpenNet Initiative: <https://opennet.net/research/map/socialmedia>.

Poladian, C. (2013, May 15). *Amy's Baking Company owner Amy Bouzaglo's criminal past surfaces after 'Kitchen Nightmares' meltdown.* Retrieved May 18, 2013, from International Business Times: <http://www.ibtimes.com/amys-baking-company-owner-amy-bouzaglos-criminal-past-surfaces-after-kitchen-nightmares-meltdown>.

Silverstone, A. (2012, January 31). *Alicia Silverstone.* Retrieved May 20, 2013, from Twitter: <https://twitter.com/AliciaSilv/status/164441392263872512>.

Smith, J. (2009, January 14). *Whopper sacrifice forced to disable behavior by Facebook (updated).* Retrieved May 17, 2013, from Inside Facebook: <http://www.insidefacebook.com/2009/01/14/whopper-sacrifice-shut-down-by-facebook/>.

Twitter. (2012, June 25). *Terms of service.* Retrieved April 12, 2013, from Twitter: <https://twitter.com/tos>.

Twitter. (n.d.). *The Twitter rules*. Retrieved May 29, 2013, from Twitter: <http://support.twitter.com/articles/18311-the-twitter-rules#>.

United Nations. (1948, December 10). *The universal declaration of human rights*. Retrieved May 29, 2013, from United Nations: <http://www.un.org/en/documents/udhr/index.shtml#a19>.

United States of America vs. Amanda Patricia Bossingham. 02CR00477-001-PHX-MHM (United States District Court, District of Arizona, June 27, 2008).

Wendy's. (2011, October 3). *Wendy's*. Retrieved May 20, 2013, from Twitter: <https://twitter.com/Wendys/status/120996561772752896>.

West Midlands Police, Birmingham South Policing Unit. (2013, February 28). *Missing teen found safe and well*. Retrieved May 27, 2013, from West Midlands Police, Birmingham South Policing Unit: <http://www.west-midlands.police.uk/np/birminghamsouth/news/newsitem.asp?id=12204>.

Risks of Social Media

INFORMATION IN THIS CHAPTER:

- Risks of social media
- Public embarrassment
- Once it's out there, it's out there
- False information
- Information leakage
- Retention and archiving
- Loss of data and equipment

Risks of social media

You'll find that the risks you face with social media are the same ones encountered by large organizations. This shouldn't be too surprising. Even the largest company's social media presence is handled by a person or small group, with employees using social media in ways similar to you. Everyone faces similar concerns when they're interacting with others, including embarrassment, misrepresentation, losing data, or sensitive information falling into the wrong hands. The scale may be different, but they're accessing the same sites, using the same apps, and need protection from the same threats.

When it comes to social media, you'll often find that the risks you face fall into two categories: technology and the people using it. Technical problems can be dealt with by implementing proper security and having the right tools in place to handle any issues that arise. When it comes to people, you need to change their behavior through policies, training, and communication. The user-generated problems of social media are diminished as a person learns what they should and should not do.

Sources of risk

People recognize risks based on their education and experience. If you'd ask people to identify the risks associated with social media, you'd get different answers related to their expertise or profession. A member of your IT department would see viruses or malware as a major threat and be worried about the impact of data loss to the company. A lawyer would be concerned about potential litigation from such things as discrimination, sexual harassment, and liability from personal messages. A records manager would be concerned about retention of data, data leakage, and sensitive information sharing. An educator or a parent might see cyberbullying as a primary risk and the lack of safeguards to protect children. While some problems may be unique to a person or business, many share similar risks that can be handled in similar ways.

Because everyone focuses on risks that affect them directly, it's always wise to gather input from a diverse selection of people. Departments in an organization will be able to identify any would-be issues that are unique to them and provide input on how to mitigate those risks and their potential impact. You can also benefit by asking peers, partners, and others who have similar situations.

If you feel improvements could be made in safeguarding yourself from potential threats, you're not alone. The Ponemon Institute conducted a survey of IT professionals and found that 63% saw social media as a serious business risk, and only 29% felt their companies had adequate controls to manage the risk. All too often, people will jump into using social media without recognizing the pitfalls and taking proper precautions. However, even if you've been using social media for a while, you can backtrack and take steps to protect yourself in the future.

Public embarrassment

People are concerned about their reputations and want to be viewed in a positive light by peers, coworkers, family, and the public. It's basic human nature to want acceptance. For individuals, it makes for a happier life and successful career. For companies, a reputation will affect their ability to do business and impact sales. Because of this, it should come as no surprise that people and businesses are concerned about elements that negatively impact their reputation and see public embarrassment as a major risk of using social media.

As we saw in previous chapters, there are many ways to embarrass yourself and your company. Making derogatory or outrageous tweets, or posting inappropriate content and uncensored blog entries, can be a concern for businesses and individuals alike. Put simply, there are times when you regret what you post. When this happens, delete it and apologize. No one goes through life without making mistakes, so people will generally understand or at least won't judge you as harshly. An apology shows that you care about how it may have affected others and will go a long way to making amends.

Prior to posting a comment, image, or video on a site, you should consider how it may be viewed by others. If the content compromises the reputation or safety of others or yourself, then don't post it. As we said earlier in this book, imagine your parents or employer viewing the post and then decide whether it's appropriate. A moment of consideration will go a long way to avoiding problems.

The content you post can and will be held against you

If you post something that could be seen as threatening, potentially violent, or slanders another person, it could result in serious consequences. The hurtful breakup of a relationship may have you spitting venom about the person, or a bad day at work may have you venting about your boss or job. Even if you meant nothing by it, a coworker could show your boss what you said or be concerned as to whether your comments are an indicator of workplace violence. Similarly, bashing someone online could be seen as libelous and results in a civil suit. Again, if this happens, delete it and make a generic apology that doesn't contain your original comments. After all, you don't want to repost what you just deleted. The fact that you deleted the offending remarks and apologized may be taken into consideration by those you'll have to answer to.

As we'll discuss later in this chapter, prior to deleting a post that could get you in hot water, make sure you make a copy of it. This could involve making a screenshot, printing the page, or making a backup of the content. If you need to defend yourself, you may need a copy of the post to accurately show what was said and what you did about it.

You should also be aware that social media sites commonly have policies that limit the types of content you're allowed to post. Sites may forbid offensive or abusive images, video, comments, or messages and may close down your account if you post content to deliberately humiliate someone. As we'll see in Chapter 7, such actions could be considered cyberbullying or harassment and lead to civil or criminal litigation.

What's allowed will vary from site to site, and sometimes differ to dramatic degrees. If you look at content communities, you would see that YouTube doesn't allow pornography, but RedTube (www.redtube.com) is a video sharing site for pornographic video. What's offensive on one site may not be seen as offensive on others. Before posting or reporting content, you should review the Terms of Service to identify what kinds of content aren't allowed.

Divorce cases and social media

While any kind of court case might use a person's social media activity as evidence, it's often seen in divorces and child custody cases. The posts and comments you make, photos you upload, and other information found on a social networking site could be used to dispute previous testimony, support claims against you, and show relationships to other people. The flirty messages you've sent or adding a past lover as a friend could corroborate an accusation of infidelity, while angry posts might strengthen claims that you have a bad temper. The people you're friends with could lend credence to allegations that you're associating with people of poor character, and perhaps have a bearing on claims that you're an unfit parent and should get reduced visitation to children. Regardless of whether it's true, as a documented record of your thoughts, feelings, actions, and intentions, social media can tell the courtroom a lot about you.

It's increasingly common to see a person's online activity used as evidence in divorce cases. In 2010, the American Academy of Matrimonial Lawyers (AAML) reported that 81% of divorce lawyers saw an increase in evidence from social networks. Of the various sites where evidence was acquired, Facebook was the most commonly used, with 66% of the lawyers finding it was a primary source, followed by MySpace (15%) and Twitter (5%). In 2013, the same organization revealed that 59% of divorce lawyers found an increase in evidence from dating sites, with 64% saying that Match.com was a primary source, followed by eHarmony (9%). You need to be careful about what you do online during a divorce, because someone may very well be watching.

Evidence isn't limited to the content you post. Your profile information may also be used to show dishonesty. In the 2013 survey by the AAML, 57% of divorce lawyers cited a person's relationship status as the most common piece of evidence, followed by Salary and Occupation (15%) and Parental Status (7%). Alton Abramowitz, president of the AAML explained that "Identifying yourself as single when you are not, or listing that you have no children when you are actually a parent, can represent some key pieces of evidence against you during the divorce process."

In terms of securing social media accounts, divorce and child custody cases are unique. During a divorce, the mutual friends of a couple will often split off into different camps, choosing which person they want to support and continue a friendship. Even if you've gone through your settings to prevent information from being public, and removed your estranged spouse and his/her family as friends, you probably haven't unfriended the mutual friends of you and your ex-spouse. Your ex can still go through those people to see what's on your Timeline, profile page, or other content you've made available. While you could remove all of your mutual friends, it gets more convoluted when your children have been added as friends to your account. You're probably not going to remove them, so you're left with the open possibility of your ex-spouse having access through your children.

While honesty is the best policy, it doesn't mean that you should allow everything to be on display. Discretion is the key. As we suggested when looking for a job, sanitizing your social media sites you use is a good step to putting your best foot forward. You should remove any posts, photos, and information that could potentially be used against you in divorce proceedings. In your profile information, you should review what's said and make certain that it's accurate or removed. Your own words, contents, and actions can be used to support accusations against you, so you need to be careful about what appears on your social media.

To prevent your ex-spouse from seeing everything on your account, modifying the information, and possibly posting as you, you need to prevent others from logging with your password. During the marriage, you've probably used the other person's computer, meaning your passwords may have been saved in the browser. Also, your husband or wife may know your password or at least some of the common ones you use. Because of this, as soon as the relationship ends, you should change your password immediately.

Removing videos from YouTube

Old videos and photos of us being silly can be a major source of embarrassment. While anyone might be mortified at being featured in an online video, some are better able to keep it somewhat private. In 2013, the Tajikistan President Emomali Rahmon had to relive awkward moments from his son's 2007 wedding, when a home video was uploaded to YouTube under the title of "Drunk Tajik President Sings a Song." The video shows the leader merrily dancing and singing out of tune and was viewed almost 300,000 times. To prevent people in his country from seeing the video, YouTube access was blocked in Tajikistan.

Since most of us can't block content in this way, we have to settle with privacy controls on the videos we post. On YouTube, you can set a video to any of the following visibility levels:

- *Public*, which allows anyone to view the video.
- *Unlisted*, which allows people to view the video if they have the link. It won't appear in search results or YouTube's public spaces.
- *Private*, which allows you and up to 50 other people you invite to view the video. Like the unlisted setting, it won't appear on your channel or search results.

Even if a video is unlisted, people can still view it if they know how to find it. You or another person may have shared a link on other sites or acquired it via email. Your settings also won't stop people from viewing and sharing any copies that have been downloaded from YouTube and uploaded elsewhere. To change the privacy setting of a video on your YouTube channel:

1. Log on to YouTube and go to your Video Manager at www.youtube.com/my_videos.
2. Choose the video you want to change the privacy settings for, and click the *Edit* button.
3. In the *Privacy Settings* dropdown menu, select Private.
4. Click *Save changes*.

Of course, these settings only apply to the videos you uploaded to YouTube and not those belonging to other people. If you're uncomfortable with the content of a video, you can report it by flagging it as inappropriate. In doing so, YouTube staff will review the video to determine if it goes against their community guidelines and should be removed, or should be restricted so that younger users can't view it. To flag a video, you simply click on the flag icon beneath the video and check the option that applies to your complaint. Options include the video containing objectionable content or that it infringes on your rights.

You can also contact the person who posted the video and ask them to remove it. If they don't remove it or you're uneasy about contacting the person directly, you can file a complaint with YouTube through their Policy and Safety Hub at www.youtube.com/yt/policyandsafety. There are different kinds of complaints you can make, including copyright complaints where someone has copied a video that you created. If you're identifiable within a video, you can also file a privacy complaint. In doing so, the request will be reviewed, so the video can be removed from the site.

Removing photos and tags that others post on Facebook

Embarrassing photos can cause problems for businesses and individuals alike. A person may indicate where they work on their profile page and then upload a photo that doesn't mesh well with the corporate image. Perhaps it's a silly image that looks unprofessional, shows the employee drinking or involved in drunken antics, or depicts something unflattering or even offensive. Depending on the picture, once it's associated with an employer, it could damage the brand or reputation of the company.

Even if an employee is mindful of the photos they upload, others may not be. You may appear in a photo taken by another person that's uploaded to Facebook. The photo might focus on you or show you in the background, where you would have gone unnoticed if someone hadn't tagged the photo and identified you. By tagging you in the photo, others will see who you are and be able to follow the tag to your profile page.

If you are tagged by someone in an embarrassing photo, you can remove the tag yourself. Untagging a photo is done from the Activity Log of your account. After logging onto Facebook, do the following:

1. Click on the Privacy Shortcuts icon, which is shaped like a padlock in the upper right-hand corner of the page.
2. From the menu that appears, click *Who can see my stuff?*
3. When it expands click on the *Use Activity Log* link.
4. On the left side of the page, click *Photos*. Alternatively, to only see the photos of you, inclusive to ones you're tagged in, you can click the *Photos of You* link.
5. Look through the list of photos until you see the one you don't want to be tagged in. Click the checkbox beside the photo, so it appears checked.
6. At the top of the page, click the *Report/Remove Tags* button.
7. When the box appears, select the option you want:
    a. I want the photo untagged, which removes the tag from the photo.
    b. I want the photo untagged and taken down, in which the tag is removed and you can ask the person to take down the photo.

Once a tag is removed, the photo no longer has a link indicating you in the picture. However, the photo is still visible to others. People will be able to see it in the album of whoever posted it, when it's shared, and may still appear in search results. If the photo is truly embarrassing or damages your reputation, send a request to remove the photo so that no one will see it.

Removing posts on Facebook

Facebook also provides ways to report other people's posts as abusive or offensive. When you click the *Report Story or Spam link*, you have the option of clicking

FIGURE 6.1

Reporting a post.

undo, hiding all stories from that person, or submitting a report (Figure 6.1). If you click submit a report, the post is flagged for review.

Hiding content

There may be content that you find offensive, but others may not. In such a case, you may want to hide the post so that you and others don't see it on your Timeline. As mentioned in the previous section, when you hover your mouse over a post on Facebook, an image of a downward arrow appears. As seen in Figure 6.1, if you click on the arrow, a menu appears with a link titled *Hide....* When you click on it, the post is hidden and a message will appear giving you the chance to unhide it and the option of hiding all posts from that person.

When you hide content in this way, it isn't deleted. You may not see it, but it is still available on the poster's Timeline. To view your Timeline, click on your name in the upper right-hand corner of Facebook and you'll see the status updates and other content you've posted. To hide one of your posts:

1. Hover your mouse over a post. An icon that looks like a pencil will appear in the upper right-hand corner. Clicking on this icon, a menu will appear.
2. Click on the *Hide from Timeline* menu item.

While the post will no longer appear on your Timeline, it will still appear in searches, news feeds, and other areas of Facebook. If you want one of your posts to be completely removed, then instead of clicking *Hide from Timeline*, you should click the *Delete* menu item.

Reporting abuse

In addition to the methods already mentioned, sites commonly have an email address or a process in which you can report abusive users, such as those who are harassing you. The methods of reporting abuse vary from site to site, with some providing email addresses and others using online forms that you use to submit a report. Some resources to report abusive behavior include:

- Twitter, https://support.twitter.com/forms/abusiveuser
- Facebook, www.facebook.com/help/reportlinks
- LinkedIn, abuse@linkedin.com

These aren't your only options. You should always contact the police if threats are made, and/or you're concerned about your safety. A threat is a threat, and there's no difference between threatening someone in person or online. By contacting the authorities, an investigation can be conducted and the person may be charged.

If you see content that is illegal, you should also make an effort to report it. For example, if someone uploaded child pornography or posted information on child prostitution, molestation, or sexual tourism involving children, you should contact authorities immediately. In the United States, you can make an online report through the National Center for Missing and Exploited Children's CyberTipline at www.missingkids.com/cybertipline. In Canada, you can make an online report to the Canadian Centre for Child Protection at www.cybertip.ca. Once a report is made, the appropriate law enforcement agencies will be notified.

Once it's out there, it's out there

There's a common belief that once something is on the Internet, it's there forever. The permanence of social media requires you to accept that once data is released online, it may be available forever. While not necessarily true, it can sure seem like it, especially when it's embarrassing. The Internet can have a long memory for moments you wish were forgotten.

Every year, you'll see new photos on social networking sites of drunken parties and young women flashing a crowd at Spring Break or Mardi Gras. While it may seem unlikely when your entire life is ahead of you, such photos can haunt you years later, especially when a potential employer, significant other, or your child sees how you led your life. Such photos can be shared, copied, and downloaded, making them available for years. Even if they aren't online now, they may be later.

A reason why data has such longevity on the Internet is due to the ease of sharing it. In 2012, a girl posted a sexual image of herself on a social networking site, which was then distributed through text messages to other students at Golden Bay High School in New Zealand. The parents expected the school to aid their daughter, but since the images were posted outside of school hours, there was little they could do. Unfortunately, as the images are shared, there are more and more copies that can be further distributed, making them harder to get rid of. The more scandalous or salacious the content, the more likely it won't be deleted.

Embarrassing content can create significant problems even years later. In 2008, Carmen Kontur-Gronquist was the Mayor of Arlington, Oregon, when lingerie photos taken of her at a fire hall were noticed on MySpace. Even though the photos were taken 4 years earlier, it resulted in a recall election where she was voted out of office.

A similar problem was encountered by Stacy Snyder, who posted a photo of herself at a party, drinking and wearing a pirate hat. The caption of the photo was aptly titled "Drunken Pirate." Years later, the photo was discovered on MySpace.

Days before her graduating as a teacher from Millersville University School of Education, she was denied her degree. The school felt that she was promoting drinking online, where underage students would be exposed to it. They claimed she wouldn't have received the degree even without this incident, but Snyder sued on the grounds that her First Amendment rights had been violated, and she had done nothing illegal. Unfortunately, in 2008, the judge rejected her claim, stating that the photo wasn't protected because it didn't relate to matters of public concern.

While this chapter discusses a number of ways to remove data from social media sites, the process can be difficult. In some cases, you may even have to bring in legal assistance to fight the battle in court, making it a lengthy and an expensive process. Even when information no longer appears to be online, it may still be there. As we discussed earlier, content on social media sites may be hidden or you may be blocked from seeing it. For example, in 2012, Afghanistan blocked YouTube in an effort to prevent people from watching the film *Innocence of Muslims*. Even though the content has disappeared to some, it didn't mean it was gone.

The best way to avoid embarrassing photos, videos, and comments from coming back to haunt you is to be proactive. Carefully consider what you're uploading or writing before you make it available to others. If you believe that it may be around forever, you may think twice about posting it in the first place.

False information

While the Internet is a great resource for information, not all of what you see is true. Beyond the hoaxes we discussed in Chapter 5, people will make false or misleading claims, which are then shared with others. Because a friend or someone you follow has shared the information, it can lend credibility to it, making it seem even more believable.

Often, the user-generated content and crowdsourced information on social media sites lack any process to verify the facts or will be available for public consumption before the errors have been edited out. Sites like Wikipedia rely on other users reading the articles and identifying errors that are then edited out. While the article will eventually become a valid source of information, people consider it to be a valid source between the time it's written and the false information is removed.

This isn't to say that social media isn't a vital part of sharing information. According to a report by the Pew Research Center, as events were unfolding during the Boston Marathon bombing in 2013, 6% of people used social network sites to keep in touch with friends and family. The report also showed that a large number of people got their news from social networking sites. Twenty-six percentage of people overall got their information from sites like Twitter and Facebook, and younger Americans (56%) aged 18–29 were more likely to use social media to obtain updates. For many people, social media is an important source of the latest information.

Unfortunately, while much was said, quantity doesn't always mean quality. Due to the competitive nature of news outlets trying to report a story first, journalists

FIGURE 6.2

Tweet making false claim during Hurricane Sandy.

covering the bombing saw false information on social media sites and reported it as fact. An example was a campaign on Reddit called "Find Boston Bombers," in which amateur sleuths attempted to identify the bomber. It turned into a witch hunt, where innocent people were misidentified as suspects and targeted by news outlets and social networking users as having a connection to the attack. One "suspect" on Reddit was Sunil Tripathi, a missing student from Brown University whose family was harassed after the misidentification. During the furor of dangerous speculation, Tripathi was found dead due to unrelated circumstances. The quality of information on social media sites can be debatable, sometimes dubious, and quickly compound a tragedy.

This isn't the only time-sharing false information that had serious consequences. As seen in Figure 6.2, during the onslaught of Hurricane Sandy, Shashank Tripathi (@ComfortablySmug) tweeted false information that caused additional panic. While not the only one spreading lies that were retweeted hundreds of times, it was reported by CNN and New York Magazine as truth. The lies resulted in him losing his job as a congressional campaign manager and facing the possibility of criminal charges.

In 2011, Gilberto Martinez Vera (@gilius_22) and Maria de Jesus Bravo Pagola (@MARUCHIBRAVO) started a series of lies about gunmen holding children hostage at a school in Boca del Rio, Mexico. The rumors were spread on Facebook and Twitter and mentioned multiple schools, causing a panic especially among parents of students. The two were later jailed on charges of terrorism and sabotage.

Every day you can find false information shared and retweeted on social media sites with little concern to its accuracy. While information flows quickly online, verifying it can be slow. A tweet or post can go viral in a short time, but it will take a while for comments to appear about how the claims are false. To ensure you're getting the right information, it's wise to take a moment to do a quick search in Google or Bing to see if what you're reading is true. If you simply share bogus information without verifying it, your credibility will suffer. If you make serious claims that are false, you could lose your job and face civil suits or criminal charges.

Misrepresenting yourself

The Internet gives a false impression of anonymity, and many people use it to create an artificial persona. Many people will tweak their age to look a little younger or change minor details to appear more interesting. Others will go farther. A person may provide false information about their experience, education, or personal details to misrepresent themselves to potential employers, clients, or romantic partners.

Omitting information or providing some misleading information may be used as a defensive measure. For example, rather than providing the city you live in, you might exclude that information from your profile or say you live in a nearby larger city. However, there is a difference between protecting yourself and creating a façade.

If you use dating sites or social networking to meet others, you'll want to stay honest. If you misrepresent yourself, eventually the ruse is discovered when the other person meets you. As you associate yourself with others on the basis of similarities and common interests, you'll also miss out on making genuine connections if the facts about you are false.

In chat rooms, it's common to find people who have created a false profile, complete with fake pictures and personal details. In some cases, it's harmless. The false information may be used as a defensive measure to keep others at a safe distance, or the person may be uncomfortable about his or her appearance and post a picture of someone more attractive. Of course, the person may have more sinister reasons. Serial killer John Edward Robinson met many of his victims in chat rooms and became known as the Internet's first serial killer. As we'll discuss in Chapter 7, pedophiles, rapists, and other predators may introduce themselves to victims through social networking sites or chat rooms prior to meeting them. The false persona may be used on social networking or chat room sites to deter you from finding a criminal record or an inclusion in a sex offender registry.

If you use sites like LinkedIn to interact with colleagues or meet potential employers, you'll want to be honest about your education and experience. If false credentials are used as part of your application for employment, you can be fired for misrepresenting yourself. Again, whether it's in person or online, honesty is the best policy.

Misrepresenting your business

Under no circumstances you want to misrepresent your business on social media sites by making false claims about your company or its products. Just as consumer protection laws prohibit making misleading or deceptive claims about products and services in traditional media, these same laws apply to false claims made online.

Not only can you be subject to litigation, but the negative public relations of showing you can't be trusted will damage your brand.

You also don't want customers or fans making false claims. If a person makes a comment that misrepresents your business, you should address the comment and correct them and/or delete the misleading comment. For example, let's say someone said your company's product was 100% environmentally friendly, but it was incorrect or there was no research to support the claim. Alternatively, a fan of your brand might make negative comments about a competitor that you know is false. Leaving such comments unaddressed is essentially the same as endorsing it as being valid. As a business, you need to be responsible for the claims you make and those of people posting on your page.

False information isn't necessarily bad

While falling for a hoax or spreading false information can make you appear foolish, a good campaign can use false information to promote a product or brand. Every year, the BBC, Google, and other companies create false commercials and news reports as a joke for April Fools Day. When it's good-natured fun or well crafted, most people laugh off the hoax and appreciate how it was done.

A great example of how false information can promote a brand is seen in the 2007 campaign in which a ghost was seen in the window of a house in downtown Toronto, Ontario. The ghost of the young girl was actually an image from a holographic projector, which passersby could see skipping, walking, and doing other movements. In the second week of these sightings, a video of the apparition was posted on YouTube, Google Video, and other sites. It quickly went viral and became the topic of discussion on blogs and various sites. A second video was released a short time later, and the two generated an excess of 2.1 million hits. When the address of the house was "leaked," even more people visited it, hoping to catch a glimpse of her nightly appearance.

After 3 weeks of the engineered phenomena, the ghost was seen in the window holding a sign that said "Get scared more often" with the logo of a subscription horror channel called *Scream TV*. The paranormal promotion was advertised as a hoax in television commercials, online, and by media outlets covering the story. For a cost of $50,000, the campaign resulted in an immediate subscription increase of 35%.

Another horror example that used the Internet is *The Blair Witch Project*. The 1999 movie was the first movie to use the Internet as a primarily target for marketing, spreading rumors in chat rooms, message boards, and other online venues that the film was authentic found footage. The claims were "verified" as legitimate by a Web site, which provided manufactured television news clips about the disappearance of people in the movie. Box office sales resulted in it becoming one of the most profitable independent movies of all time. Results like this show that if you can make the false information entertaining, it can have a positive effect on what you're selling.

Information leakage

One of the most significant risks for businesses and individuals is sensitive information being leaked. There are many kinds of information that could result in financial losses or embarrassment if it was shared with the wrong person or publicized online. Such information may be proprietary, such as trade secrets or a new product under development being revealed too early, or could reveal information that compromises security. Businesses and their employees may also be at risk by personally identifiable information being revealed. It can be dangerous when people reveal sensitive facts about themselves, the business, or their work.

Be clear about what's private

Since revealing company information can jeopardize your job and devastate a business, it's important to understand what can and can't be discussed in public. Training and policies can assist in this regard, showing employees how they should handle the information available to them in their day-to-day work. If you're unsure what you can share, then follow a basic rule: if it's not in a press release, don't discuss it.

You should determine whether your organization uses an information classification scheme, which categorizes records and data based on their sensitivity. Strict policies and procedures may exist as to what kinds of information can be shared with the public and under what circumstances it can be accessed or released to others. For example, information may be categorized as follows:

- *Secret*, which restricts who can view the data to a small people with a high clearance level.
- *Confidential*, in which information is restricted to people who need to know it. This might include client or employee information like Social Security Numbers, medical history, criminal records, or other confidential data. It may also be restricted under legislation or regulations, such as the Sarbanes–Oxley Act, Payment Card Industry, or privacy acts that protect personal data.
- *Internal*, which means the data can't be shared outside of the organization without specific permission. This might include such things as employee information (addresses, phone number, etc.), corporate policies, and so on.
- *Public*, which means it is unclassified and has few or no restrictions. Such information can be disseminated to the public and could include such things as press releases, public job postings, promotional material, and so on.

Organizations may also use a more basic scheme, consisting of classified and unclassified data. Classified information may consist of information about technology being used and current and upcoming projects. Unclassified information might be anything that can be discussed openly with partners, vendors, or even the public. Whatever method your organization uses, it's important to identify it before you accidently reveal something that could cost you your job.

Providing too much information

Everyone's had the experience of getting or giving a little too much information. Someone may tell you the indiscrete details of a personal experience or some office gossip they heard at the water cooler. Some people have trouble keeping their own information private, so you can understand why a business would be concerned about the confidentiality of corporate data.

The terminology that strangers are "friends" on social networking sites can lull you into a false sense of security. You can feel like you're addressing your family and friends and forget that a post may be read by coworkers, acquaintances you barely know, or even strangers you've added to play games. People using their personal accounts to discuss work-related information can cause dramatic problems for themselves and the business. They may cause damage to the corporate image by complaining about staff or the brand itself, violate privacy by mentioning employees or clients, or mention a key piece of information that a competitor may use to their advantage. A tweet or public post can be displayed for the world to see, and even more secure posts may be copied or shared for others to see. What you say on social media can be a public announcement.

Information security is important on both a personal and work-related level. A 2010 survey conducted by the Consumer Reports National Research Center found that 38% of people posted their full birthdate and 8% posted their street address. The same study projected that approximately 1.7 million online households had been victims of identity theft over the previous year. The number of victims is not surprising when you realize how transparent some people's personal information is on social networking sites.

As we've seen throughout this book, the tidbits of information you reveal about yourself or your work can be compiled into a telling profile. As we'll see in Chapters 7 and 11, the address on a LinkedIn profile, a birthdate on your Facebook page, and other fragments of information can be useful for the purposes of identity theft or to identify passwords and other security information that can leave you and your organization vulnerable.

Small bits of information can be accumulated from any number of sources, even the most unlikely ones, and used to access other information. During the 2008 US presidential election, vice presidential candidate Sarah Palin's email account was hacked by David Kernell, the son of Memphis Democratic state representative Mike Kernell. The hacker obtained Palin's birthdate and other personal details from a Wikipedia page and then used the information to reset the password with Yahoo!'s account recovery for forgotten passwords. The password was posted by Kernell on the site 4chan, and screenshots of the email account were uploaded to WikiLeaks. What started as a few innocuous factoids became clues to hack her account, so that private emails could be leaked to the public.

WikiLeaks

Leaking information can be done in a number of ways. It may be done directly, as in the case of someone writing a blog or post and mentioning sensitive facts about the organization or its employees. It can also be done through traditional methods, where the data is given to a journalist who then parrots what you've provided or does additional investigative reporting. With the Internet, people can now leak information to third-party sites that make the information available to everyone.

One such site that has received much publicity and been the focus of controversy is WikiLeaks (www.wikileaks.org). Since 2007, the whistle-blowing site has published classified and sensitive material belonging to government and high-profile organizations. The site provides a secure drop box, where people can upload files anonymously, which is then reviewed by members of their staff and volunteers who are part of mainstream media outlets or journalists. The information is then published on their site, but unlike many wikis cannot be edited by visitors to the site. This keeps the content unaltered from its intended publication.

Sites that post leaked documents are seen as a serious security risk. In 2010, WikiLeaks released a list of infrastructure sites that was compiled to protect US interests from terrorist attacks. It's one of numerous incidents that have led to WikiLeaks being called a threat to national security. Another issue is that some information has been provided by hackers. In 2012, WikiLeaks began publishing over 5 million email messages belonging to the global intelligence company Stratfor. In 2011, a hacking group called *Anonymous* admitted to stealing email and credit card information from the company and uploaded the data to WikiLeaks.

While such sites are an obvious risk for organizations and governments, they're also not without merit. Content on WikiLeaks has been widely reported by mainstream news. In 2010, WikiLeaks released classified footage taken by US Apache helicopters on July 12, 2007 showing civilians being injured or killed in air-to-ground attacks. The video showed a group of eight men (including two Reuters war correspondents) being shot at with 30 mm cannons. After the first airstrike, one of the correspondents was dead and the other was severely wounded and tried crawling away. In an act of compassion, a father and his two children saw the wounded man and decided to pull over, and several others tried to carry the correspondent into their van. When the helicopter opened fire again, the father was killed and his children were seriously wounded. Audio on the video shows the children were denied evacuation to the military hospital. Instead, they were given to Iraqi police and sent to a local hospital. The soldiers are heard blaming the Iraqis, saying "it's their fault for bringing their kids into a battle." After the incidents, Reuters requested the video under a Freedom of Information Act request but their request was denied. The US military defended the incident as correct actions taken against insurgents. It wasn't until the classified video appeared on WikiLeaks that the truth was revealed publicly.

When you leak information to the public, it's important to realize that you're putting your job at risk and making yourself vulnerable to civil litigation and criminal prosecution. In May 2010, Bradley Manning was arrested for leaking the Baghdad airstrike video and hundreds of thousands of other documents to WikiLeaks. It is the largest leak of classified documents in the US history. The FBI discovered his involvement through a hacker named Adrian Lamo, who confided that Manning admitted in their online chats to leaking the information. In 2013,

Manning pled guilty to a number of lesser charges, and at the time of this writing is facing trial. If convicted, he could face life imprisonment.

Corporate espionage

Governments and corporations will use social media to obtain intelligence. While a government agency will spy on a person or group of interest for national security reasons, *corporate espionage* is used to gather and analyze on competitors for commercial reasons. By obtaining privileged data that's available to insiders of a company, a competitor gains a clear advantage over other businesses in an industry.

Gathering sensitive data doesn't necessarily require finding a disgruntled employee or whistle-blower that's ready to hand over the keys to the kingdom. Often, anyone will do. By doing a simple search for a company name, you'll find numerous accounts where people mention their place of employment. You can then follow their tweets and posts to scrape together key pieces of information that can be used to your advantage. Often, it involves getting the big picture by gathering smaller pieces of a puzzle.

In 2011, the security company CyberRoam released information about an online study they conducted on 20 businesses over a 6-month period. By looking at the tweets made by the sales director, a department head, and designers of a company in Singapore, they saw that several people were looking elsewhere for employment and salaries were not being paid. Obviously, if this was public knowledge, you would think twice before applying for a job, being a supplier or even being a customer. CyberRoam was able to accurately predict they'd file for bankruptcy.

Another company in the study targeted the financial director of a New York firm. Finding that he was recently divorced, a male consultant for CyberRoam created a fake Facebook account and posed as a female. By appealing to loneliness and desire for romance, confidential information was obtained. In initial chats, the financial director mentioned that he couldn't disclose the revenues of his company but later revealed that they were $6.5 million.

Such confidential information doesn't have to be obtained through full-time employees of the company. It can be acquired through partners, vendors, temporary employees, volunteers, or anyone else who has inside knowledge of the company. Consider how many businesses take coop students from high schools, colleges, and universities. The students may only be at an organization for a short time, but may be exposed to volumes of information. If they work in an IT department, they gain knowledge of the network, know procedures, and may even have administrator passwords. Students may be aware of upcoming projects, the release dates of new products, or overhear information that indicates the stability of the business.

To protect your organization, it's important that employees know that they shouldn't discuss business-related information through their own accounts. The disclosure of information should only come through official channels, as in the case of an official social media account. By employees not mentioning anything that's business-critical, or involving ongoing or upcoming projects, your organization will be much safer online.

Retention and archiving content

Organizations are often required to retain and archive records for specific periods of time. Even if regulations mandating the retention of records don't apply to you, it's still a good idea to keep copies of your social media. If you ever needed to refer to an old post or a tweet that was deleted, such as for evidence in a legal case or to verify something, it is useful to have a snapshot of what you did online.

For many organizations, retaining records is a must. As we'll discuss further in Chapter 8, public companies are required to comply with legislation like the Sarbanes–Oxley Act of 2002, which defines what records are to be stored and for how long. It doesn't limit this to paper records. Information is information, which is why any business records, including those in an electronic format are to be saved for not less than 5 years.

If your business has a records manager. it is wise to discuss the obligations for archiving social media content. They may be able to provide you with a records retention schedule, which outlines how long a record has to remain active and why it needs to be an active record. In some cases, the records need to be available for certain lengths of time for legal or fiscal reasons, while in other cases, it needs to be retained as a historical record for a specific time or indefinitely.

Beyond individual organizations, there are also institutions that archive social media for historical purposes. In January 2013, the Library of Congress announced that it would be archiving the tweets sent by Twitter users. In 2010, an agreement was signed with Twitter, allowing them to access tweets dating back to 2006, when Twitter was founded. While there are an estimated 400 million tweets sent each day, the daunting task of archiving an estimated 170 billion tweets for posterity is done through a social media aggregation company in Boulder, Colorado called Gnip (www.gnip.com). By keeping these tweets archived, they provide a snapshot of our interests, concerns, and activities in the twenty-first century.

There are different ways of keeping records of social media activity. According to the Environmental Protection Agency's (EPA) guide entitled *Interim*Guidance for EPA*Employees who are Representing EPA Online Using Social Media*, the records created or received by the agency "using social media tools must be printed to paper and managed according to the applicable records schedule in a recordkeeping system." As we'll discuss later, making copies to a hard disk, which can then be backed up with other data is another option. Finally, there are services on the Internet that can be used to back up your social media, so that the content of any given time can be referred to when needed.

eDiscovery

The content posted on social media sites is subject to the same laws and regulations as other information. Because a record is a record regardless of its form, it may be used as evidence in criminal or civil legal cases. *Electronic discovery* or *eDiscovery* is the process of searching, locating, and securing information for the purpose of using it as evidence.

Digital information is extremely useful as evidence. When you save a file, it's time-stamped to show the date and time of its creation and the last time it was accessed. Such files are also easy to search, unlike paper documents that need to be scrutinized manually, and can be quite revealing. People tend to be less reserved when conversing in email, chat rooms, or other electronic methods of communication. In many cases, people will reveal information that they normally wouldn't through traditional documentation.

As social media has become a popular medium for communication and publishing information, it has also come into focus as important evidence. In 2011, Gartner, an information technology research and advisory company, predicted that by the end of 2013, half of all companies will have been asked to produce social media content for eDiscovery. Even in personal law suits or court cases like divorce or child custody battles, the information you post on social media sites can be used as evidence.

If you don't have the information backed up and available when needed, you could face strict penalties. For example, the Sarbanes–Oxley Act has strict regulations regarding information that may be used in an investigation, including documents in an electronic format. It imposes fines, imprisonment, or both for "altering, destroying, mutilating, concealing, falsifying records, documents, or tangible objects with the intent to obstruct, impede, or influence a legal investigation."

Inappropriate use of social media is a major problem for organizations, and many employees have been fired for mistakes they've made. If someone made a libelous comment about you, you wouldn't want the evidence disappear by someone deleting it. At its most basic level, printing out the page containing the comments or taking screenshots could be useful evidence to support your claim. Similarly, if an employee deleted content that was contrary to confidentiality agreements, social media policies, or legislation, you might be unable to prove it occurred if it was removed from the site. Archiving the site, printing, or taking screenshots will be necessary to support any discipline taken against the person.

If you're the person who needs to defend against something that was posted or tweeted, it's equally important to have an accurate copy of any content that is relevant to the accusations. This would include a copy of the information, as well as dates it was posted and deleted, and actions taken afterwards, such as an apology or updates that were posted.

Backing up social media

A *backup* is a process or system where a copy of the data is stored separately from the original, protecting you from potential data loss. While you're probably familiar with backing up hard disks, it's also possible to back up your social media content. There are many tools available to store copies of your data online or download it to your computer.

While you might think that the content you upload is safe, this might not be the case. There are no guarantees that a social media site is backing up the photos, videos, and other information you've posted. If a server storing the data failed, it might be gone for good.

As we'll discuss later in this chapter, once you've downloaded a copy of your social media content, you should include it in your backups. Doing so serves multiple purposes. First and foremost, if anything happens to the data, you can restore it from the backup. It also provides an archive of information from different dates, allowing you to view snapshots of your social media experience.

TOOLS & TIPS...

Keep Backups Safe

If you archive your social media by copying the content to your hard disk, you need to keep it safe. The information you download can contain private information that may not be visible to others viewing the site. It may contain personal and contact information, security and privacy settings, and more. Due to the sensitive nature of such information, it should be stored in a safe location. You don't want others accessing it through shared folders or a desktop that's shared by other users of the computer. Any backups of the computer or downloaded social media content should also be stored in a safe location, as anyone with access to the backup files could restore your data to another machine.

Archive Facebook

Facebook provides a feature to download a copy of the content you've posted online. This includes status updates, photos, videos, messages, chat conversations, information from your profile, and more. To download your Facebook content, follow these steps:

1. After logging onto Facebook, click on the gear-shaped icon in the upper right-hand corner of the page.
2. Click *General* in the left pane of the page.
3. Click on the *Download a copy of your Facebook data link*.
4. When the *Download Your Information* page appears, click the *Start My Archive* button.
5. Enter your password when prompted, and click the *Submit* button.
6. Click the *Start My Download* button when prompted.
7. A dialog box will appear informing you that an email will be sent to the address associated with your account when the download is ready. Click *Okay*.
8. Check your email, and when you find the email sent by Facebook, click the link to download your data.
9. When the page to download your data opens in the browser, click the *Download Archive* button.

The link you receive in the email from Facebook will only work for a few days. After that, you'll need to repeat the process again. The content will be downloaded as a compressed zip file and can be quite large depending on the amount of photos and other content you've published since joining Facebook.

Once you've downloaded and extracted the contents of the zip file to a folder, you can open a file called *Index.html* to navigate between your settings, photos, and other content. The Web page opens in your browser and provides a quick and concise way of viewing your information and finding specific content in your profile.

TOOLS & TIPS...

Getting More Than You Asked for

In June 2013, Facebook reported an issue some people's private information was compromised through the feature to archive your Facebook account, which they call the Download Your Information (DYI) tool. The problem was related to how Facebook generates friend recommendations. If you use the feature to find friends, you can allow Facebook to connect to your email, which uploads information in your contact list. This information is stored and cross-referenced with existing accounts to find people in your contact list. Even though someone in your contact list hasn't provided this to Facebook, the site now has it.

Due to a bug in the DYI tool, approximately 6 million Facebook users had their email addresses and telephone numbers shared. If I added you as a friend, you might not have shared this information with me. However, in downloading an archive, I get a list of people I've added as friends and could possibly see the information that someone else provided to Facebook through their contact list. A statement by Facebook reports that the problem is fixed but admits that for "almost all of the email addresses or telephone numbers impacted, each individual email address or telephone number was only included in a download once or twice."

Archive Twitter

Twitter also provides a feature similar to the one we just discussed. In archiving your Twitter account, every tweet you've made since starting your Twitter account will be available to view on your computer.

1. After logging in, click the gear icon in the upper right-hand corner, and click *Settings* on the menu that appears.
2. Scroll to the bottom of the page. You'll see a section entitled Your Twitter Archive.
3. Click the *Request your archive* button.

After following these steps, you'll be emailed a link that allows you to download all of your tweets. After clicking the link, the page that appears has a button you'll click to download your Twitter content in a compressed zip file. By opening a file called *Index.html* in the zip file, you'll see a graphical display of the number of tweets you've made each month and can navigate between the months to view tweets you've made.

Multisite third-party tools

There are a number of tools and services on the Internet that can be used to backup your content. Many social media sites provide Application Programming Interfaces (APIs) that developers can use to access services and content on the sites. The backup tools query your account through the APIs, gaining access to the data so it can create a copy of new and updated files. Before choosing a tool, it's important that you compare features and identify how often it backs up data, what it backs up, and the sites it can access. Not all of services are the same, so it will require some shopping.

A popular social media backup site is Frostbox (www.frostbox.com). Using the site, you can create a copy of multiple social media accounts, including Facebook, Twitter, LinkedIn, Foursquare, Flickr, Instagram, and Gmail. The backups are performed weekly and stored securely on their server. The site also provides other tools, such as social media dashboards for monitoring various sites from a single location.

Backupify (www.backupify.com) is another online service that will automatically back up Gmail, Facebook pages, Twitter accounts, Google Sites, and more. The data is backed up to their site, but information can be exported. For example, Twitter feeds can be exported to PDF files, allowing you to keep a copy on your local computer. Should you need to restore the data, it provides an easy one-click restore. The free version of the service allows you to back up to three services on a weekly basis, but subscriptions are available for daily backups and an increased number of sites.

While the previous services back up your content to their site, SocialSafe (www.socialsafe.net) is an application that backs up social network content to your computer. After installing it, you can authorize SocialSafe to connect to numerous sites and back them up to your machine. The sites you can backup through it include Facebook, Twitter, LinkedIn, Google+, Pinterest, your blog, and others. New updates to your social networking can be automatically downloaded and organized for your review. As seen in Figure 6.3, by clicking on icons in the left pane, you can search through content, navigate through all of your social network interactions by date, or view photo albums from all sites using a single interface. It also provides information on the most popular photos, posts, days with the most activity, and other information about your social network use.

Other tools for individual sites

In addition to the multisite tools, there are some useful tools for individual sites. Downloadr (www.janten.com/downloadr/) and FlicrEdit (www.sunkencity.org/flickredit) are tools for downloading copies of the photos you've posted on Flickr. Both will allow you to search and backup photos, but FlickrEdit also provides the ability to edit and upload new versions of the picture.

Free YouTube Download (www.dvdvideosoft.com/products/dvd/Free-YouTube-Download.htm) is a tool that allows you to save and convert videos found on YouTube.

FIGURE 6.3

SocialSafe.

This not only includes individual files, but all the videos from a playlist or channel. You can convert them to MP4, AVI, and WMV formats and also save the download history of the video.

Loss of data/equipment

Even if you've taken steps to archive content, it may not be completely safe. If you've downloaded it, your hard disk could crash, and you'd lose anything on the machine. Data could also be lost on your cell phone or tablet, losing any pictures or information on those devices. If you think it's rare, think again. According to a 2012 survey commissioned by Seagate Technology, 54% of American adults have and/or know someone who has lost data.

On the other side of the coin, there are times you won't want the data to be available. You may be selling or trading in your device, or it could be lost or stolen. In such cases, you'd want to find it, lock it so it can't be used, or wipe it to remove any personal information. There have been many situations where people and companies have sold such equipment, not realizing there are photos, documents, and other files that can be accessed on the machine. To protect yourself, you'll want to install the proper software, so that the data is still accessible to you and not others.

Selling and recycling equipment

The latest technology doesn't stay cutting edge for very long. The computer, tablet, mobile phone, and other devices that you buy today will become outdated and need to be upgraded or replaced. There are good reasons to upgrade your equipment. Once a device has reached a certain age, the cost of maintaining and supporting it increases, and it may be more exposed to security risks. Devices will run slower, break down more often, may not support the latest operating system and software, and have more known vulnerabilities than newer equipment. While a person or company may avoid replacing devices during tough times like a slow economy, Intel recommends that the optimal time to upgrade a computer is every 2–4 years.

To recoup some of the cost of upgrading, or environmental concerns of old devices going to a landfill, many people and companies will resell or refurbish equipment. For example, a mobile phone you're leasing might go back to the manufacturer, where it's restored to its original working condition and resold to someone else at a cheaper price. Similarly, you or your company might sell an old computer at auction or donate it to charity. When you purchase new equipment, the vendor may have a "buy your old device" option, where they'll offer a rebate or discount for trading in your old one. In doing so, they may promise to wipe your old data, and in the case of a phone, erase your SIM card. However, are you comfortable enough with any company that you'll trust them to do it for you?

While keeping up-to-date with technology is important, there's a serious security risk in improperly disposing of old equipment. There are countless stories of people buying a used computer or hard disk, only to find it was full of information. In 2008, an IT Manager in Oxford, England bought a computer on eBay, only to find it contained sensitive information on several million bank customers. The old server was sold by a company that archived data for American Express, NatWest, and the Royal Bank of Scotland, but the data on its hard drives had never been properly erased. Similarly, in 2010, NASA sold a number of computers that were used for the Space Shuttle program. The hard disks contained highly sensitive information, but the data hadn't been properly deleted. Unfortunately, residual or undeleted data on used disks isn't uncommon.

According to a 2009 study by Kessler International, a computer forensics firm, over 40% of the hard disks for sale on eBay contains personal, private, or sensitive information. Similar results were found when BT Security Research Centre and the University of Glamorgan bought disks from the United Kingdom, France, Germany, Australia, and the United States. Of the 300 hard disks purchased, 34% contained personal information, inclusive to medical records and bank account details. One disk purchased on eBay contained details of test launch procedures for a ground-to-air missile defense system, while another contained security logs from an embassy in France.

Wiping hard disks

As we'll see in the next chapter, even if a hard disk has been formatted, there are still forensic tools that can be used to retrieve deleted data. These tools can read and restore files, so long as they haven't been completely overwritten by other data. Because of this, it's important that you use software that will not only erase your information but overwrite it with patterns of data so that the previous data is unrecoverable.

When you delete a file, it is no longer visible in the computer's file system. The operating system removes a reference to the file from the file system table but doesn't remove the data. It will remain on the hard disk until the area of the disk where the file resided is overwritten with other data. Using any number of undelete utilities on the Internet, you can easily recover it. Even if it's partially overwritten, it's still possible to recover the remaining data using forensic software.

To securely erase data, you can use any number of tools. Some of these include:

- Eraser (http://eraser.heidi.ie)
- Active@ KillDisk (www.killdisk.com)
- Darik's Boot and Nuke (www.dban.org)

Using such tools, the existing data is destroyed by overwriting it with other data, as either a single pass wipe or overwriting it dozens of times. The more sensitive the data, the more passes you'll want to use.

Lost or stolen phone/tablet

A problem with mobile devices is they're mobile; they can be taken anywhere, so it's easier for them to be lost or stolen. When this happens, sensitive data stored on a tablet or mobile phone could fall into the wrong hands. This is where location and remote wiping features may provide a layer of protection.

As we'll discuss in Chapter 9, mobile devices commonly have a location aware-ness feature, which is used to determine the physical location of a device using Global Positioning System, Wi-Fi data, or by identifying its position between radio and cell phone towers. By activating the "Location On" feature of a mobile phone or tablet, you can then use software or visit a Web site to see where the device is at that particular moment. This can be useful if you've forgotten the device some-where and can still retrieve it.

If you're concerned it's irretrievable, then you should consider remotely wiping the device. When a device is wiped, personal information and other data on it are deleted. If it belongs to your company, you may need to contact your IT department. Depending on the systems and devices used by your company, they would send a command to the phone through mail server like Microsoft Exchange Server or mid-dleware like Blackberry Enterprise Server. The command might have the handset erase all data, do a complete factory reset, and/or completely disable the device.

If you have a small company or using a personal mobile device, you can still protect your information if it's lost or stolen. There are a number of apps available that will provide security and allow you to remote wipe a device. One example is Lookout Security and Antivirus, which runs on iPhone and Android devices. After going to the app store on your mobile phone or tablet and installing the app, you're prompted to set up an account using your email address and a password. An email is sent with a link to confirm the new account, and you'll receive notification emails whenever someone uses the app to locate your device, remote wipe it, or use other features. These notifications are useful in alerting you if someone has accessed your account, and may be using it to track your whereabouts or perform other remote actions.

Once the app is installed on a mobile phone or tablet, you can interact with it on Lookout Security and Antivirus' Web site (www.lookout.com). On the site, you can view devices setup to work with your account, locate your device, and see the results of anti-malware and malware scans Lookout has run against your device. As seen in Figure 6.4, by clicking on the *Find My Device* tab on the left side of the screen, you'll see a map appear showing the location of your device. At the top of the screen, you can click any of the following buttons to interact with it:

- *Scream*, which will cause the device to emit a loud alarm sound. The blaring noise is useful if you've misplaced it in your house, car, or another location you have access to, and may make a thief think twice about keeping it.
- *Lock*, which will prevent access to the device. When you remotely lock the device from the Web site, you're provided a numeric code to unlock it. Phone functions won't work until a code has been entered, so it can't be answered if you call it. Optionally, if someone enters the wrong code three times, a photo of the person will be taken with the front facing camera of the device and emailed to you.
- *Wipe*, which will erase the following from the device: contacts and call logs, calendar events, browser history, associated accounts, text messages, data in the SD card, and all pictures, videos, and documents.

Wiping your device should be considered a final solution. In doing so, it's reset to factory defaults, so it's just like when you first bought the device. Your data, apps, and settings will be gone. If you tried using Lookout or another tracking app to locate the device, it wouldn't work because the apps would no longer be on the device.

TOOLS & TIPS...

There's no such thing as a free lunch

When you install apps on a mobile device, you get certain features for free, but others may only be available for a fee. With Lookout Security and Antivirus, you need to upgrade to a premium subscription to use certain features like locking and wiping the device.

FIGURE 6.4

Lookout site finding a missing device.

While remotely wiping or locking a device provides an element of protection in preventing others from having your information, it isn't foolproof. These methods require a command being sent to the device, so circumventing it simply requires cutting off its ability to receive that command. In other words, if it can't connect to the Internet, it can't be located, locked, or wiped remotely. The easiest way to do this is to turn it off. However, even if it wasn't turned off, the device couldn't be wiped if it was in a location where it lost service or didn't have a data plan and it couldn't connect to a nearby Wi-Fi.

There are also methods of jamming a mobile device so that it can't connect to a data network. Jammers are devices that emit radio waves on the same frequencies as a digital cell phone. Even if a phone works on multiple bands, jamming a single band can prevent it from connecting to the network to send and receive calls. Jammers are illegal in most countries, as in the United States where federal law prohibits the operation, sale, and use of these devices. However, even if a country makes jammers illegal, there are often exceptions. Military installations or government agencies may use them as a security measure. Prisons might use them to prevent gang members from texting each other or other unauthorized communication by prisoners. Some countries like France and Japan have permitted jammers in areas where calls may disturb others, such as theaters, public performances, art galleries, and other venues. However, if someone were stealing a mobile device to acquire your information, would you really expect them to adhere to legalities of jammers?

Backup and restore

Losing personal photos and videos can be devastating, and losing company data like orders, contact lists, or important documents could equate to serious business losses.

When you consider the consequences, you'd expect most people regularly backup their data, but this isn't the case. The 2012 survey commissioned by Seagate found that 90% of people don't back up data on a daily basis and 89% don't use continuous backup, where the data is backed up at regular intervals or when changed.

While everyone agrees backups are important, there are many reasons why they don't. Traditionally, lack of storage has been a common excuse. Backup devices used to be fairly pricey, and if a computer had an extra hard disk, the space was used instead of dedicating it to storing backup files. Fortunately, this is no longer an excuse. A person can use a rewritable DVD to back up important files, and the price of hard disks have dropped considerably, with a 1TB external hard drive costing just over $100. People can even back up their data to the cloud, so it's stored on secure servers on the Internet.

Another perceived issue is cost. There are a number of excellent commercial solutions, such as Norton Ghost to back up files and make an image of your machine. The cost of such software is often marginal. If you're looking for a free solution then you can use Windows Backup, which is included with the operating system and discussed in the next section.

Companies are usually better at having a backup plan than individuals, as the continuity of a business can depend on the stability of data. Since backups are handled by an IT department, this provides a worry-free solution for most people. In a larger organization, files are backed up using software designed for networks, such as CommVault (www.commvault.com), and saved to tapes that can then be stored offsite. In companies using SharePoint, files are uploaded to document libraries, with the actual data saved in a backend SQL Server. CommVault then backs up this data using SharePoint agent, which allows the software to back up and restore individual sites and documents. However, even in the best of places, not everything on a network is backed up. You'll often find that a company will back up files on the network but not those saved on workstations, mobile devices, and social media sites. Policies or settings may be used to enforce where users should save their files and restrict them from saving files to a local hard drive.

Using windows backup

A backup and restore utility has been included with Windows since its earliest versions. Like a lot of tools bundled with their operating system, older incarnations have been less than inspired, difficult for a novice user, and hardly a competition for third-party tools. Windows Backup could be daunting and intimidating if you were new to computers. However, if you haven't looked at it since Windows XP, then you're in for a pleasant surprise.

Windows Backup has undergone radical changes, providing an easy-to-use interface that takes you step by step through the process of backing up and restoring files. It performs incremental backups of your files, including just the files that are newly created or modified since the previous backup. If several versions of the same file have been backed up, you can choose which version you want to restore. Once you've gone through the process of setting up your first backup, you can schedule it so that the system will automatically back up your files.

To set up a Windows 7 machine to back up files on your computer, you would do the following:

1. Click *Start|Control Panel|Backup and Restore*. (Alternatively, you can click Start and type "Backup and Restore" in the search field, and press Enter on your keyboard.)
2. Click *Setup backup*.
3. When the *Setup backup* dialog box appears, select the drive where your backup will be saved. Click *Next*.
4. To choose the files to back up, click *Let me choose*. Alternatively, you could select "Let Windows choose (recommended)." Click *Next*.
5. On the *What do you want to back up?* screen, you'll see files saved in libraries, on user desktops, and default Windows folders have already been selected. Select any additional files or folders you want to back up.
6. Uncheck the *Include a system image of drives* checkbox, as we'll discuss this later. Click *Next*.
7. In the *Schedule* section, click *Change Schedule*.
8. Ensure that the *Run backup on a schedule (recommended)* checkbox is checked.
9. In the *How often* dropdown list, select whether the backup will run monthly, weekly, or daily.
10. In the *What day* dropdown list, select the day on which the backup to run.
11. In the *What time* dropdown list, select a time that the backup will run.
12. Click *OK*.
13. Click *Save settings and run backup*.

Once you've completed these steps you'll notice the backup of your files is running, and a backup file will be saved where you created. Also, if you return to the *Backup and Restore* app in Control Panel, you'll see your new backup job listed. To reconfigure what you've done, simply click on the *Change settings* link to rerun the wizard.

To restore your files, you could click on the *Restore my files* button. This will start a wizard that will walk you through the process of selecting which files or folders you'd like to restore. Once you've selected what to restore, you then can chose whether to restore it to the original location or another location.

You can also create a system image of a disk, which will create an exact copy of a drive. This is extremely useful if your computer fails or the hard disk crashes. The image contains your operating system, drivers, programs, and any other data on the disk. By restoring the image file, you're completely restoring the computer to the point that the image was created.

To create a system image on Windows 7, you would use Backup and Restore in Control Panel, and click on the *Create a system image* link in the left pane. Once the program starts, you would then follow these steps:

1. On the first screen, select where you would like to save the backup. Your options are on a hard disk, DVD(s), or a network location. After specifying where to save the backup, click *Next*.

2. The screen that appears will show the system drive (containing the operating system) checked. If you have additional hard disks on your computer, you can check the checkbox beside each drive to include it in the image. Click *Next*.

3. Click *Start backup*.

When backing up a computer, there are some things you should take into consideration. You shouldn't back up files to the same hard disk that Windows is installed on (i.e., your system disk) or to the same hard disk as the original files. After all, if the computer fails or the hard disk crashes, you wouldn't be able to access the original or backed up files. Also, because anyone who has your backups can restore the files to their machine, you should store any external disks, rewritable DVDs, or other storage media containing your backups in a safe place.

Keeping your backups secure is important. Remember that anyone who has access to the external hard disk or other storage media could simply walk off with it. For home use, you may choose to keep it in a locked room, a locked fire box, or somewhere else that's not easily accessible to guests. Businesses will often keep backups in a secure server room or safe and keep older copies offsite in case there is a fire or other disaster.

TOOLS & TIPS...

How not to secure your backups

The worst security for backups I have ever encountered was a number of years ago and involved a finance company. To protect the financial records of their clients, they regularly backed up data on their computers. Unfortunately, they would keep the storage media containing the backups on a shelf in the back room, in a cardboard box labeled "Backups of computers." Since the room was storage for office supplies and the photocopier, the door was always propped open and accessible to everyone. The manager went pale when I pointed out the obvious. I could have put the backups in my bag, gone home, restored the data to my computer, and returned them the next day. In doing so, I would have everyone's financial records, and they would never have been the wiser.

Web-based solutions

While storing data in the cloud is touted as if it were a new craze, web-based backup solutions have been around for years and provide some advantages over backing up files and folders to a local drive. For personal use and small businesses, the option of keeping backups off premises may be impractical or impossible. With online backups, data is stored offsite on a secure server. Your data is automatically uploaded to a server on the Internet, so it remains safe even if your disks were damaged or stolen, or your premises falls victim to a disaster.

One of the more mature sites is Carbonite (www.carbonite.com), which provides unlimited storage for files on your home computer. If you have multiple computers or servers that need to be backed up, there are also packages for businesses.

The basic home package will back up files on your computer, but there are also packages that will mirror your hard disk, so that you can restore the entire system if needed. As with a number of other companies, Carbonite allows you to upload data at higher speeds until you reach an upload limit and then lower the speed at which data is transferred. Therefore, if you have a large system, it may take longer to back up once you reach this limit. Being that it constantly runs in the background on your computer, any new or modified files are automatically encrypted and uploaded to the server on a regular basis. This means that using the service requires little interaction after the initial setup.

Backing up a cell phone or tablet

For some, losing the data on a mobile phone or tablet can be devastating, as it may contain important contacts, files, or other information. If that's the case, then prior to losing your mobile device, you should consider using apps that will back up and restore the data.

Many online backup sites provide apps for mobile devices. For example, Carbonite offers free apps for tablets and mobile phones, which will automatically back up photos and videos to their secure servers. The backed up data can then be accessed from your computer, allowing you to view, share, and restore them as you would other data backed up from your computer. These apps also offer security features that were discussed earlier in this chapter, where you can lock or wipe a device remotely if your phone or tablet is lost or stolen.

There are a number of apps that you can install on a device to back up your cell phone or tablet. A tool we previously discussed is Lookout, which can back up the device remotely through the following steps:

1. After logging onto Lookout's site (www.lookout.com), click the *Backups & Restore* tab on the left side of the screen.
2. Click the *Backup now* button on the top right of the screen.
3. When the confirmation screen appears, click *Yes, backup*.

Restoring the device is just as easy and also done remotely through their Web site by following these steps:

1. Click the *Restore to a device* button on the top of the screen.
2. In the *Data to restore* dialog that appears, select the device that data was backed up from in the *Data to Restore* dropdown list.
3. In the *Restore To* dropdown list, select the device this data should be restored to.
4. Click *Start*.

Personal data or equipment

Some employees will use their own devices for business purposes or use corporate equipment for personal use. A phone or tablet might be set up to access work email or have additional apps installed to back up and wipe data. If your device is set up this way, you may be vulnerable to having the data wiped by your employer.

As we discussed earlier, a device can be locked or wiped by sending a command to it. If the employer installed security apps with this capability or set up the device to access work email, there is a possibility that your data could be destroyed accidentally or on purpose. If your employment was terminated or a command was accidentally sent to do a remote wipe, you would lose any personal and business data on the phone or tablet.

Another risk involves backups of data. An employee may do unauthorized backups of data on corporate devices they were issued. If he or she were fired, the employer could wipe the device but wouldn't be able to delete any data the employee had backed up to a site like Carbonite. The fired employee could simply restore the data to another device at a later time.

To ensure the security of business and personal data, you should keep the two separate. A business laptop, phone, or tablet should be used for business purposes and locked down to prevent the user from installing any additional apps. In the same way, personal devices should not contain business data. While this might mean you have to carry two phones, it would protect the employee and business from data being destroyed or copied without authorization.

The other potential liability is related to damage of equipment. If you installed personal apps on a work tablet or phone, or malware was installed while visiting social networking sites without authorization, an employer might fire you or hold you responsible for repairs. Similarly, an organization might be held responsible for any personal equipment and data loss if they allowed employees to use their own devices for business purposes. A policy outlining proper use of equipment can help to clarify these matters and the rights of the employee and employer. As additional protection, if you get the IT department to configure a personal device to use corporate email, have them clearly explain what was installed and whether they have the ability to remotely lock or wipe the device.

BYOD

Even though it may be safer to keep corporate and personal devices separate, there is a growing shift toward allowing employees to use their own devices. If you own a business, you may have had job candidates asking about the company's BYOD policy or asked a potential employer about it yourself. BYOD is an acronym for "Bring Your Own Device," which permits employees to use their own mobile devices in the workplace. While the person owns the device, it is connected to the corporate network, allowing them to do work on devices that aren't owned by the company.

BYOD does have a number of positive points. Since the employee is bringing their own device to work, this saves the company equipment costs. As the person is already familiar with their own mobile phone, tablet, or laptop, this can increase their productivity and decrease training time on how to use it.

As we mentioned, there are drawbacks in people using their own devices. Noncorporate devices are now connected to corporate resources and services, which create a security risk. Since it's owned by the employee, he or she has the right to install any apps or visit any sites without restriction, increasing the possibility of malware and viruses being installed. As we mentioned earlier, if a person lost their phone or tablet, anyone finding it could now retrieve any unsecured data on the device. Added to this is the risk of what happens when a person leaves the company. Even if the corporate data is wiped from a mobile phone, the company doesn't own that phone number. Business contacts may continue calling the former employee, allowing the person to steal customers if he or she goes to work for the competition.

To address these problems, the company needs a BYOD agreement that sets conditions on the use of personal devices at work. It also gives the company permission to manage the person's device. *Mobile Device Management* (MDM) software can be used to monitor and manage devices, make configuration settings, remotely lock and wipe the device, distribute applications, and more. Some popular MDM systems include:

- SOTI (www.soti.net)
- Symantec Mobile Management (www.symantec.com/en/ca/mobile-management)
- MobileIron (www.mobileiron.com)
- Airwatch (www.air-watch.com)

Being that BYOD is increasingly common, you'll find that there are a wide range of choices in MDM systems. You will however want to ensure that the MDM supports a wide range of platforms. Employees may have devices running Android, iOS, Windows, or other operating systems. You never know what someone is going to bring to work, but you'll want them all protected.

Bibliography

@ComfortablySmug. (2012, October 29). *Tweet by @ComfortablySmug*. Retrieved July 25, 2013, from Twitter: <https://twitter.com/ComfortablySmug/status/263083953152466947>.

American Academy of Matrimonial Lawyers. (2010, February 10). *Big surge in social networking evidence says survey of nation's top divorce lawyers*. Retrieved August 13, 2013, from American Academy of Matrimonial Lawyers: <http://www.aaml.org/about-the-academy/press/press-releases/e-discovery/big-surge-social-networking-evidence-says-survey->.

American Academy of Matrimonial Lawyers. (2013, February 11). *Dating websites providing more divorce evidence says survey: nation's top matrimonial lawyers cite Match.com as most common source*. Retrieved August 13, 2013, from American Academy of Matrimonial Lawyers: <http://www.aaml.org/about-the-academy/press/press-releases/divorce/dating-websites-providing-more-divorce-evidence-says>.

Arghandiwal, M. (2012, September 12). *Afghanistan bans YouTube to block anti-Muslim film*. Retrieved June 23, 2013, from Reuters: <http://www.reuters.com/article/2012/09/12/us-afghanistan-youtube-idUSBRE88B0SC20120912>.

BBC News. (2008, August 26). *Bank customer data sold on eBay.* Retrieved June 4, 2013, from BBC News: <http://news.bbc.co.uk/2/hi/uk_news/7581540.stm>.

BBC News. (2009, May 7). *Missile data found on hard drives.* Retrieved June 4, 2013, from BBC News: <http://news.bbc.co.uk/2/hi/uk_news/wales/8036324.stm>.

BBC News Technology. (2010, December 8). *NASA sells shuttle PCs without wiping secret data.* Retrieved June 4, 2013, from BBC News Technology: <http://www.bbc.co.uk/news/technology-11947721>.

Buchholz, D., DeVetter, D., Gonzalez, J., Livne, O., & Mahvi, J. (2012, July). *PC Lifecycle managment: boosing productivity and IT efficiency.* Retrieved June 4, 2013, from Intel: <http://www.intel.com/content/dam/www/public/us/en/documents/best-practices/pc-life-cycle-management.pdf>.

Choney, S. (2012, November 1). *Man who made false tweet about Sandy apologizes; could face prosecution.* Retrieved July 25, 2013, from NBC News Technology: <http://news.yahoo.com/blogs/abc-blogs/superstorm-sandy-rumors-cost-congressional-campaign-manager-job-140408935--abc-news-politics.html>.

Facebook. (2013, July 21). *Important message from Facebook's White Hat Program.* Retrieved August 13, 2013, from Facebook: <https://www.facebook.com/notes/facebook-security/important-message-from-facebooks-white-hat-program/10151437074840766>.

Garrett-Walker, H. (2012, April 12). *Teens warned about posting dodgy images online.* Retrieved June 24, 2013, from The New Zealand Herald: <http://www.nzherald.co.nz/nz/news/article.cfm?c_id=1&objectid=10798360>.

Gartner, Inc. (2011, February 17). *Gartner says by year-end 2013, half of all companies will have been asked to produce material from social media websites for E-Discovery.* Retrieved July 30, 2013, from Gartner: <http://www.gartner.com/newsroom/id/1550715>.

Hernandez, D. (2011, September 1). *Terrorism charges for 2 in Mexico who spread attack rumor on Twitter, Facebook.* Retrieved July 25, 2013, from Los Angeles Times: <http://latimesblogs.latimes.com/laplaza/2011/09/twitter-tweets-veracruz-mexico-terrorism-drug-war-censorship-rumors.html>.

International Business Times. (2013, June 9). *Odd News: Tajikistan president ordered YouTube shutdown for uploading his "Bad Dancing and Singing" at son's wedding.* Retrieved June 19, 2013, from International Business Times: <http://au.ibtimes.com/articles/476420/20130609/takijistan-president-emomali-rahmon-youtube-bad-dancing.htm>.

ISACA. (2010, June). *Top five social media risks for business: New ISACA white paper.* Retrieved June 13, 2013, from ISACA: <http://www.isaca.org/About-ISACA/Pressroom/News-Releases/2010/Pages/Top-Five-Social-Media-Risks-for-Business-New-ISACA-White-Paper.aspx>.

Kessler International. (2009, February). *Is your confidential information being sold on eBay?* Retrieved June 4, 2013, from Kessler International: <http://www.investigation.com/press/press75.htm>.

Pew Research Center for the People & the Press. (2013, April 23). *Most expect 'occasional acts of terrorism' in the future.* Retrieved June 24, 2013, from Pew Research Center for the People & the Press: <http://www.people-press.org/2013/04/23/most-expect-occasional-acts-of-terrorism-in-the-future/>.

Ponemon Institute. (2011, September). *Global survey on social media risks.* Retrieved June 13, 2013, from Websense: <http://www.websense.com/assets/reports/websense-social-media-ponemon-report.pdf>.

Rosen, J. (2010, July 21). *The web means the end of forgetting.* Retrieved June 24, 2013, from New York Times: <http://www.nytimes.com/2010/07/25/magazine/25privacy-t2. html?pagewanted=all>.

Sarbanes–Oxley Act of 2002. (2002, July 30). Retrieved July 30, 2013, from Office of the Law Revision Counsel: <http://uscode.house.gov/download/pls/15C98.txt>.

Seagate. (2012, June 12). *Seagate reinvents backup for your digital life.* Retrieved June 10, 2013, from Business Wire: <http://www.businesswire.com/news/ home/20120611005277/en/Seagate-Reinvents-Backup-Digital-Life>.

Sonwane, A. (2011, July 9). *Privacy disasters in social media – how vulnerable is your organization?* Retrieved July 25, 2013, from <http://www.lsec.be/upload_direc- tories/documents/110906_SocialNetworkingThreats/6_Sonwane_Abhilash_ Cyberoam_110906_2.pdf>.

Stanglin, D. (2013, April 25). *Student wrongly tied to Boston bombings found dead.* Retrieved July 25, 2013, from USA Today: <http://www.usatoday.com/story/ news/2013/04/25/boston-bombing-social-media-student-brown-university-red- dit/2112309/>.

Tapellini, D. (2010, May 4). *Consumer reports survey: Social network users post risky information.* Retrieved June 19, 2013, from Consumer Reports: <http://news.consumer- reports.org/electronics/2010/05/social-networks-facebook-risks-privacy-risky-behavior- consumer-reports-survey-findings-online-threats-state-of-the-net-report.html>.

The Telegraph. (2013, January 22). *Library of congress is archiving all of America's tweets.* Retrieved June 24, 2013, from <http://www.businessinsider.com/ library-of-congress-is-archiving-all-of-americas-tweets-2013-1>.

Travers, L. A., & Oster, S. (2010, January 26). *Guidance: Representing EPA online using social media.* Retrieved July 1, 2013, from Social Media Subcouncil: <http://govsoc- med.pbworks.com/w/page/21329932/Guidance%3A%20Representing%20EPA%20 Online%20Using%20Social%20Media>.

WikiLeaks. (2010, April 5). *Collateral murder, 5 Apr 2010.* Retrieved July 25, 2013, from WikiLeaks: <http://wikileaks.org/wiki/Collateral_Murder,_5_Apr_2010>.

YouTube. (2013, May 16). *Video privacy settings.* Retrieved June 20, 2013, from YouTube: <http://support.google.com/youtube/bin/answer.py?hl=en&answer=157177>.

zig. (2007, June 15). *An online phenomenon that started in a house.* Retrieved June 19, 2013, from zig: <http://www.zigideas.com/screamtv/pdf/campaign_rollout.pdf>.

The Dark Side

INFORMATION IN THIS CHAPTER:

- Cybercrime
- Social engineering
- Hacked accounts

The dark side of social media

Every community has areas that are on the wrong side of the tracks. The virtual world can be a wonderful place, allowing you to interact with networks of people, enjoy the isolation of a game, or chat with groups or one-on-one, but not everyone or everyplace is safe. The Internet can be deceptive and make you overconfident and unwary of predators, charlatans, and scams.

As we've seen throughout this book, there are many threats on the Internet, but a person is especially vulnerable when using social media. Social platforms rely on sharing information, engaging others, and having trust. Social media is about friends, followers, connections, and sharing. These words instill trust, giving us faith in the links we click, the programs we install, requests that are made, and questions asked. Unfortunately, trust is also necessary to take advantage of someone.

Cybercrime

Cybercrime is a criminal activity that involves computers and the Internet. A cybercriminal may use online resources to obtain information about a person, as a medium to contact potential victims, gain access to systems, and/or damage data and bring down systems. The types of offenses will vary, but they will always involve technology and connectivity.

The targets of cybercrime may be computers or people. A cybercriminal may focus an attack on systems using viruses or other malicious code, which we'll discuss in Chapter 8, or by directly hacking a system to gain unauthorized access. They may also focus their attention on people to steal their identity, commit fraud, stalk, or bully them. It may also be a precursor for other offenses, where the crime is initiated online, but later violates or injures the person through later physical contact.

Scams

Online scams aren't new to the Internet but have evolved and taken new twists on social networking sites. Cybercriminals can gain in-depth information from your profiles and may make connections through friend requests. This has made many of the scams sent through email more personal and believable.

Grandparent scams have been typically done over the telephone and involves an elderly person being called by someone claiming to be a relative or grandchild. The person may claim that they've been in a car accident or in some other trouble and needs money wired to them. With social media, the scammer may make a friend request to the victim first, establishing a relationship as a long-lost relative before trying to get money through online chats, instant messages, or over the phone.

Shared stories are a common way for scammers to gain money. A link may be shared to a controversial video, interesting app, or something else that will entice people to click it. This may be an offer for a discount at a popular store or some fake feature offered by the site (such as a dislike button on Facebook). When the link is clicked, people are taken to online surveys or other sites that pay the scammer referrer fees.

You'll also see bogus job offers on Twitter or through direct messages on other sites like LinkedIn. They'll say you can make large amounts of money by working from home and may require you to pay a start-up fee. In other scams, a bogus perspective employer will try and get sensitive information from you, such as your Social Security Number or other information that should only be given after you're hired by the company. You should always be careful about work-at-home offers, jobs that require no previous experience, or online requests for sensitive information. The offers seem too good to be true, because they generally are.

According to the 2012 Internet Crime Report, created in partnerships between the Federal Bureau of Investigation (FBI) and the National White Collar Crime Center, one of the most frequently reported Internet crimes is the *Hit Man Scam*. There have been variations over the years, but the basic premise involves an email being sent to you by someone pretending to be a hit man, who's been hired to kill you or someone you care about. If you pay a certain amount, then the kind killer won't fulfill the contract. To convince you that the threat is legitimate, scammers have begun to use social media to get personal information about you or facts that can make it seem more convincing. After all, if they have your name, address, phone number, and other tidbits of data, it would certainly scare you into believing the person knew how to get at you.

Scams are designed to get something from you and are usually financially motivated. To protect yourself, you need to be wary of strangers, the offers they make, and the sites you visit. To ensure your accounts haven't been compromised, you should monitor your statements and look for any strange charges. If you find any transactions you didn't make, contact the credit card company or bank to inform them the account may have been compromised.

Using secure browsing

Secure browsing is an important feature on any site containing personal information or where you make online transactions. It's important that any communication between your computer and the sites used for banking or online purchases is secure. Browsers should use Hypertext Transfer Protocol Secure (HTTPS) to safely exchange data with a site, as this provides encrypted communication and secure identification of a network's Web servers.

You can tell whether HTTPS is used by looking at the address bar in your browser. The Uniform Resource Locator (URL) should begin with *https://*. Your browser may also display a padlock icon to show if the site is secure. Newer versions of Internet Explorer display a padlock icon on the right side of the address bar, while Firefox provides a Site Identity button to the left of the address bar. Clicking on these will display information about the site, inclusive to whether the site is verified, who owns it, and if communication is encrypted. By ensuring the site is correct and communication is secure, there's less chance of a scammer getting your information and stealing your money or identity.

Of course, just because you're using a secure connection doesn't mean your protection is absolute. If a site has been compromised, then the connection may be secure, but the end point of that connection won't be. When the site is hacked, your credentials can be taken regardless of how you're connecting to a site. An issue occurred in February 2013 when the customer support vendor Zendesk was hacked, allowing the hackers to download the email addresses of people who contacted Twitter, Pinterest, and Tumblr for support. While passwords weren't obtained in this attack, it doesn't mean they can't be acquired through a follow-up phishing attack, as we discuss later in the chapter, or other security breaches.

Issues can also arise when the apps you use to connect to sites have security vulnerabilities that are exploited. In July 2013, Tumblr (www.tumblr.com) had a security issue with their iOS app, which allowed passwords to be detected. The site released a security update for iPhone and iPad users and recommended that users to change their passwords.

Many social media sites provide features for secure browsing but generally need to be activated. As we saw in Chapter 3, LinkedIn provides a setting you need to activate, while on Twitter HTTPS is used by default. On Facebook, you can turn on secure browsing through the Security Settings page of your account. To activate the feature, do the following:

1. Click on the Settings menu, which is the gear-shaped icon in the upper right-hand corner of the page. When the menu appears, click *Account Settings*.
2. In the left pane of the page, click *Security*.
3. In the *Secure Browsing* section, ensure the *Browse Facebook on a secure connection (https) when possible* checkbox is checked.
4. Click *Save Changes*.

Cyberstalking

Cyberstalking is a form of repeated harassment that involves the Internet and methods of electronic communication like email, online chat, and instant messages. Just as an offline stalker will follow or stakeout a victim, an online stalker will use electronic and Internet-based tools to track the object of their obsession. Victims of cyberstalking may be threatened, receive viruses or malware in email, and have false accusations or statements posted online to encourage others to join in the harassing of the person. For obvious reasons, cyberstalking can be terrifying for the victim.

Unfortunately, social media is an excellent tool for cyberstalkers to track and monitor a person. Social networking sites can provide information on where a person works, their location, who they associate with, likes and dislikes. Using this, you may be able to identify where a person is at a given time and meet them face-to-face or engage them online.

When reported in the news, stories of cyberstalking are often strangers stalking celebrities. An example of this occurred in 2011, when actress Patricia Arquette quit Facebook after an alleged incident where she was harassed. Her final post warned people about adding strangers as friends. However, cyberstalkers aren't necessarily strangers, and the victims aren't just celebrities.

In 2010, Lee David Clayworth dated a woman named Lee Ching Yan for several months while teaching in Malaysia. After they broke up, she stole his laptop, hacked his email account, and began harassing him. Contacting people in his account's contact list, she posed as Clayworth and sent messages about how he'd had sex with underage students. The laptop she stole contained nude photos she'd taken of him, which she posted on various sites. The cyberstalking progressed with her posting hundreds of comments and false accusations, to the point that a Google search of his name showed links to how he was involved in deranged or criminal behavior.

Although harassment is illegal, it doesn't mean it's always enforceable. Clayworth sued Yan in Malaysia, and the court awarded him the equivalent of $66,000 in damages. She continued with the defamation, so the court found her guilty of contempt of court. She moved out of the country and continued her harassment.

Attempting to remove the content from sites was difficult for Clayworth. While some sites have been helpful, Yan has reposted the false information after it's taken down. Other sites like liarsandcheaters.com have opposed his actions to have content removed. The manager of the site wrote that he would relocate the site to Germany, so Clayworth would have to go through German courts to have it removed. The manager stated that until then "the post will remain permanently for the rest of your life."

While it can be difficult or impossible to find a legal resolution if the cyberstalker resides in another country, you should still make an effort to report the abuse to sites and police. The person harassing you may be lying about their location and reside in the same country or same city as you. It's better to take action and view the situation as a genuine threat.

Protecting yourself

As with real-life stalkers, a cyberstalker's motivation is to control the victim, and this is done through intimidation. In cyberspace, the stalker may feel even bolder, hidden behind aliases, and believing in the anonymity of the Internet. Being the victim can feel paralyzing, but there are ways to take control and protect yourself. To combat cyberstalking, you need to limit the information you post online, remove their ability to access information, and prevent them from contacting you.

Many victims have been involved in some kind of relationship with the cyberstalker. They might be a former girlfriend or boyfriend, an estranged or ex-husband/wife, or someone else you've had an intimate relationship with. They might even be a former friend or roommate. Because they had a relationship with you in the real world, they had access to your computer, mobile device, wireless router, and other equipment.

As we'll see in Chapter 10, keyloggers or other monitoring tools can be installed to record the characters you type and take screenshots of what you're doing on your computer. As you enter passwords or visit sites, the information is captured and can be emailed to a person or uploaded to a site. If the cyberstalker had access to your machine, he or she could have easily installed such software. As we'll discuss in Chapter 8, anti-malware/antivirus tools can be used to detect and remove such malicious software.

Your first reaction to reading any messages received by a cyberstalker is probably to delete it. However, unless it's a file that's been quarantined or deleted by antivirus software, you shouldn't delete anything from a cybercriminal. The messages can be important evidence, and a forensic investigation may reveal important information on who sent the email and where it originated. If you've received a direct message on a site, simply don't delete it. If you've received it in the inbox of your email account, you can move the offending message into its own folder. When you do contact police to file a complaint, you may be asked to forward it to the officer.

Because the person may have had access to your passwords before, you should change your passwords. This includes the ones for social media sites you use, email, your Internet Service Provider (ISP) password, and banking sites. As we'll discuss in Chapter 10, strong passwords should be used, and these should be changed regularly. If you have a home security system, you should also change the access codes and any verbal passwords used when talking to the security company. It does little good changing the codes, if the person can talk to the security company, tell them a password, and have them disable the alarm.

If you have a wireless network in your home, you should also change the passwords on the router. Wireless routers have an IP address that displays an administration site that's used when you set it up. You should go onto this page and change the administrator password, any password used to join the network, and remove any devices your stalker has previously set up to connect to the network. If the person had previous access, the person could change these passwords and lock you out of your own network. He or she could also use a network protocol analyzer like Wireshark (www.wireshark.org), which will capture the packets of data sent across the network. Using such a tool, the person would be able to see any passwords sent in clear text or any sensitive data. To ensure the data you send and receive is secure, you should make sure that encryption on your wireless router is turned on through the administration page.

Regardless of whether you know the stalker personally or not, you should send a single response telling the person to stop harassing you. Tell the person to leave you alone and that you will contact authorities. If they want to talk about it, never agree to meet face-to-face and don't involve yourself in any further discussions.

In addition to the steps we've already discussed, you should use methods discussed throughout this book to secure your social media, including:

- Use features to block the person's access to you. In Chapter 9, we'll see that by blocking the person from visiting a page or blog, you'll restrict them from making comments and viewing your information.
- Know what's being said about you and where. As we'll see in Chapter 10, there are ways to perform online searches of people. It is wise to do a search of your own name and family members and remove any personal or revealing information from these sites.
- Report Abuse. As we saw in Chapter 6, abusive behavior is a violation of the Terms of Service for many sites and ISPs.
- Be wary of revealing your location. As we'll discuss in Chapter 9, be careful of apps or making posts that show where you are or where you'll be.

It is always advisable to contact authorities and consider legal action if threats are made or you're fearful of your safety. If you're concerned the person will contact you in real life, restraining orders may be used to restrict the person from coming within a specified distance of you and may also have conditions from contacting you in other ways.

Cyberbullying

Cyberbullying is another form of online harassment, where a person or group bullies a victim using the Internet and/or other methods of electronic communications. If this sounds like cyberstalking, you're not wrong in making the comparison. Both involve many of the same methods to terrorize a victim. The cyberbully may post abusive comments, send threatening or demeaning messages, make audio or video records of someone without their consent, or disclose personal information with the purpose of humiliating or intimidating them. As with any bully, they like the power that comes through humiliating and demeaning another person.

An extreme example of cyberbullying occurred in 2006, when a 13-year-old girl named Megan Meier started an online friendship through MySpace with a 16-year-old male named "Josh Evans." Messages to the girl started out complimentary but eventually turned vicious. Emails to her said he didn't want to be friends as she wasn't nice to her friends, and messages posted on the page stated "Megan Meier is a slut. Megan Meier is fat." Devastated by the betrayal of friendship and public humiliation, the 13-year-old girl hung herself.

What was discovered later was that Josh Evans never existed. The account had been created by an adult named Lori Drew, who was the mother of Sarah, a former friend of Megan. The mother had created and monitored the profile and had been aided by her daughter Sarah and an 18-year-old employee named Ashley Grills. Although they had bullied Megan to the point of committing suicide, Lori Drew was indicted and convicted of a misdemeanor for violating the Computer Fraud and Abuse Act for breaching the MySpace Terms of Service. In 2009, the conviction was overturned by Judge Wu of the Central District of California.

Since that time, there have been many laws passed directly dealing with cyber-bullying and online harassment. California state legislature passed Assembly Bill 86 2008, which allows schools to suspend or expel students for bullying online or offline. Many school codes have also been amended to include provisions that deal with bullying, and it's common for schools to implement anti-bullying programs that address this problem.

While cyberbullying often refers to behavior where a child or an adolescent is bullying another minor, adults can also be bullied online. As with children, if an adult is bullied, it's important to speak up and tell others. For those experiencing workplace bullying, you should explain the issues to management and/or a union representative. Many organizations have policies that address harassment and would (or should) take such complaints seriously for fear of being vulnerable to a potential lawsuit.

For children or teenagers, it's important to tell an adult. If the adult doesn't take the problem seriously, then tell another adult who will. According to the 2011 report by Pew Internet and American Life Project, when teens sought advice about a problem like mean behavior on the Internet, 53% turned to friends and 36% confided in their parents. Almost all said the advice they received was helpful.

It's also important to tell the bully to stop. The person may see the unwanted behavior as a joke or posting what they said as acceptable. In telling them it's not acceptable, they can't say they didn't know and excuse it as a prank. Sending a single message telling them to stop can serve as evidence against the person when you contact police, employers, or school officials.

Sometimes, a cyberbully is a former friend or pretended to be one. As we discussed with cyberstalkers, if the bully had access to your computer, you should change passwords. The same applies if you used their computer. If your password was logged or the site was set to remember you on your next visit, the bully could log on to the site as you. To protect yourself from any monitoring tools or devices, you should check your computer for any USB sticks or devices that may have been plugged in and run a scan for any malicious software that may have been installed. In addition to this, follow the steps we discussed in the previous section to protect yourself.

Cybersex and other intimate issues

Social media is used to make connections, but many use it to engage others more intimately. Many people use chat rooms, dating sites, and social networks to make romantic or sexual connections. Others use these same forums to make a connection with potential victims. The person may be looking to initiate a virtual relationship that leads to stalking or sexual assault, as a precursor to blackmail, or any number of online scams.

Romance scams

A common scam involves the promise of love and companionship. A cybercriminal will use chat rooms or sites to find and romance a victim. According to the 2012 Internet Crime Report, with the exception of men who are aged 20–29, women in every age demographic are more frequently victimized by this scam. Gathering information on your profile page, a person might see what books, music, movies, and other pastimes you like and claim a shared interest. Using this, posts on your wall or tweets you've made, they can determine your likes and dislikes. The scammer may post flattering comments, entice you with promises, and gain your interest with fake pictures that are supposed to be of them. Once you trust the person, the scammer will ask for favors. You may be asked for money, requested to help by receiving and reshipping a package, or do something else on their behalf. The scam generated 4467 complaints to the Internet Crime Complaint Center (IC3), with victims collectively losing more than $55 million.

Romance scams work because they play on your emotions. The person will often say how you were meant to be together and claim to love you or have feelings within 24–48 hours of first meeting online. They may ask you for your address to send you a gift, and in some cases, you might actually receive something, such as flowers or some other token of affection bought with a stolen credit card. In time, they may even ask for some money so they can visit you or ask another favor that will cost you.

Chat rooms

There are many ways in which people will interact online. There are discussion boards and chat room sites like Dephi Forums (www.delphiforums.com), where people can create accounts and join in public chats with groups of people or private chat rooms of two or more people. Virtual gaming worlds and social worlds provide the ability to engage in conversations with other players, and even games on Facebook may provide features where you can type back and forth to other users. Once two people get along, they may decide to break away from the site and use Instant Messaging (IM) or chat clients, which are designed for exchanging messages and may have features like audio/video chat, the ability to exchange files, or clickable links so that people can visit sites or see the same content.

Because you can share links and files through chat sites and client software, you need to be careful of what you click and receive. As we'll discuss in Chapter 8, a file you receive could be malicious software or contain a virus, and sites offering pornography are notorious for having malicious code that may install viruses or other software on your machine.

The software used to chat should also be a concern. In 2011, Facebook partnered with Skype to introduce a video call feature, which scammers took advantage of.

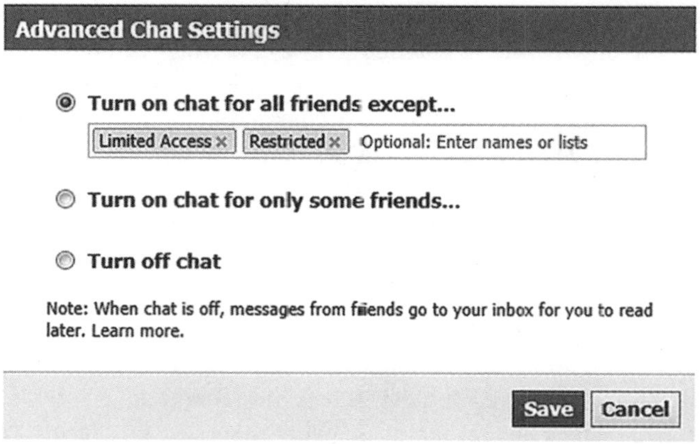

Advanced Chat Settings

◉ **Turn on chat for all friends except...**

| Limited Access × | | Restricted × | Optional: Enter names or lists

○ **Turn on chat for only some friends...**

○ **Turn off chat**

Note: When chat is off, messages from friends go to your inbox for you to read later. Learn more.

Save | Cancel

FIGURE 7.1

Advanced chat settings.

Clicking on a link to "Enable Video Calls" that was shared on Facebook, you were asked to install an app, which requested permission to access your data and information (even when it wasn't being used), and post on your wall and newsfeed. After allowing this, SPAM would be sent to your friends with links to surveys. The scammers profited from referral fees, as people were sent to the sites.

Blocking chat in Facebook

Facebook provides a chat feature that shows people who are available to chat in the right-hand side of your page and newsfeed. By clicking someone on the list, a small chat pane will appear where you can type your messages back and forth. If a person is unavailable for chat, any messages you send will appear in their inbox, where they can be read later.

Facebook provides a number of settings to control who can chat with you. In the lower right-hand corner, at the bottom of the sidebar, you'll see a gear-shaped icon for controlling your chat settings (Figure 7.1). On the menu, you could click *Turn Off Chat* so the chat feature is no longer active during your current session, but chat will turn back and be available when you next log on. For greater control over the chat feature on Facebook, you would click *Advanced Options* to get a dialog box of options.

The first option on the *Advance Chat Settings* dialog box is *Turn on chat for all friends except*, where you can specify individuals or lists of people you'd rather not chat with. In selecting this option, you would enter the names of any lists or people who can't chat with you. As we'll see in Chapter 9, you can use existing lists or create your own custom lists of people. Anyone not mentioned will still be able to chat with you.

Another option is *Turn on chat for only some friends*, which allows you to specify that certain people will be able to chat with you. When you select the option, a box appears where you can add those elite individuals and lists of people who will have the ability to engage you in chat. Everyone else won't be able to chat with you.

The final option is *Turn off chat*. Unlike the option on the settings menu that we mentioned earlier, this setting will turn off chat and keep it off. When you next log on, it will still be turned off and remain off until you change this setting. Turning off chat doesn't completely isolate yourself from others, as people will still be able to send messages to your inbox.

Cybersex

Online conversations aren't always G-rated. *Cybersex* is a term that describes a sexually explicit conversation that simulates a sexual encounter. Those chatting with each other often don't know each other in real life. Their conversations may involve flirting, or extend into a sexual dialog of what they like or sharing fantasies, and may be used as stimuli for masturbation. Assuming it involves consenting adults, there's nothing illegal about it.

While you might think such activities are rare, you'd be wrong. According to a 2004 study, out of 1828 people surveyed, 658 women and 800 men claimed to use the Internet for online sexual activities, and almost one-third of the men and women reported they'd engaged in cybersex. While popular, it isn't without its share of risks.

Chat sites often use aliases, where you create an account with a username to prevent others from seeing your real name. The anonymity is a powerful and attractive feature, but it's important to realize that it goes both ways. You don't really know who you're chatting with. The person who asks you to engage in cybersex or *cyber* may claim to be in their 20s or 30s, but it could also be someone who's 13 or 63. If the person is underage, you may wind up having to address the additional legal issues of having inadvertently corrupted a minor, Internet luring, or (if photos or video were exchanged) being charged with receiving child pornography. Everything about the person, even their gender could be a lie. Alternatively, it could also be a coworker or someone you know, causing great embarrassment. Just as the alias isn't your real name, the personal information and photo on a profile page could also be fake.

Anonymity can be empowering. It can make you feel like you can say anything, as if you're protected behind a secret identity. A person can reveal what excites them and talk in a way they never would to even a real-life partner. It also provides a mechanism for sharing personal details, intimate secrets, and discuss personal problems with work and relationships. The information you give could be used by a cyberbully or cyberstalker to gather information about you or (as we'll see later in this chapter) as a social engineering ploy. As with other online sexual activity, cybersex often isn't discussed or admitted to in real life. Because it's a secret, a spouse or boyfriend/girlfriend discovering these virtual relationships may see it as a betrayal or an infidelity. If a real-life partner sees it as cheating, it can destroy the relationship, causing embarrassment or even legal action, as in the form of divorce or child custody proceedings. Prior to engaging in cybersex, you should understand how your real-life partner feels about online sexual activities and respect their opinion.

Virtual relationships can go beyond cursory ones. If two people meeting online like each other, they may add one another as friends, creating an online relationship. The ongoing exchange can also invoke real feelings, evolving it into an online affair or even a real-life one. Unlike real-life relationships, you experience the person in fragments, only seeing the aspects they want to reveal which may be completely fabricated, and filling the rest in with fantasy.

The best way to approach a chat room is the way you would a bar. You'll meet people seeking friendly conversation, those who are lonely and want companionship, and others seeking sex. While many people are nice, there are also those who will try and get what they can from you. Once they have you in private, some may use mind games or trickery.

Whether it's to scam or play you, a person who's trying to get something will often use sweet talk. Almost everything they say is positive, encouraging, and something you want to hear. While peppering you with compliments, they may also make subtle jabs against any current relationships you have. They may say *If I were your boyfriend/girlfriend, I would ...* followed by a positive comment. The wording places a suggestion to think of that person in a relationship role and insinuates they'd make a better partner than your real-life one. If he or she can undermine current relationships, it may keep you from turning to others and talking about the chats. The person wants gain your trust, so they can get what they want.

The person may ask for your phone number to call and talk in person, ask you to call him/her, or suggest a video chat. While the person may genuinely want to connect with you, the request could also be part of a blackmail scheme or some other scam. A phone conversation may turn sexual and recorded, while a person using a webcam may be lured into remove clothing or even perform sexual acts. The blackmailer will take screenshots or capture the video and then demand payment or some other favors in exchange for not posting the images or video to the Internet.

Before any chats or online dating goes too far, you should do a little detective work. As we'll discuss in Chapter 10, online tools can be used to find detailed information about a person. Even a simple check can be revealing. By typing a phone number, email address, account name, or other information provided by the person, you can establish whether the details they provide appear true. Because many scams involve sending packages or money to another country, if they claim to be local and say they're out of the country, be suspicious.

When it comes to video chatting, you need to be careful. If you're chatting with someone you haven't met in real life, you should try and determine if it's a live feed. Scammers may hide their identity by using prerecorded video of someone else. Maybe they're fooling you into thinking they're more attractive, hiding their age, or don't want you identifying them to police. If you're typing messages back and forth and not talking with one another, you wouldn't be able to match the audio with movements of the person's mouth. To ensure it's a real person, get them to do something like point at a corner of the screen or hold something up to the camera. If they refuse, it may be because they can't.

TOOLS & TIPS...

The Anonymity of the Internet

The anonymity of the Internet is often an illusion, especially when you consider how your IP address can be traced. When you go on the Internet, your ISP will issue your computer an IP address, which identifies it and is used when communicating with servers and other devices. Sites will often log this information, and it can be used to track a person to some degree. IP addresses are usually assigned on the basis of your geographic location, providing a correlation between who you are and where you are. As we'll see in Chapter 8, by doing a reverse lookup of the IP address, you can identify the ISP someone's using, which may be used by law enforcement as a source to finding someone's account information.

Sexting

Sexting is a variation of cybersex in which sexually explicit text messages are exchanged and may include suggestive, nude, or pornographic images or video. The text messages, images, and video are often shared using mobile phones. Unlike cybersex, where the partakers of the activity can be a real-life couple but more often involves people who don't know each other offline; sexting more commonly involves participants who know one another and have exchanged phone numbers.

While the majority of people with mobile devices haven't sent or received a sext, there are many who have. According to a 2012 study by Pew Internet & American Life Project, 15% of adult cell phone owners have received a nude or nearly nude photo or video from someone that they knew, and 6% have sent one of themselves to another person. Being that it's common for mobile phones and tablets to have a built-in camera, it's easy for someone to take advantage of the technology and include a picture or short video without thinking of the repercussions.

Sexting isn't limited to any particular age group. The majority of those receiving, sending, and forwarding sexts are younger, between the ages of 24–34, with the second largest group being 18–24. However, people of all ages have done it, including teenagers. In a 2009 study, Pew surveyed cell phone owners between the ages of 12–17 and found similar behavior, inclusive to sending and receiving sexually suggestive or explicit images. 15% of the teenagers had received a sext on their mobile phone, while 4% had sent one of themselves.

Sending such photos or videos to someone doesn't mean that it will stay with that person. You may have sent a suggestive photo or video to a boyfriend, girlfriend, or spouse, but it can easily be forwarded to other people. The 2012 study by Pew found that 3% of adult cell phone owners forwarded a sexually suggestive or explicit photo or video of someone they know to another person. Once it's shared, it could be sent to coworkers, family, or even uploaded to a porn site and be passed around for years.

Fake photos and video

Some people want to hide their identity online. It may be for protection, as in the case of someone visiting a chat room and wanting anonymity or it may be a scammer who relies on concealing his or her true identity. As part of a false persona, the person may use fake photos on profile pages. Often these are from other people's sites or from stock photo sites. For example, by going to Shutterstock (www.shutterstock.com), you can search millions of stock photos and find a photo of a model that suits your needs. Fortunately, while it used to be difficult identifying if a person's photo was fake, Google has made it easier.

Google provides a feature to find identical or similar photos of a person. By uploading a photo or using the URL of one you've found online, Google will try to find the same image or similar ones on different sites. If the image appears in a profile, you could right-click on the image, click *Properties* on the menu that appears, and then copy the URL in the Address (URL) field of the *Properties* dialog box that appears. There is also an extension for Chrome and Firefox, which allows you to right-click on an image and select *Search Google with this image*. To search for the same or similar photos on Google's Web site, do the following:

1. After going to Google (www.google.com), click on the Images link in the top navigation bar.
2. Click on the Camera icon beside the search field.
3. Either click *Upload an Image* to search using a photo on your hard disk or copy the URL of the image into the search field.
4. Click the *Search by image* button.

In using this tool, you should realize that someone could use it to find information about you. If you have a photo of yourself on one site, someone could use it to search for other images on a site providing personal information. Any photos you have on a site should not reveal any personal information about you, inclusive to logos of where you work, places you frequent, or where your children go to school. By sanitizing the personal information on sites that have photos of you, you can limit a person finding more about you than intended.

Explicit content on social media sites

Unless you've lived an incredibly sheltered life, you know that there's pornography on the Internet. While some social media sites like Facebook forbid any content that is pornographic or contains nudity and/or violence, other sites allow it. Because of this, you should review the Terms of Service for sites you use to identify what isn't included as inappropriate content for the site.

Twitter allows mature or adult content to be uploaded to their site, including media that contains nudity, violence, or shows potentially upsetting imagery like medical procedures. Indicating whether it's of a sensitive nature is up to the person who makes it available. If you do upload such content, it's advisable to indicate it through your account settings, so that people are warned before they see it. If you don't want to see such content, you can opt out of the default setting to view it. To configure this, perform these steps:

1. Click on the gear-shaped icon in the upper right-hand corner of the page, and click *Settings* on the menu that appears.

2. Scroll down until you see the *Tweet media* section. Click on the *Display media that may contain sensitive content* checkbox so it is unchecked.
3. If you're uploading sensitive content, click on the *Mark my media as containing sensitive content* checkbox so it appears checked.
4. Click the *Save Changes* button.
5. When prompted, enter your password and click *Save Changes*.

In choosing to view sensitive material on Twitter, it doesn't mean everything is allowed. If you see any illegal content such as child pornography or other content that you want Twitter to be aware of, click the *Flag Media* link below the image or video to report it.

Explicit content of yourself or loved ones

Digital cameras and web cams are inexpensive, and cameras in mobile phones and tablets are commonplace, so it's not unusual to find people creating their own sexually explicit photos and video. The self-generated images and homemade pornography might be created for personal use and meant to be shared privately between those involved or its creator and a specific person. A couple might make a video, believing it's safe on their mobile device or computer. A lover might take a picture of his or herself, send it to a significant other via email, a sext message, or upload it to a private album or account on sites like Facebook, Photobucket, Tumblr, or Flickr. Unfortunately, such photos and video have a way of becoming public.

A 2012 study by the Internet Watch Foundation (www.iwf.org.uk) found that 88% of the homemade pornography they reviewed online had been taken from another site or location. Referred to as parasite Web sites, they get content from sites where the images were originally uploaded. It may be taken from social media sites with insecure settings, hacked accounts, chat sites, or lost or stolen mobile devices. Adults aren't the only ones at risk of this. For over 47 working hours, they looked at 12,224 images and videos on 68 sites and focused on images depicting young people (aged 13 and 20) who were performing sexual acts or posing in a sexually explicit manner.

Sometimes images are also uploaded for the purposes for revenge. A couple may break up, and one of the parties may decide to upload the photos to a social networking site or a site that specializes in pornographic photos of an ex or revenge photos. While these can cause embarrassment for anyone, if the person in the photo is underage, it's also illegal. In 2008, 17-year-old Alex Phillips broke up with his 16-year-old girlfriend. While together she had taken nude photos of herself and emailed them to Phillips. Now that they were broken up, Phillips decided to post them on his MySpace page with derogatory captions. When she realized the photos were online and available to the public, she called the police, who told Phillips to remove them. When he didn't, they contacted MySpace, who removed them immediately. Phillips was charged with criminal libel, possession of child pornography, sexual exploitation of a child and causing mental harm to a child. In 2009, he pled guilty to a lesser charge of causing mental harm to a child.

Even if an underage person takes a sexually explicit photo of his or herself, it is still child pornography. In 2008, a 14-year-old girl made headlines when she posted 30 nude photos of herself on MySpace, because she wanted her boyfriend to see them. The National Center for Missing and Exploited Children discovered the photos, notified a state task force, who then contacted local police. As she found out, even if you take a photo of yourself, an underage person can be charged with producing, possession and distribution of child pornography.

As discussed in Chapter 6, you can request a site to remove embarrassing or harassing content, and if you do see explicit content where the person is underage, it's important to report it. However, removing an image or a video from the Internet can be difficult and almost impossible, especially if it goes viral and distributed on a wide scale. If an image is uploaded to a site, it may be copied to other sites, causing it to appear in multiple places. Also, if someone downloads it, they may upload it again after you've had the image taken down.

Predators

Just as there are predators in the wild, there are those who seek out prey on the Internet. As we've seen in the previous sections, there are those who will look for potential victims for blackmail, scams, and even Internet-initiated sex crimes. Of course, adults aren't the only victims.

There are numerous studies and surveys that show how prevalent it is for children and teenagers to be solicited for sex online. According to a report funded by the National Center for Missing and Exploited Children, 70% of girls and 30% of boys who were surveyed were approached or solicited for sex, and 79% of them experienced this on a home computer. While children of any age can become the target of a pedophile, the study (which surveyed children aged 10–17) found that the majority of those who were solicited (81%) were aged 14 or older.

Teaching children and teenagers about online safety is an important deterrent against their being victimized. Some of the important topics to cover include:

- Don't talk to strangers. While it may seem cliché, only 14% of those who were solicited for sex knew the person. Young social network users should avoid talking to strangers. For the rest of us, be wary of them.
- If someone suggests meeting in person, don't. In aggressive incidents, 75% of those soliciting a youth of sex suggested meeting in person.
- Talk to an adult if you have a problem. In 56% of incidents where a youth was solicited for sex, they didn't tell anyone. This leaves them vulnerable to being groomed by a pedophile.

As we've stated before, it's also important to control the information that's posted on social networking sites. The study found that 34% has posted their real name, phone number, home address, school, and other personal information. However, it's not just children who are at fault for this. According to a 2010 survey by Consumer Reports, 45% of social network users with children posted their children's photos online. Looking at just Facebook users, the same survey revealed that 26% of users posted their children's photos along with the children's names and 7% posted their street address. Even if the names only appear in photo tags and captions, this could be enough for a predator to identify the child and start a conversation.

Even if a social media site has age restrictions, it doesn't mean that younger children aren't setting up accounts. Facebook limits the age of people using the site to 13 and under, but there's nothing stopping a child from creating an account with a fake birthdate. Regardless of their age, if you have a teenager or younger child using social media, don't allow them to be unsupervised.

The more predictable a person is, the easier it is to find them. By going on the same sites at the same time each day, it's easier for someone to know when you're online. They can then start regular chats and make consistent contact. Limit the time a child is allowed to go online and stagger those times so it's inconsistent.

To make yourself available in case problems arise, ensure the family computer is in a common area of the house, such as a living room. Let them know that if he or she has a problem, you or another adult will be available to help. The other benefit of having online activity in a common area is that the child knows that you may be watching and be less likely to do something online you'd disapprove of.

IM is commonly used by predators, allowing real-time communication between two people. While a predator may meet someone in a chat room, they'll often suggest using IM software to continue the conversation. Features of IM software can include voice over IP to allow audio communication, video chat, the ability to transfer files, and clickable links that takes the person to a site. These features allow the predator to send links to pornographic sites and coach victims into sending revealing pictures or appear in video chats. Eventually, the predator may try and arrange a meeting.

Monitoring tools

The argument of privacy versus safety is always a controversial one, even when it comes to monitoring a child or teenager's online activity. Even if you don't want to aggressively monitor them, you should have access to accounts. The email address used as the account's contact should be one that you can access, and you should be able to log into the account if needed. Should the child exhibit signs of a problem, you can log on and investigate further.

Parental control systems are useful in monitoring and controlling what a child does online. Free software like Norton Family (www.onlinefamily.norton.com) allows you to monitor sites that are visited, control the time spent online, view what a person searches for online, and track activity on social networks. The premier version also provides additional features, such as the ability to monitor Android smartphones, so you can block sites and texts and monitor what apps are being installed.

If you're concerned about a child or teenagers already having problems with their online activities with a mobile device, then you may want to use more aggressive monitoring tools. Mobile Spy (www.mobile-spy.com) provides features that allow you to monitor text messages, IM, sites visited, videos that were watched on YouTube, and calls that were dialed and received on the phone. Some of the more invasive features allow you to listen to the phone's surroundings, track Global Positioning System (GPS) locations, and take photos using the phone's camera without the person knowing.

TOOLS & TIPS...

Check Your Apps

Even if you don't use monitoring software, it's important to know that they exist. The same software that may be used to monitor a child's mobile phone for signs that they're in trouble can also be used to monitor what you're doing. If others have access to your phone and could potentially install apps, you don't know what might have been installed. It's a good idea to review what apps are installed to identify if something's been installed that shouldn't be there.

Social engineering

Social engineering is the practice of using various techniques to get people to reveal sensitive or personal information. Using a variety of methods, a person might get you to reveal the information by manipulating you, through technological means or through documents you've made accessible. In many cases, you won't realize it's even happened until after you're a victim, if you even realize it at all.

There are many ways to use social engineering to get private and confidential information. The simplest ways are very low tech. *Shoulder surfing* involves looking at what a person types on a keyboard as they enter a password or watch information that appears on the monitor as they type. Another is to pose as someone who's trying to help you and ask questions that get you to reveal information. For example, if I called you at work and identified myself as part of the IT department, I might say that there's a problem with your network account. Because it's in your benefit for this to be fixed, and if I drew it out long enough and was convincing, you might give me your password so I can get into the system as you to "fix the problem."

While many social engineering scams are more complex than this, getting a person's password doesn't have to be much more difficult than asking them. In 2003, Infosecurity Europe (www.infosec.co.uk) conducted a survey of office workers at Waterloo Station in London, England, in which people were asked a series of questions to get the reward of a cheap pen. The questions in the survey included asking a person to reveal his or her password, which 90% of office workers did willingly. Of this number, 75% immediately gave up their passwords when asked "What is your password?," and 15% gave up their password when some basic social engineering tricks were applied, such as asking the category their password fell into and some additional questions. For example, one person doing the survey was the CEO of a company who initially refused giving the password as it would compromise security, but later said it was his daughter's name. When asked what his daughter's name was, he replied without thinking, thereby giving up his password.

While Social Engineering is often associated with a conversation where the tidbits of truth is slowly leaked out, it can (and often does) happen in ways you wouldn't consider. One method is through questions that people distribute to one another via email or Facebook notes. The questions may be fun or silly to fill out and have recurring bouts of popularity, as they allow you to share information with others that wouldn't normally come up in conversation. If you search for "Facebook notes questions," you'll find a number of these questionnaires. Some of the types of questions might include:

- What is your favorite color?
- What is your real name?
- What city were you born in?
- What is the name of your favorite pet?
- What is your favorite food?

In glancing at these questions, they may seem fairly innocuous. However, if you look closer at the questions, you'll find that some are common security questions asked when setting up an account online. If you provided me the answers, I might be able to use an email address that can be viewed on your profile page, attempt logging onto the site, and click the link saying that I can't remember my password. By answering one of the security questions like "What city were you born in?" I could automatically obtain access, may be asked to create a new password or have a temporary one emailed to me. In the end, I now have control of your account, which could be very bad if it gives me access to your financial information, like a bank or credit card account.

Social media is a dream resource for social engineers. People post a considerable amount of information about their lives, loved ones, and interests on multiple sites. By going through this information, you can find when a person was born, their family member names, information on where they work, and their sports fans, movie buffs, and more. Individual pieces of information may not seem like much, but combined it can be somewhat revealing.

When people create passwords, they want to remember them, so they often incorporate the things they love or have interest in. As we'll see in Chapter 10, there are a number of passwords that are easy to guess and common among people. In 2012, SplashData, a provider of password management software, compiled a list of common passwords, and in looking at these you can see that many fall into specific categories. These include:

- Keyboard rolls like qwerty, asdf, 12345
- Letter and\or number combinations like 11111, abc123, or 345abc

- Names (inclusive to first names or first initial followed by surname)
- Country or city of origin
- Favorites (car, team, sport, athlete, band, song, movie character, actor, etc.)
- Affiliations (including religious words like god, jesus, etc., schools and clubs)

In using these, there may be a numerical extension. For example, the end and sometimes beginning of the password would contain a number (e.g., a number between 0 and 9, 123, 69, 007, and so on) or a significant date (such as by putting a year of birth, graduation, or marriage). When thinking about your own passwords, there's probably more than one that follows this formula.

With this knowledge in hand, now look at a Twitter or Facebook account that's visible to everyone or belongs to someone you know. In looking through, you'll probably find tweets or posts about their favorite team winning a game, mentions of their favorite movie, their child's name, and so on. These things can be leading to finding what their password is.

The information you find on people's profile pages and posts can also be compiled into more specific uses. In looking at the information a person puts in their contact information on social networking sites, you'll see instances where their address, phone number, email address, and other personal information is available for everyone to see. In many cases, they didn't want the information available to everyone, but mistakenly thought their security settings prevented others from seeing this.

Sites like LinkedIn are a goldmine for social engineers, as it's designed to display information like an online resume. In addition to possibly seeing contact information, you can see the schools they attended, current and past positions with organizations, how long they've been working at a job, interests, groups and associations, awards, and so on.

To show how vulnerable this makes you, consider how easy it would be for an attacker to look at your LinkedIn profile page and see where you're currently working. By using a site like WhitePages (www.whitepages.com), the person could call you at work or possibly at home. While talking to you, the attacker could pose as someone in authority to get you to reveal more information. By saying he or she is from your bank and wants to confirm information, the person could recite what you've published on your LinkedIn page, and then slip in a question or two like "For confirmation purposes, can I get you to tell me your Social Security Number?" Between a phone conversation and your LinkedIn page, it would be easy for the attacker to apply for an online credit card, loan, or take other measures to steal your identity.

Protecting yourself from social engineering requires being aware of potential security risks and taking steps to minimize them. Primary to this is being aware of the information you make available on the Internet, and keep in mind that strangers could have access to this information. Some tips for your safety and information security include:

- Be thoughtful about what you're saying online. Don't mention projects you're involved in, answer questions that reveal personal or business information, and avoid mentioning the names of coworkers and loved ones in tweets or other public forums. If someone could use it against you or your business, don't say it.

- Leave contact information like addresses, phone numbers, and so on blank.
- Ensure security settings on social media sites limit what strangers can see.
- Don't accept friend or contact requests from anyone who asks. The chances of the wrong person viewing your information increase if you accept these requests from strangers.
- Review the friends and contacts you have. If you have hundreds of friends, how many of them do you really want seeing your posts?

Dumpster diving

If you've ever thrown something in the garbage that maybe should have been put in a shredder, you should wonder who might have access to it. *Dumpster diving* is a low-tech way of getting information, which involves pulling documents containing information from the trash. A person may throw out a piece of paper with a password on it, a work document, pay stub, bill, or something else containing sensitive information. One in the trash, anyone with access to the waste basket, a trash bag the janitor throws it into, or the outside dumpster can pull it out and use it. Even if the information isn't as direct as a piece of paper with a password written on it, the information on multiple documents can be compiled into something the attacker can use.

Organizations should implement a policy that any documents containing confidential information should be shredded and not thrown out with regular trash. However, even if your business follows such policies, this doesn't protect you from employees taking information home and throwing it out there. In the second annual Infosecurity Europe survey mentioned earlier, it was found that 80% of employees took confidential information home with them when they changed jobs. Even if an attacker didn't have access to information at your business, it doesn't mean that they can't get it through current and former employees.

Trying to restrict what information an employee can and can't take home from work can be difficult if not impossible. Many people in a workplace use tablets, laptops, and other devices that store considerable amounts of data and walk in and out of a business on a regular basis. As such, education and policy are important, so that workers take this responsibility seriously.

For employees, there is a greater need to control what they leave the building with on their last day of work. If a former employee is angry enough to leave a business with confidential information, they are also probably more than willing to share it with anyone who asks. Some may even be angry enough to start posting confidential information on social networking sites, or as we discussed in Chapter 6, uploading documents to various sites like WikiLeaks (www.wikileaks.org).

Phishing

One social engineering technique is *phishing*, which is pronounced as "fishing." The term comes from the philosophy that if you cast a big enough net, you'll catch a few fish. It involves sending out bulk email or instant messages to as many people as possible, asking them to provide information or click a link. The link often takes them to a fake Web site that looks like a legitimate site. For example, it may look like a login screen for Facebook, Twitter, PayPal, or a credit card company. You're asked for your username and password, credit card information, or some other data that a criminal is trying to obtain. The site may require a number of questions filled out, many of which are innocuous, but buried between the questions are ones that do ask for your personal or financial information.

Phishing may also be focused on specific targets, such as individual employees or groups within an organization, which is referred to as *spear phishing*. For example, let's say I know you and a couple of others in your company are in charge of social media, and I send you an email posing as the IT department. The email might state that we're updating our records and want you to confirm the username and password of social media sites "our" company is using. Without thinking twice, you may think this is a legitimate and reasonable request and respond to the email. Even if I don't get a response from all of the people using social media, even one response can give me everything I want.

Whaling is another variation, in which the attacker targets bigger fish within the company. The target is a senior executive or some other high-profile person within the company. By focusing on these people, there is a better chance of acquiring more privileged information that a low-level employee wouldn't be privy to.

Context phishing can also be used to gain a person's trust. Using this method, I look at your online activity, using sites like eBay to discover your bidding history, Facebook to find your birthday and friends, or MySpace to discover your interests. By mentioning bits and pieces of information I know about you, I can know how to gain your trust and have a better chance of your providing me additional information. By compiling enough of this information, it is possible to use the data to commit identity theft.

As is the case with other kinds of cybercriminals, phishers go where people go. As social networking sites have increased in popularity, incidents of people using social media sites for phishing expeditions have also increased. Many people will ignore or question the validity of request in their email to click a link or answer a question, because they've been educated to be wary of these requests. However, the same people will think nothing of doing it when the message is received in through a social networking site. The fact is, no matter what the medium, you need to be careful of the message.

Fake sites

A common ploy in social engineering involves getting a person to enter information into a fake site. The site may look like the real thing, but it's been created to try and capture personal or sensitive information. As you log into it or enter data into fields under the guise of verifying information, it is stored and reviewed later by the criminal who runs the site. Now that he has your information, the person can log onto the site you thought you had gone to and pose as you online.

While some sites used for phishing and other scams can be quite elaborate, most are not. When you visit the site, you may notice a number of things that can make you question the site. For example, words may be misspelled or have poor grammar, images on the site may be of poor quality, or the design of the site may look different from what you're used to. If you have been to the site before or see things that make you question whether it's legitimate, trust your instincts, don't enter any information, and leave.

Another way to identify a fake site is to look at the protocol being used to communicate with the Web server. A *protocol* is a set of rules, and in terms of networking, it is how computers communicate with one another over a network. In many cases, a browser will use HTTP to request a page or resource from a Web server, but on more secure sites, a different protocol is generally used. Secure sites like banks will generally use a protocol called HTTPS, which provides encrypted communication and secure identification of a network's Web servers. As we mentioned earlier in this chapter, if the site is using HTTP, you'll see in your address bar that the URL begins with "http://," but if it's used HTTPS you'll see that it begins with "https://" and will show a padlock symbol next to the address bar. If the site isn't using HTTPS but is using some other protocol, you should be concerned because the data is being transmitted over the Internet insecurely.

Fake sites for purposes other than phishing

Fake sites may also be created for criminal and noncriminal purposes. There are humorous parodies of commercial sites, and ones that are created as a form of Internet activism called *cyber-activism*. When considerable work is done, these may look like the real thing and can easily fool you. It isn't until you delve deeper into the site's content that you recognize that it's a fake. Examples of these include:

- *Police Guide FBI Records Search* (www.policeguide.com/cgi/criminal-search.cgi), which allows you to enter personal data to search FBI records. Well, not really. The FBI doesn't allow public searches of their records system, and it is obviously a joke when the search is completed.
- *World Trade Organization* (www.gatt.org or www.gatt.org/homewto.html). While the real site is located at www.wto.org, these sites, searching on Google, include a description of the site as the "Official web site of the World Trade Organization." The site is one of many created by the Yes Men, who create prank sites as part of cyber-activism. A list of some of their archived sites is available at www.yeslab.org/museum.
- *Apple iPhone* (http://apple-cf.com.yeslab.org) is another parody from the Yes Men, but worth mentioning because it was so close to the real site that Apple worked fast at having it shut down. The site offered a "conflict-free" iPhone 4 that doesn't use minerals from mines in the Congo that isn't controlled by rebel groups and a free upgrade by going to Apple store on 5th Avenue.

In looking at these sites, you can see the varying levels of effort involved in creating a site that impersonates another organization. The first site offers a service to check FBI records, and although it's obviously for amusement, it does ask you to provide information. By pretending to be a legitimate site, people are lured into a sense of security. A site gets you to enter personal data by offering something you really want or a service that benefits you, enticing you to give up information you'd normally keep private.

Although the Apple iPhone site wasn't built for the purposes of scamming people out of money, there are a number of online scams that are for this purpose. When a new iPhone is released, people are enthusiastic to upgrade, and offers have appeared on the Internet that get people to pay for an upgraded phone prior to its release or when they were sold out. It's a common element of many scams to offer something too good to be true.

Even if fake sites aren't designed for purposes of phishing, scams, or other criminal endeavors, they can cause considerable problems for a business. For the iPhone site, Apple needed to pay legal fees to have it shut down and dedicate resources to address allegations on the site. These and other fake sites can cause public relation issues for companies by publicizing unethical or unpopular business practices or by publicly embarrassing them by portraying them as unprofessional or foolish.

Fake or shortened URLs

When you do visit a site, you need to be careful that the site you've visited is the correct one. For example, let's say you click on a link to take you to LinkedIn. If the address bar at the top of the browser starts with www.linkedin.com, you know you're at the right place. However if it looks different, showing something like http://linkedin.example.com or http://linkedin.com@example.com, you are not on the correct site. You'll notice that the domain name in these URLs is example.com, meaning you never reached the LinkedIn site. In such cases, you should immediately leave the site and not enter any username or password.

For fake sites, you'll often find that a domain name similar to the real one is used. For example, if you saw a link for www.linkedin.cm, you might miss that the URL doesn't use the .com domain suffix. It's actually using the .cm suffix, which is reserved for sites registered in Cameroon. Another common ploy is to use the domain suffix of the real site but use a slightly different spelling to the name. Unless you're paying attention, you might miss that the link is taking you to www.linkdin.com instead of www.linkedin.com.

Although the suffix of a domain may be an indicator, this isn't always the case. It's important to note that many legitimate sites will register domain names that don't end in .com, or ones that aren't related to the country the business actually resides in. For example, you may have seen domains ending in the suffix .tv, which are often used by television stations or sites with rich media. The .tv domain suffix is a country code for the islands of Tuvalu, which is a Polynesian island nation that is $26\,km^2$ in size, and as of 2013 has an estimated population of 10,698 people. In 2000, they started leasing the domain name .tv to Verisign for $50 million in royalties over a 12 year period, which was then renewed under undisclosed terms until December 31, 2021.

Before clicking on any links, it's always a good idea to take a moment and see where it will take you. If it's a link on a Web page, you can hover your mouse over it and see the URL of the link in your browser's status bar or in a tooltip that displays beside the link. Depending on the email program you're using, the same will occur if you've received a link in email.

As we discussed in Chapter 4, shortened URLs can be used to make a long URL smaller. You may see a site starting with tinyurl or bit.ly, such as http://bit.ly/10TjJ3v. When you click on it, you find yourself taken to a site with a different and significantly longer Web site address. Generally, there is no problem with this. The reason it occurs is because the URL is being resolved by a site like TinyURL or Bitly. Clicking the link takes you to their service, which resolves that URL to one in its database, and redirects you to the proper site. The shortened URLs make it easier when you're making a post or tweet and limited to a certain number of characters. However, it also masks where you're going. If you were to click the link, you couldn't be sure if you were going to what appeared to be a legitimate site, or one that a hacker setup to obtain information or install malware to your system. If you believe a site isn't legitimate, you should contact the shortened URL service and notify them, change any passwords you may have entered on the site, and run anti-malware software on your machine.

Norton Safe Web

A useful tool for checking links on a page or newsfeed is Norton Safe Web, which is available through Facebook's App Center at www.facebook.com/appcenter/norton-safeweb. In visiting the page, click on the *Go To App* button. When using the app for the first time, you'll be asked to allow it to have certain permissions on your account. As seen in Figure 7.2, a page will display that analyzes the links that have been shared in the last 24 hours, showing which are safe and what ones you should be concerned about. By hovering your mouse over the red slider in the upper right corner and holding down the left mouse button, you can move the switch to the *Auto-Scan On* position. This will set the app to automatically check any links on your newsfeed.

When Norton Safe Web automatically scans your wall, it will post an update to tell you if any malicious links have been detected. If it's something you posted, you should delete it from your profile. If someone else posted it, you can then use a *Warn Your Friends* option to notify them about the link. If nothing malicious is found, the app will post a message every 30 days to notify you that your wall is safe.

Anti-phishing protection in browsers

Newer versions of browsers have features that will detect whether a site has been reported as a known for phishing or malware. *Malware* is programs that contain malicious code that's designed to damage or disrupt your computer, gather private or sensitive information, and may even download additional software or viruses. Browsers like Internet Explorer and Firefox will compare the URL you're attempting to visit to lists of reported sites and will block you from going to the site if there's a problem. Browsers like Opera and Google Chrome will also use

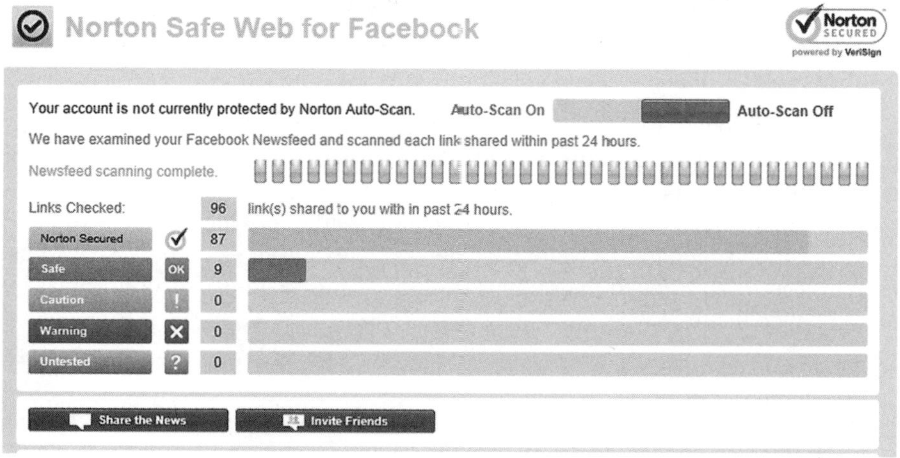

FIGURE 7.2

Norton Safe Web for Facebook.

sandboxing techniques, in which the browser is isolated from other information on your computer. They will also do such things as block access to a site if the URL in a certificate doesn't match the URL of the site you're visiting. If the two don't match, then this is a sign that the site you're visiting is a fake one.

Internet Explorer provides a *SmartScreen Filter* feature that runs in the background while you're using the browser. In versions 7 and 8 of Internet Explorer, this was called a *Phishing Filter*. When you attempt to go to a site, it will compare the URL to a list of sites that have been reported to Microsoft that's stored on your computer. It will then determine if the site has any features that are common to phishing sites, and (if you've permitted it) may then send information to Microsoft to check the site against an updated list of problem sites. If the site is on a list, the browser displays a warning page, and you can then choose whether to continue to the site.

By default, SmartScreen Filter is not turned on, so to use it you need to activate it in your browser. To do this, you would follow these steps:

1. In Internet Explorer, click on the *Tools* menu.
2. Select *SmartScreen Filter* from the menu, and click *Turn on SmartScreen Filter*.
3. When the dialog box appears, make sure that the *Turn on SmartScreen Filter (recommended)* option is select, and click *OK*.

If you don't have SmartScreen Filter turned on, you can still check the site by doing the following:

1. In Internet Explorer, click on the *Tools* menu.
2. Select *SmartScreen Filter* from the menu, and click *Check this web site*.

3. When the dialog box appears, click *OK*.
4. Wait for the site to be compared against a list on Microsoft's site to determine if it's unsafe. A dialog box will appear showing the result.

Google Chrome provides features that will check a site and display messages if you are visiting an unsafe site that contains malware or is suspected of being a phishing site. If you want to continue to the site, you have that option, but it is recommended to leave and find the information you're looking for on a safe site. By default, phishing and malware detection is turned on. If you don't want to use it, you need to go through the settings to turn off this feature. To confirm that it's turned on, do the following:

1. In Google Chrome, click on the menu button (which has three strips on it) in the upper right of the browser.
2. Click *Settings*.
3. At the bottom of the page that appears, click *Show advanced settings*.
4. When additional settings appear on the page, look in the *Privacy* section and ensure the checkbox labeled *Enable phishing and malware protection* is checked.

Mobile devices can also benefit from security apps that will scan sites for malware and phishing risks. As we saw in Chapter 6, Lookout Security and Antivirus is a tool that can be installed on iPhones and Android devices. One of the premium features is Safe Browsing mode, which scans sites for malware and phishing risks.

Hacked accounts

Hacking is a mainstream term that has come to refer to anyone who breaks into a computer system. While for ease of understanding we use the term throughout the book, the original definition of a *hacker* referred to a computer enthusiast. It was someone who would hack away at a keyboard, programming, or working in some other way on a computer. A *cracker* is what most people are actually referring to when they discuss hackers. A cracker is someone who will try to crack the security of a system, breaking into computers or cracking passwords.

There are many laws that have been designed to deal with the unauthorized access of systems and data, and the damage that can result from such actions. In the United States, individual states have specific laws that address the issues of unauthorized computer access, identity theft or fraud resulting from accessing data, destruction of data, and other issues related to hacking. In terms of Federal law, the Computer Fraud and Abuse Act (CFAA) of 1986 has been amended numerous times, inclusive to the enactment of the USA PATRIOT Act of 2001. The CFAA makes it a federal crime to access a computer without proper authorization and came under additional scrutiny in 2013.

In 2011, Aaron Swartz, the cofounder of Reddit, was arrested for downloading millions of academic articles from a database using a guest account. If that doesn't seem like hacking, you would have been in disagreement with the government.

He was arrested by police and a US Secret Service agent. While many of the articles were public domain, there was also copyright material, which they believed Swartz planned to share via peer-to-peer networks. He also spoofed the MAC address of his laptop, as MIT had used the number to block the computer from the network. He was arrested on counts of wire fraud and violations of the Computer Fraud and Abuse Act, which could have resulted in a million dollar fine and up to 35 years in jail.

In 2013, Aaron Swartz committed suicide by hanging himself. No suicide note was found, so there is no indication as to what his specific reasons were. However, one can only imagine the stress of facing those kinds of charges. As a result of his death, an amendment to the Computer Fraud and Abuse Act has been proposed that will prevent people from being charged for violations of terms of service, contracts, or other agreements.

Hacking attempts can cause serious problems for an organization. While many people associate hacking with accessing the protected systems of large organizations, hacking social media accounts can have far-reaching implications. On April 23, 2013, the Twitter account of the Associated Press (@AP) was hacked, and a tweet was sent out saying that there had been two explosions in the White House, and Barack Obama had been injured. The incident caused US markets to plunge within minutes of the tweet. Associated Press used their Twitter accounts to tell everyone that the tweet was false, and that the account had been hacked. They advised people to ignore tweets from the accounts, as they'd been compromised. A hacker group called the Syrian Electronic Army later claimed responsibility.

An example of how hacking works

In the case of the parody news site the Onion (www.theonion.com), the hackers used phishing attacks that were focused on the email accounts of staff members. Employees received an email that had a link to the Washington post, which seemed to have a story about their organization. The link eventually took them to a page that asked for their Google App credentials, before redirecting them to a Gmail inbox. Once the hackers had access to a Gmail account, they sent the same phishing email to staff. Because it seemed to come from a trusted source, people were more willing to click the link. Unfortunately, one of those who fell for the ruse had access to the Onion's social media accounts.

When the IT staff realized an account had been compromised, they emailed staff and notified them to change their passwords. A short time later, the hackers sent out a duplicate email, which contained a link to change their passwords. At least two staff members fell for this, and the hackers now had additional access to accounts. This allowed the hackers to continue sending tweets. However, since the hackers hadn't sent the duplicate email to any member of the IT staff, they were unaware that it had been sent.

In what has got to be one of the oddest ways of identifying a compromised account, the Onion then insulted the hackers. Being a satirical news site, the editorial staff began writing about the incident, and one article called "Syrian Electronic Army Has A Little Fun Before Inevitable Upcoming Deaths At Hands Of Rebels" upset the hackers to the point where they tweeted responses through the Onion's Twitter account. When the IT staff realized this, they reset all of the accounts, regaining control of their social media.

Protecting yourself

Monitoring your social media is important in determining whether a problem has occurred. If you notice unexpected tweets or posts appearing, it could be a sign that a social media account has been compromised and/or someone has gained access to your account. Being aware of what's going on is important to identifying a problem.

As we mentioned in Chapter 5 and will discuss further in Chapter 11, tools like Hootsuite allow you to interact with multiple accounts at the same time and don't require having multiple people having access to the password for these accounts. Because fewer people have the password, there's less chance of it being obtained through social engineering tactics or tools that capture passwords.

If a problem occurs, you need to lock it down as fast as possible. This would include changing passwords to social media accounts, so the hacker is prevented from further access. If you can identify how a person got into the account, deal with fixing that problem so they can't get into the system the same way.

Communication is important. As we saw in the case of the Associated Press Twitter account being hacked, they let people know what had happened, so false information wasn't being passed on to the public. By letting people know when information isn't credible, people will know that you're a trusted and reliable source the rest of the time.

When the problem occurs, you should let employees know about it. They can help in securing the system by changing passwords and notifying IT staff of anything that may have caused a security breach. If possible, use methods other than internal email, as this may have been compromised. If you have an intranet, text messaging to managers, or other internal communication methods, use those to get the word out.

Education is important to avoid problems and keep them from getting worse. By educating users about phishing and Internet safety, they'll be less likely to fall victim to a social engineering attack and can help in identifying security breaches. Users should know that you won't send links for password changes, as this is often used in phishing as user's password.

As hacking is illegal, you should report the incident. Contact police so that they can investigate the crime and obtain evidence that could be used in convicting the person(s) responsible. So that they have a full understanding of what occurred, document the events as soon as possible, including screenshots of affected pages, and any steps taken to secure the site after the incident occurred.

Defaced sites

When an account is hacked, the hacker may use the access to modify the content of your site. You may find odd text on pages saying that someone was there, notice new graphics, or find that links have been changed to point to new locations.

In some cases, the Web page may even be modified to include malicious code that will download malware to a visitor's machine.

In 2013, the Financial Times (www.ft.com) was hacked by the Syrian Electronic Army. How did we know it was them? The various blog posts stated "Syrian Electronic Army Was Here" and used Twitter accounts to invite people to see it. Others targeted by the group have included Harvard University whose site displayed a photo of Syrian president Bashar al-Assad with a statement of the group claiming responsibility. The groups have also hacked the BBC, CBS News, E! Online, and the Turkish Ministry of Interior's Web site, gaining access to sites and/or Twitter accounts.

If your account has been hacked, it's important to review the content of your pages. This means reviewing any recent tweets, new and updated pages, and any new content that you don't recognize from before. For Web sites, and any sites where you have the ability to upload content, you should consider restoring the content from a backup that is dated prior to the attack. In doing so, you'll be certain to change the pages back to their previous state and avoid missing any changes that have been missed.

Keeping track of who's logged on

Unfortunately, most sites don't provide a history of recent logins, which would allow you to monitor when the account was accessed. Because of this, you need to look at your profile page, recent tweets, and other activity to see if anything appears amiss. There are however some useful security features that will tell you when the account is being used.

A feature on Facebook provides a listing of active sessions, showing who is logged into your account. To view current sessions, do the following:

1. Click on the gear-shaped icon in the upper right-hand corner of the page. When the menu appears, click *Account Settings*.
2. In the left pane of the page, click *Security*.
3. In the *Active Sessions* section, click *Edit*.

The area will expand to show current sessions using your account. It may show some of your recent logins if you or another person hasn't properly logged off. In looking at the listing, you'll see the device used and the approximate location of the person using the account. It's important to realize that the location shown may not entirely be accurate. If you're using a computer, your ISP may be located in another city, so it will show that you're logged in at a different location.

Another feature on some social media sites will notify you when someone has logged onto your account. On Facebook, it's found on the *Security Settings* page we just used to view current sessions. To set up notifications, follow these steps:

1. In the *Login Notifications* section, click on the *Email* checkbox so it appears checked.
2. If you want to be notified by text message, click on the *Text message/Push notification* checkbox so it appears checked.

3. If you haven't previously added a mobile phone number to your profile information, you'll be prompted to provide one. A confirmation text message will be sent to that number that contains a code. Enter the code into the field on this dialog box, and click *Confirm*.
4. Click *Save Changes*.

Trusted contacts

At times, you may forget your Facebook password or be prevented from accessing the account because someone's changed the password. You could try using the *Forgot my Password* option on the main page and have a link sent to you to reset your password. Unfortunately, if the email has been compromised, this could be an issue too. In such a case, you'd need to provide Facebook with a new phone number or an email address to reach you, so they can give you control of your account.

Facebook also provides a feature where you can select several friends who can help you regain access to your account. Once it's setup, you have the option of using this if you can't log on. The contacts you specify would give you access codes, which could be used to regain control. To use this feature, go to the *Security Settings* page discussed in the previous section and follow these steps:

1. In the Trusted Contacts section, click on the *Edit* link.
2. When the section expands, click on the *Choose Trusted Contacts* link.
3. When the dialog box appears, click the *Choose Trusted Contacts* button.
4. Select three to five friends, and click *Confirm*.

When you have a problem logging onto your account, you would contact the people you selected. They would follow instructions to obtain security codes, which you'd enter to regain access. Because you're trusting them with a combined ability to access your account, you should only choose people you can explicitly trust, such as family members or close friends. If you have a falling out with a friend or family member, make sure that you review your Trusted Contacts in Facebook to remove them from this list.

TOOLS & TIPS...

Passwords are Sent in Different Ways

Different protocols are used on networks to communicate information between your computer and a server. Some protocols are secure and support encryption, but others do not. For example, POP-3 may be used by an email client to log on to a mail server but transmits the username/password as clear text. If hacker used a software tool called a *packet sniffer* to grab data off of a network, he or she could look in a packet of data and see the username/password used in authentication. If you used the same username and password on multiple sites, it wouldn't take long to hijack those accounts. Even if this wasn't the case, by cracking your email account, he or she could visit each site and click the "Forgot password" link. The hacker could then simply access your email account and respond to the notifications containing a link to change the password.

Bibliography

ABC News. (2007, November 19). *ABC Good Morning America.* Retrieved March 15, 2013, from Parents: Cyber Bullying Led to Teen's Suicide: <http://abcnews.go.com/GMA/story?id=3882520&page=1>.

Brenner, J. (2013, February 14). *Pew internet: Social networking (full detail).* Retrieved March 10, 2012, from Pew Internet & American Life Project: <http://pewinternet.org/Commentary/2012/March/Pew-Internet-Social-Networking-full-detail.aspx>.

Central Intelligence Agency. (2013, March 26). *Central Intelligence Agency (CIA).* Retrieved April 4, 2013, from The World Factbook: <https://www.cia.gov/library/publications/the-world-factbook/geos/tv.html>.

Daneback, K., Cooper, A., & Månsson, (2005).S. -A. (2005). An internet study of cybersex participants. *Archives of Sexual Behavior, 34(3)*, 321–328.

Digital Media Law Project. (2009, March 6). *Wisconsin v. Phillips.* Retrieved July 17, 2013, from Digital Media Law Project: <http://www.dmlp.org/threats/wisconsin-v-phillips#description>.

Federal Bureau of Investigations and the National White Collar Crime Center. (2012). *Internet Crime Report.* National White Collar Crime Center.

Internet Watch Foundation. (2012, October 22). *Young people are warned they may lose control over their images and videos once they are uploaded online.* Retrieved July 17, 2013, from Internet Watch Foundation: <http://www.iwf.org.uk/about-iwf/news/post/334-young-people-are-warned-they-may-lose-control-over-their-images-and-videos-once-they-are-uploaded-online>.

Lenhart, A., Madden, M., Smith, A., Purcell, K., Zickuhr, K., & Rainie, L. (2011, November 9). *Teens, kindness and cruelty on social network sites.* Retrieved July 7, 2013, from Pew Internet & American Life Project: <http://pewinternet.org/Reports/2011/Teens-and-social-media.aspx>.

Leyden, J. (2003, April 18). *Office workers give away passwords for a cheap pen.* Retrieved April 5, 2013, from The Register: <http://www.theregister.co.uk/2003/04/18/office_workers_give_away_passwords/>.

Onion Inc.'s Tech Blog. (2013, May 8). *How the syrian electronic army hacked the onion.* Retrieved July 14, 2013, from Onion Inc.'s Tech Blog: <http://theonion.github.io/>.

Ranieri, V. (2009, August 28). *Conviction in Lori Drew MySpace Case Thrown Out.* Retrieved March 15, 2013, from Jolt Digest, Harvard Journal of Law and Technology: <http://jolt.law.harvard.edu/digest/jurisdiction/9th-circuit/united-states-v-drew-3>.

Smith, A. (2012, November 30). *The best (and worst) of mobile connectivity.* Retrieved August 13, 2013, from Pew Internet & American Life Project: <http://pewinternet.org/Reports/2012/Best-Worst-Mobile/Part-V/Activities.aspx>.

SplashData. (2012, October 2012). *Worst passwords of 2012—and how to fix them.* Retrieved March 12, 2013, from SplashData: <http://www.splashdata.com/press/PR121023.htm>.

Tapellini, D. (2010, May 4). *Consumer reports survey: Social network users post risky information.* Retrieved June 19, 2013, from Consumer Reports: <http://news.consumer-reports.org/electronics/2010/05/social-networks-facebook-risks-privacy-risky-behavior-consumer-reports-survey-findings-online-threats-state-of-the-net-report.html>.

Tomlinson, K. (2013, May 6). *Teacher 'powerless' to stop ex-girlfriend's cyberstalking.* Retrieved June 24, 2013, from CBC News: <http://www.cbc.ca/news/canada/british-columbia/story/2013/05/03/bc-cyber-stalking.html>.

Wolak, J., Mitchell, K., & Finkelhor, D. (2006). *Online victimization of youth: Five years later.* Retrieved July 14, 2013, from National Center for Missing and Exploited Children: <http://www.missingkids.com/en_US/publications/NC167.pdf>.

Risk Management

INFORMATION IN THIS CHAPTER:

- Risk management
- Laws and regulations
- Insurance
- Forensics
- Police use of social media
- Malware, viruses, and exploit distribution

Risk management

There's an old saying that *nothing ventured is nothing gained*. There are many potential problems that could happen in using social media, but there are also considerable benefits. However, before we discuss the risks of social media, we should clarify what we're actually talking about. A *risk* is the possibility of a problem occurring and not the inevitability of it happening. The distinction is important to recognize. In identifying risks, you are not saying that something is going to happen, you're just saying that it could. You're trying to detect the possible things that could go wrong and how they'll affect you. Once you know what you're dealing with, you can then manage those risks to reduce or remove their potential impact.

Managing risks is a process of identifying, assessing, and dealing with possible threats. If this sounds difficult, don't worry. As we saw in Chapter 6, you'll often find that people are aware of the problems that could affect them. Some of these may be unique to a person or business, while others are common to almost everyone.

Assessing risks

Using the knowledge of people in your organization, you can assess the risks by following several basic steps:

1. *Identification*, where you determine what potential threats you may be faced with.
2. *Evaluation*, where you look at the potential threats and determine their impact and the likelihood of them happening.

3. *Mitigation*, where you document and implement ways to minimize or remove a potential threat.
4. *Monitor*, where you examine whether a risk has become an actual problem or if the steps you've taken are working.

It's important that you don't make your risk assessment more complicated than it needs to be. You're looking at where problems might be, how they'll affect you, and how to deal with them. In identifying these potential hazards, you'll need to determine which are more serious than others and which are more likely to happen than others. This will help you to prioritize one item over another.

To give a basic illustration of how the process works, let's look at a simple situation of buying a box of cookies. I might identify a *risk* of my kids eating them all. They're kids, so the *likelihood* is pretty high. The *severity* of doing this would be low, as they're cheap and we could buy more. Now, remember that there is a cause and effect relationship between risk and impact. Therefore, the *impact* might be getting cavities, weight gain, and the cost of replacing them. To *mitigate* the problem, I might put the box on a high shelf that they can't reach. We could then *monitor* the situation and see if it's working (the box is full), the risk has occurred (the box is empty), or if changes need to be made (hiding them elsewhere).

When you create a list of risks and their related impact, you'll want to prioritize them and handle the most serious ones first. Some problems are more likely to happen than others, with them being remote, occasional, or probable. In Table 8.1, we've listed our risks and ranked the likelihood of each with a number, ranging from 1 to 3 (with 1 being a remote chance of happening and 3 being probable). Some problems can also have a more severe impact than others. In Table 8.1, we've rated this from 1 to 5, with 1 being negligible and 5 being catastrophic. Now that we have these

Table 8.1 Example of Risk Assessment

Risk	Impact	Probability	Severity	Avoidance/Contingency
Social media person uses wrong account	Public embarrassment Inaccurate information sent	1	2	Limit access to account Require people to fully log off the Twitter account after using it
Virus\Malware	Damaged data Security compromised Embarrassment of spreading virus to others	2	3	Install antivirus and anti-malware software Ensure that antivirus signatures are up to date

numbers, let's use a calculation of Risk = Probability × Severity. If we multiply the value in the probability column by the one in the severity column, we can immediately see that risks with the highest numbers need to be addressed first and foremost.

If the risk actually happens, then it can influence a number of aspects to your business and\or personal life. Since situations can change, risk management is an ongoing process, so you should review your strategy on a recurring basis. If there are changes, you would update your assessment and implement new ways of dealing with potential threats. By being prepared and creating strategies to avoid problems or contingency plans to deal with them, you'll be better equipped to handle situations as they arise.

Sources of risk revisited

While individuals and businesses will encounter risks unique to them, there are a number of common ones that we discuss throughout this book. In 2010, the Information Technology association ISACA (www.isaca.org) identified the top five potential risks for social media as:

1. *Viruses/malware*, which we'll discuss later in this chapter
2. *Brand hijacking*, which we'll discuss in Chapter 10
3. *Lack of control over content*
4. *Unrealistic customer expectations of "Internet-speed" service*
5. *Noncompliance with record management regulations*, which we discussed in Chapter 6.

One of the biggest risks that companies identify is the lack of control they have over content. Unlike traditional media that's one-sided and professionally created, social media content is informal, conversational, and user generated. Even when the information is representative of the company, comments from others can quickly veer the conversation in another direction. This doesn't mean that you don't have any control, just that you need to assert it in different ways.

While loss of control can be expected, you can influence conversations and redirect them back to the original point of your post. As with a verbal conversation, as people begin talking about something completely different from an original topic, you can circle them back to the original conversation by mentioning a key point of what you wanted to discuss. As we'll discuss in this chapter, monitoring and engaging people in conversations can have a dramatic effect on catching problems early and influencing the discussion. As we'll discuss in Chapter 10, you can also use the alternative approach of moderating conversations, publishing posts that have been vetted, and/or turning off the feature to add comments.

Policies and training on proper use of social media can go a long way in preventing employees from posting content that embarrasses or misrepresents the company. As employees learn the dos and don'ts of social media, they'll understand what is expected of them, and how inappropriate content posted to their own accounts or those of the company can affect their job and the public perception of the business.

When a business looks at making social media accessible on company computers, there is always a risk of employees excessively using social media during work hours. Management will say the impact of this risk is a loss of productivity. After all, if a person is tweeting about their day and watching YouTube videos that aren't educational, research or otherwise job-related, they're not getting work done. A similar fear was seen over a decade ago when businesses considered giving employees access to the Internet. The fear that surfing the Web would sink the business was unjustified, and companies implemented policies, firewall restrictions, content filters, and other controls to monitor and restrict how employees conducted themselves online. By applying similar policies and controls, you can mitigate problems related to accessing social media sites.

The IT department will see a different impact to excessive use of social media. The large amounts of data streamed from a content community may cause network utilization issues, causing employees to find the corporate network slow. In some cases, the internal network infrastructure or Internet connectivity may be out of date and unable to handle the bandwidth used by accessing video or other significant downloads. Many organizations have had to increase their Internet bandwidth to accommodate the use of social media. However, even if the infrastructure can normally handle the network traffic, it may be adversely affected during peak hours of usage. To address such issues, the IT department could restrict access to sites like YouTube so they are only accessible during low periods of network use or create a secondary network that off-loads such traffic from the corporate network. Since a cardinal rule of network security is to only give people the access that they need to do their job, you could also restrict access to content communities. In doing so, people would need to specifically request network access or use personal devices that are off of the corporate network.

Not implementing social media might seem like a solution to these risks, but avoiding it is a risk in itself. By not engaging in social media, you're avoiding the possible benefits. You've removed an opportunity to reach new and existing customers, prevented employees from interacting or collaborating with other professionals, and given your competition a clear competitive advantage. Sticking your head in the sand and hoping social media will go away isn't an option. Those who never face risk, never benefit from its possible rewards.

Laws and regulations

It's easy to break the rules if you're unaware of them. In using social media for business purposes, it's always wise to check with a lawyer to ensure you understand the laws and regulations that apply to your company. As we'll see in the sections that follow, there are many laws and regulations that apply to specific industries and may be unique to your type of business.

It's important to realize that the content you post and your online behavior can also make you vulnerable to criminal charges or civil litigation. While a full discussion of existing legislation and the legal implications of social media is outside the scope of this book, in the sections that follow, we'll discuss a number of rules and laws that are commonly violated through social media use.

Privacy policies and terms of service

Social media sites have rules that should be reviewed prior to deciding to setting up an account and periodically reviewed afterward to identify any changes. The *Terms of Service* outlines the limitations and conditions of using the site. In using the site, you're consenting to those rules, so you should read them to know what you're agreeing to. You should also determine whether the terms of a social media site are contrary to the terms used on your company's Web site. If you link to a social media presence from your site, you should indicate in the Terms of Service on your site that your company is not responsible for terms and conditions applicable to third-party sites.

Social media sites will also provide a Privacy Policy, which outlines how personal information is handled by the site and any restrictions placed on you when capturing data from other users. As we'll discuss in Chapter 9, a developer might create an app and make it available through the site, which will access information on a user's account. Because of this, apps available on a site may also have their own privacy policies that should be reviewed. Infringing on a privacy policy may result in the site closing your account and could also violate privacy laws. As we'll discuss in the sections that follow, there is government legislation protecting the privacy of people online, and companies can be penalized for violating them.

Sarbanes–Oxley act

In response to the financial scandals involving Enron, WorldCom, and other companies, the Sarbanes–Oxley Act (SOX) was enacted in 2002 to protect shareholders and the public from fraudulent business practices. It regulates financial disclosures from corporations and prevents fraudulent accounting and ensures the validity of records. The Act applies to all public companies in the United States, any company (foreign or domestic) that has registered equity or debt with the Security and Exchange Commission, and accounting firms that provide auditing services for them. Noncompliance with SOX can result in fines, imprisonment, or both.

Section 409 of SOX requires companies to disclose material changes in their financial conditions and operations and keep this information up to date. While companies regulated under the act are required to communicate the information through traditional disclosure mechanisms, many have made use of social media sites to disseminate financial statements. In doing so, they need to ensure that they reflect current and updated information is published to these sites and monitor them to ensure compliance with legislation.

The SOX also defines what records are to be stored, and for how long they're to be available. Such regulations can have a dramatic effect on the retention and archiving of data. As we'll discuss in Chapter 9, it's important that records retention policies also address information posted on social media. Because documents are documents regardless of whether they're digital, it's important to archive social media content in case there are questions of whether your company has violated SOX or other regulations.

Health insurance portability and accountability act

The Health Insurance Portability and Accountability Act (HIPAA) of 1996 is a legislation that (among other things) provides privacy protection for health care information. The act outlines the policies and procedures for keeping a patient's identifiable information secure, inclusive to any data that is in an electronic format, and sets penalties for any violations.

Under HIPAA, health care providers, insurance companies, and other individuals and organizations that have access to your health care information can't disclose protected information. The status of your health, health care provisions, and payments are all protected information that is linked to a person and could identify them.

The right to privacy isn't limited to adults. The act also extends the right to privacy to younger people, aged 12–18. However, there are exceptions. If a child was suspected of being abused, then the health care provider is required to notify child welfare services and release the relevant medical history to the agency.

Social media provides a new way for information to be disclosed, and there have been numerous violations throughout the world of health care providers infringing on a patient's right to privacy. If you work in health care, commenting on a patient's social networking site that they have an appointment or making a post about a difficult patient you had that day could put you in hot water. In some cases, privacy infringements have been more blatant. In 2010, a 60-year-old man was brought into St. Mary Medical Center in Long Beach, California, after being brutally stabbed multiple times. Nurses and other staff at the hospital took pictures of the man and posted the images on Facebook, leading to three staff members being disciplined and four being fired.

HIPAA also provides clear guidelines on how digital information is handled through information systems. For example, any data that's sent over an open network needs to be encrypted, and systems that store the data must be protected from intrusion. Even though you'd expect any site to try and prevent intrusion, public sites would not have the same level of protection as closed networks. The messages you post or send to mailboxes on social networking sites would not be encrypted, as many social media sites don't even use HTTPS for secure communication, although this is improving.

Fair information practice principles

The United States Federal Trade Commission created a set of guidelines related to privacy protection called Fair Information Practice Principles (FIPs). FIPs isn't an enforceable piece of legislation but has served as the basis for other laws and regulations. There are five core principles designed to protect consumers when personal information is collected and used:

1. *Notice/Awareness*, which relates to being informed prior to personal information being collected. The person is notified who is collecting data, how it's collected, how it will be used, potential recipients of it, and steps taken to ensure confidentiality, integrity, and quality of the data.
2. *Choice/Consent*, which provides consumers with a choice of how the information may be used or the ability to opt-in or opt-out of data collection.
3. *Access/Participation*, which allows consumers to review any data collected on them, so they can verify or contest its accuracy or completeness.
4. *Integrity/Security*, which states that data must be accurate and secure.
5. *Enforcement/Redress*, which addresses the fact that policies of collecting and using data must have some form of enforcement or redress to ensure it's followed. This may be through self-regulation, private remedies, or government enforcement.

Payment card industry data security standard

The *Payment Card Industry Data Security Standard* (PCI DSS) addresses the protection of debit, credit, and cash card transactions, and the personal information of cardholders. It is a widely accepted set of policies and procedures that applies to any company that processes, stores, or transmits card information. In other words, it applies to any business that accepts payment with a credit card/debit card, which is any merchant that has a Merchant ID (MID), and ensures that any data related to the card, cardholder, and transactions is transmitted and maintained in a secure environment. In complying with PCI DSS. the sensitive information that's handled by payment processors and merchants is secure, and information related to their payments and purchases is protected.

Payment Card Industry Security Standards Council (PCI SSC) was created in 2006 by MasterCard, Visa, American Express, Discover, and JCB as an independent body to manage the standards and improve the security of account transactions. In doing so, it sets the standards and improves on them, so that the disclosure of information about credit cards and cardholders is regulated. The council does not enforce the standards, as this is the responsibility of the payment brands.

In relation to social media, PCI DSS provides protection on any purchases you make online. It also protects you from your credit card information or information about you as a cardholder appearing on sites or being available as a public download. The unauthorized release of such information could result in a business paying higher processing fees, receiving fines or penalties, and possibly reimbursing a cardholder for damages related to the breach of information.

Digital millennium copyright act

The Digital Millennium Copyright Act (DMCA) is an American copyright law that protects the ownership of digital information. Through it, any images, video, music, or other digital media that you create or own can't be shared or sold in ways you indicated it not be used, or that prevent you from making intended profits. If you were to reproduce, distribute, publicly display, or have a public performance of copyright material, it would be a violation of Federal law. This protects the person who created or owns the work from unauthorized copies being made, distributed, or sold without their consent.

DMCA has a significant impact on a variety of areas related to social media. In creating a blog or maintaining a page, adding photos or other content that was protected by copyright would be a violation of the act. As we'll discuss in a later section, using the intellectual property of another person or company without permission means that they can't profit from the work they did. You've taken their product, used a professional service they provide, but didn't pay for it. Since this is stealing, you don't want to add any professional content that you haven't created yourself on a page, or you could face serious penalties and/or litigation.

Through this Act, any photos, video, or other data you create are protected. This prevents online marketers, competitors, or other parties with access to your data from using your material if they haven't obtained permission. The Act also provides protection from others who publish pictures or video of you, or digital media in which you own the rights to. Under Section 512, it is illegal to post an unsolicited photo of you without your consent. If you found a site was hosting an image of you, you can submit a take-down notice, which requires them to remove the photo. If they don't, they could be liable for infringement.

Removing content from Google

An example of how you can use the take-down procedure to remove your copyright material from sites is Google's tool at www.google.com/dmca.html. Visiting this page, you're provided with a list of products, including Blogger, Google+, Web Search, Picasa, and others. After selecting the product containing content you believe violates applicable laws, you then specify why it should be removed. There are numerous laws that could be violated and justify the removal of content, which makes the tool useful for numerous purposes. For example, you might identify child pornography, information that reveals personal information, or violates laws and/or your rights in other ways. If you were to specify Image Search, an option appears to have it removed because it may violate your copyright.

Intellectual property and trademark infringement

Intellectual property is a creative product that is owned by an individual, group, or organization. It can include such things as trademarks, designs, or copyright material, as in the case of written works, movies, music, or other works. Because of person's livelihood or a company's profits may depend on the revenue generated from such property, it's important that their property is protected and not used without authorization or proper license.

Social media causes unique problems for organizations. Since the content isn't professionally created, issues like adhering to copyright or trademark restrictions may be overlooked. Consider a person who copies and pastes a poem or short story on his or her blog, or someone who uses a photo taken by a professional photographer. The artist has not only lost money that comes from selling his or her work, but others may now consider it as public domain and take and share the content further. Because the content has been used without permission, this can leave the organization vulnerable to lawsuits.

The issues of intellectual property rights and trademark infringement can also take the form of counterfeit products being sold online. According to the 2012 Internet Crime Report, the FBI received 56 complaints from people who purchased thought they were buying designer merchandise from Jeannine Buford through an online auction. While some paid and failed to receive their orders, others got counterfeit products. In total, people had lost $145,333. As a result of the crime, Buford was sentenced to 57 months in federal prison, had to pay $225,500 in restitution, and forfeited the contents of her bank account, 2011 Camaro, and other items. As you can see from this, sometimes crime not only doesn't pay, it can cost you much more than you earned.

Counterfeit products consist of almost any good you can think of, including watches, jewelry, clothes, CDs, DVDs, software, and even cigarettes. While you'll find them sold almost anywhere, a 2013 report by the United Nations Office on Drugs and Crime (UNODC) stated how prevalent it is for them to be sold and sought out by consumers online. The UNODC also reported that according to the World Customs Organization, between 2008 and 2010, approximately 75% of the counterfeit goods seized worldwide were manufactured in East Asia, with most of it coming from China. Despite the financial losses to genuine manufacturers, cost to taxpayers in losses of duty and sales taxes, and potential health risks of buying counterfeit products, it continues to be big business. In 2010, an estimated $24.4 billion worth of counterfeit goods from East Asia were sold to the United States and European Union.

Discrimination

As we saw in Chapter 3, discrimination is a serious concern in social media. If a potential employer viewed information about a candidate on a social networking site, they might see the person's photo or personal information. From this, they could determine the person's age, race, religious beliefs, and possible disabilities. If an employer reviewed the photos, likes, or posts of an employee who's considered for a promotion, it's possible they might ascertain the person's sexual orientation or other information they were previously unaware of. In each of these cases, they would see identifiable aspects that are protected by legislation. By not offering the candidate a job, an argument could be made that the company discriminated against the employee.

Discrimination can also occur in workplaces between employees. An employee may add coworkers as friends or make a post that reveals a protected characteristic, resulting in the person being excluded or treated unfairly. The coworkers may even discriminate against the employee through social media, such as by creating an event on Facebook and inviting other employees, but excluding that one person. As we'll see in Chapter 9 when we discuss policies, such discrimination can result in the company being vulnerable to a civil lawsuit or may be part of a larger pattern of workplace harassment.

Defamation

Defamation is the act of making false accusations or misrepresenting someone in a malicious way. It can occur through *slander*, which is a spoken statement, or through *libel* where a person is defamed in a permanent record. In terms of social media, such records can include posts, email or direct messages, tweets, or videos and images that are uploaded to a site. False or malicious comments can cause serious damage to your reputation, causing embarrassment or financial loss.

Defamation isn't limited to individuals, and many businesses have suffered from statements that have made them infamous on the Internet. Clay Nissan, a car dealership in Massachusetts, had the misfortune of experiencing this in 2013. In 2012, Jill Colter was fired for inappropriate interactions with employees and customers. Her brothers Adam and Jonathon started a social media campaign, rallying people to boycott the company, and claiming that she was fired because she had cancer. They also claimed that other employees had been fired for having cancer, and that the company had a policy of discriminating against cancer patients. Their Facebook called "Boycott Clay Nissan" had 30,000 followers by August 2012, and the company suffered significant losses from loss of business. After suing the brothers, the court awarded Clay $700,000 in damages.

Harassment

As we saw in Chapter 7, issues dealing with harassment should be a serious concern when using social media. *Harassment* is a behavior or a conduct that annoys, threatens, intimidates, or makes a person fearful of their safety. The person is demeaned and may be the target of derogatory comments or representations that allude to the victim's race, color, gender, religion, or other aspects of who they are. Due to the seriousness of the crime, states and countries have created laws to protect victims, making it enforced through civil litigation and/or criminal penalties.

Even if you weren't the one who initially set out to harass someone, you could still be held responsible. In 2013, Jennifer Pawluck posted an Instagram photo of graffiti depicting a local police officer named Ian Lafreniere with a bullet hole in his head. Even though she didn't create the graffiti, taking a photo of it and posting it online was enough for her to be charged with criminal harassment and intimidation. Posting or sharing content that promotes violent or unlawful action against someone could be seen as endorsement of a threat.

You should always be careful about sharing or posting content that demeans or could make a person fearful. If you wouldn't want to be the focal point of such attention, then don't do it to someone else. This not only applies to personal use of social media but also in the workplace where you may find people being bullied or sexually harassed. As we'll discuss in Chapter 9, even the harasser's conduct doesn't result in criminal harassment charges, an organization should have policies in place to deal with such problems and help employees who are victimized.

Insurance

Mistakes in social media can be expensive. Courtney Love discovered this in 2011, when she had to pay a reported $430,000 plus interest for comments made on Twitter and MySpace. After hiring designer Dawn Simorangkir to create a number of outfits, the business relationship went sour, and the singer began a rant of tweets and posts in March 2009. According to court documents, one of Love's tweets stated "Austin police are more than ecstatic to pick her up she has a history of dealing cocaine, lost all custody of her child, assault and burglary," while others accused her of prostitution and other activities that attacked Simorangkir's reputation and negatively affected her business.

As you can see from this, the content you post can expose you to possible lawsuits and result in paying excessive legal fees and settlements. While you might think that making a tweet or updating a blog is different from a journalist publishing an article, you can still be held to the same level of accountability. Publishing content on social media can expose you to copyright infringement, plagiarism, libel, and other possible liabilities.

To protect yourself, you should contact your insurance provider to make sure that any existing liability insurance is enough to cover possible lawsuits and covers publishing social media content. Companies should have adequate liability insurance, and any employee using social media as part of his or her job should be covered for any issues under the employer's insurance policies. For personal use, you should check with your agent to see if potential lawsuits resulting from social media use is covered under Personal Injury coverage under your existing home or rental insurance.

Forensics

Forensics is a term used to describe the process of using techniques and tools to gather evidence for civil and criminal trials. *Digital forensics* is specific to the identification, preservation, recovery, and examination of evidence, in relation to digital media, such as computers, mobile devices, networks, and other sources. Once the data has been analyzed, it may then be presented in court, tribunals, trials, or other forums as evidence.

When you've heard of forensics, it's probably been in association with criminal cases. For example, in the years I worked as a computer forensic analyst, I examined computers involved in cases related to homicides, child pornography,

Internet luring, and other crimes. The information gathered from machines might be used to identify individuals involved in a crime and/or presented as evidence in court. However, corporations also use digital forensics to analyze computers and mobile devices for internal issues, such as policy violations, disciplinary matters, or to support accusations by other employees. At times, the information discovered on a machine may uncover illegal activities, requiring further investigation by law enforcement.

When you use a computer or mobile device, traces of your activities are stored on the machine and external systems like the servers you connect to. Looking at a browser's history, temporary files, logs, and files saved to the hard disk or other storage media can help create a timeline of what was done and who you interacted with. Looking at the various sources of information, you're able to establish a person's online behavior and gather evidence of their activities.

Digital data may be acquired from numerous sources, including hard disks, external storage, networks, and backups. Because passwords may be saved in a browser, forensic software products are used to view them, enabling an investigator to retrieve information needed to access the sites you visit. As we'll see in the section that follows, there are also tools for extracting evidence from mobile devices, inclusive of any apps and files saved on the device.

Digital forensic software

If you go on the Internet, you'll find a number of security tools that allow you to recover data from a computer or mobile device. However, if the data was recovered using a hacking tool or some program that could modify the time stamp of files or other data, it might not be admissible in court. While that might not seem important when you first use such tools, you never know what you might find, and whether it could lead to testifying about the evidence in court. Because of that, it's always best to use proven digital forensic tools whenever possible.

SANS Investigative Forensic Toolkit (SIFT) is a free VMWare appliance that can run in VMWare Player and comes with preconfigured forensic tools. The SIFT workstation can be downloaded from http://computer-forensics.sans.org/community/downloads. Because the tools are open source and frequently updated, it provides an excellent platform for learning and performing forensic investigations.

While there are many security and forensic tools that can be used to analyze information on various systems, not all of them are available to the public. EnCase and Cellebrite's forensic software and tools are examples of this. Both are widely used by law enforcement and military but only available to approved corporations.

EnCase is a suite of products from Guidance Software (www.guidancesoftware.com) that's used for performing computer forensics. It copies data by creating an exact, bit-for-bit copy of the drive. By having the bitstream image saved as a file, it can be stored and analyzed later using a user-friendly graphical user interface. By saving an image of the drive, you analyze the copied information in the file, rather than data on the actual machine. This prevents time stamps and other information on the computer from accidentally being modified.

Celebrite's (www.cellebrite.com) Universal Forensic Extraction Device system is used to perform digital forensics on mobile devices. The series of products allow you to perform a bit-for-bit extraction of data and do an in-depth analysis of mobile devices, inclusive to phones, tablets, GPS devices, and more. The solutions not only allow you to view easily accessible information on a device but can also break codes, acquire data from flash memory, extract hidden and deleted information, and decipher encrypted data. You can view a person's contacts, call logs, messages, saved files, trip logs, and any other data stored on the device.

As we discussed in Chapter 6, mobile devices can be remotely wiped or locked. To prevent this from happening before evidence can be acquired, it's important to turn it off as soon as you get it. If you contacted police or a forensic investigator, they would put the phone, tablet, or other device into a Faraday bag or Faraday cage. The Faraday bag or cage is made from a material that prevents the device from receiving a signal from the phone plan carrier or connecting to a Wi-Fi. Since the device is cut off from the Internet and service provider, it never receives any messages to wipe or lock the device.

Whenever you're using or analyzing a computer for your business or personal use, if you discover anything you feel is illegal, it's important to stop what you're doing and contact police. Continuing to examine the machine could easily modify data on the computer or device and possibly alter evidence. You should also document any steps you've taken prior to contacting police and give it to them as soon as possible. Your documentation may be used as evidence or part as your statement. It's also incredibly useful for future reference in case you need to testify.

Don't delete messages

Even though forensic software can recover deleted data, that doesn't mean it's an open invitation to erase it. While you might be tempted to remove threatening or upsetting messages, you should never delete them, as they may be used as evidence. Even if you print out a copy of the messages the person has sent, keeping the original digital message is important. An email contains message headers or MIME (Multipurpose Internet Mail Extensions) information, which will show the path an email took crossing mail servers, IP addresses, and other valuable data. Using this will trace the email back to the original sender. The email headers will often be hidden but becomes visible when configured to do so. For example, on Gmail, you would view the message headers by doing the following:

1. Open the message, and (at the top of the message pane) click on the down arrow next to Reply.
2. When the menu appears, click *Show Original*.

Using information in the email, you can identify where it originated. In looking at the information in the headers, you'll see a line beginning with "Received: from" followed by a series of numbers between square brackets. These numbers are an IP address that identifies the computer that the message originated from. For example, the line may look similar to the following:

Received: from exprod8mx241.postini.com ([64.18.3.141] helo = psmtp.com)

Once you have this information, you can then use a number of different tools to acquire information about the sender, which could include the person's approximate geographic location and the email service or Internet Service Provider (ISP) used to send the email.

Reverse lookups

Once you have the IP address, you can then use tools like ARIN WHOIS IP Address Database Search (www.itools.com/tool/arin-whois-domain-search) to do a reverse lookup. Using this tool to search for the IP address we previously gave as an example, you'll see that the email originated from Postini, which is an email security and archiving service owned by Google. In other searches, you'll often get the ISP of the person who sent the email. In addition to seeing who the IP address is registered to, you're also provided with their address, country, and other contact information. Using this, law enforcement could contact the company to obtain the account information of the person who sent the email, which could include such details as the person's real name, address, phone number, and other details.

Finding the approximate geographic location

Tools like the Visual Trace Route Tool at www.yougetsignal.com/tools/visual-tracert/ allow you to see the approximate location of where a person is located. After entering the IP address into the search field, you're provided with a graphic display, showing a map of the route that data traveled between your IP address and the one you entered. If you entered the IP address of a person who sent you an email, you're given the approximate geographic location of the sender. While the person's ISP might be in a nearby larger city, it will provide an indicator of the area they're in, inclusive of the possible city, state, and country where they reside.

Using Facebook

Facebook allows you to search for people using an email address. Using the email address of the person who sent you a message, you can search Facebook accounts and see if the email is associated with anyone. If you get results, you can then look at the person's profile photo and other public information on the account.

Acquiring information from social media sites

When investigations involve social media, the sites will try and accommodate law enforcement requests. Police can (and do) make requests to sites asking for account information, log files, and details about specific posts, tweets, and messages. The evidence through these requests can be crucial to tracing a post or message to the person who wrote it and acquiring supporting personal information about a suspect.

To protect users, requests need to be in accordance with American law, inclusive to the Stored Communications Act, 18 U.S.C. Sections 2701-2712, where a valid subpoena, court order, and/or search warrant is provided asking for the user's records to be disclosed. For International requests, the officer requesting the person's account records needs to make an international Mutual Legal Assistance Treaty request. This helps to prove that the request is coming from a law enforcement agency and is not an arbitrary attempt to see personal information about a user of the site.

When a request is made, police need to be as specific as possible. The site needs to know the account you're trying to get information about, specific posts or tweets you're trying to gather facts about, dates and times, and any additional details you can provide. The facts provided help to isolate the information you've requested.

When a request is made to preserve evidence, sites will do so for a limited time. For example, Facebook will try and preserve the account information for 90 days from the time the request was made. Doing so allows an investigation to take place without any of the information being modified or deleted. Facebook online requests by law enforcement can be made at www.facebook.com/records, while requests to preserve account information on Twitter can be made at https://support.twitter.com/forms/lawenforcement.

Police use of social media

Law enforcement has been using social media in a variety of ways for years. Police will post information on missing or wanted individuals, press releases, and other information online in the hopes of gaining additional information. Does it work? According to a 2012 survey by the International Association of Chiefs of Police (IACP), 74% of law enforcement agencies surveyed found that social media has helped solve crimes in their jurisdiction. As a tool, it's proven to be extremely beneficial in investigations, sharing information, and providing assistance to the public.

According to the 2012 IACP survey, 94% of agencies use social media, with 61.7% using it to gather intelligence and 77.1% using it for investigations. The ways social media may be used in an investigation include:

- Reviewing the social media profiles and activities of suspects (86.3%)
- Reviewing the social media profiles and activities of victims (49.4%)
- Using a fake profile or undercover identity to monitor someone or gather information (53.3%)

Being that police most commonly use social media for investigations, whether you're a victim or suspect, you need to seriously consider that your social media presence could be examined or monitored by law enforcement. Information found online can reveal a lot about a person and can incriminate you. The posts and tweets you make could be used to establish your character, invalidate testimony, or be used as circumstantial evidence in a trial.

Incriminating yourself

There are many instances where people incriminate themselves on social media sites without thinking. Controversial comments, compromising photos, or any number of posts or tweets could be used against you as evidence in a criminal or civil trial. Before admitting to anything online, think before you post.

In some cases, the content people post online provide everything that's needed for an arrest. In 2012, 19-year-old Hannah Sabata sent a text message to her ex-boyfriend about how she had robbed a bank, along with a link to the 7-minute video called "Chick Bank Robber" that she posted on YouTube. On the video, she brags about stealing a car, shows the drugs in her possession, and flashes a wad of cash she stole from the Cornerstone Bank in Waco, Nebraska. By the time the former boyfriend called police about it, people had already informed police about the video. In June 2013, she was sentenced to 10–20 years in prison.

Even if you're not posting facts about crimes you've committed, being friends with a suspect would show you're associated with that person. The Facebook friends of gang members, drug dealers or users, terrorists, or other criminals can be used to identify their associates, who might be involved in crimes or a criminal enterprise. After all, social media is extremely useful in showing connections between people.

In 2012, New York Police Officer Michael Rodrigues went on Facebook and friended several members of the Brower Boys gang. Using their posts, he was able to identify gang members, track their movements based on what they said, and set up surveillance to arrest them. Members of the gang even posted pictures of their crimes, providing more evidence. Ultimately, 14 members of the gang were arrested.

Defending yourself online

While you have the right to remain silent, it doesn't happen too often on social networking sites. On July 10, 2013, Matthew Oliver saw his photo on Facebook page of the Pasco County Sheriff's Office (www.facebook.com/pascosheriff). The page featured him as their "Fugitive of the Day," which inspired hundreds of comments, including ones from Oliver himself. Rather than turning himself in or calling a lawyer, he began commenting on his own wanted bulletin and used it as a forum to argue his innocence. Obviously, the conversation that was generated didn't always go his way, and he was soon responding to off-topic remarks about the size of his ears, and how he was grinning in the wanted photo. Despite the ongoing dialog of that day, he failed to win over the police and was arrested 2 days later.

While it may be tempting to argue your case online, it's not wise to do so if it's related to an ongoing or upcoming trial. A lighthearted quip to a fellow poster could make you seem unremorseful, while kvetching about the police could make you appear as though you have a problem with authority or disregard of the law. If it's a legal issue, let the lawyers handle it.

Outdated content

Since news can become outdated quickly, you need to be discerning when it comes to crime-related content. As we discussed in Chapter 5, there have been many instances where a person goes missing, and an email or a post on a social networking site asks for help finding them. In many cases, the requests continue to circulate long after the person's found. The same can apply to bulletins about a wanted person. Even though a person is no longer a fugitive or wanted for questioning, the initial post still indicates a person is wanted and can be shared long afterward.

The problems aren't difficult to imagine. If you were identified as a suspect on a social networking site, turned yourself in and/or later found innocent, you would no longer be a wanted person. An employer or clients could still see a post stating you were a fugitive, people might continue writing posts that defamed you, or someone might try to be a hero and restrain you until the police were called. Such incidents could injure you or your livelihood, and all have the markings of a potential lawsuits.

The way that information is updated on a social networking site can be a legitimate problem. On Facebook, you can delete or hide a post but not edit it. Posting a comment under the post to update people isn't enough, as it can be buried in countless other comments. If you're the subject of outdated information, you can request police to remove it from the site. However, while this takes care of the original source, you may still experience problems from it appearing on other people's pages, where they've shared or reposted it. If you're reading such posts, it's important to verify that the information's valid by searching online and visiting the police department's official Web site.

Direct use of social media to solve crimes

In 2011, the Vancouver Police used social media during and after the riots that broke out during the final game of the Stanley Cup. On June 15, 2011, it's estimated that over 100,000 people were gathering in downtown Vancouver, watching the hockey game on large screens that had been set up. In the final minutes of the game, fights broke out, bottles were thrown, and escalated to cars being lit on fire or flipped over. Over 100 people were treated at hospital for injuries, and there were millions of dollars in property damage. Police used Twitter to disseminate information to the public, including transportation routes people could use to leave the area.

While the riot was in progress, people began a campaign to identify and shame rioters, posting photos and video on Web sites, blogs, Twitter, and Facebook. It resulted in people who were identified as being harassed, and in one case a rioter's family was threatened. People were fired from their jobs, and even their employers experienced backlash from their employee's involvement. As a result of the shaming, 34 people turned themselves into police between June 15 and July 20.

The police and public interactions through social media were staggering. The tweets made by police were retweeted an estimated 75 times, extending the information to a wider audience. There were so many people linking to their press releases from Twitter that the server crashed. During the riot, the Vancouver Police provided instructions on how to submit photos and video as evidence, so that people involved could be identified. Police also encouraged members of the public to tag any photos of people they knew, which assisted law enforcement in the investigation that followed. According to the 2011 Stanley Cup Riot Review prepared by the Vancouver Police, within 5 days of the riot, they had received 4300 email tips, 15,000 images, and 1500 hours of video from the public.

Malware, viruses, and exploit distribution

There are many kinds of programming-related problems that can affect your computer, network, and data. You may be the victim of an attack that takes advantage of bugs in the software you're using, or install a malicious program by opening a file you've received, or being tricked into installing it when visiting a Web site or clicking a link. As we'll see in this section, there are many different kinds of computer security threats that you'll come across using the Internet, which can be combatted using specialized software.

Malicious code (or *malcode*) or malicious software (also called *malware*) are terms for code that's been created to cause damage to your data, bog down networks, steal important information, or cause other problems. There are many different classes of malicious software, including viruses, Trojans, worms, and bots.

Viruses are programs that will insert a copy of itself into another executable, so that it spreads from file-to-file, computer-to-computer. Generally, viruses attach themselves to executable files on your system. The program a virus attaches to may run as expected, hiding the fact that it's infected. Once the virus is activated, it may do any number of things, including damaging data, using up memory, and/or cause the computer not to respond to requests from other machines in a denial of service (DoS) attack.

Trojans are programs that may provide a legitimate function, or at least appear to, but contains harmful code that is designed to perform a malicious action. Unlike viruses, Trojans don't self-replicate or infect other files. Just as the Greeks discovered when they received the Trojan horse, it needs to be opened for the attack to begin. You might open an email attachment or download a program from the Internet believing it's not harmful, and it may not initially appear to be. Even if you haven't opened any file attachments, simply receiving the email and viewing its contents in your email client can be enough to activate it. Once activated, the Trojan may annoy you with pop-ups, download additional malware, delete files, or transmit data to an attacker. It might also exploit vulnerabilities on your computer, providing a backdoor for hackers to access your system.

Worms are stand-alone programs that replicate by making copies of itself, which may spread through networks and/or vulnerabilities on a system. While a worm will often damage the files on a system, by corrupting or deleting data, this isn't always the case. Because the worm replicates across a network, the increased network traffic eats up bandwidth, slowing down the network.

Bots are another type of malicious program, getting their name from the word "robot." They self-propagate on a system and communicate with a centralized server. The server(s) act as command-and-control (C&C) center that transmits, instructs, and/or receives data from the bots that have infected computers.

The attacker can have remote control over the bots and instruct it to flood a particular server with requests, causing legitimate requests to be denied (i.e., a DoS attack) and even crash the server. The bots may log keystrokes and obtain information like passwords or financial data and send it back to the C&C.

Scareware/ransomware

Malicious software isn't only used to damage data and devices. There is malware designed to extort money, get people to provide credit card information, or buy bogus products. A common scam involves *scareware*, which is malware that scares you into believing your computer is infected with a serious virus. A pop-up may appear on your screen saying that you've been infected and won't allow you to close the screen. It will say you need to click on the button to buy antivirus software, which is actually a fake product. In clicking the link, you may be asked to provide credit card information, or malicious code will be installed on your machine.

A variation of scareware scams involves phoning you, where a person claims to be from a trusted company like Microsoft Support. The person will tell you that they've identified a virus on your computer and try to get you to purchase bogus antivirus software. You may be directed to visit a Web site, where malicious code runs and infects your computer. The software installed may give the cybercriminal remote access to your machine.

Ransomware is similar to this but will lock you out of your computer until you pay to have malware removed. When the malware is installed, it may overwrite explorer.exe, write information to the Windows Registry, or other data needed by your operating system. One type of worm is called Citidel ransomware, which installs malicious software called Reveton. Whenever the computer loads, an imposing warning appears on the screen that appears to be from the FBI or other law enforcement, telling you how you've violated federal laws. It may even state that you've visited child pornography sites or may take over your webcam to give the illusion that you're being recorded. To unlock the computer, it gives instructions on how to pay a fine using a prepaid money card.

Removing these threats can be difficult, but you should never follow the instructions they give. Instead, use another computer to visit a legitimate antivirus or anti-malware site and find the steps required to remove the malware. In some cases, running anti-malware software like *Malwarebytes* (www.malwarebytes.org) may be able to remove the scareware or ransomware. If you can open *System Restore* on a Windows computer, you can also try restoring it to a previous state, before it was infected. To use System Restore on a Windows machine, do the following:

1. Click on the *Start* menu.
2. Click *Control Panel.*
3. Click *System and Security.*
4. In the Action Center section, click *Restore your computer to an earlier time.*
5. Click the *Open System Restore* button.

6. When the wizard opens, click *Next*.
7. Select a restore point from the list, and click *Next*.
8. Click *Finish*.

Baiting

One method of infecting a person with malware is associated with social engineering. *Baiting* is a technique in which a CD-R, DVD-R, USB flash drive, or some other storage media is left in a location, in the hopes someone to use it on their machine. For example, I might leave a CD labeled with something intriguing like "employee salaries" by the entrance to your business, and you might pick it up and decide to see what information is on it. When you opened a file on the disk, malicious software would then be installed on your machine. If the computer was set to auto-run programs as soon as storage media is inserted, your computer would be infected after you inserted it in the CD/DVD-ROM. For social engineering, a Trojan might be used to send information on your computer to an Internet site or it might download additional viruses or exploits to your machine.

Browser hijacking

Redirection to an incorrect site has been a longtime problem on the Internet. By adding some simple JavaScript to a page, a person can be sent from a legitimate site to a fake one. Because of this, it's always important to look at the address bar of your browser to make sure that you're on the correct site and haven't been redirected to a fake one, before you start entering personal data, passwords, and other sensitive information. Unfortunately, fake sites can also be a source of infection by malicious code. This happened in 2012 to almost 30,000 WordPress blogs when such code was added, taking visitors to a site that displayed what appeared to be an antivirus check finding malware and viruses on the person's system. Such sites can exploit outdated browsers and plug-ins, causing Trojans and malware to be installed.

Browsers can also be redirected through malware. Add-ons, plug-ins, or other software on your machine may change the settings of your browser, so when you open your home page or default search engine, you're redirected to another site. Restoring your browser back to the way it was can require various degrees of work. In more serious cases, you may need to revert your system to a previous state using System Restore, as we discussed earlier. In many cases, running antivirus and anti-malware software that we discuss later in this chapter will remove the malware. You can also try uninstalling the software affecting your system by doing the following:

1. On the *Start* menu, click *Control Panel*.
2. Depending on the version of Windows you're using, click *Uninstall a program* or *Add and remove programs*.
3. When the list of programs appears, look at the recent programs and uninstall any recent ones that you're certain should not have been installed.

Browser hijacking often occurs through *Browser Helper Objects*, which are plug-ins that provide additional functionality to the browser. Malicious software posing as add-ons, extensions, or toolbars may be installed on a system. Generally, antivirus and anti-malware software will identify malicious ones and attempt to remove them. You can also disable them through the browser. On Firefox, you would click the *Tools* menu and then click *Add-ons*, while on Internet Explorer, you would click the *Tools* menu, click *Manage add-ons*, and then click *Toolbars and Extensions*. Once the dialog box opens, you can then review the list of add-ons for ones that you can't identify and probably shouldn't be there. Selecting the unwanted add-on and clicking the *Disable* button will prevent it from loading in the browser.

Once you've removed or disabled the cause of the problem, you'll still need to restore your home page and default search engine settings in the browser. If you don't, you could wind up reloading the page that caused the malware or add-on to be installed in the first place. To restore your home page in Internet Explorer, do the following:

1. Click on the *Tools* menu, and then click *Internet Options.*
2. When the *Internet Options* dialog box appears, click on the *General* tab.
3. In the *Home Page* section, enter the URL of your home page in the browser. For example, you might enter www.google.com.
4. Click on the *Programs* tab, and in the *Manage Add-ons* section, click the *Manage add-ons* button.
5. When the *Manage Add-ons* dialog box appears, click on *Search Providers* in the left pane.
6. If there are any unrecognized search providers in the right pane, click on it, and then click on the *Remove* button at the bottom of the dialog box.
7. Click on the *Find more search providers* link at the bottom of the dialog box.
8. When the Web page appears, select a search provider, and then click the *Add to Internet Explorer* button.
9. When prompted, click *Add.*
10. On the *Manage Add-ons* dialog box, click *Close.*
11. On the *Internet Options* dialog box, click *OK.*

Protecting yourself from backdoors and exploits

Backdoors are undocumented ways of accessing systems. A programmer may have included one to access a system without needing to be authenticated or may be created when a system is compromised by a virus, worm, or other malicious software. Once the backdoor is in place, a hacker can use it for continued access to a system, until the software providing the backdoor has been patched by updated software.

It's important to keep up to date with installing patches, updates, and service packs on computers. When operating systems and software are released, there may be bugs or glitches in the software that a hacker or malware can exploit. An *exploit* is a command, method, or software that will use a vulnerability in a system to gain additional access, download additional malware, or run commands that can damage your data or system. As bugs and vulnerabilities are identified, software vendors will release patches, bug-fixes, and other updates that will fix the problems to make the system more stable and secure.

The other way to protect systems is to limit what's installed. Organizations commonly set up security on computers, network group policies, and corporate policies that restrict the download and installation of software. By preventing users from downloading unauthorized apps, widgets, and programs, there's less chance that malicious software will also be downloaded by mistake.

Protecting yourself from viruses and malware

There are numerous tools available on the Internet that will detect, block, and remove viruses and malicious software. In using antivirus and anti-malware software, you'll need to update the signature files that contain information used by the program to detect viruses and malware. In many cases, you'll find that apps will do this for you, and programs installed on your machine will provide the option to run in the background and install updates as they become available. If signature files aren't regularly updated, you're putting your computer and mobile device at risk, because it won't be able to detect the latest malicious code that's become known and thereby will unable to block or remove it from your system.

Symantec provides a number of security products that are commonly used for business and home use. Norton Anti-virus, Norton Internet Security, and Norton 360 are all products from Symantec that provides protection from viruses and other malicious code, such as spyware that will monitor your computer, and provides free technical support. It also comes with Norton Safe Web, which scans your Facebook newsfeed for downloads that it knows are dangerous, and will automatically warn you and people you've added as friends. To purchase any of these products you can visit www.norton.com.

Norton Mobile Security (http://us.norton.com/norton-mobile-security) is another tool from Symantec for mobile devices. It runs on iPhone, iPad, and Android devices and provides protection from viruses and other threats to mobile devices and detection of phishing that can compromise personal and sensitive information. It also provides features to remotely locate, lock, and wipe a device and remotely take a photo of someone who has it. If you're concerned about a particular person contacting you, it allows you to block calls and messages from phone numbers you specify, as well as unknown or anonymous numbers. If you're concerned about security on your phone or other mobile devices, it is definitely worth looking into to safeguard your security.

There are many antivirus and security programs which offer a free trial and then require you to continue using their service by purchasing the product or buying a subscription. If you don't have the money to spend right now, it doesn't mean that you need to be exposed to viruses and malware. There are tools that provide limited protection for free. Through them, you get free antivirus protection and can get additional features if you like the program and want to get more out of it.

As we've discussed in previous chapters, Lookout Security and Antivirus is a tool that will check and block viruses and other threats to a mobile device and provides security features, such as the ability to remotely lock, find, and wipe a device. Even if you only use the limited features, you can upgrade to use more premium features at anytime.

Avast (www.avast.com) is free antivirus software that provides protection against viruses and malware. It is an exceptional tool at detecting and removing viruses and supports remote assistance so that a friend can assist if there's a problem. If you want more advanced security, they also provide an Internet security suite that provides a virtual browser window, firewall, antispam, and additional features.

AVG Free Anti-Virus (http://free.avg.com) is free software that will scan your computer for viruses and malware and remove it from the system. It also has features that will scan links to detect whether clicking it will take you to sites that are known for having malicious software, viruses, phishing scams, and so on. A family safety feature can also be activated to prevent access to inappropriate sites containing mature content.

AVG also has free antivirus software for Android devices. AVG Antivirus for Android (http://www.avg.com/us-en/antivirus-for-android) will scan the device for viruses and malware and also provides features to locate, lock, or wipe a device. They also have family safety software for Windows phone (http://www.avg.com/us-en/avg-family-safety-mobile-win) that will block a child from accessing inappropriate sites and also those that are known for having malicious software, phishing scams, and so on.

While you should only run one antivirus program on a computer to avoid conflicts, there is additional software that you can install will scan your system and remove malware. If your computer has already been infected by malware, you should consider Malwarebytes (www.malwarebytes.org) to remove it. As with other software we've discussed, it uses signature files to identify malicious software, modified Registry keys, and other threats that have been downloaded and installed on your machine. It's an exceptional tool that you should run regularly to identify any potential threats that other antivirus/anti-malware software may have missed.

In choosing a product, you should only download and install antivirus/anti-malware software that is known and trusted. As we discussed earlier in this chapter, there are programs that will pretend to be a legitimate product but are actually scams or actually malware that will install additional programs on your system. Even researching new products can be dangerous, as some sites will actually do a drive-by download, where malicious code on the page downloads malware to your system. If you're unsure what products to trust and decided against any of the ones mentioned here, consider asking a professional in your IT department at work or ask someone who's well versed with computers and can personally vouch for products.

Bibliography

Commonwealth of Massachusetts, Superior Court Civil Action No.12-01138. (2012, September 10). *Clay corporation vs. Colter.* Retrieved July 23, 2013, from Governo Law Firm: <http://governo.com/_documents/News/News670_1.pdf>.

Constantin, L. (2012, March 6). *30,000 WordPress blogs infected to distribute rogue antivirus software.* Retrieved March 15, 2013, from PC World: <http://www.pcworld.com/article/251374/30000_wordpress_blogs_infected_to_distribute_rogue_antivirus_software.html>.

Digital Media Law Project. (2011, March 3). *Simorangkir v. Love.* Retrieved July 24, 2013, from Digital Media Law Project: <http://www.dmlp.org/threats/simorangkir-v-love#description>.

Federal Bureau of Investigations and the National White Collar Crime Center. (2012). *Internet crime report.* National White Collar Crime Center: <http://www.ic3.gov/media/annualreport/2012_IC3Report.pdf>.

Hennessy-Fiske, M. (2010, August 8). *When Facebook goes to the hospital, patients may suffer.* Retrieved July 22, 2013, from Los Angeles Times: <http://articles.latimes.com/2010/aug/08/local/la-me-facebook-20100809>.

International Association of Chiefs of Police. (2012). *2012 Survey results.* Retrieved July 24, 2013, from International Association of Chiefs of Police: <http://www.iacpsocialmedia.org/Resources/Publications/2012SurveyResults.aspx>.

ISACA. (2010, June). *Top five social media risks for business: New ISACA white paper.* Retrieved June 13, 2013, from ISACA: <http://www.isaca.org/About-ISACA/Pressroom/News-Releases/2010/Pages/Top-Five-Social-Media-Risks-for-Business-New-ISACA-White-Paper.aspx>.

Kazia, A. (2013, April 17). *Montreal woman's arrest highlights legal risks of social media.* Retrieved July 23, 2013, from CBC News: <http://www.cbc.ca/news/technology/story/2013/04/16/f-policing-social-media.html>.

Locker, M. (2012, December 5). *WATCH: Woman brags about bank robbery on YouTube, gets arrested.* Retrieved July 24, 2013, from Time Newsfeed: <http://newsfeed.time.com/2012/12/05/women-brags-about-robbery-on-youtube/>.

Martinez, J. (2012, May 31). *Cop tracked Brooklyn gang Brower Boys by'friending' them online.* Retrieved July 24, 2013, from New York Post: <http://www.nypost.com/p/news/local/brooklyn/facebook_em_gang_busted_5ZTTJeeMG2U5BJVztT4CjN>.

Pasco Sheriff's Office. (2013, July 10). *Pasco Sheriff's office.* Retrieved July 24, 2013, from Facebook: <https://www.facebook.com/pascosheriff>.

PCI Security Standards Council. (n.d.). *PCI SSC data security standards overview.* Retrieved August 14, 2013, from PCI Security Standards Council: <https://www.pcisecuritystandards.org/security_standards/index.php?id=pci_dss_v1-2.pdf>.

Simorangkir v. Love, BC410593 (Superior Court of the State of California for the County of Los Angeles March 26, 2009).

United Nations Office on Drugs and Crime (UNODC). (2013, April). *Transnational organized crime in East Asia and the Pacific: A threat assessment.* Retrieved August 13, 2013, from United Nations Office on Drugs and Crime: <http://www.unodc.org/documents/southeastasiaandpacific//Publications/2013/TOCTA_EAP_web.pdf>.

Vancouver Police Department. (2011, September 6). *2011 Vancouver Police Department 2011 Stanley Cup Riot review.* Retrieved June 24, 2013, from City of Vancouver: <http://vancouver.ca/files/cov/2011-stanley-cup-riot-VPD.pdf>.

Weber, K. (2013, July 12). *Fugitive Matthew Oliver caught after commenting on his own wanted picture on Pasco Sheriff's office Facebook page.* Retrieved July 23, 2013, from 10 News: <http://www.wtsp.com/news/local/article/324834/8/Fugitive-comments-on-his-own-Facebook-wanted-picture>.

Policies and Privacy

INFORMATION IN THIS CHAPTER:

- Policies
- Privacy
- Blocking users
- Controlling app privacy
- Location awareness

Policies

While there are tools and methods to mitigate potential threats, the key element in addressing many of the risks associated with social media is user behavior. Through training and enforceable policies, users learn not to use social media for unauthorized nonbusiness purposes, and its proper usage as a work-related tool.

A *policy* is a set of directives that addresses a particular aim or goal and provides information on how to accomplish it properly. It allows employees to gain insight on the decisions their employer has made on important areas of the business and the courses of action you need to follow to adhere to those decisions. Policies will generally include or reference *procedures*, which are a set of steps or guidelines that employees can use to follow the policy properly.

As with other policies, a social media policy provides information on what a person can and cannot do, and how the business expects it to be used and its expectations carried out. Because social media can have a far-reaching effect across an organization, a wide variety of other policies will also need to be updated. You may find that social media use will impact existing policies dealing with workplace harassment, corporate conduct, records retention, and other areas of the business. By not mentioning social media in these policies and its effect on a particular issue, a policy could be considered invalid when it's violated through social media.

Pros and cons

As with anything, policies have a number of pros and cons associated with them. They can make a person's life easier or be so complex or pointless that they're

217

never used. In deciding whether to implement a policy, you need to determine if a policy is needed or whether issues are covered effectively in existing policies.

A benefit of having good policies is that it can provide a mechanism to prevent legal issues. If the policy provides information on legislation or regulations that the company must follow, then outlining them in a policy will provide employees with the information they need to adhere to those rules. In Chapter 8, we discussed a number of laws and regulations that are designed to protect the privacy of clients and to control how information is handled. By explaining relevant portions of a law or regulation and how it applies to social media, an employee is less likely to violate those restrictions. Explaining this not only protects the employee but also makes the organization less vulnerable to litigation, fines, or other penalties.

Established policies and procedures help to protect the company from liability, as it shows the organization has made a formal attempt to achieve compliance with standards or laws. It shows that the business tried to communicate the importance of a rule and showed how to comply with it. With this in mind, if the policy has been written simply to protect the business and consists of difficult to follow legal jargon or impossible to achieve procedures, it can also be used to show why compliance wasn't achieved.

Policies can enhance professionalism, as they outline a consistent way of doing business, which carries from one employee to another. Any business will experience times when employees leave their current position and a new person takes over the job. Even if the last person in the job stays for a time to train the new person, he or she may forget to train the new person on certain things. After all, no one remembers everything, so they may overlook certain rules or the related procedures of how the company wants a particular course of action to be followed. Policies provide a remedy for this, as they're a documented reference of business practice, and often provide information on the procedures and laws that relate to that work.

Policies should never become a replacement for effective management. They aren't meant to make supervisors automatons that recite rules verbatim or make them unable to make proper business decisions. At times, management will need to decide when a policy doesn't apply or failed to address an issue. For example, your policy may state that the social media person is the one with access to an account, but you might need to violate this rule by having your IT staff access the account during a security breach. Policies should provide guidance and support and clarify how to deal with specific issues. They're meant to be weighed with common sense and applied appropriately.

Creating a policy

Policies have common features that should be universal regardless of what they're addressing. A good policy is relevant to a particular purpose, concise, and clear in expressing its ideas. It should provide understandable actions and guidelines to achieve a goal or deal with a problem or a situation.

For a policy to work, it needs to be timely and current. If you're reading a social media policy that addresses the company's use of a site that no longer exists or your company no longer uses, it isn't much help. Because of this, the policy should be reviewed annually, and each version of it should have a date when it was last reviewed, when it's to be reviewed next, and a version number. In looking at the policy, people will know whether they're looking at the current version.

The first part of your policy should explain its purpose. Is it to promote your public image, provide a way to engage customers, or all of these reasons? Explaining why the policy exists enables people to understand why it's important and why they should follow it.

Identifying the purpose might expose a need to create multiple policies, so that you're meeting the requirements of various departments. For example, a corporate social media policy would address how to use accounts to represent the business, while a Human Resources policy would outline how social media is used to recruit potential employees and issues related to background checks. If the purposes of your social media policy are diverse enough, consider creating multiple ones.

Definitions of common terms are another important section of a policy. Just because you understand terms like social media, social networking, and content communities doesn't mean everyone else does. If you don't include clear definitions of the terms used in a policy, you're giving people an excuse not to follow it. If they break the rules, they can simply say that they didn't understand what it was talking about.

The bulk of a policy will explain the correct way of using social media and adhering to the business' expectations. It would be here that you answer such questions as:

- Who is the official spokesperson of the company through Twitter, Facebook, and other sites? Is it a particular department or a specific position that's held by someone?
- What are the names and URLs of official accounts? This helps to clarify whether a tweet or post was the official voice of the company or the ramblings of a coworker or fake account.
- What restrictions are there in engaging customers and followers of your social media presence? To comply with regulations, you may be restricted from posting information about a person's account, so customers should be referred to a call center or help desk.
- Who owns the content? As we'll discuss later in this section, ownership of the content that's created and posted should belong to the company and not violate any copyright or intellectual property agreements.

Online social behavior

A social media policy should address online or social behavior. This identifies how you expect employees to conduct themselves online and outlines what can be communicated and when. As we discussed in Chapter 5, basic rules of netiquette can also help a person understand how to behave online and represent the business in a manner that won't offend others or incite negative comments.

A social media policy should also address personal use. Regardless of whether the business likes it or not, employees will continue to use Facebook, Twitter, and other social networks. Employees will comment on political, religious, or other topics that a business would not address through its corporate accounts, and an organization should respect your right to do so. However, this becomes a problem if employees used personal accounts to conduct business such as when a sales representative tried to attract new customers online. To remove your business from personal views, your policy should recommend separate business and personal accounts. If a personal comment is made on an account that identifies your relationship to the organization, the employee should state that it is not necessarily the views of the business.

Enforcing policies

One of the biggest problems with policies is when they aren't enforced. According to a report by the Ponemon Institute, 65% of the IT professionals surveyed believed that their organizations didn't enforce acceptable use policies for social media or were unsure. The top reasons that they weren't enforced were:

- Lack of governance and oversight (44%)
- Other security issues were a priority (43%)
- Insufficient resources to monitor compliance with the policy (41%)

An important step in enforcing policies is to provide a mechanism for reporting violations or filing a complaint. It may be by notifying a supervisor or manager, informing a department like Human Resources, or telling a union representative. By showing the process for how violations are to be reported, people will have a better understanding how to report them, and managers will be able to handle complaints accordingly.

Information on who to notify may also be found in other documents such as a risk register. As we discussed in Chapter 8, when you assess risks, you need to identify the probability and impact of a potential threat and determine how to mitigate and address potential problems. This information may be documented in a risk register with details on who is to be notified and take action when a problem occurs. Table 9.1 gives you an idea of some of the information you'll see in a risk register. By referring to it when needed, you can see what needs to be done, by whom, and within what time frame.

Policies should provide information on how they're to be enforced. A policy may contain a blanket statement that any violations may result in disciplinary action, up to and including termination of employment. It may also provide options, which managers can use as part of a disciplinary process. The employee could receive a verbal or written warning, suspension with or without pay, a fine or penalty, or in extreme or recurring violations be fired. If policies are enforced in a fair and equal manner, then employees will recognize it and take the rules seriously.

It's also important for employees to recognize how they're protected when reporting violations of policy or possible crimes that have been committed.

Table 9.1 Example of a Risk Register

Category	Risk	Probability	Severity	Avoidance/ Contingency	Action By	Action Within
Social media	Inaccurate information posted or tweeted	2	2	Approval process/Issue retraction/ Correct mistake by reposting update	Social Media Officer	30 minutes
Security	Compromised account	1	3	Reset passwords on all social media accounts	Social Media Officer/IT Department	30 minutes

For example, section 806 of the Sarbanes–Oxley Act provides protection for "whistleblowers" of publicly traded companies who report or assist in investigations where fraud or a violation of legislation or specific regulations has occurred. The act states that no member of a company "may discharge, demote, suspend, threaten, harass, or in any other manner discriminate against an employee in the terms and conditions of employment because of any lawful act done by the employee."

Under no circumstances should any disciplinary measures violate existing legislation, regulations, labor laws, or contracts. If elements of a policy are shown as illegal or in violation of your contract, it makes the policy unenforceable. Any actions taken to enforce the policy could leave a company vulnerable to a civil dispute and possible fines from government labor agencies.

Getting people to read it

Even though a considerable amount of work may go into creating a policy, it doesn't serve a purpose if people are unaware of it or doesn't read it. Larger organizations may have hundreds of policies providing directives on countless issues and activities. Trying to read all of these is a pointless endeavor, and employees simply won't retain all of that information. To ensure that people understand policies that relate to their job, managers need to identify which ones their staff should be aware of and communicate that they're to read and understand those ones. In reality, anything beyond those few are the ones that they'll refer to as needed.

While organizations create policies to communicate their directives, they need to identify how people will access them and be aware of changes. In small businesses, you can let people know at staff meetings or by pinning a copy on a bulletin board. For larger organizations, communicating that there are new or updated polices can be more challenging. A business may save copies on a shared network drive, but employees won't know when they're updated unless they look at the date and time the document was last modified. You can send out emails, but they may be forgotten over time or lost in more pressing day-to-day messages. By using an intranet Web site that's only accessible to employees, people can have easy access to updates on policies. For example, sites built with Microsoft SharePoint will allow employees to set alerts on changes and list new documents that have been uploaded.

Organizations also need to know if an employee actually read a policy. You could simply send a corporate communication saying they must read a policy and/or have employees sign a printed document stating they've read and understood it. The policy could also be made into an electronic form and have a checkbox that users must check to indicate compliance. If you made this form into a portal to your intranet, it could be a mandatory step to read and acknowledge the policy before entering the site. You could also make the policy into a Microsoft Infopath form with checkbox or button to indicate they've read and acknowledged the policy. The InfoPath form could be set up to add the time and date it was completed and has a workflow that automatically saves and/or emails a completed copy to a supervisor. As you can see, there are numerous options for controlling whether employees have reviewed the policies and confirmed their understanding.

Policies affected by social media

Social media can impact existing policies in ways you haven't considered. Employees create and publish their own content, access social media sites in the workplace, and use the Internet in ways that hadn't been previously considered when the policies were developed. When social media becomes a part of how your company does business, the policies need to reflect this change.

A social media policy should refer any other procedure or procedures that may be applicable. You want to keep any policy concise and understandable so copying and pasting sections from other policies will lengthen it needlessly. There are many other policies that can be affected by social media and cross-referencing them may be necessary.

Acceptable use

Many companies have an Acceptable Use Policy (AUP) that outlines the proper use of computers, networks, Internet, software, and other technologies. As you might expect, this type of policy is created by IT departments that focuses on systems they manage or control access. The AUP addresses the employee's responsibilities in using corporate equipment and their access to information systems provided through the company.

When a company creates a social media presence, the person responsible for it may be issued a mobile phone with apps that allow him or her to connect to social media sites. The AUP may need to be updated to mention these mobile devices and how additional apps can't be installed on them. Adding apps that aren't approved increases the chance of malicious software being installed, expose personal information, and could cause issues with the devices.

While the AUP will state that equipment should only be used for business purposes, it should also mention social media accounts. It should state that only business social media accounts should be used on mobile phones and other devices issued by the company. If a person uses an app to connect to both the business account and a personal account, there is a greater chance the person will accidently make a personal tweet or post using the wrong account.

Antidiscrimination and antiharassment

No organization should allow a work environment to become intolerable by undermining and devaluing the people who work and do business there. *Discrimination* occurs when a person is treated differently, in an unfair or unjust manner, on the basis of a defining characteristic. A person may be the targeted because of their race, skin color, national origin, religion, sex, sexual orientation, age, disability, marital status, or other identifiable characteristics or protected statuses. *Harassment* is a course of comments or actions that are unwanted and should be known to be unwelcome by any reasonable person. In an effort to make a clear statement that such behavior isn't tolerated, policies that provide a set of standards and expectations for employees should be created.

When a person is excluded, intimidated, or degraded in an organization, it has a negative effect on everyone. The person who's the target of a comment or action may feel humiliated or belittled, while those seeing the behavior may feel uncomfortable being in the workplace. It can poison the environment making it intolerable to work there.

From the standpoint of an employer, this can also have a negative impact on the business. An employee who's bullied or discriminated against will be preoccupied with the way he or she is treated and may spend a considerable amount of time documenting the events. Morale will suffer, and employees may also have lower productivity out of concern for a coworker or that they may be treated the same way. If it's a current or prospective client, vendor, or supplier who experiences this treatment, it may cost the company their business. Those suffering from the behavior may also file complaints against the harasser(s) and even file a lawsuit against the employer.

While some businesses may create separate policies to address types of harassment, organizations may create a single antidiscrimination and antiharassment policy. Such policies are used to show how the behavior is inacceptable in the workplace, and that staff, coworkers, vendors, customers, and other individuals cannot be treated this way.

As we saw in Chapter 7, harassment and bullying aren't limited to face-to-face encounters. Online harassment and cyberbullying can involve derogatory or prejudiced comments on blogs, posts, or tweets, or embarrassing or demeaning photos posted on content communities or social networks. The content may appear on intranet sites that are accessible to employees or on public sites where the harassment or discrimination extends out of the workplace.

Another type of harassment is *sexual harassment* in which a person is targeted by unwanted attention, inclusive to comments about gender, physical attributes, or advances for sexual favors. Both men and women can be victims, just as harassers may be of the same or a different gender. When harassment is of a sexual nature, it may be verbal, physical, or related to comments and other content posted online.

When a person's conduct is unwelcome and recurring, it can be extremely distressing. However, even a single instance may be enough to violate a policy or existing laws, or to press criminal charges against a harasser. For example, if your manager threatened your job unless you went on a date or provided sexual favors, or a coworker touched you in an inappropriate manner, you would want to report it. You don't need to wait for repetitive behavior and risk threats to your safety or employment.

As with other forms of harassment, sexual harassment also has a cyber-aspect. An employee may make sexual comments about a fellow employee in posts or on a blog, or display inappropriate content in the office. If you allow employees to access social media from their workstations, they may be able to access images or videos that contain nudity or pornographic content. Even if the IT department has restricted such content from most sites, a person could still use Twitter to view such images making employees, customers, or others with access to the area uncomfortable.

Failing to mention Internet usage in such policies could give the impression that their conduct online is exempt. Because harassment and discrimination isn't acceptable in real life or electronic forms, it needs to be indicated in your policy. The behavior is the same regardless how it's shown.

Confidentiality

Sometimes, a job requires you to keep certain information secret. The company may have a trade secret such as a recipe or process that's needed for the business to survive. In other cases, an agency or business may have access to a client's personal, medical, criminal, or financial information, creating a need for privacy. If the information ever got out publicly, it could cause embarrassment, put a person's safety at risk, or cause a possible loss for the organization or client.

For information to stay private, the people with access to it need to understand what they can't share or discuss with others. Agreements that address information disclosure are sometimes needed to serve as contracts between an employer and employee, or parties doing business together. *Confidentiality agreements* or *nondisclosure agreements* are used to outline what a person isn't allowed to discuss outside of the workplace or the course of their duties. The discussion of privileged information includes verbal, written, or electronic means of communication.

In many cases, the need for confidentiality is a legal requirement. For example, as we saw in Chapter 8, legislation like the Health Insurance Portability and Accountability Act is designed to protect a patient's privacy. Unfortunately, while health-care workers should know better than to publish anything that could identify a patient on social media sites, it hasn't stopped it from happening, resulting in many hospitals blocking employees from using social networking sites at work.

Tri-City Medical Center in Oceanside, California, has experienced several problems over the years with social media. In 2007, five nurses and five other staff were fired after taking photos using their mobile phones of patient x-rays and a suicidal patient, which was then posted on Facebook. In 2010, the hospital faced further embarrassment when several nurses were found to be discussing patients on

Facebook. Five nurses were fired as a result, and the hospital required its employees to sign an agreement that stated "Even if the patient is not identified by name or by the medical record number the information you disclose may identify that patient."

Intellectual property

Agreements or policies may also need to be created that protect work products, so they are clearly the intellectual property of the business. After all, in paying employees to do work, you don't want them leaving with it under the belief that they can now sell it to a competitor or use it for their own purposes. You should clearly establish that any systems, processes, templates, or methods created by the employee on company equipment and/or during company time are owned by the organization.

As we discussed in Chapter 8, the use of intellectual property is a serious concern for businesses. People in an organization need to understand that the logos, trademarks, account names, and other elements used in a social media presence are the properties of the business. Just because you wrote a blog entry or created a brilliant infographic, the content is owned by the business and not the creator. Similarly, just because you found an image on Google Images or some other site doesn't mean that it's public domain and can be used without the explicit written permission of the owner.

Records retention

As we discussed in Chapter 6, organizations will archive and retain records to comply with legislation or industry regulations. A document may need to be active for a certain number of years, archived in case someone needs to refer to it, and finally deleted. Records retention policies are used to provide employees with the information and procedures needed to preserve records for specific periods of time.

The policy provides rules that are used to identify which documents need to be kept and for how long. To facilitate records retention, organizations will use *Enterprise Content Management* (ECM), which the Association for Information and Image Management International (www.aiim.org) defines as "strategies, methods and tools used to capture, manage, store, preserve, and deliver content and documents related to organizational processes." Larger organizations may organize and store the data in ECM systems running on servers, which will automate the process of archiving and purging data based on rules associated with different types of documents.

Because a record is a record regardless of its location or format, the content you post on social media sites can be considered as a record that needs to be retained and archived. For example, let's say you created a graph about sales and saved it as an image. It might need to be available to people as an active document for a year, archived for two, and then finally deleted. Whether you save the graph to a network server, ECM system, or upload it to a social networking site, the same rules apply.

Moonlighting

Moonlighting is a term for secondary employment outside of one's regular job. It may be a second job you have or may be a part-time business you've started. Organizations often have policies regarding secondary employment. While some may prohibit it, however, many recognize that a position elsewhere gives the employee additional skills and experience that can be beneficial to the organization.

When secondary employment is allowed, policies commonly state that it must be legal, doesn't damage the organization's reputation, and will not use company resources. Obviously, no employer wants to see his staff using LinkedIn at work to find a second job or posting ads for a part-time business on corporate blog or profile page of their intranet social networking site. Like church and state, you want to keep your secondary job separate from your primary one.

Moonlighting policies commonly stress that your secondary employment can't be in conflict with your regular job. An example of this occurred in Manukau, New Zealand in 2012, when the manager of a salon went to post a status update on the salon's Facebook page only to find an employee's Facebook page open on the work computer. Entries on the page of Ammy Hull, a beauty therapist at the salon, showed that she was seeing clients at her home. The case went before the Employment Relations Authority, and Hull was ordered to pay a "nominal amount" in damages. By poaching customers and treating them at home, it caused a loss of business for the salon that was seen as a breach of good faith.

If you're unsure whether a private business or secondary employment might be in conflict with your regular job, you'll often find a policy that states if there's a possible conflict, the employee must get written permission. In doing so, the business is aware of the second job, and you're assured they don't have a problem with it.

Noncompete and nonsolicitation agreements

When a person leaves a company, they may have their own social media accounts that have friends and followers who are existing customers. With this information, important clients could be coaxed away from your company, costing you their business. By having partners and employees sign an agreement that restricts them from using this information, you can avoid ex-employees from soliciting customers away from doing business with you. Even if they have the contact information for existing clients, they won't be able to solicit their business without violating the agreement and facing penalties or a possible lawsuit.

Similar to this, a noncompete agreement is a document that restricts employees from using insider knowledge of your business to become competitive. After immediately leaving your company, you don't want a partner or employee using their knowledge to start their own business and using what they've learned against you. The agreement may set conditions saying they can't compete within a specific geographic space and/or within a set amount of time after leaving the company.

Code of conduct and ethics

A *Code of Conduct* or *Code of Ethics* is a policy that addresses how colleagues or employees interact with each other and clients. While used in businesses, you'll also find these codes in schools and venues like conferences. The code of conduct allows students and attendees to understand how they're expected to behave and how to report problems.

A code of conduct provides guidelines on behavior during business hours and may have information related to other policies, describing issues of harassment or confidentiality. The code may also provide ethical guidance on how to deal with clients, such as by telling employees not to accept gifts from vendors or suppliers as it may be considered a bribe or influence purchases.

How not to report a violation

Social media may be a great way of sharing information, but it's not the way to report a policy violation. An example of using social media to register a complaint was seen in March 2013 at PyCon, an annual Python developer conference in Santa Clara, California. During the conference, Adria Richards overheard two developers sitting behind her, who were making jokes about dongles and forking. The jokes were sexual innuendo, and while the tech terms sound like dirty words, they're actually not. Finding it inappropriate, she decided not to tell them she was offended. Instead, she took a photo of the developers (and others surrounding them), and as seen in Figure 9.1, tweeted a complaint to the PyCon hashtag

FIGURE 9.1

Adria Richard's tweet about inappropriate behavior.

PyCon approached Richards, who pointed out the developers who made the remarks. The pair was taken out of the conference, the matter was discussed privately, and the developers apologized. As a result of the incident, PyCon updated their code of conduct. It provides information on how to properly report harassment or inappropriate behavior by contacting a member of the conference or hotel staff. PlayHaven, the employer of one developer, also took action by later firing their employee.

Richards was also fired from SendGrid, where she worked as a developer evangelist. While SendGrid stated they respect her right to report inappropriate behavior, however, they did not agree with how she did it. CEO Jim Franklin wrote in a blog that "Publicly shaming the offenders—and bystanders—was not the appropriate way to handle the situation."

The incident became a point of controversy. The situation and related firings were debated on social media sites and became heated. After firing Richards, SendGrid experienced a Distributed Denial of Service (DDoS) attack. People also noted that while Richards claimed she was taking a stand against the sexist comments and jokes with sexual overtones, as seen in Figure 9.2, she had made them herself during the week of the conference, prior to the incident.

As is the way of the Internet, additional information about Richards appeared on sites. Her previous history at conferences was reported by tech conference organizer Amanda Blum, who wrote on a blog (http://amandablumwords.wordpress.com/2013/03/21/3/) about Richards' past conduct. During a New York conference, there had been a session by Danielle Morrill (www.daniellemorrill.com) called "Getting the Money Shot," which jokingly made reference to thinking like a porn director while creating a screencast. Richards took offense, but didn't say anything to the speaker or conference organizers. Instead, in a podcast, she threatened to boycott the conference for promoting porn, and when speaking at a session, spent her time talking about how porn had no place at the conference.

FIGURE 9.2

Inappropriate tweet by Adria Richards.

Privacy

As we've seen throughout this book, privacy issues on social networking sites are a serious concern. Your privacy can be at risk through the facts you provide, what's revealed by others, and what you allow people to see. As we'll see in the sections that follow, by limiting the availability and visibility of personal data, you can prevent it from becoming public or being seen by the wrong people.

Your own worst enemy

If you wanted to point a finger at who's the worst culprit at violating your privacy, you'd probably be pointing at yourself. In the 2010 Consumer Reports State of the New Survey, they found that large numbers of people post a significant amount of personal information on social networking sites. In it, they found that 56% of Facebook users and 52% of all social network users posted information that could put them at risk and expose them to potential problems. As seen in Table 9.2, a wide variety of data can be obtained from the social networks used by a person, and when combined together, it can create a comprehensive profile about them.

What friends say about you

Even if you're careful with your information, your friends may not be. They may post comments or photos that reveal sensitive or embarrassing information that you would never consider publishing on the Internet. When you do notice them doing

Table 9.2 Information People Post About Themselves on Social Networking Sites

	Facebook (%)	All Social Networks (%)
First and last name	84	80
Photos of themselves	63	57
Email address	51	49
Birthdate with year	42	38
Birthdate without year	30	26
Photos of children	24	21
Names of friends, family members, or associates	19	16
Employer	17	16
Names of children	16	13
Street address of their home	7	8
Cell phone number	7	6
Home phone number	4	4
Information that they are home or away	3	3

this, you'll need to make the effort of asking them to remove the content or deleting comments yourself.

The people you're friends with on social networks can say a lot about you. People tend to be friends with comparable interests, education, and other similarities. If most of your friends went to a particular school, it could indicate your alma mater. If many of them worked in the same field or for the same employer, it could signify that you were in the same profession and they were coworkers. By looking at the qualities of your social networking friends, you'll find that it can reveal a lot about you.

According to a 2010 study, researchers found that they could infer information about a person based on what was known about their social networking friends. Using information from as little as 20% of users, the algorithm they created that could identify the personal attributes of a person with a high degree of accuracy. Some of the details they could infer included a person's education level, hometown, the university he or she attended, and other facts.

Using Facebook lists

Facebook allows you to organize people you've added as friends in lists. Using these lists, you can group people together to control how you see their posts and whether they can see yours. While you can create custom lists, there are ones created with your Facebook account, including:

- *Close Friends*, where you'd add people whose posts are a priority to you. If a person is added to this list, you'll see more of their posts in the newsfeed and get notifications of when they post.
- *Acquaintances*, where you'd add people whose posts you don't really care to follow. If a person is added to this list, their posts will show up less frequently in your newsfeed.
- *Restricted*, where you'd add people you've added as friends, but should only see public content.

When you make a post in Facebook, you can choose who will see it using the audience selector. As seen in (Figure 9.3), by clicking on the drop-down list beside the post button, you can select whether the post will be *Public*, only visible to people you've added as *Friends*, seen only by you, or visible to lists of people. If you wanted the post to appear to your friends, but not those in the Acquaintance list, you would select *Friends except Acquaintances*. To see additional lists of people, you'd click the *See all lists ...* menu item at the bottom.

As we'll discuss later, you can change the default settings of the content you post so that only certain audiences will see your posts when you make them. In changing the default settings, you won't have to change the audience on every post you make so that certain people are excluded.

FIGURE 9.3

Audience selector on status update.

Create new lists

While the few lists provided by Facebook is a start, it isn't comprehensive enough to group together people who have commonalities. You might want to group your coworkers into a list, so a post is only visible to those you work with. By creating this list, you could click the *Custom* menu item on the audience selector and make a post visible to everyone except those on the coworkers list. By creating new lists, you have granular control over who will see the posts you make. To create a new list, you would do the following:

1. Visit the Timeline of the person you want to add to the list. Click on the gear-shaped icon in the lower right hand of their cover photo, beside the message button.
2. When the menu appears, click *New List*.
3. When the *Create New List* box appears, click *Next*.
4. In the *List Name* box, type the name of your new list.
5. From the list of options below, select who will be able to see this list. To prevent others from seeing the list and who's on it, select *Only Me*.
6. Click *Done*.

Restricted list

The Restricted list is probably the list you'll want to use most often. There are times when you'll add someone as a friend, even though you don't want the person to view most information on your Timeline. The person may be a boss or coworker you felt obligated to add, or someone you've added to gain additional allies or neighbors in a game. The person may be someone you're uncomfortable unfriending, as it might cause a confrontation if they noticed you'd removed them. By adding the person to the Restricted list, you'll continue to appear as friends, but the person will only be able to see public content on your Timeline.

The Restricted list can be accessed through the *Manage Blocking* page we discussed previously in this chapter. By going to the *Restricted List* section, you would click on the *Edit List* link. This will display a list of people currently on the list. By clicking on a picture of someone you don't want on the list, they'll be removed. By selecting *Friends* from the drop-down list in the upper left-hand corner, you can add people to the Restricted list by clicking on their names. A check mark will appear on the photo of each person you've added to the list.

Restricting who can see your Facebook posts

Rather than changing the audience of individual posts on Facebook, you can also control who will see your content by default. In changing the default settings, you can modify whether your future posts will be visible to everyone or only specific audiences. To access the default settings for posts you would go into the *Privacy Settings and Tools* section of your account. To access this area:

1. Click on the gear-shaped icon in the upper right-hand corner of your screen.
2. Click *Privacy Settings*.

When the page appears, you'll see a number of options in an area entitled *Who can see my stuff?* The first part of this section is titled *Who can see your future posts?* It's used to set the default groups who will see any posts made on your Timeline. By clicking the *Edit* link, you'll see the area expand to show a *Customize* button. Clicking this button displays a menu of possible audiences:

- Public
- Friends
- Friends except Acquaintances
- Only Me
- Custom

You can select an individual group from the menu or click *Custom* to display a dialog box where you can restrict multiple lists of people. As shown in Figure 9.4, the top section allows you to choose people or lists who will be able to see the posts you share from a drop-down list. By clicking the *Friends of those tagged* checkbox, anyone who is tagged in a post will also be able to see it. In the bottom section, you can type the names of people or lists who will not see your posts. As you type in the name in this field, Facebook will show you a list of possible matches, which you can select for inclusion. To remove a person or list, you would click on the "X" beside their name. Once you're finished securing who will see your posts, click *Save Changes*.

Alternatively, you can also modify these settings by clicking on the Privacy Shortcuts icon, which is shaped like a padlock and appears in the upper right-hand corner of the page. By clicking *Who can see my stuff?*, the menu expands to show

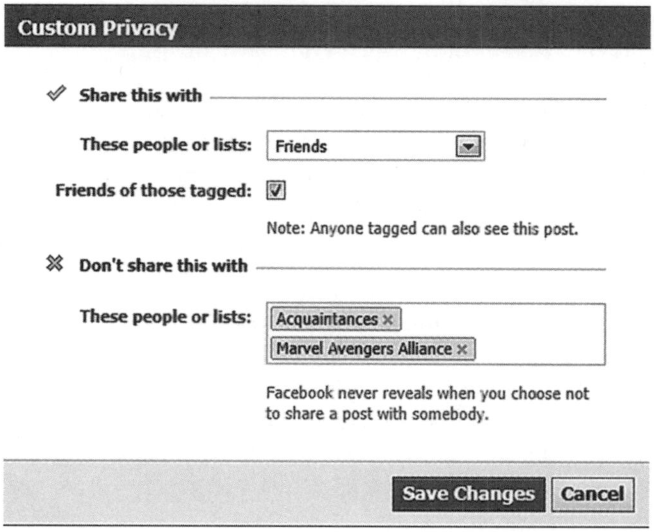

FIGURE 9.4

Custom privacy dialog box in Facebook.

additional options. By clicking *Who can see my future posts?* menu item, you can select different groups who can see your posts.

You can also control who can see individual posts. If you're making a status update and want it to appear only to specific people, you can use the audience selector button. This button appears next to the *Post* button on your status update and provides a drop-down list of potential audiences that you can choose from. In using this, only the lists of people you select will see the post.

Limiting past posts

Changing the default settings will control who can see your future posts, but it doesn't affect previous posts in your Timeline. If you're concerned about previous posts being available for everyone to see, you'll need to change the visibility of past posts.

If you've used older Facebook apps on a mobile phone that didn't provide an in-line audience selector for the posts you created, then these posts would be visible to everyone. To change who can see these posts, you would use an option in the Apps Settings section of your account by doing the following:

1. Click on the gear-shaped icon in the upper right-hand corner of the page.
2. Click *Account Settings* on the menu that appears.
3. In the left pane, click on *Apps*.
4. Scroll down until you see the section entitled *Old versions of Facebook for mobile*. Click the *Edit* link.
5. When the area expands, click on the button and select the audience that you want to view these old posts.

Facebook also allows you to change the audience of all your past posts that were visible to the *Public* or *Friends-of-Friends*. In using it, everything previously posted on your Timeline that was seen by these groups will only be visible to *Friends*. It is however a one-way process, so you can't revert your past posts to the previous audiences once this is used. To change them, you'd need to manually go through each post, and change the audience from *Friends* to something else. To limit the audience of past posts, do the following:

1. Click on the gear-shaped icon in the upper right-hand corner of your page, and click *Privacy Settings* on the menu that appears.
2. In the *Privacy Settings and Tools* section of your account, you will see an area entitled *Limit the audience for posts you've shared with friends-of-friends or Public*. Click on the *Limit Past Posts* link.
3. When the section expands, click on the *Limit Old Posts* button.
4. Confirm the change, and Facebook will automatically modify the audiences associated with your previous posts.

Restricting who can see your friends and who you follow

When someone visits your Timeline, they'll be able to see a box containing thumbnail images of your friends, and any lists and people you're following. This can cause privacy issues, as others will be able to see those you've accepted friend requests from, and those you're following. To restrict the visibility of this information, do the following:

1. Click on your name in the upper right-hand corner of the page.
2. Scroll down the page, until you see the *Friends* box in the left pane, which shows photos of your friends.
3. Hover your mouse over the *Friends* box, and you'll see an edit icon shaped like a pencil. Click on the icon, and when the menu appears, click *Edit Privacy*.
4. When the *Edit Privacy* dialog appears, click on the drop-down list below *Friends List*. Select the list of people who should see your friends.
5. Click on the drop-down list below *Following*. Select the list of people who should see your followers.
6. Click Close.

Even if you restrict who can see your friends and followers, it won't be completely hidden. If someone visits your Timeline, they'll see any mutual friends. You will also appear in the friend's list of anyone you're friends with.

Protecting your tweets

By default, any of the tweets you make are public. Anything you say can be read by anyone, even if they don't have a Twitter account. For some, this is exactly the kind of behavior you want from Twitter. If you have a hashtag campaign, or using it to promote your brand, you'll want everyone to read what you have to say.

Twitter has the ability to send private tweets, which only go to followers you've approved. This is the best option for people who use Twitter to communicate with friends, colleagues, and others who are approved followers of your account. In using this setting, the tweets won't appear in any search results and can't be retweeted by others. Also, if anyone tries to follow you, you'll have to grant permission for the person to become a follower. To protect your tweets, follow these steps:

1. Click on the gear-shaped icon in the upper right-hand corner of the page, and click *Settings* on the menu that appears
2. Scroll down until you see the *Tweet Privacy* section. Click on the *Protect my tweets* checkbox so it appears checked.
3. Click the *Save Changes* button.
4. When prompted, enter your password and click *Save Changes*.

Unfortunately, this is an all or nothing process. If you protect your tweets, only the ones you make after enabling the setting. Any tweets you made prior to this are still public and will appear in search results. If you decide you don't want your tweets protected anymore and disable the setting, then all of your tweets become public, regardless of whether they were previously protected.

Checking the risk of a site

Privacy Score (www.privacyscore.com) is a tool that allows you to check the privacy risk of using a site. By entering the URL of a site on the page, it will provide a score of how it handles personal and tracking information. As seen in Figure 9.5, using the site, you can see a site's overall score out of 100, who tracks you when visiting the site, how long information on you is retained, user anonymity, and links to view the site's privacy policies. By hovering over areas of the page, you can view information on how the scores were represented and make an educated decision on whether you want to visit or sign-up with the site.

Another useful tool for determining privacy issues with the sites you're using is Privacyfix (www.privacyfix.com). The app is available for Firefox and Chrome, and will review privacy settings on Facebook, LinkedIn, and other sites you use. The app is also available on the Chrome Web Store (https://chrome.google.com/web-store). As seen in Figure 9.6, after installing it on your browser, you can log on to sites and review potential privacy issues with your settings. By clicking links beside each issue, you can automatically fix them.

What is interesting about Privacyfix is that it provides estimates of how much various sites make from your activity, and the percentage of sites you're tracked on. It also provides easy to view information on how exposed you are based on your security and privacy settings. As you change your privacy settings, it's useful to review the findings to determine whether your exposure has minimized or whether there are still issues.

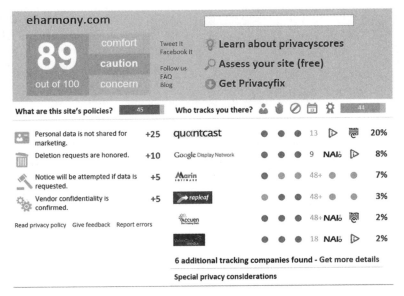

FIGURE 9.5

Privacy score results.

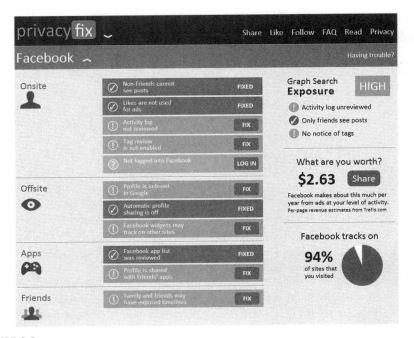

FIGURE 9.6

Privacyfix on chrome browser.

FIGURE 9.7

Privacyfix healthbar.

By turning on the Privacyfix healthbar, you'll be able to view potential risks as you visit sites. The tool will use your current URL to identify the ratings associated with the site, and trackers that gather information on the sites you're visiting. To view results of a site, you would click on the healthbar icon beside your address bar in Chrome, and a display similar to that in Figure 9.7 would appear. To block tracking attempts, you would click on *Block* in the *Ad Trackers* section. The other sections provide important information regarding the site's policies on data sharing and other concerns you should be aware of.

Blocking sites through the browser

There are times when you'll come across a site that's of particular concern, and you won't want anyone accessing it from your computer. If you're using a multiuser computer such as one shared by your family, you can block the site from being accessed through the browser. On Internet Explorer, do the following:

1. Click on the *Tools* menu, and then click *Internet Options*.
2. When the *Internet Options* dialog box appears, click on the *Content* tab.
3. In the *Content Advisor* section, click the *Enable* button.
4. Click on the *Approved Sites* tab.
5. In the *Allow this Web site* field, enter the URL of the site you want to block.
6. Click *Never*.
7. When you're done adding sites you want to block, click *OK*.

The *Ratings* tab of the Content Advisor dialog also allows you to control the kinds of content that users are allowed to see in the browser. You can set rating levels to enforce parental control, or if you have a small business that wants to restrict employees from accessing certain types of content. Using a slider control on the tab, you can set the level of restriction, so that users are prevented from seeing such things as nudity, sexual material, depictions of violence, or even content that sets a bad example for young children.

Controlling the content viewed by someone is an issue that can be of great importance to a parent, school, or other locations where inappropriate content isn't allowed. In browsing the Internet, you can find images and video showing excessive violence and pornography, sites that promotes hate, or other content unsuitable for a child. If a young child sees this, it could be emotionally damaging and have a long-term impact on their development as a person and how they viewed the world.

Parental control software

As we discussed in Chapter 7, there are a number of monitoring tools that can also control what a person can and cannot see. By installing parental control software, you can block pornography, mask profanity, and perform other actions that will censor the kinds of sites a child can visit. Norton Family (https://onlinefamily.norton.com/familysafety) and Net Nanny (www.netnanny.com) are both popular products with a range of features, inclusive to controlling the time a child spends online, the sites they can visit, and the ability to send you alerts or reports of a person's activity. Such software is configurable to allow children and others using the computer to only see what you're comfortable allowing them to see.

Blocking users

Sometimes, there are people who cause too many problems or who you don't trust. You might have someone constantly posting inflammatory comments, badgering you, or being a general nuisance. When this occurs, one way to deal with them is to be rid of them. If all else fails and it gets too much, you may have the ability to block the person or restrict their access. As we'll see in the sections that follow, many sites provide the ability to block a user so that they can't post to your page or contact you.

Blocking users on Facebook

When you block a user on Facebook, the person won't be able to see what's posted on your Timeline, can't tag you, or invite you to events or groups. They also won't be able to add you as a friend or start a conversation with you. It removes almost all contact with the person through Facebook itself.

Facebook allows you to block anyone, regardless of whether it's a friend or not. You don't need to add them or accept a friend request prior to blocking them. As we'll see shortly, you provide an email address or name, and if multiple accounts are found, a list of potential matches is displayed so you can pick the person you want to block. This allows you to be proactive and block people before they cause actual problems.

There are however exceptions to the rule. Even if a person is blocked, you'll still see them in any groups the two of you participate in, and it won't block them in apps or games used by the two of you. For example, if the person was your neighbor in a game, you'd still see them in the game. If the game provided the ability to chat with others, as in the case of games like Farmville or Yoville, they could still start a conversation with you through those games.

To block users in Facebook, you would follow these steps:

1. Click on the gear-shaped icon in the upper right-hand corner of the page, and click *Account Settings* on the menu that appears.
2. In the left pane, click *Blocking*.
3. When the *Manage Blocking* page appears, as shown in Figure 9.8, scroll down to the *Block users* section.

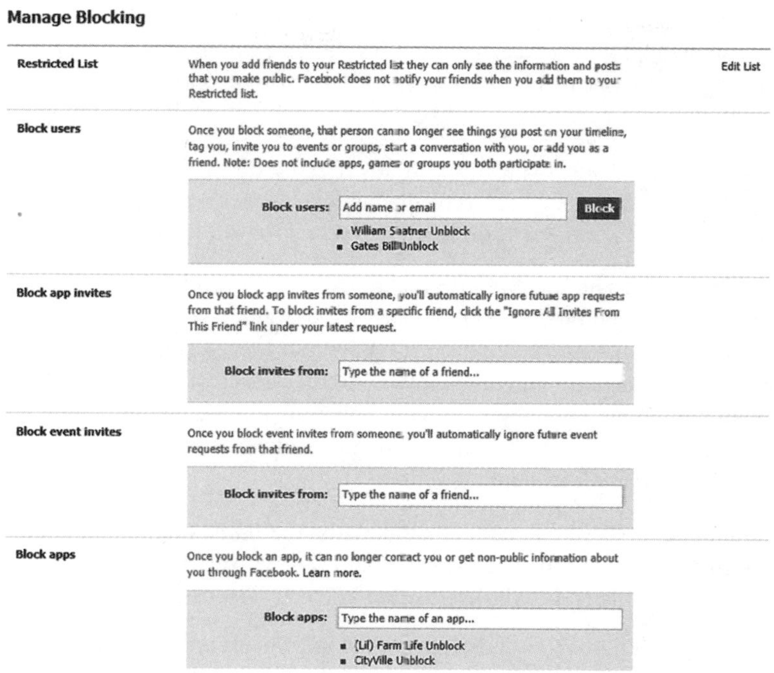

FIGURE 9.8

Manage blocking settings on Facebook.

4. In the *Block users* field, type the name or email of the person you want to block, and click the *Block* button.
5. Because there may be more than one user with the name you entered, a dialog box will appear showing you a list of possible people to block. Find the person you want to block, and click the *Block* button.

Unblocking users

Once you've blocked a person or app, they will appear in a list beneath the appropriate section. For example, if you blocked a user, his or her name appears under the *Block users* section. To unblock a person, simply click on the *Unblock* link beside the name, and click the *Confirm* button when prompted.

Blocking invites

Sometimes, you may not want to completely block a person, but don't want to get invitations to play games or use a particular app. Many games require a person to have neighbors or allies, so people will send invitations to their friends to play so they can advance in the game. After awhile, the requests can become annoying. By blocking the invites, you don't need to be rude and tell the person to stop, and get the relief of never receiving a request.

Blocking invitations for apps can be done in two ways. When you receive an invite to use an app, you can click *Ignore All Invites from this friend* on the request. However, doing this only blocks app invites from that one person. To block all invites for a particular app, you would do the following:

1. On the *Manage Blocking* page, scroll down to the *Block app invites* section.
2. In the *Block invites from* field, type the name of the friend to ignore. As you type, a listing of friends will display that you can select from. Select the name.

Event invites are another type of invitation you may receive in Facebook, where you're invited to a particular event hosted by a friend. While it sounds friendly enough, not all events are welcome ones. People a long distance away may invite you to events you'd never travel to, invite you to parties where products are sold, or send invitations to events you'd never agree to attend. Rather than constantly decline them, you can block the person's invites and never have to see them. This is done through the following steps:

1. On the *Manage Blocking* page, scroll down to the *Block event invites* section.
2. In the *Block invites from* field, type the name of the friend to ignore. As you type, a listing of friends will display that you can select from. Select the name.

As we saw with users, the names of blocked individuals are listed in the area where you've blocked them. To unblock a particular person, click on the link beside their name.

Blocking users on Twitter

Twitter also allows you to block users. If your tweets are public, they'll still be able to see what you've tweeted, but it will prevent them from doing certain actions. They won't be able to follow you, see your profile picture in their Timeline, or add you to lists. Also, any replies or mentions they make won't appear in your mentions tab. To block a user, do the following:

1. Visit the profile page of the person you want to block. Beside the Follow button near the top of the page, click on the person icon.
2. On the menu that appears, click *Block*.

Blocking users on YouTube

If you post videos on YouTube, you may have a problem with other users. To prevent them from contacting you through private messages or posting comments on your videos or Channel, you can do the following:

1. Go to their channel page. You can reach this by clicking on their name beneath one of the videos they uploaded, or by going to the URL www.youtube.com/user/<username>, where <username> is their actual account name.
2. Click on the *About* tab.
3. Click on the flag icon, and when then menu appears, click on the *Block User* menu item.

Blacklisting users on WordPress

While a private blog allows you to control who can see what you've posted, most blogs are public so everyone can read what's said. Because of this, you can't directly block users on sites like WordPress. You can however prevent a known troublemaker from posting comments.

As we'll see in Chapter 10, WordPress provides complete control over moderating the comments that people make and allows you to preapprove comments before they're posted. It also allows you to add certain words to a list, which is used to mark comments as SPAM instead of holding them for moderation. Unless you review the SPAM that attempted to be posted on your blog, no one will see what the troublemaker had to say. To add a person to the blacklist, do the following:

1. After logging in, you're taken to your Dashboard. If you're already logged in, hover your mouse over your username in the upper left-hand corner, and click *Dashboard* from the menu that appears.
2. In the left pane, hover your mouse over *Settings*, and then click *Discussion* on the menu that appears.
3. Scroll down until you see the *Comment Blacklist* section. In the box, enter the name and email of the person you want to block on separate lines.
4. Scroll to the bottom of the page and click *Save Changes*.

You should note that while you could add the IP address used by a troll to the blacklist, it often isn't a good idea. An *IP address* is used to identify your computer on a network like the Internet, allowing communication to take place between your machine and servers. An Internet Service Provider will issue an IP address to a computer for a limited time, so if you blacklisted a troll's IP address, there's no guarantee he or she would have it the next time they went on the Internet.

Controlling app privacy

On social media sites, certain information is public. On Facebook, this includes your name, username, gender, profile picture, cover picture, and networks. If it wasn't public, then you wouldn't be able to see other people and add them as friends, contacts, or colleagues.

In the same way that people can view certain information, it's also accessible to apps. This allows games to show others who are playing, send gifts, and send invites to those not playing. Some apps wouldn't function or provide the social aspects you'd expect if they couldn't view this information.

If an app on Facebook wants additional permission, it will need to ask for it. For example, it's common for apps to request permission to post to your wall or send email to you. It may need this so that you can ask friends for help with games, notify you, or simply to advertise the app and coax more people to use it.

Unfortunately, when you install an app on social networking sites, you're initially left with the choice of allowing it or not. When you install an app on Twitter, it will inform you of the permissions you're allowing, but your choice is to either sign in and accept the app or cancel the install. However, just because you've installed an app doesn't mean that you're stuck with it. You can revoke access to an app after it's installed. Some sites will also allow you to edit the permissions given to an app or block access to ones you're concerned about.

Managing apps on Facebook

The apps you install on Facebook can be managed through the Apps Settings page. To view this page, do the following:

1. Click on the gear-shaped icon in the upper right-hand corner, and click *Account Settings* on the menu that appears.
2. On the left pane of the page, click *Apps*.

On the page, you'll see a section called *Apps You Use*, with a list of apps that have been installed. The list may not be complete, but if you scroll down, you'll see a link at the bottom of the list entitled *Show All Apps*. Clicking this link will expand the list to show every app you've installed.

By clicking on the *Edit* link beside the name of an app, it will expand and show you detailed information about the app, its use, and the permissions it has to your account. The first line of this expanded area shows when the app was last used. As we'll discuss later in this chapter, if you haven't used it for some time, you should consider removing it completely to limit the number of apps accessing your account (Figure 9.9).

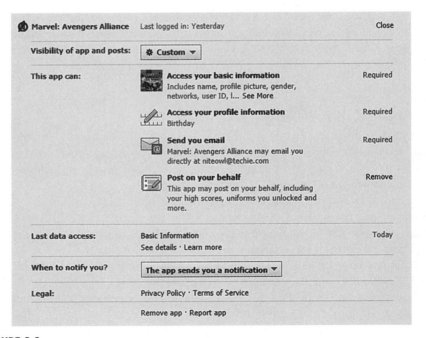

FIGURE 9.9

Editing the settings of a Facebook App.

The *Visibility of app and posts* section allows you to control who will be able to see the app and any posts it makes. By clicking on the button, you're provided with a drop-down list of possible audiences. As we'll see later in this chapter, the audience you choose may be everyone (i.e., public), only you, or other lists of Facebook users that you're willing to share the information with.

The section(s) below this will show you the permissions given to the app. The privileges an app uses will vary, but you'll commonly see that it needs to access your basic information, which is public. It may also have other requirements based on what it does, such as needing to send you email, access specific profile information, and so on. If you installed the Hootsuite app on your Facebook account to manage social media, you'd see it requires the ability to manage pages, post on your behalf, access messages on a page, and manage advertisements. In using the tool (which we discussed in Chapter 5), these permissions make perfect sense. However, if a privilege makes no sense, such as a calculator app needing your current city, address, or other information, you should question it and consider removing it or not installing it to begin with.

You should always review privileges that an app requests but aren't required for it to function. For example, while you can control the visibility of the app and any posts it makes, do you really want it to make posts? Some apps will make a considerable number of posts of activities to promote its use, and there are many games that have been on Facebook that post significant requests for items needed by a player. If you don't want the app to perform an action or view information that isn't needed, click on the *Remove* link beside that privilege.

You should also be wary of allowing an app to make read requests or access your friend's data. By making read requests, apps have been able to access private communications in a person's mail. Being able to access a friend's data gives the app a pipeline to the information you have access to. This could include the person's political views, current location, and other private information. When an app requests such permissions, you'll see the types of information it wants to access or actions it wants to perform below the privilege. After reviewing what's being accessed, you can then decide whether having the app is worth sharing that information.

Determining what privileges to give may require some forethought and research. Try and think why the privilege is needed. If it wants to access your data even when you're not logged on, is it a reasonable request? If you're unsure, click on the *Privacy Policy* link in the *Legal* section at the bottom of the area you expanded to view the app's information.

If you're concerned how often the app is connecting to your account, you can see this in the *Last data access* section. Here you'll see what information was accessed and when. By clicking the *See details* link, a dialog box will appear providing details of what specific information on your account was accessed.

Finally, apps may want to contact you by sending a notification. By clicking on the drop-down list in the *When to notify you* section, you can select whether or not the app can email you notifications. This is an important feature, especially if you're dealing with a game that's bombarding you with updates and notifications of gifts sent to you.

Checking the privacy of apps before you install

As we saw earlier in this chapter, Privacy Score is a useful site for determining the privacy risk of a Web site you plan to visit or sign-up with. The URLs of various apps on Facebook and other sites can also be entered to identify possible privacy issues before you install them. A version of Privacy Score that addresses Facebook app privacy is also available at https://apps.facebook.com/privacyscoreapps.

Removing apps

Just as you'll sometimes want to prune back other areas of your online presence, it's a good idea to occasionally review the apps you've installed. Over time, you'll find that the apps you installed previously may no longer be used, meaning there's no point for it to have access to your personal information and privileges to your account. Rather than keeping them, it's better to remove the ones that are no longer useful.

On the *Apps Settings* page of Facebook, you can click the "X" to the right of an app's name to remove any that you recognize as no longer being used. If you're unsure, you can click on the *Edit* link to the right of the app's name to expand the area and view more information. By looking at the top line, you'll see the date you last logged into it. If it's been a considerable amount of time since it was last used, and you don't see yourself using it in the future, click the *Remove App* link at the bottom of the area showing this app's information.

If you don't use apps on Facebook, log on to other sites using your Facebook account, or use plug-ins or applications that interact with your account, you could also consider turning off the app platform on your Facebook account. This will prevent you from using apps on Facebook, so you should seriously consider whether you want to remove this functionality from your account. On the first line of the *Apps You Use* section of the *Apps Settings* page, you'll see an option asking if you *Use apps, plug-ins, games, and Web sites on Facebook and elsewhere?* If you click the *Edit* link beside this, it will expand the area, and display a *Turn Off Platform* button. Clicking this button shuts down integration with third-party apps.

Twitter doesn't provide the granular control over apps that Facebook does, but it does also allow you to remove any app you've installed. Once removed, the app will no longer have privileges to access your account. To revoke privileges from an app, do the following:

1. In the upper right-hand corner, click on the gear-shaped icon, and click *Settings*.
2. On the left pane of the page, click *Apps*.
3. When the *Applications* page appears, you'll see a list of apps that have access to your account. Each app will show when you approved it and the permissions it's been given. For each app you want to remove, click the *Revoke access* button beside the apps name.

Blocking apps in Facebook

Facebook provides the ability to block apps, so that it can't access information that isn't public and will be unable to send messages to contact you. Blocking apps is done through the *Manage Blocking* page as we discussed earlier in this chapter. To block an app, you would follow these steps:

1. Click on the gear-shaped icon in the upper right-hand corner of the page, and click *Account Settings* on the menu that appears.
2. In the left pane, click *Blocking*.
3. When the *Manage Blocking* page appears, scroll down to the *Block apps* section.
4. In the *Block Users* box, type the name of the app to block, and click the *Block* button.

Unblocking apps

After blocking an app, its name will be listed in the *Blocking apps* section. If you change your mind and want to unblock an app, simply click on the *Unblock* link beside the app's name, and click the *Confirm* button when prompted.

Location awareness

It's common for mobile devices to have a location tracking feature that uses GPS or the nearest Wi-Fi hotspot to determine your location, and even show where you are as you're moving. The feature does have benefits. As we discussed in Chapter 6, apps like Lookout Security and Antivirus, Norton Mobile Security, and AVG Antivirus for Android can use this feature to find lost and stolen devices. Location tracking can also be an issue when you consider others may be able to track where you are using this feature.

Rather than risk a breach of privacy, many turn off location tracking on their mobile devices. According to a 2012 study by Pew Internet and American Life Project, 19% of cell phone owners turn off the location tracking feature out of concern others will be able to access information on where they are. Those most likely to turn off the feature are people between the ages of 25 and 34 (32%) and parents (25%).

The concern for privacy is a valid one. If you're worried about an ex-spouse, someone you had a bad relationship with, or someone else of concern, you need to be wary of revealing your location. If someone wanted to monitor you and track your activity, a person with access to your device could install an app that tracks its location. The person could also try and acquire your password to a site that shows where a device is, which is why you should change your passwords to such sites every few months or whenever you're concerned of a security breach.

TOOLS & TIPS...

The Location Isn't Always Exact

Tracking devices can be useful to determine where employees and vehicles are, as in the case of shipping vehicles and delivery trucks. For example, UPS and FedEx use GPS tracking devices to know the exact location of their vehicles in their fleet, which helps determine estimated delivery times. From time to time, you'll also hear of employers installing location tracking apps on company phones to monitor employees. Recently, I was told about the experience of a salesperson who works for a firm in a large city. The manager has such apps on his employee's smartphones and visits a site to track the whereabouts of staff in real time. It makes the manager feel he has greater control over people doing sales calls or handling existing accounts. Many employees don't like this. Some are quietly looking for other jobs, while others find ways to fool the software. One person parks his car in the underground garages of buildings in the downtown area. The manager sees a general location where several clients have offices and has no idea his salesperson is actually grabbing an afternoon nap in the car. While such ingenuity won't earn an employee-of-the-month award, it does show that people will find ways to avoid being monitored.

Being aware of your location and situation

In using location-aware apps, it's important to consider where you are and your situation. Depending on the apps you use, your location could broadcast your home address, where you work or go to school, or whether you're far from home. If you were on vacation or out for an evening, a tweet or post that includes your location would show that your house is empty and unattended. As we've mentioned before in previous chapters, advertising this is like putting a sign on your front lawn saying no one's home, and it's an open opportunity for robbery.

Other people seeing your location can also make for some hard to explain situations. You might tell your spouse you were going to one place, but checking your location would reveal that you were somewhere else. It could also jeopardize a person's job if an employer or coworkers saw their colleague was frequenting a bar on company time or enjoying the beach on a sick day. If you think this is farfetched, you should realize that some apps, SMS messages, and data contained in photos can contain GPS coordinates that could be used to identify an exact location. As we'll discuss later in this chapter, searching for these coordinates in Google can reveal where you are in Google Maps or other sites.

Depending on your career, revealing your location could be dangerous. The US military advises service members and their families about using social media and stresses that they shouldn't reveal any information that could put an operation or soldiers at risk. Facts about the leave and return dates of service members, their names, and locations could be used to piece together information on troop movements, and the identities of those involved. If a soldier had location tracking turned on while deployed, it could be used to view the real-time movements of troops. You lower the possibility of problems by controlling the details you reveal online.

Location-based social networks

It's common for social networks to provide options to show your location, and there are many apps that use location tracking. However, there are some social networking sites that are built to use location awareness as part of its basic functionality. One of the most popular location-based social networks is Foursquare (www.foursquare. com). Using it, you can view venues that are close to your physical location, view comments about a business, and "check in" to show that you visited it.

As with many social networking sites, Foursquare has had features and bugs that have created controversy over privacy issues. In 2010, a developer named Jesper Anderson found a security hole in Foursquare allowing him to log who had checked into venues in San Francisco over a three-week period. What he realized is that when a Foursquare user checks into a location, a photo of the person appeared on a page for that location. It didn't matter how a person had configured their privacy settings, the page always showed a random selection of 50 people who had recently been there. Writing a script, he loaded this information on locations in San Francisco, logged changes in recent visitors, and recorded the differences. It allowed him to record 875,000 check-ins and create a history of where people had gone within that period of time. Once Foursquare became aware of the privacy leak, they fixed the problem so that the "who's here now" section of the venue page adhered to the privacy settings of the user.

It wasn't the first time the "who's here" information raised privacy issues. Girls Around Me (www.girlsaround.me) is an app that has caused controversy around the location-based social network. The app collected data from Foursquare to show users where women and men were located nearby, and provided photos and other information found in their Facebook profiles. Using it, you could scan for women, men, or a location to find people you wanted to meet. Looking at photo previews, you could then pick someone you liked and then do homework on them through information on their Facebook page.

Privacy concerns caused Foursquare to prevent the app from accessing its data and changed how they showed the "who's here" information on a venue. Rather than showing everyone within an area, you can only view who else is checked into a place. If you're not checked into the venue, then you'll only see people you've added to your social circle and a total number of people who are checked in there.

However, this isn't to say that similar functionality isn't available elsewhere. Banjo (www.ban.jo) is another app that uses other social networks to compile data on people. The app connects to your Twitter, Facebook, LinkedIn, Instagram, Google+, or Foursquare account to find people near you. It will display photos of them on a map so you can see how far away they are from your location and allows you to review recent tweets, posts, and photos that are public.

Removing location information from Facebook

When you post a new status update, Facebook will display the last location you specified. As shown in Figure 9.10, the last location I specified in a post was

FIGURE 9.10

Removing the location from a status update.

"Nowhere." To remove the location, hover over the location button at the bottom left of the status and click the "X." The location won't appear in your update.

If you wanted to provide a new location, you could click on the same button again and enter a new place. However, as we've mentioned, the less people know about where you are, the safer you'll often be.

Removing location information from Twitter

Twitter provides several settings to control whether location information appears in your tweets. In the account settings, you can opt into having a location added to your tweets. By default, this feature is turned off in Twitter. If turned on, when you make a tweet, you can click on a location icon to select a location you're tweeting from or search for a neighborhood or city. You also have the option of turning it off for individual tweets. Third-party apps can also be used to tweet your exact location such as an address or coordinates.

If you have been tweeting your location, the information about where you've been is stored with each tweet. Anyone viewing your past tweets could see where you go, when, and even possible addresses or coordinates of your home, friend's houses, or other places you frequent. To turn this feature off and remove about where you've been from previous tweets, do the following:

1. In Account Settings, scroll down until you see the *Tweet Location* section. Ensure the *Add a location to my Tweets* checkbox is unchecked.
2. Click the *Delete all location information* button.
3. When prompted, click *OK*.
4. Click the *Save Changes* button.
5. When prompted, enter your password and click *Save Changes*.

Hiding events

When you accept an invitation to an event, it will state where and when it occurs, so others will be able to see when and where you are at a given time. To prevent others from viewing the events you're attending, you hide the Event section on your profile page. To modify the visibility of Events, do the following:

1. On your profile page, click on the *More* menu below your cover photo, and then click the *Events* menu item.

2. Click on the Edit icon that's shaped like a pencil in the right corner of the *Events* section.
3. When the menu appears, click *Hide Section.*

Privacy of photos

Photos can reveal a considerable amount of information. When taking a photo, it can have recognizable features in the background that show where you are. Aside from the obvious identifiers like standing in front of a business sign or having your kids posing beside a school logo, even the most innocuous photos could be enough to identify where they were taken.

As we saw in Chapter 7, using Google you can search for an image and find similar matches. While we've already discussed how it can be used to identify a person, it can also be used to identify a place. If you used Google Image Search to find visually similar images to a photo showing a building, storefront, or other landmarks, it could return results of other images. In looking at the page where the photo originated, you might find a name or address of where the photo was taken.

People and locations can also be identified by the comments and tags people make. While we discuss tagging in Facebook in Chapter 10, you should consider setting audiences on who can view the albums of photos you upload to Facebook. By doing the following, you can limit who can view the photos decreasing the chance that someone will provide more information than you intended:

1. In Facebook, click on your name in the upper right-hand corner of the page.
2. Beneath your cover photo, click on the *Photos* tab.
3. When the *Photos* page appears, click on *Albums.*
4. In the lower right-hand corner beneath an album, click on the gear-shaped icon, and choose the audience who will be able to view the photos.

Geotags

Geotagging is a process of adding GPS information to a photo, showing the latitude, longitude, and other geographic attributes about where the photo is taken. If you have a newer digital camera or smartphone, it may have the ability to automatically add this information to your photos. Geotags are useful if you use programs to organize your photos by location or want to pinpoint exactly where it was taken. Unfortunately, it can also be a serious privacy concern if others look at the photo and use the information to determine your home address or places you frequent.

When a digital photo is taken with a camera that supports geotags, it will save additional information about the photo in the photo's *metadata*, which is basically additional data about the data. It will store facts about the type of camera used, lens, aperture, flash, and other details like the latitude, longitude, and altitude. If the image was uploaded to a content community or social networking site, anyone could download the image and see this information. By entering the GPS coordinates provided into Google Maps or the GPS system in your car, you could get the exact address and directions to where the photo was taken.

Viewing the information stored in a photo isn't difficult. Called Exchangable Image File (EXIF) data, it can easily be retrieved using sites like Jeffrey's EXIF Viewer (http://regex.info/exif.cgi). Here you can enter the URL of a photo or upload a copy and see the information stored in the image.

The GPS coordinates and other details in a photo can also be viewed in Windows by simply looking at its properties. By right-clicking on a photo and clicking *Properties* on the menu that appears, a dialog box providing information related to the image appears. As seen in Figure 9.11, by clicking on the *Details* tab, you'd be able to see a *GPS* section providing the coordinates of the photo's location.

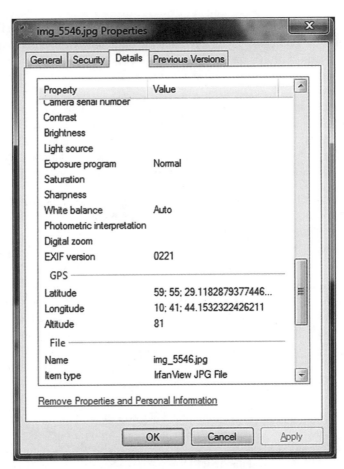

FIGURE 9.11

Geolocation information in an image.

Fortunately, Windows makes it easy removing the geotagged data. By clicking on the *Remove Properties and Personal Information* link on this tab, a dialog box appears that allows you to select what details you'd like to remove. If you'd like to keep everything as it is, but want a second copy of the image to post on Facebook, the dialog box also provides the option of making a sanitized copy that's had every possible property removed.

Of course, the best way to avoid having images with this information available on the Internet is not to have it included in the image's metadata. You should check your manual to see if the camera or phone supports saving geotagged or EXIF data, and change your camera or privacy settings on the device so it's turned off. On an iPhone, you would do this as follows:

1. On the home screen, tap the *Settings* icon.
2. Tap the *Privacy* menu.
3. At the top of the screen, choose *Location Services*.
4. Change the *Camera* setting to *Off*.

If you have any apps that use the camera on your mobile device such as Instagram or Facebook Camera, you should disable location services on them as well. Camera apps that support geotagging could still add the GPS information after the photo was taken, so it's always best to disable this feature so you don't accidentally reveal your location.

Bibliography

Forking and Dongle Jokes Don't Belong At Tech Conferences. (2013, March 18). Retrieved July 29, 2013, from Andria Richards: <http://butyoureagirl.com/14015/forking-and-dongle-jokes-dont-belong-at-tech-conferences/>.

Backhouse, M. (2013, May 17). *Moonlighting beauty therapist caught by social media trail.* Retrieved July 29, 2013, from New Zealand Herald: <http://www.nzherald.co.nz/nz/news/article.cfm?c_id=1&objectid=10884381>.

Blum, A. (2013, March 21). *Adria Richards, PyCon, and How We All Lost.* Retrieved July 29, 2013, from Amanda Blum: <http://amandablumwords.wordpress.com/2013/03/21/3/>.

Boyles, J. L., Smith, A., & Madden, M. (2012, September 5). *Privacy and data management on mobile devices.* Retrieved July 29, 2013, from Pew Internet & American Life Project: <http://pewinternet.org/Reports/2012/Mobile-Privacy/Main-Findings/Section-2.aspx>.

Brodkin, J. (2013, March 21). *How "dongle" jokes got two people fired—and led to DDoS attacks.* Retrieved July 29, 2013, from arstechnica: <http://arstechnica.com/tech-policy/2013/03/how-dongle-jokes-got-two-people-fired-and-led-to-ddos-attacks/#.UUxk6WZm8B0.pocket>.

Franklin, J. (2013, March 21). *A Difficult situation.* Retrieved July 29, 2013, from SendGrid: <http://blog.sendgrid.com/a-difficult-situation/>.

Hennessy-Fiske, M. (2010, August 8). *When Facebook goes to the hospital, patients may suffer.* Retrieved July 22, 2013, from Los Angeles Times: <http://articles.latimes.com/2010/aug/08/local/la-me-facebook-20100809>.

MC&FP Office of Military Community Outreach. (n.d.). *Military community and family policy: Social media guide.* Retrieved July 29, 2013, from Military One Source: <http://www.militaryonesource.mil/12038/MOS/ResourceGuides/Social_Media_Guide.pdf>.

Mislove, A., Viswanath, B., Gummadi, K. P., & Druschel, P. (2010). You are who you know: Inferring user profiles in online social networks: *WSDM '10 Proceedings of the third ACM international conference on web search and data mining.* New York, New York: Association for Computing Machinery (ACM). pp. 251–260.

Noller, J. (2013, March 20). *PyCon's response to an inappropriate incident on March 17th.* Retrieved July 29, 2013, from PyCon: <http://pycon.blogspot.ca/2013/03/pycon-response-to-inappropriate.html>.

Ponemon Institute. (2011, September). *Global survey on social media risks.* Retrieved June 13, 2013, from Websense: <http://www.websense.com/assets/reports/websense-social-media-ponemon-report.pdf>.

PR Newswire. (2010, May 4). *Consumer reports survey: 52 Percent of social network users post risky information.* Retrieved June 19, 2013, from PR Newswire: <http://www.prnewswire.com/news-releases/consumer-reports-survey-52-percent-of-social-network-users-post-risky-information-92748344.html>.

PyCon. (2013). *PyCon 2013.* Retrieved July 29, 2013, from Code of Conduct: <https://us.pycon.org/2013/about/code-of-conduct/>.

Richards, A. (2013, March 13). *@adriarichards Twitter Account.* Retrieved July 29, 2013, from Twitter: <https://twitter.com/adriarichards/status/313417655879102464>.

Richards, A. (2013, March 14). *@adriarichards Twitter Account.* Retrieved July 29, 2013, from Twitter: <https://twitter.com/adriarichards/status/312265091791847425>.

Sarbanes–Oxley Act Section 806: Whistleblower Protection. (n.d.). Retrieved July 28, 2013, from SOX-Online: <http://www.sox-online.com/act_section_806.html>.

Singel, R. (2010, June 29). *White hat uses Foursquare privacy hole to capture 875 K check-ins.* Retrieved May 23, 2013, from Wired: <http://www.wired.com/threatlevel/2010/06/foursquare-privacy/>.

What is Enterprise Content Management (ECM)? (n.d.). Retrieved July 29, 2013, from Association for Information and Image Management (AIIM) International: <http://www.aiim.org/What-is-ECM-Enterprise-Content-Management>.

Security

INFORMATION IN THIS CHAPTER:

- Security
- Fake accounts
- Passwords
- Privacy and information sharing
- Content security

Security

Not everyone takes security seriously. It's not uncommon for people to create a social media account and never look beyond the default settings. In the same way, they'll buy a mobile device, computer, or some other equipment to access those sites and accept that it's set up in a way that best protects them. Often, the default settings provide the greatest ease of use but are also the least secure. It's never a good idea to trust someone else has your security in mind, so you should check and configure these settings yourself. Fortunately, in reading this book, you've already shown how you're willing to do that.

Security is a trade-off. The more you lock down a social media account, restrict content from appearing on your profile page, and prevent people from accessing photos and other content, the less chance people will have finding you in searches. This not only means people you'd rather avoid, but also any old friends and family members you'd like to connect with. A decision can make your social media use more secure, but it can cost you functionality and/or ease of use.

The trade-off of security applies to almost anything you can think of in technology, accounts, network access, equipment, and content. As we've seen throughout this book, and discuss further in this chapter, there are many threats on the Internet and many tactics, settings, and tools to protect you and your systems. The level of security you choose to use is subjective, where it's up to you how much and how little you use. Ultimately, you need to decide how much you're willing to expose yourself to risks, and what level of vulnerability you can live with.

Keeping track of accounts

When you're exploring the different social media sites available, it's easy to create accounts and forget the ones you don't use. This can leave a security hole, especially if you've set up posts on one site to automatically tweet an update or publish to another site. If a hacker gained access to it, it could be confusing at first trying to figure out why strange posts were appearing, not realizing it was coming from another site. Since you haven't used that account for awhile, when you do realize what's happening, you might also realize you've forgotten the username and password for the site.

To keep track of your accounts, you should consider creating a master list. It should state the URL of the site, the account name, and password. Keeping a master list of administrator passwords is a practice of IT departments in organizations, in which administrator accounts and passwords are documented and stored in a secure location. It's important that you don't keep it someplace where people will be able to read it or as a document on your computer. If it's stored as an electronic document on your computer or network, as in the case of a spreadsheet or Word document, you can add an extra small measure of security by password protecting it. As changes occur, update the list so the information is there when you need it.

The other benefit of keeping a list of accounts and passwords is that it shows you where the same passwords are being used on multiple sites. If a site was hacked, your credentials could be compromised, and the hacker could now potentially gain access to any site using the same passwords. When this occurs, you'd need to change the passwords on any sites using them. In referring to your list of passwords, look for ones used multiple times, and then change them so a unique password is used on each site.

TOOLS & TIPS...

Setting up Social Media for a Business

IT departments should have authority over the technical aspects of social media and be involved in setting up and maintaining accounts. While they aren't difficult to set up, it ensures that people who are well versed with security are configuring the account correctly and in a consistent manner that follows social media security guidelines. Any settings they initially make could be modified later by a person using the account, but at least you're assured it's done correctly at setup or since the last security audit.

Security reviews

Threats change, so security needs to change and address them. Even if you've done everything right in configuring your security settings, there's no guarantee that new settings won't be introduced or old settings may be reset. Changes can occur anywhere. It may be on your computer or other devices used to access the Internet, or on the sites themselves.

Social media sites often make changes to their security to address identified or potential issues. While some sites notify you of updates and new settings, others may implement them without your knowledge, leaving you unaware of what's happened. How often this happens, and whether you're notified depends on the site. Because of this, you should review your settings from time to time to ensure they're configured the way you intended.

When a social media site changes its security, it can affect the options that are available. While you may have thought security was set up properly, the options may have changed. In some cases, the changes may reset your security settings to their default settings or provide additional options that may need to be set. The site may decide to turn on a setting that you don't want or make the option available and turned off. To benefit from the available security options, you need to review them and make sure they're set properly.

Being that social media involves using a computer or other devices, you also need to review how they're protected. You should evaluate the effectiveness of any security tools used to protect your computer, network, and mobile devices. Antivirus software needs to have signature files updated on a regular basis so it can identify any potential threats and block, quarantine, or remove them accordingly. To ensure you're protected, you should check the software to ensure it's being updated automatically, and that your system is being scanned on a regular basis.

The operating system and software installed on a system will need to be updated from time to time. Doing so will patch any known vulnerabilities, which can be exploited by malicious software. This applies not only to your computer but also to any mobile devices you use.

It's equally important to reevaluate strategies used to keep your organization and employees secure. The Social Media Officer should work with the IT department to provide information on changes that have occurred, and the IT staff should be aware of the social media sites being used when configuring security settings on equipment. Browsers, operating systems, and other tools may be updated, so it's necessary to identify and resolve any issues that could occur in using social media on these devices.

Businesses also need to audit their security so they're aware of changes in requirements. A company may have initially been fearful in using social media but now wants the sites accessible in the workplace. Conversely, they may have allowed users free reign over the social networking sites they visit but now want to limit access due to a number of incidents. These require changes to the existing firewall rules, how users are trained to use Internet resources, and may require changes to existing policies.

Security strategies

One of the major benefits and problems of social media is that you don't need any additional hardware or software to begin using it. Despite the hidden costs we'll discuss in Chapter 11, a person can simply create an account and begin using it. This allows employees to bypass the normal channels of employing new technology, along with any risk assessment and safeguards provided by an IT department. So long as they're able to go online and access social media sites, they're essentially out of your control.

The purpose of a social media security strategy is to give people the ability to do what's needed without compromising security. In creating one, you need to identify what areas need to be secure, how security will be achieved, and who will be responsible. The strategy should encompass any areas related to using social media, inclusive to the corporate workstations people may use, mobile devices issued to employees, network security, and firewall restrictions.

The security of corporate networks and computers is maintained by members of an IT department, who can grant or deny the ability to access features, resources, and perform certain actions. Because public social media sites are external to your network, this level of control doesn't extend to those sites. Don't expect the same level of support for an external site that you would for your intranet Web site or another network resource.

There is greater control over private social networking sites that your company may use. For example, if they have sites created with SharePoint, the Administrator can control who within the organization can view, contribute and approve content added to pages, as well as documents and other files that are uploaded. Because applications deployed to this environment may have their own security controls, the IT staff may have granular control over what people can do. In creating a security strategy, you'll need to identify what sites are effected (e.g., Facebook, Twitter, or your corporate intranet) and create rules and procedures that are applicable to them.

The other area where the IT department needs to be consulted is in relation to the firewall settings. A *firewall* is a hardware and/or software security system that controls what is allowed to pass in and out of the network and will use content filtering features or tools to look at the content to determine if it should be allowed. It blocks unwanted content through rules that are created and looks at the data packets entering or leaving the network to determine whether they match those rules. For social media use, content filtering tools like Websense (www.websense.com) could be used to allow or block sites like Facebook and Twitter, or sites that fall into specific categories, such as social networking. It's important to work with the network administrator in your IT department so that the security settings can be configured to allow employees to access the sites.

If you want people to use certain apps, the IT department will also need to be aware of these requirements. For example, some apps use Adobe Flash, which means it needs to be installed on the computer being used. In other cases, the site may use HTML 5 to deliver content, which isn't supported by all browsers. Because employees probably (and should) have restrictions on what they can install on corporate computers, the IT staff would need to have these programs installed.

The level of support an IT department gives is another important topic to discuss, as social media can be accessed from home computers and personal mobile devices. A Social Media Officer may feel that the IT department's help desk should provide social media support to employees, but the IT staff may have a different opinion. They're probably not going to suddenly provide technical support to equipment that isn't owned by the company. They also wouldn't want to touch a personal mobile phone or tablet brought into the office, as the company could be liable for infringing on someone's personal privacy and any problems occurring later with the device.

This isn't to say that a company should ignore the fact that employees will use personal devices to access social media or the potential risk. As we've mentioned in previous chapters, an employee could fall victim to social engineering and give away their password or other sensitive information, or have their home computer infected with a virus or malware. To prevent this, the company should train employees on security-related issues and also look into corporate discounts for them to purchase antivirus software and other security tools for home use.

TOOLS & TIPS...

Don't Expect Miracles

The same security controls available on your personal social media account is what's available to a business one, so don't expect the IT department to configure any settings beyond what you can see. Also remember that they won't be able to access any settings if they haven't been given the account's username and password. Due to their technical background, your IT staff can be useful in recommending the best possible settings and provide insight on how to configure them to achieve the results you want.

Fake accounts

Like it or not, fake accounts are part of the social media landscape. People will create accounts with false information for a variety of reasons, many of which are innocuous. A person may create accounts to have additional neighbors or allies needed in a game, or as a parody to satirize a person or an organization. Some people will also use false information when creating their account to hide their true identity, whether as a defensive measure or to make it more difficult for police to trace back their actions.

A common reason why people create fake accounts is because they wouldn't otherwise be allowed on a site. The person may be banned from a site or chat room, or unable to create a legitimate account because it would violate the Terms of Service. As we mentioned in Chapter 4, according to a 2011 survey by Consumer Reports, approximately 7.5 million of the minors who use Facebook were younger than 13, and of this, more than 5 million of them were 10 and under. Younger users create fake accounts to access to the site, providing a bogus birthdate to bypass the age restriction. If the fake account is removed, many people will simply get a new email address and create a new fake account.

Hacking an account isn't the only way to pose as another person. It's common for new accounts to be created by someone posing as another person. I can visit your page on Facebook and download your profile picture or use an editing tool like Editor by pixlr.com (www.pixlr.com/editor/) to obtain and edit the photo using the URL of the picture. Looking at the personal information you've allowed to be visible, I could duplicate it in a new profile. Viola ... I now appear to be you. Once this is done, any disparaging remarks I make under that account will be attributed to you by the general public, damaging your reputation, costing you clients, and making you the target of public outrage.

Sometimes, online impersonation can lead to tragic events. In 2010, David Russell created a fake account on Facebook, pretending to be a popular British musician. He began seducing a 19-year-old woman named Maricar Benedicto and convinced her to travel from California to England. Once there, he took her to a secluded forest, blindfolded her, slit her throat, and attempted stabbing her to death. He was sentenced to 17½ years for kidnapping and attempted murder.

In using social media, you need to realize that the person you're interacting with may not be the person they say they are. If a family member or friend tries to add you as a connection, try to email or phone them and confirm the request is real. If it's a long-lost friend or someone you have limited contact with, then temporarily add them to a Facebook list that gives restricted access. Once you've confirmed who they are, you can remove them from the list and give them greater access to your Timeline, blog, or page.

Brandjacking

Brandjacking is a term that refers to someone creating a false representation of your brand. The site, page, or account appears to belong to you or your organization or individual but has been created by someone else. It may be created as a parody, protest, or to pose as a legitimate company and sell counterfeit products.

In some cases, brandjacking is an attempt to squat on a good Twitter name in the hopes the actual owner will pay for it. This is similar to *cybersquatting*, in which people would register good domain names that might be wanted by businesses or major organizations. As it's illegal and most sites won't allow the transfer of account names, attempting to take on an account name for this purpose is pointless.

An example of brandjacking occurred in 2008, when a Twitter account called @ExxonMobilCorp was created with the appearance of belonging to the multinational oil and gas giant, Exxon Mobil Corporation. It showed the company logo and appeared to be representative of the company. It was eventually found to be a fake, with Exxon having no idea who was behind the account. Even when a brandjacked account does no visible damage, it can make the actual company appear incompetent and not in control of how they're represented.

Brandjacking as part of an attack

Brandjacking can also be part of a multipronged attack, incorporating other tactics to attack an organization or individual. Such attacks aren't limited to big corporations. It can happen to anyone, even those who seem to revel in negative attention.

The Westboro Bapist Church (WBC) is an independent church noted for its anti-gay movement, inclusive to a Web site called godhatesfags.com and picketing funerals of murdered homosexuals. They are also known for picketing the funerals of those who have died in military service. In 2012, the WBC announced that they were going to picket funerals of those killed in the Sandy Hook Elementary School shooting. The announcement of picketing the funerals of 20 children and 6 staff members attracted public attention and also that of a hacktivist group called *Anonymous*.

Anonymous became vocal about the WBC on social networking sites. Conversation about it started on the *Anonymous News Network* Facebook page, and through a hashtag campaign they started called #OpWestboro. Tweets called for people to stop protesters, leading to walls of people arriving at the funerals to shield mourners from WBC protesters. Anonymous stepped up their attack and called for people to obtain and share information about WBC's membership. Within hours, the call for action achieved results. Links to sites like Pastbin (www.pastebin.com/ARASaC1h) showed the names, addresses, phone numbers, and work locations of WBC members. A hacker named CosmoTheGod hacked the Twitter accounts of church spokesperson Shirley Phelps-Roper and the pastor's son Fred Phelps Jr.

In 2013, it was news outlets reported that Anonymous had hacked the WBC's Facebook page, but this wasn't the case. The WBC was actually brandjacked. The Westboro Baptist Church page on Facebook appears to be legitimate, with some markings of a hacked page, including a blurb that attributes the church leaders as the names of various hackers. Some of the posts on the brandjacked page promote tolerance, recognize the sacrifice of those killed in combat, and encourage people to sign a petition for the US government to recognize the WBC as a hate group.

Defensive profiles to prevent impersonation

Even if you or your organization don't use social media, it is important to set up profiles for the business and key members of your organization. If you don't, there is always the possibility that someone else will. By setting up fake profiles, someone can impersonate a business entity and its spokespeople, sending out false information and publicly embarrassing them.

There have been a number of cases where businesses, celebrities, and other people have been impersonated on social media sites. One notable case from 2009 involved St. Louis Cardinals manager Tony La Russa, where a fake Twitter account was created posing as him. Tweets involved a number of disparaging and vulgar comments against him and the team intended to cause public embarrassment. After an attempt to notify Twitter, La Russa sued Twitter in the first case of a celebrity lawsuit against the social media site. How the case ended depends on who you listen to. It was reported the two had come to a settlement involving Twitter paying La Russa's legal fees and making a donation to his Animal Rescue Foundation, but Twitter says this is untrue.

Two days after the initial report, Twitter said the settlement details were erroneous and went on to announce a new verification program, where a person could apply online and have their Twitter account verified as being legitimate. As seen

Bill Gates ✔
@BillGates

🐦 Follow

FIGURE 10.1

Bill Gates Twitter account showing the blue verified account badge.

in Figure 10.1, any verified accounts have a blue check mark on them. Since the verification program became active, Twitter has since closed it to the public and only uses for business partners and "highly sought users in music, acting, fashion, government, politics, religion, journalism, media, advertising, business, and other key interest areas." Facebook offers similar verification with comparable limitations.

While the verification program helps people identify they're following a legitimate account, it isn't foolproof. In 2012, a fake account was created for Wendi Deng, the wife of News Corp Chief Executive Rupert Murdoch, and was verified by Twitter with the blue tick mark. Some of the tweets that were followed included flirting with celebrities, and the account was followed thousands of people who thought it was the real person. By the time the verified account was announced as fake, the incident proved more embarrassing for Twitter, who lost credibility in their ability to verify the legitimacy of their accounts.

Another way people fake Twitter verification is by adding an image of the blue check mark on their profile page's background or header photo. At first glance, the profile will appear to have been verified because it includes a blue tick. However, as seen in Figure 10.2, to determine a profile is really verified, hover your mouse over the blue check mark and the words "Verified account" will appear. If it doesn't do this, then the person has merely included the blue tick in their header photo and the account isn't really verified.

Twitter of course isn't the only place where fake accounts impersonating others can be created. Accounts have been created to impersonate businesses and individuals on MySpace, Facebook, and countless other social media sites. As we saw in Chapter 7, when we discussed the tragic case of Megan Meier, profiles can also be created on social networking sites for fictitious people for dubious or malicious reasons.

FIGURE 10.2

A verified account profile shows the words "verified account" when you hover over the blue check mark.

Reporting fake accounts on Facebook

While you'll find many fake accounts on Facebook, they aren't actually allowed. If you find an account pretending to be you or impersonating someone else, you can report them. You can also report pages that have been created that are impersonating or harassing you.

1. Click on the gear-shaped icon of the fake Timeline, which appears beside the Message button. Click *Report Page* from the menu that appears.
2. When the dialog box appears, make the appropriate selection from the list to report the page or account. Click *Continue*, and follow the instructions to file a report.

If you don't have an account on Facebook and find a page or profile impersonating you, Facebook provides the ability to report it. However, they don't make it easy. When you're logged off of Facebook, you can go to www.facebook.com/help and search for information on reporting a page, and follow the link www.facebook.com/help/contact/?id=169486816475808. On this page, you'll be presented with three options:

1. Someone is using my email address on their account.
2. Someone created an account for my business or organization.
3. Someone created an account pretending to be me or a friend.

After selecting the option that applies to you, you would then continue through a series of steps to report the page.

Reporting inappropriate profiles on LinkedIn

LinkedIn also provides methods of reporting fake or inappropriate accounts. When a profile is flagged as inappropriate, it's later reviewed by the site. To flag a profile, you would do the following:

1. On the person's profile, click on the down arrow next to the *Send a Message* button.
2. When the menu appears, click *Flag as inappropriate*.
3. When the dialog box appears, select the reason it's inappropriate from the drop-down menu.
4. Optionally, you can provide additional details in the *Details* field.
5. Click *Send*.

Fake profiles can also be reported through an online Notice of False Profile form. If you believe someone has posted inaccurate or unlawful information on their profile, you could fill out the form and submit a claim regarding the problem. Unfortunately, finding the claim form isn't easy, although you can find it by searching for "False Profile Policy" at http://help.linkedin.com or visiting http://help.linkedin.com/app/answers/detail/a_id/30200 and clicking on the link to report the person.

Passwords

Passwords are an important part of security, especially when it comes to social media sites. As we mentioned, many sites like Facebook, Twitter, LinkedIn, Tumblr, and so on ask two things to log on:

1. Username or email address
2. Password

Since your username may be visible for anyone to see, and your email address is generally treated as public knowledge, the only thing really preventing someone from accessing your account is the password. To protect yourself, it's vital that secure passwords are used on all social media accounts, especially Facebook and Twitter. Many other social media sites like Pinterest allow you to log on using your Facebook or Twitter account, so if these are compromised, countless others will be as well.

You also don't want to use the same password on multiple sites. If your password is compromised on one site, then someone with that password can use it to successfully log on to any other sites you're a member of. You might not think it very important if your site on LinkedIn was compromised, as financial information isn't stored on there. However, it may provide the work employment history needed for a credit card or loan application, and if the same password was used to access banking or credit card sites, you'd have an even more serious problem.

TOOLS & TIPS...

The most Important Password in Social Media

One of the easiest ways to hijack social media accounts is through an email account. If a person has access to your email or cracks the username/password for it, he or she could visit each of the sites and click the "Forgot password" link. The attacker would then use the email notifications containing a link to change the password. In doing so, you no longer have the correct password, but the other person does. To avoid this problem, make sure you use a secure password for your email accounts and limit who has access.

Bad passwords

In creating passwords, you don't want to use ones that are weak or easy to guess. Although you've probably heard this one before, many people don't follow this rule and continue to use passwords that are uninspired. SplashData (www.splashdata. com), a provider of password management software, compiled a list of common passwords in 2012 from password lists posted on the Internet by hackers. Of these, the top 10 were:

1. password
2. 123456
3. 12345678
4. abc123
5. qwerty
6. monkey
7. letmein
8. dragon
9. 111111
10. baseball

If an attacker were to use password cracking tools, it wouldn't take long to break them. For some, it won't even take long to guess. Except for one, all of the passwords are either numbers or letters (not a combination of both), do not use upper and lower case letters, and do not contain any special characters using symbols on your keyboard. They contain words found in the dictionary and patterns that password recovery software checks to crack your password.

Commonly used passwords have common characteristics, which can be broken down into different categories. As we mentioned in Chapter 7, these similar features make them easier to guess when social engineering tactics are applied, so you'll want to avoid passwords that consist of:

- Keyboard rolls like qwerty, asdf, 12345
- Letter and/or number combinations like 11111, abc123, or 345abc
- Names (inclusive to first names or first initial followed by surname)
- Country or city of origin

- Favorites (car, team, sport, athlete, band, song, movie character, actor, etc.)
- Affiliations (including religious words like god, jesus, etc., schools and clubs)

When common passwords are used, a person will sometimes add a number to the end. This may be due to password restrictions, which require a combination of letters and numbers, or because the person thinks that by adding these, the password is suddenly secure. Some of the common numerical extensions include:

- Adding a number ranging from zero to nine (0–9)
- Numbers that have a personal meaning, such as the person's birth, graduation, marriage date
- Numbers that have a social meaning, such as 007, 69, 666
- A random series or combination of numbers like 123, 0000, 77777

Good passwords

While looking at the elements of a bad password can tell you a lot, there are a number of qualities that make a strong, secure password. The best passwords should contain the following:

- Does not contain any words found in the dictionary
- Does not contain the name of your company, your username, or real name
- At least eight characters (although more is better) consisting of the following:
  - Uppercase letters, such as A, B, C, etc.
  - Lowercase letters, such as a, b, c, etc.
  - Numbers, such as 0, 1, 2, 3, 4, etc.
  - Special characters, which are symbols found on your keyboard like: ` ~ ! @ # $ % ^ & * ( )_ - + = { } [ ]\|:;"'<>,.?/

There are many ways to create a password that's complex and difficult to crack, but it is important to create one that you'll remember. You've probably known someone who created a difficult password, wrote it on a sticky note, and attached it to their monitor. The worst I've seen was when I walked into a large public office and saw the name of an application and its associated username/password written on a whiteboard in large letters. These are terrible breaches of security. Anything you create should be memorable, stored in password management software, or documented and kept in a safe place.

A good trick to create complex passwords that you'll remember is to create a meaningful sentence and use the first letter of each word. For example, "Today I will use Facebook with a complex password" becomes *TIWUFWACP*. To make it stronger, you can use a combination of upper and lowercase letters. If we were to use the grammar of the sentence, it becomes *TIwuFwacp*. However, you could also use a pattern of making the first and last few letters uppercase and then leave the rest lowercase, so that it becomes *TIWufwACP*. In looking at this, you can see how quickly it becomes complex but remains memorable.

You can expand on this technique and increase a password's complexity by adding numbers and special characters. If we're to continue using the same password, we could add punctuation to the sentence, adding an exclamation point to the end making it *TIWufwACP!* We could also add a meaningful number to make it even stronger. For example, I started dating my wife in 1993, so I could make the password *93TIWufwACP!* Even though this last item is unrelated to our core sentence, it's memorable enough for me to remember. By using a number that's meaningful to you, it will be easy to include as you think of your sentence and type the first letter of each word.

If your password is compromised, a hacker could use it indefinitely, which is why you should change your password on a regular basis. Unfortunately, many do not. Even on corporate networks, it's not uncommon to see the same Administrator or system password used for years at a time. You'll often find that the password security for user accounts is better, as there are network policies that force people to change it, often every 90 days. Because social media sites generally don't require a person to change their password on a recurring basis, it's up to you to follow good practices and change it every few months. Obviously, if you do change it more frequently that's great.

When a password is changed, it should be different from previous passwords. After all, if I cracked your password and you flip-flopped between using two different passwords, half the time your compromised password will allow me access. It would only be a matter of time before you reused your old password, and attackers count on this.

If you want to see whether a password is strong and difficult to crack, there are tools on the Internet to check the strength of a password. For example, Microsoft has a tool at www.microsoft.com/security/pc-security/password-checker.aspx, which will not store any password entered on the page but will show you whether it's secure. As seen in Figure 10.3, as you enter a password into a box, the page shows you whether it's strong or not. In this case, the password entered was "Password1". Even though a number of the requirements for creating a good password were met, the checker still found it weak because it wasn't very complex and used a word found in the dictionary.

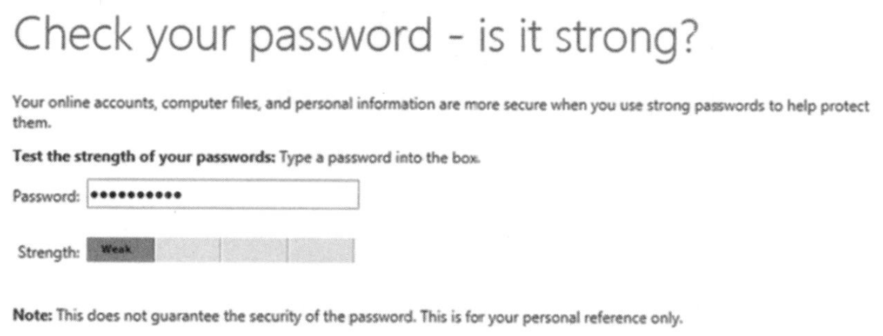

Check your password - is it strong?

Your online accounts, computer files, and personal information are more secure when you use strong passwords to help protect them.

Test the strength of your passwords: Type a password into the box.

Password: ●●●●●●●●●

Strength: Weak

Note: This does not guarantee the security of the password. This is for your personal reference only.

FIGURE 10.3

Password checker on Microsoft's safety and security center site.

Hacking 101

Obtaining passwords aren't as difficult as you might think. People may make the mistake of sharing their passwords with others or use settings that can make your account less secure. There are also many password recovery tools on the Internet. By running these programs, you can retrieve passwords from different programs and systems with little effort.

The easiest way to get into someone's account is to open a browser after someone else has logged into a social networking site. If you checked the checkbox to remember you or leave you logged when you logged onto the account, the next person who opened the browser and went to the social media site would automatically be logged on. Even if you had stringent security limiting what others can see, that person would be able to see all of your information and settings because they're logged on as you.

There are many programs on the Internet that allow you to recover passwords stored in Web browsers, which you may have forgotten. One such tool is NirSoft's *WebBrowserPassView* (www.nirsoft.net/utils/web_browser_password.html), which enables you to recover passwords from Internet Explorer, Mozilla Firefox, Google Chrome, Safari, and Opera. To determine the browser versions you can recover passwords from, you should visit the site and look at the latest version.

When running the program, you're presented with a graphical user interface that lists the URL, username, and password, as well as the browser it was acquired from. If you wanted to be covert in obtaining passwords using WebBrowserPassView, you could save the program to a USB stick and create a batch file containing the following code:

```
@echo off
CD /d "%~dp0"
IF NOT EXIST LOGRESULTS/nul (mkdir LOGRESULTS)
WebBrowserPassView.exe/shtml LOGRESULTS/Passwords.html
exit
```

In running the batch file, it would create a folder on the USB called LOGRESULTS and store a Web page in it named Passwords.html. You could slip the USB stick into a computer, run the batch file, and walk away. At your leisure, you could open the HTML file and view a listing of the sites, usernames, and passwords the person visited. You could then use this information to gain access to the person's accounts on Twitter, Facebook, LinkedIn, Gmail, or any number of other social networking, mail, banking, or credit card sites.

Keyloggers are another common way of acquiring a person's passwords and monitoring their activity. For example, *Blazing Tools Perfect Keylogger* (www.blazingtools.com/bpk.html) is a tool that can be installed on a computer and has features to run on Windows startup and that hide it so the person is unaware it's installed. After installing it on a machine, you can see a textual display of every key they pressed on their keyboard, showing you the sites they visited and the passwords they typed. You can also take screenshots at intervals to see everything the person saw on different dates and times. If you won't have access to the computer to retrieve this information, you can have it email it to you or upload it to an FTP server at specified intervals.

Of course, it's even easier if someone's already acquired the passwords for you. While the common depiction of a hacker is a lone individual pounding away at a keyboard, you'd be surprised how much they interact with one another online. If a hacker manages to acquire a list of usernames and passwords such as by downloading a database from a site, he or she might decide to share it with others. For example, in June 2012, 6.5 million LinkedIn and 1.5 million eHarmony (www.eharmony.com) passwords were uploaded to a Russian hacking site. This allowed others to download and decipher the encrypted passwords, which as we discussed in Chapter 3 isn't that difficult to do with the right software.

Verification for password resets

Twitter provides a feature that adds an extra layer of protection when resetting a password. By default, all that's needed to reset a password is your account name. If you have this set, when you forget your password, you'll also need to enter your email address or phone number as additional confirmation of your identity. To set this verification feature, follow these steps:

1. Click on the gear-shaped icon in the upper right-hand corner of the page, and click *Settings*.
2. Scroll down to the *Password reset* section, and click the *Require personal information to reset my password* checkbox so it appears checked.
3. Click *Save Changes*.

Protecting your account with two-step verification

As we'll saw in Chapter 7, some social network accounts provide a notification feature, which allows you to be emailed or texted when someone logs on using your account. There are also features that will restrict who can log on from a computer or device that hasn't previously been used to access your account. When this is set, a person will need to enter a code to log on from an unknown browser.

Facebook provides a Login Approval feature that will send a security code to your mobile phone when you log on using an unknown browser. When you receive the code, you must then enter it in addition to a username and password to access the account. To set this feature on Facebook, do the following:

1. Click on the gear-shaped icon in the upper right-hand corner of the page. When the menu appears, click *Account Settings*.
2. In the left pane of the page, click *Security*.
3. In the *Login Approval* section, click *Edit*.
4. When the section expands, click on the *Require a security code to access my account from unknown browsers* checkbox so it appears checked.

5. When the dialog box appears, click *Get Started*.
6. Click on the option that describes the type of phone you use (i.e., Android, iPhone, iPod Touch, or Other). Click *Continue*.
7. If you haven't previously activated Code Generator to get security codes on your phone, open the Facebook app on your phone, tap on the menu button, and then scroll down to Code Generator. After tapping Active, return to your computer and click *Continue*.
8. Test the code, and then click *Confirm*.

On Twitter, you can also set up your account to use a verification code when logging in. To use this feature, you need to add a phone to your Twitter account and have the Twitter mobile app installed on your mobile phone. Once this is done, you can activate the feature by doing the following:

1. Click on the gear-shaped icon in the upper right-hand corner, and click Settings on the menu that appears.
2. Scroll down to the *Account Security* section, and click the *Require a verification code when I sign in* checkbox so it appears checked.

Once you've set the feature, a step-by-step process will begin similar to what we previously discussed with Facebook. You'll be sent a message to your phone, which you use to confirm the process. Once complete, you'll need to enter your username, password, and a six-digit code that's sent each time to your phone when you try to access the account.

LinkedIn also has a two-step verification logon process that can be activated through the settings of your account. To activate this, you'll need to have the LinkedIn mobile app installed on your mobile phone and perform the following steps:

1. Click on your name in the upper right-hand corner of the page. When the menu appears, click *Settings*.
2. Scroll down the page, and click on the *Account* tab.
3. Click *Manage security settings*.
4. In the *Two-step verification for sign-in* section, click *Turn On*.
5. Select the *Country* you reside in from the drop-down list.
6. Enter the phone number of your mobile phone. The number won't appear in your profile.
7. Click *Send code*.

Privacy and information sharing

An important part of social media security is the privacy of personal and sensitive information.

According to a 2012 report by Consumer Reports, 13 million Facebook users in the United States don't use privacy controls, meaning that the details about them are visible for anyone to see. Accepting the defaults and never changing your privacy settings exposes your information to other Facebook users and makes it available to anyone using a search engine.

Locking down personal information

When you set up an account, you're asked to provide information about yourself. Some of this may be kept private and retained by the site in case there's a problem. For example, if your account was compromised, they might want your phone number so they could call you and help clear up the matter. However, some of the personal information may appear on your profile page and available to anyone who searches for it or looks at your profile.

In Chapter 3, we showed you how to lock down personal information on a LinkedIn account, and many of the same principles apply to other sites. To protect yourself, you'll want to review the personal and contact information appearing on your profile. Settings may be available to lock down who can view the information, and you can simply delete a lot of the details about yourself so there's no chance of it ever being seen by others. What you choose to make available to others often depends on your situation. If you run a business, you'll want people seeing the location of the business, phone number, and other details. For personal use, you probably don't want others seeing this or only a select number of people. As we'll see in the sections that follow, Facebook provides a number of options for securing this information.

Contact information on Facebook

The contact information in the *About* section of your Facebook profile allows you to provide numerous ways for people to reach you. If you've provided this information and the security settings aren't configured, you could advertise your address, phone number, and other facts that someone can use to find you. If you think people don't share sensitive information like this, browse some Facebook profiles and you'll be amazed how much some people share with the public.

While you might be tempted to remove everything, some information may need to be handled differently, and you'll want to limit who can view it. For example, if you have a mobile phone setup for use with your account, you might want to leave that information for apps to function. Instead, you would select the audience who will be able to see that information and set it to an extremely limited audience so that those you don't want viewing this information won't see it To secure contact information on your Facebook account, do the following:

1. Click on your name in the upper right-hand corner.
2. When your Timeline appears, click on the *About* tab below your cover picture.
3. Scroll down to the bottom of the section and click *See All*.
4. In the *Contact Information* section, click the *Edit* button.
5. In the *Email* section, click on the *Friends* icon to the right of each email address, and change the audience to one you're willing to share that address with.

6. Click on the *Hide from Timeline* icon beside each email address, for any email addresses you don't want publicized on your page, click *Hide from Timeline* so the email address doesn't appear on your Timeline.

7. In the *Contact Information* section, click the *Edit* button.

8. In the *Mobile Phone* section, click on the icon to the right of the section and choose *Only Me* from the drop-down list.

9. In the *Other Phones* section, remove any phone numbers.

10. In the *IM Screen Names* section, click on the icon to the right of the section and select an audience that you want to allow instant messaging with, such as *Friends*.

11. Unless the profile is for a business and you want people to know the address, remove the information from the Address, City, Zip, and Neighborhood fields.

12. Click *Save*.

As we discussed in Chapter 3, you should limit access to your email address on your profile pages or change the settings to limit its visibility. Because LinkedIn, Twitter, Facebook, and other sites allow users to send messages to one another, you will still be able to communicate with other users without relying on a people contacting you directly via email. If you really want an email address on your page, you might consider the alternative of creating a second email account; one to log on with and another to post on your page so that people can email you directly.

Basic information on Facebook

The basic information in the *About* section of your profile allows you to provide a considerable amount of information about who you are. As seen in Figure 10.4, the *Basic Information* section provides fields to reveal your gender, birthday, marital status, anniversary, languages, sexual preference, religious and political views. In looking at this, you can see that much of the information is related to protected statuses and could be used to discriminate against you if an employer or someone influential viewed it. It could also be useful for scraping information used in your password, or for identity theft as it provides answers to personal questions you might find on a credit card or loan application.

To secure basic information on your Facebook account, do the following:

1. In the *About* section of your Timeline that we were previously in, go to the *Basic Information* section and click on the *Edit* button.

2. When the screen shown in Figure 10.4 appears, if you don't want your *Gender* showing on your Timeline, click on the *Show on my timeline* checkbox so it's unchecked.

3. In the *Birthday* section, click on the drop-down list below the birthdate fields. The most secure solution would be to select *Don't show my birthday on my Timeline*. However, if you want people wishing to see your birthday, select *Show only month & day on my Timeline*. After all, people don't need to know the year of your birth to wish you a Happy Birthday.

4. If you don't want your *Relationship Status* showing, click on the drop-down menu and select "---". If you want to limit visibility for this section, you can also click on the icon to the right, and select the audience.

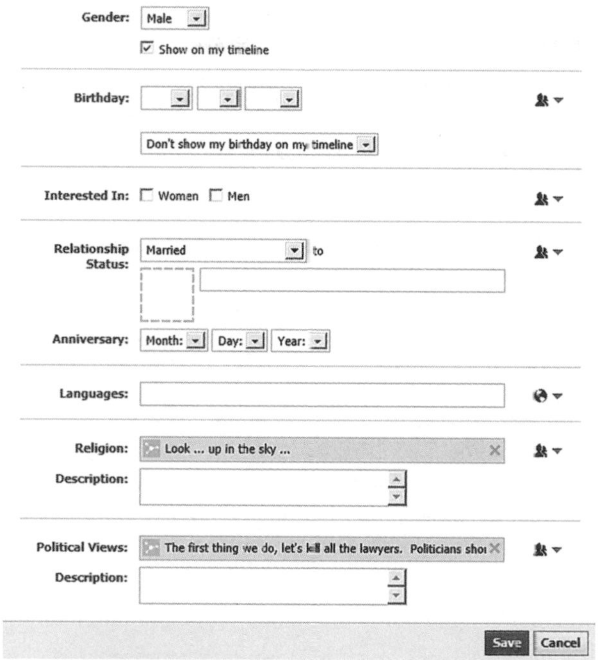

FIGURE 10.4

Basic information in Facebook.

5. In the *Anniversary* fields, click on the *Year* dropdown so that it isn't showing a year. If you don't want any of this information showing, change the fields so that a *Month* and *Day* aren't selected.
6. If there are any *Languages* that you don't want listed, which could reveal your nationality, leave the field blank.
7. Remove any religions that you don't want others seeing from the *Religion* field.
8. Remove any political affiliations or views that you don't want others seeing from the *Political Views* field.
9. Click *Save*.

Alternatively, you can select the icon shaped like a person to the right of each section, and select an audience who can view this information. However, you should consider removing information that you don't want others seeing, as someone accessing your account would be able to see this information regardless of the audience.

Likes on Facebook

You might not realize it, but what you like says a lot about you. You may not have stated your religious beliefs in your Facebook profile, but according to the 2012 report by Consumer reports, a projected 7.7 million people have liked a page on Facebook that shows a religious affiliation. Similarly, your basic information may not have mentioned whether you're interested in men or women, but an estimated 2.3 million liked a page that indicates their sexual orientation. Looking at what a person has Liked on Facebook can tell you about a person's interests, activities, places they frequent, and much more.

As we saw in Chapter 9, Facebook allows you to configure lists of audiences, and these can be used to control who sees sections of information on your profile. To use these lists to control the visibility of what you've Liked, do the following:

1. Click on your name in the upper right-hand corner of Facebook.
2. When your Timeline appears, click on the *More* tab below your cover photo, and click *Likes* from the menu that appears.
3. Click on the Edit icon in the upper right corner of the *Likes* section, and then click *Edit Privacy* on the menu that appears.
4. The *Edit Privacy of Likes* dialog box will appear, shown in Figure 10.5. Beside each item, click on the icon to the right, and click the name of the audience who will be allowed to view that information.
5. Click *Close*.

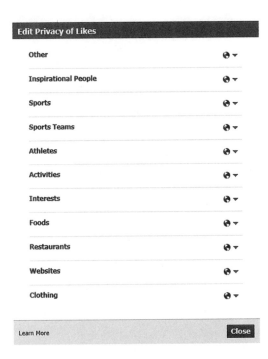

FIGURE 10.5

Edit privacy of Likes in Facebook.

The Likes section of your profile isn't the only place where your interests are shown. After you completed the previous steps, you may have noticed there were a large number of sections on the page below the Likes section. In scrolling down, you'll see sections showing the TV shows, Books, Movies, and Music you like. For each of these, you should do the following:

1. Click on the Edit icon in the upper right-hand corner of the section, and then click *Edit Privacy* on the menu that appears.
2. When the dialog box appears, click on the drop-down menu and select the audience who should view your Likes in that section.
3. Click *Close*.

Privacy shortcuts

As we saw in Chapter 9, and discuss further in this chapter, there are numerous settings you can use to lock down your account and make it secure. Privacy settings can be configured through the *Privacy Settings and Tools* page, where you can control who can see your information and content, who can contact you, and who can look you up. To make it even easier accessing these settings, Facebook added Privacy Shortcuts in 2013. These shortcuts provide an easy way to find and configure the privacy settings and allow you to make changes quickly from a drop-down menu.

In the upper right-hand corner of the page, you'll see a lock-shaped icon. When clicking on it, a menu appears with various questions like "Who can see my stuff?," "Who can contact me?," and "How do I stop someone from bothering me?" Clicking on a question related to a privacy issue you're concerned about provides additional options, which you can use to configure your privacy settings. At the bottom of the menu, you can click the *See More Settings* link, which takes you directly to the *Privacy Settings and Tools* page that we discussed in Chapter 9.

Doxxing

Doxxing is a technique that involves tracing information about a person by using Internet sources. By using various sites and tools, you can obtain significant amount of personal and even financial data. The term "doxxing" comes from the word "docs" (short for documents), and referrers to the act of tracing a person's information through available online documentation and/or uploading the revealing information to a public site or forum (such as one related to hacking). Someone doxxing a person may acquire bits of information and compile the sensitive information into a comprehensive profile about you. Once a hacker acquires the data, they may use it against a person or dump the information and related documents on a site for others to use.

If this sounds something that is overly complicated or requires significant skill, rest assured it isn't. If you think it's illegal to look up information about people on the Internet, it's not. The technique involves searching public records on the Internet and is no more illegal or immoral than using Google (which can be used as a doxxing tool) for searching. Where it does become illegal is when you reveal that information and/or place another person at risk. Doxxing is a serious threat when an unscrupulous person conducts the search and uses it to publicly embarrass or coerce someone, put them in possible harm, or for when used for such illegal activities as stalking, hacking, identify theft, fraud, blackmail, and so on.

An example of doxxing occurred on March 11, 2013, when a group of hackers posted information about celebrities and political figures on the site Exposed.su. The .su domain suffix was a top-level domain that was reserved for use by the no longer existent USSR, and an increasing number of sites have registered to use this suffix for illegal activities. As seen in Figure 10.6, when initially discovered and reported, www.exposed.su was used to post personal and financial information on such celebrities and public figures as Kim Kardashian, FBI Director Robert Mueller, Hillary Clinton, Los Angeles Police Department (LAPD) Chief Charlie Beck, Mel Gibson, Ashton Kutcher, Donald Trump, Al Gore, and others.

By clicking on links on this site, you could view pages of the different celebrities and see such information as their full names, birthdates, social security numbers, current and previous addresses, phone numbers, and a copy of their credit reports. While still being investigated at the time of this writing, if you're wondering how someone can get your credit report, this can be acquired through a site like annualcreditreport.com, which allows a person to access his or her own credit report for free (or someone else's if you have the right information). As you can see by the counter on the site, it was viewed 215,656 times when the screenshot was taken on March 12, 2013 but was over half a million people the next day. You'll also note that the hackers advertised to follow them on a Twitter account and gave the opportunity to follow tweets for additional information.

You might think that once discovered, they would have stopped and shut down or walked away from the site. Not a chance. On March 13, 2013, additional personal and financial information was added to the site on such people as Kanye West, Tiger Woods, and Bill Gates.

FIGURE 10.6

Exposed.su Web site.

Doxxing 101

The basic techniques of doxxing are relatively simple, and there are videos showing how to do it on content communities like YouTube. Using these techniques, you can search what information is on the Internet about you and your organization and can reveal potential threats to your security.

You and others you know have probably searched for information about yourself on Google or other search engines. In doing so, you may have found photos, links to sites mentioning you, or other information. However, there are other search engines that provide more detailed information, which index data sources that standard search engines do not. These can include Web pages, court records, property records, news articles, databases, documents, social media sites, and other sources on the Web. The searches may also result in finding current and previous addresses, phone numbers, and other contact information related to a person. The end result gives you more comprehensive results than a simple Google search and provides links to other sites where you can acquire additional information.

To illustrate how this works, go to Pipl (www.pipl.com) and enter your email address into the first field on the screen. Alternatively, you could also search using a name, phone number, or a username that you use in chat rooms or online gaming (inclusive to any online games played on X-Box or Playstation). To narrow the search, you can also enter a location (i.e., city, state/province, or country) into the Location field. After entering the information, click on the button to begin the search. When the search results appear, you'll see information related to what you entered. If results appear, you know where information appears about you on the Internet and should consider changing security settings and removing anything that could be considered a risk for you (i.e., phone numbers, addresses) on those sites. Once done, you should check again at a later date to ensure such information no longer appears in search results.

TOOLS & TIPS...
Search Sites

Pipl isn't the only site you can use for searching personal information available on the Internet. There are numerous ones, some which charge a fee for their use, including those discussed in Chapter 3 when we talked about screening candidates for employment. Another useful site that provides results for free is 123 People (www.123people.com) for searching names and email addresses. This site will show you results broken into groups of social networking, documents, business professionals, blogs, and more. Another site for looking up phone numbers and addresses is Whitepages (www.whitepages.com).

The human flesh search engine

The *Human Flesh Search Engine* is a phrase that's commonly associated with Internet use in China, in which crowdsourcing is used to research and share information on people, often to publicly humiliate them or for the purpose of vigilantism. Using microblogging sites like Weibo, social networking sites, blogs, and other forums, users of the sites collectively look for information and share it. They may form a manhunt to find a particular person, expose political corruption or extramarital affairs, or other social unacceptable behavior or criminal acts. The resulting exposure is sometimes followed by the person or organization being the focus of defamation, hate email, threats, cyberattacks, and/or real-life consequences when their employers or families are informed about what happened.

In 2013, the Human Flesh Search Engine proved incredibly effective when a Chinese tourist visiting Egypt photographed graffiti scratched into a sculpture in the 3500-year-old Luxor Temple. The graffiti said "Ding Jinhao was here," and a photo of it was shared on Weibo and shared almost 90,000 times by outraged users. Within a day, the vandal was identified as 15-year-old Ding Jinhao from Nanjing, East China's Jiangsu Province. His parents went to the media outlets and publicly apologized for their son, and the Web site of the boy's former school was hacked so that you had to click "Ding Jinhao was here" to enter the site.

As we've seen in previous chapters, a public rallying to gather information to address an acknowledged or perceived injustice isn't limited to one country. Unfortunately, while there has been some positive results from this, there have also been people mistakenly accused of crimes they've had nothing to do with. In Chapter 6, we discussed how the Reddit campaign "Find Boston Bombers" attempted to identify the bomber of the Boston Marathon, resulting in false accusations that caused innocent people to be harassed. While it may start with the best of intentions, the results of the Human Flesh Search Engine aren't always accurate.

Facebook graph search

In 2013, Facebook introduced *Facebook Graph Search*, which allows you to search by different categories of information. Using it, you can search Facebook for people, photos, places, and interests using preconfigured search parameters or by entering your own criteria. Depending on the security and privacy settings on your account, you'd be surprised at the search results you're appearing in.

When you click on the search bar at the top of a Facebook page, you're presented with a drop-down menu of items you might like to search for. This includes such things as photos of your friends, music and movies you might like, and games your friends play. Once the list is presented, you can click on one of the categories to view results. The tool is easy enough for a child to use and becomes a little creepy when you realize that it allows others to see information and images that might have been forgotten or unnoticed. For example, if you went through other people's photos and clicked Like on certain ones, you could view them at any time by using the search bar's menu item to view photos you'd previously liked. Essentially, it's the same as creating an album of other people's photos.

Searching in Facebook also allows you to find very specific information about groups of people. It's great to use for finding people you're looking for, but it comes with a share of risk. For example, let's say you were looking for a potential date and wanted to see the unattached friends of your friends. Using the tool, you could search for "Friends of my friends who are single" and be presented with a list of matches. If you entered "Women who live in North Hollywood, California and who are single and like Serial Killers," you be presented with a list of people in the city you mentioned, who had the marital status you were looking for. Of course, if you considered how the tool could be used in the wrong hands, it could be very dangerous appearing in a shopping list of people matching those parameters.

What appears to people in Facebook Graph Search is based on the information you've provided on your profile, and the privacy settings you've configured on elements of your account. If you want to limit what others can see, you should lock down your account as we discussed earlier in this chapter. What people see in the results is largely up to you.

Controlling exposure to search in Facebook

As we discussed in Chapter 9, social networking sites commonly provide settings that allow you to control whether the posts you make are public or limited to certain groups of friends, followers, and acquaintances. Based on the visibility of the information you publish, it can effect whether search engines will see what you've posted or tweeted.

Facebook provides a setting that will prevent search engines like Google or Bing from linking to your Timeline. By appearing in search results, a person could click on a link to your page and view any content you've made visible to the public. To prevent your Timeline from appearing in search results, follow these steps:

1. Click on the gear-shaped icon in the upper right-hand corner of your screen. When the menu appears, click *Privacy Settings*.
2. In the *Who can look me up?* area of the page, go to the section entitled *Do you want other search engines to link to your timeline?* Click on the *Edit* link.
3. When the area expands click on the checkbox, so it no longer appears checked.
4. When the dialog box appears, click *Confirm*.

Facebook also provides settings that prevent people from looking you up based on your email address or phone number. By default, anyone can search for you on Facebook using this information. To prevent such searches, go to the *Who can look me up?* area of your Privacy Settings, which you just finished using, and do the following:

1. In the section entitled *Who can look you up using email address or phone number you provided?* Click on the *Edit* link.
2. When the area expands click on the button, select the audience that you want to allow this access.

Content security

The details you add to your profile aren't the only pieces of information that need to be protected. There are sections of your Timeline that you'd probably rather hide, so the information isn't readily available to others. Once set, you'll want to verify that the settings are correct, and a mistake hasn't been made that allows others to see the content you've added through your account.

You also need to be concerned about the content and comments posted by others. If you have a blog, you don't want trolls making rampant comments that could be embarrassing or reveal personal information. Similarly, you don't want people posting inappropriate or sensitive details about your life on your Timeline. To control this, you'll want to use the settings available through your account to control the visibility of what others say and share.

Preapproving or turning off comments

If you have embarrassing or offensive comments posted on your page, you can delete the comments and block the user. As we saw in Chapter 9, blocking users prohibits them from visiting your page, preventing them from bothering you. Of course, they could simply create another account on the site and continue their efforts. If that happens, then consider making a complaint to the site or contacting police if behavior becomes harassing or threatening.

In some cases, you might expect negative comments and want to have greater control over what other people say. This may be the case if you're posting content while doing damage control, such as during a scandal or time you're getting negative publicity. If other people's comments are a serious concern, a number of sites provide the ability to turn off comments or require them to be preapproved before they're viewed publicly.

Some social media sites, such as blog sites like WordPress and content communities like YouTube, provide the ability to control how comments are handled. One way is for comments to be preapproved before they're published, so that only the ones you've confirmed are appropriate are seen by others. Comments can also be turned off, preventing anyone from posting an opinion. While this certainly kills the possibility for social interaction, it does allow you to maintain your YouTube channel or blog as an information source, without having to worry about what others do on it.

On YouTube, you can configure the default settings of your account by logging in and going to http://www.youtube.com/account_defaults. When visiting this URL, you can scroll down the page until you see a section entitled *Comments and responses*. By default, all of the options in this section are turned on, but you can click on any of the checkboxes to uncheck them and turn them off. Options in this section are:

- Allow comments, which has a dropdown beside it allowing you to choose whether *All* comments or only those comments that are *Approved* will be published.
- Users can vote on comments.
- Users can view ratings for this video.
- Allow video responses, which has a dropdown beside it that allows you to choose whether *All* responses or only those that are *Approved* will be published.

Once you configure these settings, they become the default settings for any videos that are uploaded to your YouTube channel.

WordPress also has settings that control how comments are handled on your blog. On the *Discussion Settings* page of your settings, you can configure when you'll be notified about new comments, and whether people are allowed to post comments on new articles. These settings are important, as they keep you aware about interest in your blog and controls how people interact with it.

Your blog can be configured so that comments don't automatically appear as soon as someone makes them. For most situations, you should have it set so that the first comment a person makes on your blog must be approved before it appears to others. Unless someone's persistent in bothering you, or you're extremely concerned about the comments people make, this should be adequate. For more restrictive control over comments, you can also set it so that every comment must be preapproved before others will see it. To configure this, do the following:

1. After logging onto your blog, hover your mouse over your name in the upper left-hand corner and click *Dashboard*.
2. In the left pane, click *Discussion*.
3. Scroll down to the section entitled *Before a comment appears*.
4. To preapprove comments, click on the *An administrator must always approve a comment* checkbox so it appears checked.
5. To have only the first comment a person makes approved, click on the *Comment author must have a previously approved comment* checkbox so it appears checked.
6. Scroll to the bottom and click *Save changes*.

Stop people from posting on your timeline

By default, anyone you add as a friend has the ability to post content to your Timeline. If you ever have a problem, or you're concerned over what people add to the Timeline of a business account, you'll probably want to change this. Limiting the access so that only you can post to your Timeline doesn't affect your friend's ability to make comments on posts, such as status updates or photos you've added. To restrict security so that only you can add to your Timeline, do the following:

1. Click on the gear-shaped icon in the upper right-hand corner of the page, and click *Account Settings* on the menu that appears.
2. In the left pane of the page, click *Timeline and Tagging*.
3. In the *Who can add things to my timeline?* Section, click on the *Edit* link.
4. When the area expands, click on the button and select *Only Me* from the menu.

Another way to control the content that appears on your Timeline is to restrict the posts friends tag you in. If a friend uploads a picture to their Timeline and tags you in it, it will appear on your Timeline and show that you were tagged in the photo. Depending on the content, this could be a good or a bad thing. After all, you might not want coworkers seeing a photo of you having a night on the town or family seeing a picture someone took at a party. To prevent unwanted content from being published on your Timeline, you can set your account so that you have to review any posts friends tag you in before they appear on your Timeline:

1. On the *Timeline and Tagging* page, go to the *Who can add things to my timeline?* section. Click on the *Edit* link.
2. When the area expands, click on the button and select *Enabled* from the menu.

Controlling what others see

Even if you allow others to post content or tagged content to appear on your Timeline, you have some control over who will see it. The *Timeline and Tagging* page allows you to specify the audience that has access to view this content. As we discussed in Chapter 9, the lists you use can be customized to specific groups of people you've added as friends.

It's important to remember that these settings only limit the visibility of content on your own Timeline. It doesn't affect others seeing the same content posted to another person's Timeline. To restrict who can see the posts you've been tagged in, you would perform the following steps:

1. On the *Timeline and Tagging* page, go to the *Who can see things on my timeline?* section.
2. Click on the *Edit* link beside *Who can see posts you've been tagged in on your timeline*.
3. When the area expands, click on the button and select the appropriate audience from the menu.

Restricting who can see the content others have posted on your timeline is also controlled through the *Who can see things on my timeline?* section. To modify these settings, perform the following steps:

1. Click on the *Edit* link beside *Who can see what others post on your timeline?*
2. When the area expands, click on the button and select the appropriate audience from the menu.

Controlling tags

When a tag is added to a photo or other content you've posted, the person who's tagged and their friends are able to view it. When someone you're not friends with adds a tag, you're asked to review it. If you don't approve it, then the tag isn't set. However, by default this doesn't apply to friends. If a friend tags content, it's immediately available for their friends to view. This can be a problem if that person is friends with people you don't want seeing the content.

To force any tags to be reviewed, even those that are set by friends, you would use the settings on the *Timeline and Tagging* page:

1. Scroll down to the *How can I manage tags people add and tagging suggestions?* section. Click on the *Edit* link.
2. When the area expands, click on the button and select *Enabled*.

The settings for controlling tags aren't all restrictive. On any posts that you're tagged in, you can also extend the audience to lists of people who are your friends. Maybe you want a list of family members to be included in an audience, so they can see photos you've been tagged in. If they aren't already in the audience, you can change the settings so that they're automatically added:

1. On the Timeline and Tagging page, scroll to the *How can I manage tags people add and tagging suggestions?* section.
2. Click on the *Edit* link beside *When you're tagged in a post*, who do you want to add to the audience if they aren't already in it.
3. When the section expands, click on the button and select the appropriate audience from the menu.

Hiding sections of a timeline

Facebook allows you to hide different sections on your Timeline so that others won't see them. This keeps areas that reveal your interests, likes, notes, events, places you've been, and other pieces of information from being displayed on the Timeline for others to see. While individual stories from apps, Likes, and other activities may still appear in your Timeline, the section itself won't be visible.

As you add certain apps to your Timeline, they may add a section on you Timeline revealing information about what you've done on Facebook or other sites. For example, if you joined Pinterest or Foursquare, you may have authorized an app on Facebook to log on to those sites. This gives it the ability to post information from their site in the section that's been added to the Timeline, which may reveal more than you're comfortable with sharing. To hide sections, do the following:

1. Hover your mouse over one of the sections, such as the About box on the left side of your Timeline. When the edit icon shaped like a pencil appears, click on it and then click *Edit Sections* when the menu appears.
2. When the *Edit Sections* dialog appears, you'll see a list of sections. Click on the checkbox beside the name of one you want to hide, so that it's unchecked.
3. At the bottom of the dialog box, click *Save*.

Some sections like *About*, *Photos*, and *Friends* cannot be hidden. For these, you'll need to change the audience who can view that content, as we discussed in Chapter 9 when we told you how to control the privacy of Photos and how to restrict who can see your friends. In changing the audience, these areas will still appear on the Timeline, but the information in them will be hidden from view.

Seeing through the eyes of others

Understanding what others can and cannot see is a basic concept for managing the security of content you've posted. You can configure settings, but you'll never know if it's set correctly if you don't check it. Just because you think the public can't see it doesn't mean it's true.

A simple method of seeing what the public sees is to visit your page without logging into the site. If I visit my page on LinkedIn, Twitter, or any other social media site without logging in, I'll be presented with the content that's only available to the public. Visiting the page in this way is especially easy if you've created a custom URL. As we saw in Chapter 3 and discuss further in Chapter 11, sites like LinkedIn and Facebook allow you to create vanity URLs, which will take people directly to your page.

Facebook provides you with an easy way to identifying how others see your pages. Using a link, you can view the public content on your page or as a specific user. If you're concerned what a friend can see, or a person who's been added to a particular list can view, you can use this feature to see what they see. To use this feature, follow these steps:

1. Click on the *Privacy Shortcut* icon that looks like a padlock in the upper right-hand corner of the page.
2. When the menu appears, click *Who can see my stuff?*
3. When the section expands, click on the *View As* link in the *What do other people see on my timeline?* section.

When you've clicked on the *View As* link, your Timeline will change to display what is visible to the public. You'll also notice a black bar appear at the top of the screen stating "This is what your timeline looks like to: Public." To see how your Timeline appears to another user, you can click on the *View As Specific Person* link next to this in the black bar. A box will appear where you can enter the name of a friend. A list of friends will display as you type, and when you select one, you'll see your Timeline as it appears to the selected person.

By checking your settings, you'll be assured that the efforts you've made to secure your information are correct, and no adjustments need to be made. Because security and privacy settings can change, you should periodically use this feature to see what the public and specific people you've added as Friends can see on your Timeline. By being proactive, there's less chance the wrong person will see information you thought was private.

Bibliography

Adegoke, Y. (2012, January 4). *Twitter embarrassed by fake Wendi Murdoch account.* Retrieved March 15, 2013, from Reuters: <http://www.reuters.com/article/2012/01/04/us-wendimurdoch-twitter-idUSTRE80305620120104>.

Consumer Reports. (2011, May 10). *CR survey: 7.5 million Facebook users are under the age of 13, violating the site's terms.* Retrieved April 12, 2013, from Consumer Reports: <http://pressroom.consumerreports.org/pressroom/2011/05/cr-survey-75-million-facebook-users-are-under-the-age-of-13-violating-the-sites-terms-.html>.

Consumer Reports. (2012, May 3). *13 million U.S. Facebook users don't use privacy controls, risk sharing updates beyond their "friends."* Retrieved July 29, 2012, from Consumer Reports: <http://pressroom.consumerreports.org/pressroom/2012/05/my-entry.html>.

FAQs about Verified Accounts. (n.d.). Retrieved March 15, 2013, from Twitter: <https://support.twitter.com/articles/119135-faqs-about-verified-accounts>.

La Russa, Twitter Settle Lawsuit. (2009, June 5). Retrieved March 15, 2013, from NBC Sports: <http://nbcsports.msnbc.com/id/31105703/>.

Middleton, R. (2011, October 5). *Man who slit throat of American girl he met on Facebook and lured to Northamptonshire jailed for life*. Retrieved July 12, 2013, from Northhampton Chronical and Echo: <http://www.northamptonchron.co.uk/news/crime/man_who_slit_throat_of_american_girl_he_met_on_facebook_and_lured_to_northamptonshire_jailed_for_life_1_3117269>.

Not Playing Ball. (2009, June 8). Retrieved March 15, 2013, from Twitter: <http://blog.twitter.com/2009/06/not-playing-ball.html>.

Wong, H. (2013, May 29). *Netizen outrage after Chinese tourist defaces Egyptian temple*. Retrieved June 26, 2013, from CNN: <http://www.cnn.com/2013/05/27/travel/china-egypt>.

Worst Passwords of 2012—and How to Fix Them. (2012, October 23). Retrieved March 12, 2013, from SplashData: <http://www.splashdata.com/press/PR121023.htm>.

Where do We go from Here?

11

INFORMATION IN THIS CHAPTER:

- Where do we go from here?
- The pitch, the promise, and the reality
- Who's in charge here?
- Monitoring social media
- Keeping it fresh
- Dialing it back and taking control
- Ongoing training

Where do we go from here?

So, your social media site has been up and running, and you're done now right? Wrong. Even if you've locked down your accounts, configured security settings, and educated the people using social media, you're not finished … ever. Technology changes, people change, and you need to change with it.

Once you've created a social media presence, you need to monitor it. To be a part of the conversations, you need to know what's being said, and trends that are occurring. You'll want to know whether new sites are gaining popularity, and decide if you're going to be loyal to the site you're on, or follow others to the latest and greatest social media sites on the Web.

Social media is more than just social, it's also commercial. If you're running a business, you'll have concerns over how social media is being handled. You may have set up a committee of people to govern social media for your business, but it may not be working as well as intended and adjustments may need to be made. You may find that the needs and priorities of your company have shifted, and you need to adapt. You need to always be aware of the current state of social media, so you can keep pace with changes and use it to your advantage.

The pitch, the promise, and the reality

When you hear some people talk about social media, it can sound like an old-time snake oil salesman. It's the answer to all your problems, and will cure what ails ya; giving you profit, opportunity, and popularity. Anyone can simply setup an account with little effort, and best of all its free! Once you've started working with social media, you find the truth is a little different.

While it's true that social media costs nothing, there can be hidden costs associated with it. These phantom costs aren't apparent until you really start analyzing your return on investment, and it can catch you by surprise when you realize how much you've spent over time. Some of the hidden costs include time, tools, equipment, and advertising.

You'll spend a considerable amount of time working on social media sites. You'll need to create content, secure settings, and get things the way you want. You'll also work at generating conversation and buzz about your brand, and monitoring what's being said. While the investment of time can seem inconsequential when it's for personal use, it can be a considerable cost for a business.

Time is money for a business because each hour worked is an hourly wage that needs to be spent. For social media, you're paying the person handling your presence, which may be a single Social Media Officer or a team of people. You're also paying marketing staff to help with campaigns to increase sales, customer service representatives to follow up on resolving complaints, managers to meet and discuss their needs for social media, and senior management to set priorities and policy. There may also be members of Human Resources who will use social media as part of a recruitment process, and legal costs related to protecting any copyright or trademark material used on the sites. It all adds up.

As we've seen in previous chapters and discuss further in this one, tools may be used to manage social media. Tools like *Hootsuite* (www.hootsuite.com) may be used to schedule content at certain times, monitor multiple sites, and provide analytics to show you what's working. Such tools will cost money, and should be considered as a potential cost of implementing social media.

To use social media in the manner you want, you may need to purchase additional equipment. Maybe you want access to Twitter and Facebook 24 hours a day, 7 days a week, and need to purchase a smartphone or tablet. If you want to create videos or podcasts, you may need to purchase a camera and additional software. These costs can be expensive depending on your needs, wants, or desires.

Advertising costs are another factor to consider. Sites like Facebook make money from selling ads for posts and pages you create. While you can set the daily budget for these ads, they can mount up quickly. In addition to this you might pay a photographer to take professional photos, a graphic designer to create images for your social media campaigns, or combine traditional advertising with social media to promote your brand. It may seem inexpensive at first, but costs will mount over time.

When you're looking into using different kinds of social media, you need to consider the motives behind the source of information. A social media firm that you can outsource the work to may focus on the benefits, but gloss over the costs of hiring them. A developer or software company will promise their tool will increase the effectiveness of using social media but play down the cost of a monthly subscription. They're in business and want to make a sale, so it's up to you to keep a level head and decide if it's worth the cost.

You'll also see pitches and promises made in some of the training sessions you go to. If you looked at some training sessions for collaboration and social networking products for a corporate intranet, you might notice that there are different sessions for business professionals and IT professionals. The manager will hear about how the product will increase productivity, and free up IT staff from having to create content as users will do it themselves. The IT professional will learn about the increased amount of administration and may later find that many users don't want the extra work of creating content, and continue to rely on an administrator in IT. Getting people to adopt the new technology becomes another cost added to the mix.

To gauge the costs of social media, you need to take into account all of the real and hidden costs involved. This will give you a better understanding of what you're paying for, and give you a clearer picture of what you're getting out of it.

TOOLS & TIPS...

Dealing with Social Media Before it's Too Late

Often, by the time you realize you need to take social media security seriously, its already too late. This is especially true for young people who are very open and free with social media, posting comments and photos they probably shouldn't have made public. When you later try and lock it down, you can find that it is virtually impossible. Photos may be shared, and people you didn't want to view certain information already have it. As we mentioned in Chapter 10, Facebook Graph Search makes it easy to find information about a person, and other tools can be used to gather detailed information about a person. It's important to consider social media security early, review your settings regularly, and be careful about what you post.

Who's in charge here?

When you start using social media, you have to accept a certain lack of control and trust. You have to accept that you can't control what people are going to say in comments on your page, or what they're going to tweet about you. It's the same as not being able to control what others are going to say in the privacy of their own home. In the same light, you have to trust that the comments made by those handling social media are going to be appropriate, and in line with the company's thinking. Put simply, you can't micromanage what others are thinking and saying when you aren't around.

While one of the biggest risks of social media is lack of control, it doesn't mean you can't put controls in place to mitigate this risk and get others to help. As we'll see in the sections that follow, having a team of people available to assist and provide their expertise is important in taking charge. Jumping into the social media pool alone is like jumping into the ocean without a life jacket. You might be able to swim okay, but you'll be safer with the added support.

Accountability

Accountability is the ownership and responsibility over an area or person. It provides a chain of command that allows you to understand who you answer to for certain actions, and whether you're responsible for what was done. It's an important concept as it establishes what you need to answer for and to whom you're answering.

In personal use of social media, you're accountable for what you tweet and post, and can be held liable for anything that violates the site's Terms of Use or is illegal. If you have children, they may be charged as minors for illegal acts, such as harassment or making threats, but you'd be the one held liable in a civil suit as you're accountable for them. Your children would also be accountable to the site, and could have their accounts deleted for what they do. Of course, as a parent, I'd say that would be the least of their concerns.

For business use, accountability in social media can be more complex, but still holds the basic tenet of taking ownership over your actions and being answerable to someone. A Social Media Officer in charge of the business' social media presence will often work with multiple departments in an organization, but would still require a single person to report to. Larger organizations may include the position or department responsible for social media in the business' organizational structure, clarifying who they're accountable to.

To be accountable, there needs to be an understanding of what's expected, and what a person is authorized to do. Businesses need to set rules regarding the frequency of updates, and the process used for updating information. While the Social Media Officer may be free to respond to comments, other content like press releases or official statements may need to be approved by other people. In such cases, the person who approved it would be accountable for its content.

Approval processes and workflows are important in ensuring the information available to others is authentic and correct. Even though multiple people may work on corporate blogs or collaboration sites, security can be setup on what's published on a site. As we'll see later in this chapter, if you had a corporate blog, an employee might write a blog but might not have the ability to publish it for others to see. The Administrator of the blog site would need to approve it before it became visible to everyone.

Businesses need to have strong internal communication, so that managers are aware of how social media is being used. If conversations are taking place on a social media site, you don't want that information kept in a bubble. A Social Media Officer needs to provide reports to management and the governance committee, and apprise stakeholders about how social media is being used. Sales and marketing departments, public relations, and management need to know about the feedback, compliments, complaints, and conversations that are going on so they know how to address the public and deal with possible concerns.

Accountability in a crisis

When a crisis happens, people will often equate accountability with blameworthiness. People will start pointing fingers as to who's the person at fault, so that they don't get in trouble. Employees often need to be reassured that you're trying to identify what's happened so the problem can be fixed, and it doesn't happen again. Unfortunately, if management is hardnosed and quick to discipline, employees will know better and spend more time trying to keep their job than resolve the problem.

It can also be a serious issue if finding blameworthiness is a management style. You've probably had or heard of managers that take credit for an employee's work, but quick to blame someone else for mistakes. If this is seen as a pattern, owners and senior management should wonder whether they're getting a full assessment of issues, or if the manager is covering his or her butt. If an employee made a mistake, it may have been because they had inadequate training, followed incorrect instructions, or preoccupied with the bullying of a supervisor. The problem may be in how the employees are managed.

Governance

Social media governance is the act of exercising control and authority over a business' social media presence, and providing a method or system of management. It guides and directs people on how to use social media through policies, processes, roles, and responsibilities. To achieve this, a governance committee should be created to act as the governing body over your company's social media.

A governance committee helps shape a company's social media presence, and serves as a resource for the person who handles social media and others who use it. Its members should consist of key players and stakeholders from different areas of the company. These are people who are directly affected and have a vetted interest in the business' social media, and will have the insight needed to contribute to decisions. As we discussed in Chapter 4, they may be representatives of such departments as marketing, legal, public relations, training, IT, and so on. By having a cross section of the organization, comprised of people with valuable knowledge on aspects related to your social media presence, you'll find the committee to be more effective.

Developing plans, policies, and guidelines

Governance committees can play a vital role in the documents that are created and used in an organization to use social media effectively. By having people from different departments, and diverse fields of expertise, they can have an impact on policies, plans, and guidelines that will be used throughout the organization.

The committee will have a major role in developing a social media policy, and provide guidance in changes needed to other policies. As we saw in Chapter 9, introducing social media into an organization can have a significant impact on existing policies. It should be the committee's responsibility to identify the need for changes, notify the appropriate departments responsible for those policies, and explain how and why there's a need to include provisions for social media in them.

Because a governance committee has such a major impact on policies, it follows that they should also have significant input on training plans. They can outline what areas are concerns to the organization, and need to be taught to employees. People need to be aware that they need to use social media in a way that conforms to policies and follows best practices or the organization.

Branding guidelines are an important part of successfully representing your company online. In Chapter 2, we discussed the importance of branding, and how it defines the way that you're seen by others. Guidelines should be developed so that any social media sites representing your business use the same logos, trademarks, or other content to provide a consistent look across all of the sites. You want people to identify that your presence belongs to your company as soon as they see it.

A communication plan is another important part of getting people to adopt social media and use it wisely. Communication plans outline how employees, vendors, partners, and the general public will be informed about issues related to your organization's social media. It explains how you're going to tell people about the sites you're introducing, details they need to know, and changes that affect them. This may involve different methods of relaying information. If you used Yammer or SharePoint to allow employees to collaborate on projects, you might promote it as an announcement on those sites. You could also use posters, newsletters with tips on how to use features, or host information sessions that tell people about what's being offered. For a public site, cross-promotion might be used by tweeting about a new Facebook page or adding links on the corporate Web site. You might also issue press releases, or use print advertising in stores. The decisions you make in communicating such news can have a significant impact on its success.

The scope of making decisions

A governance committee needs to understand their role and the scope of their decision-making powers. Some companies will trust the professionals on a team, allowing them to make decisions and implement changes, which are later reported to higher management. In other organizations, a committee is there to agree on recommendations, which are then passed to management for a final decision. To work effectively, the committee needs to understand its decision-making powers.

Committee members are consulted for guidance in issues, and may need to respond in a decisive and timely manner. While major decisions should be made by senior management, they should be able to take action on smaller ones. Doing so provides for quicker responses and diminishes the bureaucratic process.

A governance committee that can't make any decisions is a worst-case scenario. The meetings will feel like exercises in futility, and people needing answers will be in for a frustrating experience. Imagine trying to create branding guidelines or a security plan, and after waiting months for the next committee meeting, you find that the members can't and won't provide direction. Any work you're trying to do or problems you're trying to fix would be caught in a holding pattern, waiting for a verdict that never comes. The consequences of indecision can be as devastating as making bad choices.

Reviewing membership

Committee memberships should be reviewed from time to time. After a committee is formed, you'll often find that there are people who contribute very little or nothing at all. They may have joined as a career move, thinking it will help them get a promotion. They may have joined with the best intentions, but lost interest over time or misunderstood the level of commitment required. Sooner or later, it becomes obvious who these people are. They'll miss meetings, and offer little to those they attend. Since apathy can be contagious, you'll often find your committee will lose momentum and effectiveness. By reviewing the membership periodically, you can replace them with people who have a genuine interest, and have new ideas brought to the table.

Clear and understandable roles

It's important for people to have clear and understandable roles in managing the social media of a business. There will be a Social Media Officer, a governance committee, and stakeholders who have an interest in seeing it succeed. Even though these roles are clearly defined early in the process, there may be changes over time.

When a business first starts using social media, it's often handled by an existing employee or two, who may even split these duties with other responsibilities. In choosing the person for this role, it should be a full-time employee with an understanding of technology, communication skills, an understanding of the organization, and leadership qualities. The person has to help guide and drive conversations, and be able to respond to negative comments and criticism. You're giving this person the responsibility to speak on behalf of your company, so it's not a position you want to give an intern or coop student, regardless of how much time they spend on Facebook.

Over time, the ability to manage the social media sites may overwhelm current staff, or you may decide that the amount of work involved merits a formalizing the position. It's at this time you'll decide using a full-time person, dedicated to the job. The role of a Social Media Officer is a new one in the corporate world, and often necessary in larger organizations.

A *Social Media Officer* is responsible for the social media of an organization, inclusive to producing and publishing content. This person creates a social media strategy, which sets the goals and objectives for social media, and establishes how they'll be achieved. The person will monitor social media sites, identifying trends, looking for brand-related topics, and watching for customer issues that are made through negative and positive feedback. The Social Media Officer also serves as an evangelist, promoting social media use and the tools that can make it more effective.

If the social media presence is large enough, you might expand the number of people handling it further, so that it becomes its own department. A *Digital Media Manager* is a person who's responsible for managing multiple areas of digital media. Such a person might oversee such areas as social media and corporate sites, and supervise Web designers responsible for the Web site, a Social Media Officer, and possibly a media liaison who handles press releases.

While the Social Media Officer is responsible for creating content, it's not uncommon for companies to recruit others to do it for them. Bloggers and blog editors may be people within the organization who are encouraged to write and manage content. There are also professional bloggers, who are hired to write articles and other content on behalf of the business.

The roles within a governance committee are also important to define, and may change slightly over time. Each committee should have a chairperson or cochairs that help keep the meetings on track and guide topics that need decisions made. The members of the committee provide insight into areas related to social media, how it affects their areas of expertise, and will collectively agree on recommendations or changes that need to occur. They should understand whether the organization has put them in charge of the person who handles social media, or if they are a resource for that person.

The committee may also invite people to be advisors. For example, while an IT manager may be on the committee, he or she may not have significant knowledge of certain technologies. If you use Microsoft SharePoint, you might also want to invite the SharePoint Administrator to meetings, as this person can inform and advise you about its features and limitations. After all, social networking isn't just used on public sites; it's also used on intranets. While the advisor doesn't have voting privileges, he or she should be invited to provide input.

When first implementing social media for a business, you should form a governance committee as soon as possible, but forming one at any time is better than not at all. You'll often find that when you're creating a social media presence, the group will meet more often as this is when most of the decisions need to be made. As things wind down and the sites are being maintained, meetings will be less frequent and the committee experiences its greatest risk of falling apart. You don't want the committee dissolving after your social media is up and running, so it's important to continue meeting to report changes, the status of campaigns, and discuss decisions that need to be made.

The role of the user is important, and one that should be recognized. Employees should understand their place in a business' social media presence. A clear understanding should be established as to what's permitted and restricted in internal social networking sites, corporate blogs, and other social media owned by the company.

Anyone has the ability to create a social media account, but it doesn't mean they should. As we discussed in Chapter 9, a social media policy should list the official accounts used for Twitter, Facebook, and other social networking sites. The accounts that represent the business should be controlled, and employees should understand that they can't make their own and begin tweeting or posting about the company. Decisions should also be made on whether employees are allowed to post their own comments on the business' social media pages, or if they're advised to refrain from doing so.

The role of the IT department should also be clarified as providing technical support, and whether they're to create content. Some companies encourage employees to start their own blog, while other's frown upon it. As we mentioned earlier, if employees can publish their own content, they may revert to old habits of getting the Web designer, SharePoint Administrator, or IT staff to do the work for them. If users are responsible for their own content, they and the IT department needs to know that they can refuse such requests, and book the person for training instead.

Because social media sites are controlled by third-parties, the Social Media Officer and users within the business need to know that any support by IT staff is limited. If the site goes down, or problems arise with using the site, calling the company's help desk won't get you very far. The IT staff does however need to know whether they're responsible for working with the social media site for any problems with accounts and what their responsibilities are for technical support.

Crisis management

The best time to deal with a crisis is before it happens. If you don't already have a plan to deal with a crisis, you should create one. A public relations nightmare can spiral out of control quickly on social networking sites, with viral videos and tweets blaring negative publicity about your brand. If you do have a plan, it's a good idea to incorporate social media into responding to the public so you can engage customers quickly and address any concerns they have.

In 2010, safety recalls were tarnishing Toyota's image, so they dealt with the crisis by using Twitter. Using a number of retweetable ads and addressing consumer concerns through a Twitter account, they also created a site that would aggregate press releases, news stories, and the most popular images and videos being tweeted about the company. Responding to the crisis through social media gave them the advantage of responding to public concerns before they got out of control.

As we saw in Chapter 4, by monitoring conversations, you're able to see what's being said about your brand. However, you can also use social media to control how and where those comments are made. By creating a fan page on Facebook dealing with an issue, a person can make comments on it, allowing you to focus on those problems. Doing this will also divert the negative comments from your main page or account. By providing an email address for people to respond to, or following a customer on Twitter so that they can directly message you, you're better able to deal with them one-on-one and decrease the negative tweets.

A crisis can also result because of social media. This was seen in 2009, when Kristy Hammonds and Michael Setzer made a video of themselves preparing sandwiches at a Conover, North Carolina franchise of Dominos. The video shows him sticking cheese up his nose, sneezing on a sandwich, and sticking a sponge down the back of his pants and later using it to wash dishes. Posting it on YouTube, the video was viewed more than a million times over a few days, and resulted in the franchise calling the Health Department, throwing out all open food containers, and sanitizing the restaurant. It also resulted in the two being fired, and police charging them with contaminating food distributed to the public. Since the incident at one franchise had gone viral and was being talked about worldwide, it made Dominos realize the power of social media. They created their own video of their chief executive addressing the issue, posted it on YouTube, and created a Twitter account to address concerns.

Continuity planning

Business continuity is the ability to allow your business to function, so that you can continue critical functions. If social media is used as a necessary function of a business, you should include it in your company's continuity plan. Even if it isn't critical, you should have a continuity plan for when you can't use social media.

At times, you may find that your social media account is unavailable. Fortunately, for most sites, this doesn't happen too often. Twitter provides information on their status at http://status.twitter.com, showing its stability by being transparent about when it's been unavailable. Because sites could be unavailable when you really need it, you should be prepared for when it happens.

Because most people and businesses have a presence on multiple sites, you could use them to provide updated information. For example, if Twitter was down, you could use your corporate Web site to let people know about your presence on other social media sites, and direct them to other social networking sites you use. This allows you to continue staying in touch with people, even though your primary method isn't available.

Continuity planning should address what to do if the Social Media Officer isn't available. If the person in the role of handling social media gets sick, quits, or gets fired, the new person will need that password. Similarly, the IT department may need to access the account to handle a security issue or provide some other support. As IT departments should already keep a master list of administrator passwords in a secure location, businesses should continue this process and ensure that IT is always notified when a password is changed for a social media account.

Monitor social media

If you don't know what's going on, you won't know how to deal with it. What's being said on your social media channels, and what others are saying about it, is an important part of managing social media. To effectively handle what's going on, you need to watch the sites closely. As we'll see in the sections that follow, there are many features available on sites to be notified of issues, analytics to view statistical information, and tools that can aid you in monitoring your social media presence.

Reading is fundamental

Most of the time you spend on social media site should be reading what others have said, rather than pushing what you have to say. It's important to read the posts, tweets, and comments people make so you can understand what your customers are saying, control problems, and understand potential issues. Conversations are driven by the users of social media, and many times won't require your participation. However, without monitoring them, you won't know when your involvement is required.

A good example of interacting with customers was seen in 2012, when the British mobile phone company O2 suffered a major service disruption, and irate customers took to Twitter and Facebook to vent their frustration. Thousands of comments appeared on the company's Facebook page, and the Twitterverse was set ablaze with scathing comments. The company took ownership of the problem, and its social media team began posting updates, responded directly to people, and apologized to irate customers for the problems.

What is amazing is the level to which O2 responded to criticism in a friendly manner. Tweets that normally would be ignored by most using social media were met with cheery and humorous responses. An example is when Graham Cummings (@grahamcummings7) fired an angry tweet at O2 (which is edited here) saying "F*CK YOU! SUCK DICK IN HELL." Rather than shirk away, @O2 responded with "Maybe later, got tweets to send right now." The response inspired others to come to O2's defense. Initially the tweets against Cummings were barbed insults, but the conversation quickly changed into friendly back-and-forth jabs that sounded like something you'd hear in a pub.

Rather than parroting an official response, O2 took the position of reading what was being said and responded in a manner akin to two friends chatting about a problem. The tweets even interjected some good-natured humor, as seen in Figure 11.1.

FIGURE 11.1

Tweets between O2 and a customer.

While it's important to read and become involved in conversations on your own social media, you also need to be aware of what's being said elsewhere. Remember that your page is not the only place that people will be talking about you, or topics related to you and your business. There are pages, tweets, blogs, wikis, chat rooms, and videos created by other people that are relevant to your business or the audience you want to attract. By participating in these conversations, you'll increase awareness of your brand, promote it, and will drive traffic to your social media or your corporate Web site.

Notifications

If you want to follow the conversations on your page, it's important to know when something new has been posted. Notifications are used to have a message sent to you when something you've specified as important occurs, and you want to know about it. While many notifications are turned on by default on sites like Twitter and Facebook, you may want to adjust these settings. Getting no notifications is as bad as getting too many, as you'll find that important messages can get lost in the noise.

Setting notifications on Facebook

As seen in Figure 11.2, the Notifications Settings page on Facebook allows you to control how you'll get notifications, and what you'll be notified about. To access this page, you would do the following:

1. In the upper right-hand corner of the page, click on the gear-shaped icon. When the menu appears, click *Account Settings*.
2. In the left pane of the page, click *Notifications*.

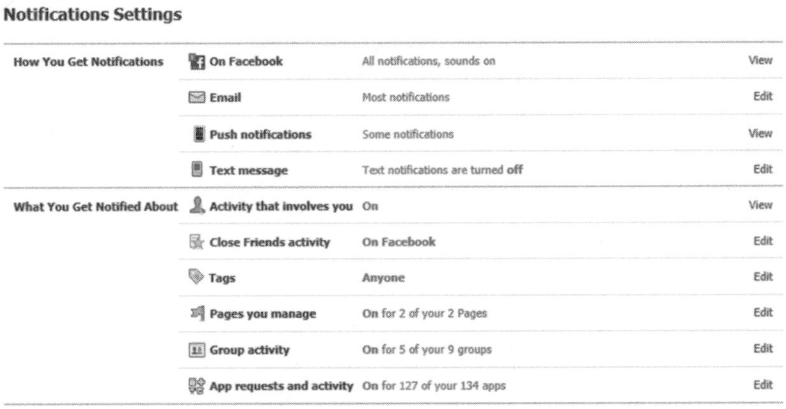

Notifications Settings

How You Get Notifications	On Facebook	All notifications, sounds on	View
	Email	Most notifications	Edit
	Push notifications	Some notifications	View
	Text message	Text notifications are turned off	Edit
What You Get Notified About	Activity that involves you	On	View
	Close Friends activity	On Facebook	Edit
	Tags	Anyone	Edit
	Pages you manage	On for 2 of your 2 Pages	Edit
	Group activity	On for 5 of your 9 groups	Edit
	App requests and activity	On for 127 of your 134 apps	Edit

FIGURE 11.2

Facebook notification settings.

The first section of this page is the *How You Get Notifications* section. In it, you'll find a *Text message* setting allows you to control whether you receive notifications through text messaging. However, it will only be available if you've associated a mobile phone with your account. The *Email* setting allows you to control whether you'll be notified via email about everything, or only those related to your account, security, and privacy.

The *What You Get Notified About* is the second section of this page. The *Close Friends activity* setting allows you to control whether you'll be notified about close friends via email and/or Facebook, or if you'd like this turned off. The *Tags* setting determines whether you're notified when anyone, a friend, or friends-of-friends tag you in a photo. Because you'll want to be aware of when you're tagged, it's advisable that you get notified when you're tagged by anyone. You don't want to be tagged in an embarrassing or inappropriate picture and find out about it later.

The *Pages you manage* setting is used to specify whether you'll be notified about pages you help administer. If you click on the Edit link for this, you'll see a list of pages you manage. If the checkbox beside a page is checked, you will receive notifications about them. For any related to your job or business, or those you want to keep up-to-date with, you should have those pages checked.

Clicking on the Edit button to the right of the *Group Activity* setting will show you the groups you belong to. Beside each group, you can select whether you'll receive notifications when anyone makes a post, a friend posts, or not at all. For the groups you're particularly interested in, you should choose all posts or those made by friends. To cut down the noise from groups you don't follow much, turn off notifications.

For most people, unwanted notifications will come from the apps you've added. When you click the Edit button beside *App requests and activity*, you'll see a list of the apps you've added to Facebook, inclusive to ones that connect you to other sites. To prevent the app from notifying you of any requests or activity, uncheck the checkbox beside that app.

Setting notifications on Twitter

Twitter also provides the ability to send emails when tweets are made, direct messages are sent, and certain events occur. To control when you receive notifications, do the following:

1. Click on the gear-shaped icon in the upper right-hand corner, and click *Settings* on the menu that appears.
2. In the left pane, click on the *Email notifications* tab.

The first section on this page involves *Activity related to you and your tweets* and contains most of the options that you'll want to monitor. Here, you'll uncheck the checkboxes that you don't want to receive emailed notifications about. The top portion allows you to choose whether you're emailed when your tweets are marked as favorites, retweeted, or marked as favorites. You can also be emailed when you're mentioned in a tweet, when those tweets are retweeted, and when your tweets get a reply. You can select whether you're to be notified when people you follow do this, or anyone.

At the bottom of this section, you should also ensure that you're notified when someone sends a direct message to you, as you'll probably want to be aware of this. Optionally, you can be notified when you're followed by someone new, someone shares a tweet, a person in your address book joins Twitter, and when someone you follow joins a conversation you're in.

The next section deals with retweets you make and what happens with them. You can be emailed when your retweets are marked as favorites, and when they're retweeted.

The final two sections are *Activity from your network* and *Updates from twitter*. While some provide useful information, you may want to uncheck many of these boxes to decrease the amount of email you get from Twitter. To keep up with top stories and tweets, you may want to consider setting them to be emailed to you as a weekly digest. You may also want to check the box that allows you to get tips from Twitter, as this can be useful if you're new to the site.

Keeping track of "likes"

When you make a post on Facebook, people have the option of clicking on a Like button to indicate their approval or enjoyment in what you've said or shared. These Likes are important to monitor. They're clear indicators as to whether people like what you've had to say, and show that you're going in the right direction. If there are enough Likes, consider posting similar content in the future.

The Like button is also an opportunity to show that you're reading what people have to say, and to give you the chance to show your appreciation. When someone makes a particularly witty or astute observation, or says something you appreciate, you can click on the Like icon below their comment. While you won't want to overdo it and Like every comment, it gives you an option other than replying to what they've said.

Hijacking

The other reason to keep track of likes and comments is because someone may use them to hijack your page or campaign. The method is relatively simple. If you're in the same industry as mine, or have a campaign or product that I can use to promote my own agenda or organization, I post to your page or make my own comments. In doing so, your customers now see my posts and may venture away from your page to visit mine.

As we saw in Chapter 9, someone who is obviously trying to do this can be blocked from your page, making it impossible for them to continue with the same account. However, a person or group can easily fall under your radar and achieve the same results by using Likes. If you posted a comment on my competitor's page, I could click the Like button on your comment. This is a positive action, and you'd see this as endorsement or approval of something you said. You'd also be notified that I liked your comment, see the name of my account, and visit my page. It's a subtle and sneaky way of unsolicited advertising (i.e., SPAM). By clicking Like on comments, I've begun to take away traffic from the competitor's page and gotten people to visit mine.

By hovering your mouse over the Likes on people's comments, you may identify accounts belonging to competitors, or organizations and individuals who are trying to cause problems. If you do see this trend, you may want to call them out or block that account from your page.

Keeping track of dislikes

It's the nature of social media that people will say what they think, and not everything will be flattering or encouraging. Trolls may post inflammatory comments to get a rise out of people, but you shouldn't dismiss every negative comment as an invalid rant. Customers will have bad experiences, find fault with a campaign, or expose problems with your business practices. By monitoring these posts, you can try and appease unhappy customers, and use constructive criticism to improve your campaigns and business. The negative comments made by people can be as valuable as the positive ones.

Monitoring hashtags

Hashtags are useful for generating a conversation in Twitter and provide the ability to monitor a related group of tweets. When you create a hashtag for a campaign, it's important to watch what's being said, so you don't lose track of important comments. If you want updates on the use of a hashtag, you can use sites like Twilert (www.twilert.com) to send you an email when someone tweets about your product, service, business, or a hashtag being used in your campaign.

Hijacking

Just as someone can hijack a campaign on your Facebook page, a group or organization can hijack a hashtag campaign by using it to insert tweets about their own products, beliefs, or crusade. Throughout this book, we've seen a number of examples of these tactics. In Chapter 5, we saw how PETA tweeted comments on McDonald's and Wendy's hashtag campaigns to promote their own agenda. Hijacking hashtags are generally met with distain. People will see it for what it is: SPAM. Its unsolicited advertising of your organization or something you're selling to others.

You want to be careful making tweets on existing hashtags, as may be seen as a cheap and obvious attempt at promoting yourself. You don't want people seeing that you're trying to wedge a plug for your brand in the middle of a conversation. As we saw in Chapter 2, the Gap and American Apparel promoted their brand using the hashtag #Sandy, which was being used to discuss the ongoing devastation of Hurricane Sandy. While both used the hashtag as a sales ploy to sell products, it could have gone completely different if they had expressed concern for people in the storm, or offered aid in some way. Imagine the positive promotion of their brand if they had tweeted that they were making a donation for victims, or giving clothes to those who suffered? It's important to have empathy for how people will receive your message and use common sense in what you say.

If you are going to use existing hashtags, you need to determine how it's being used. In Chapter 5, we discussed the mistake Celeb Boutique made, when they promoted their Aurora dress using an existing #Aurora hashtag, where people were discussing shootings in Aurora, Colorado. Looking over what's being tweeted will give you an understanding of what's being said and how it's being used before adding your own perspective. If it's generic, such as using #socialmedia being used to discuss social media topics, then jump in and make a tweet about social media. If it's being used for specific conversation on an event or someone else's campaign, avoid it.

TweetDeck

If you have trouble monitoring what's happening with your accounts, you may want to consider using software designed to aid you. TweetDeck (www.tweetdeck.com) is a dashboard application that allows you to add one or more Twitter accounts. Using it, you can view your Timeline, interactions, messages, and other activities using customizable columns on an easy-to-use interface.

Using tools on blog sites

Blog sites commonly provide tools that allow you to monitor what's happening. WordPress (www.wordpress.com) provides a dashboard that allows you to see the number of posts, pages, categories, and tags on your blog, in addition to statistics on how many people viewed different posts and which are the most popular. To view this information, after logging into WordPress, hover your mouse over your account name in the upper left-hand corner, and click *Dashboard* on the menu that appears.

If you click on the graph beside your name in the upper left-hand corner, you'll be provided even more statistical information about your blog. *Analytics* is data you use for analysis and provides important insight into what content is working on a site. In looking at this data, you'll see a graph showing the number of visitors and views over days, weeks, and months. As seen in Figure 11.3, you'll also be provided with a map showing you the views by country. Using this, you can see which locations have the greatest interest in your blog, allowing you to identify possible target audiences for future posts.

Since you can connect your WordPress blog to other social media sites, you can also see how many times your blog has been followed in Twitter and Facebook, as well as through the blog itself. You can also view which search engines and sites people followed to get to your blog, giving you an indication of who's linking to the blog and which search engines are most used to find your posts.

Top Views by Country for all days ending 2013-08-05 (Summarized)

7 Days | 30 Days | Quarter | All time

Country	Views
United States	156
Canada	100
South Africa	22
Australia	14
United Kingdom	11
Brazil	7
India	6
Germany	5
Mexico	5
Ireland	5
Philippines	4
Netherlands	3
Italy	3
Romania	3
Georgia	3
Sweden	3
Swaziland	3
Bermuda	2
Slovenia	2
Spain	2
Bangladesh	2
Palestinian Territory, Occup	2
Bahamas	2

1 ▬▬▬▬ 156

FIGURE 11.3

WordPress views by country.

Facebook insights

Facebook Insights is a tool that's free with your Facebook accounts, and is accessed through the pages you manage. The interface provides information on the page Likes, comments, shares, and clicks on posts. It also provides graphs and textual information. Demographic data can be used to see the percentage of men and women using your page, and how it compares to all of Facebook. Geographic and language information is also available, so you can see how many fans spoke a certain language and the estimated location of where they live.

Google analytics

Google Analytics is another tool you should consider using to gather data about your sites or any Android or iOS apps created by your company. By going to www.google.com/analytics, you sign into the site using a Gmail account or another account you've setup, and choose the site you want to monitor. Google Analytics then provides you with tracking code that you can add into your pages or mobile app to collect usage information that's sent to your Analytics account. You can also set specific URLs to monitor, such as those for pages on Facebook, Twitter, blogs, and other social media sites.

Monitoring multiple social media sites

If you find it difficult monitoring conversations across multiple sites, an option may be using sites like Netvibes (www.netvibes.com). As seen in Figure 11.4, after creating your account, you can add various widgets to a dashboard, connecting your various social media sites to a single page. This allows you to keep track of Facebook posts, tweets, social bookmarks you've created on Delicious, and other sites on which you have a presence.

Another tool we discussed in Chapter 5, Hootsuite allows you to monitor your accounts on such social media sites as Twitter, Facebook, LinkedIn, Google+, MySpace, Foursquare, WordPress, and mixi. You can also add apps to connect to other sites, making it extremely versatile. On your Hootsuite dashboard, click on the *Getting Started* tab, and click the button to *Install Apps*. A listing of potential apps will appear that will allow Hootsuite to connect to these sites. The list includes such sites as YouTube, Reddit, Instagram, Tumblr, Flickr, Blogger, SlideShare, and others. Upon clicking the *Install App* button beside one of the sites listed, you may be asked to confirm permission to connect to the site and provide your username and password for that site. You'll also be asked whether you want the content to appear on an existing tab or have a new one created for you that's dedicated to that site.

Once you've added the tabs, you can click on them in the interface to switch from one site to another, viewing the tweets and posts on each. As we discussed in Chapter 5, you can post and tweet new content, or use the tool to schedule tweets and posts to appear on the sites at specific dates and times.

Hootsuite also allows you to create reports to provide statistical information about the sites you're monitoring. By clicking on the *Analytics* icon in the left pane of the Interface, you can choose from multiple reports to view information on an overview of your Twitter profile or Facebook page, LinkedIn Page Insights, Facebook Insights, Google Analytics, or a custom report as seen in Figure 11.5.

SocialSafe is another tool we've discussed for monitoring multiple sites, allowing you to view a journal of posts and tweets made in different dates, a calendar

FIGURE 11.4

Netvibes.

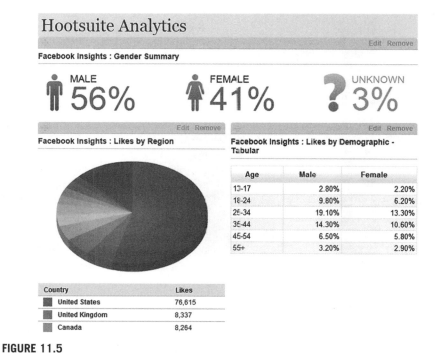

FIGURE 11.5

Creating an analytics report in Hootsuite.

view, and photos you've uploaded to sites. It provides an easy-to-use interface and, as seen in Figure 11.6, provides analytics to show you the most popular photos, updates and interactions, and days of the week that had the most activity.

The other benefit of using tools to monitor your social media accounts is that it allows multiple people to access the accounts without having to hand out passwords. If your business has several people who post content to social media sites, you don't have to give each of them the password for these accounts. They only need to connect using a single interface. If any of them leave the business or become the target of a phishing attack, you'll be protected because they won't know the passwords and won't be able to access your accounts. There's less chance of your social media accounts being compromised if fewer people know the passwords.

Keeping it fresh

Stale content is a problem for social media and Web sites. If there's nothing new, then people will stop visiting a page, following your tweets, and have less interest. They've seen it before, and will assume you've either lost interest or have nothing

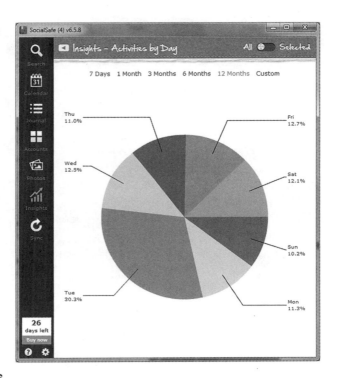

FIGURE 11.6

SocialSafe insights.

new to say. Since social media is also about building a relationship with friends and followers, you don't want to jeopardize your connections with people by falling out of touch with people.

As we saw in Chapter 5, tools like Hootsuite and Tweetdeck can be used to schedule tweets. If you know you're unavailable to create new tweets during certain times, you can use these tools to send out them out on specific dates and times. Rather than have nothing new on Twitter, you can have new tweets being sent while you're on vacation, at conferences, or otherwise unavailable. It also allows you to send tweets that are relevant to people in other time zones, those enjoying the weekend, night owls, and others who you want to reach outside of normal business hours.

Campaigns are important tools to get word out and generate interest in businesses, products, and even your social media presence. Some campaigns, like those we discussed in Chapter 5, can be extensive and involve multiple types of marketing. Others can be as simple as offering e-coupons, promotional codes for discounts, or having a prize for being the 100th person to comment or liking the page. If some campaigns worked out well, then you can reintroduce them, generating similar results with minimal effort.

There will be times when there's nothing new to say. For personal use, there may not be much happening in your life. while for a business you might have a lull in news or be in between planned campaigns. To inspire yourself, you should search news, articles and content created by other people. You may find an article or some news related to your industry that you can write about or share a link to, or some video or image that a customer has created about your product or business. There may be testimonials or positive tweets that followers have made on their accounts that you'll want to retweet or share. By showing that you're following what others are saying, you're able to acknowledge others and show that you appreciate them.

New content doesn't have to be about new things. If you post an old photo or reminisce about a positive moment in the past, you'll find that people will relate to it. For businesses, it can also show that you've been in business for a long time, and may renew interest in old products or previous methods of advertising. As seen in Figure 11.7, by posting a photo of an old garbage bag that used to be given to customers for their cars, Delta Sonic Car Wash inspired over 100 comments from people who became nostalgic and asked for the bags to be brought back. Reminding people about the past can make them reminiscent of good or better times, what attracted them to you in the first place, and how long they've been loyal to you.

FIGURE 11.7

Facebook post by Delta Sonic.

Deciding what's working and lessons learned

Before creating new content and after doing any major work, you should sit down with others and try and decide what's working and anything you've learned from experience. A simple meeting of people involved in a project can provide valuable information on tactics that worked well and mistakes that were made. It allows you to replicate successes and avoid repeating mistakes.

As we saw earlier in this chapter, you can use monitoring tools to see what people are responding to on a site. You can identify trends, popular posts and pages, and articles on blogs that are being visited and read by people throughout the world. It provides information on what content is working on a site and indicates the direction you should take for future content you post.

Social media campaigns are another area that needs management and review. When you start a campaign, you need to identify what you're trying to achieve from it. It may be to generate conversation, increase followers, raise sales, or some other objective. To determine whether a campaign was successful, you need to look at whether it achieved the results you intended and provided a return on investment. If you spend a lot of time and/or money on the campaign, but it didn't achieve the objective, then you'll need to review what was done and determine if there was anything that could have improved results.

Learning from your mistakes and successes is an important tool in making future endeavors thrive. Taking a short amount of time from a project to review similar efforts in the past will help you to avoid problems and lower the overall risk associated with what you're hoping to achieve.

Creating Facebook pages

Creating a Facebook page can help promote causes, interests, businesses and products, and people or things you're a fan of. To create a page, logon to your Facebook account and go to www.facebook.com/pages/create/. In doing so, you'll see different options to select the type of page you're trying to create. When clicking on any of these options, you'll be provided with fields to provide more information, such as the name that will be used for the page, and a category that describes it. For a local business or place, you'll also be asked to provide the address and phone number of the business so customers can know where to visit it. After filling out these fields, click on the checkbox to agree to Facebook's terms, and then click the *Get Started* button.

What follows is a wizard that takes you through the process of setting up your page. Through the steps that follow, you'll provide a description of the page, which will help in search results when people try to find it, the URL of your Web site, photos for your profile, and more. If there's any information you're unable to provide through the process, such as a good photo to upload for the profile, you can skip ahead and add it later.

Security settings

When you create a page, people have a significant amount of access. By default, it's published for everyone to see, and everyone can post content to it. Obviously, you'll want to some control over your page and how it's used, so you'll want to adjust the security settings. To change the security settings:

1. Click on the *Admin Panel* button in the upper right-hand side of the page.
2. At the top of the page, click on the *Edit Page* button.
3. When the drop-down menu appears, click *Edit Settings*.

Upon doing so, you'll see a page similar to the one shown in Figure 11.8. The first section allows you to control the visibility of the page, which we discuss later in this chapter. While you're setting up the page, it's always a good idea to unpublish the page while you're working on it, and then publish it when you're ready for others to see it. To modify the settings, you would click on the *Edit* link on the right side, configure it as desired, and then click the *Save Changes* button.

The next two sections control posts that others make on your page. The *Posting Ability* section controls whether others can post to the page's Timeline, and if they can upload videos and images to it. In most cases, you would uncheck the boxes for this to avoid everyone being able to add content to the page. If you do allow this, then the *Post Visibility* setting should be set. Here, you'll find options that control whether posts are automatically visible to others, or if they need to be approved by

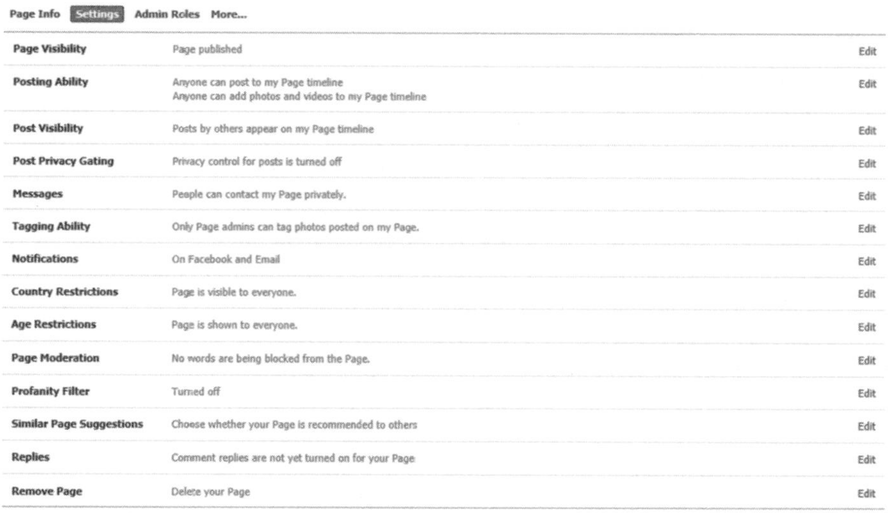

Page Info Settings Admin Roles More...		
Page Visibility	Page published	Edit
Posting Ability	Anyone can post to my Page timeline Anyone can add photos and videos to my Page timeline	Edit
Post Visibility	Posts by others appear on my Page timeline	Edit
Post Privacy Gating	Privacy control for posts is turned off	Edit
Messages	People can contact my Page privately.	Edit
Tagging Ability	Only Page admins can tag photos posted on my Page.	Edit
Notifications	On Facebook and Email	Edit
Country Restrictions	Page is visible to everyone.	Edit
Age Restrictions	Page is shown to everyone.	Edit
Page Moderation	No words are being blocked from the Page.	Edit
Profanity Filter	Turned off	Edit
Similar Page Suggestions	Choose whether your Page is recommended to others	Edit
Replies	Comment replies are not yet turned on for your Page	Edit
Remove Page	Delete your Page	Edit

FIGURE 11.8

Facebook page settings.

an administrator first. It also provides an option to have these new posts highlighted at the top of the page.

The *Post Privacy Gating* section allows you to set whether you page has a privacy control, which allows you to select audiences who will be able to see new posts. The ability to select a list of people who will see your posts is something we discussed in Chapter 9, and may be something you're familiar with when using your personal Timeline. Oddly enough, it's turned off by default for pages, but you should turn it on. While most of your posts will be public, there may be times when you'll only want certain groups seeing a post. For example, if you have a local business, you may want to post a special for local customers, and would want to select the network of people living in the same area of your business.

The *Messages* option is used to control whether a message button will appear on your page. If people click on this button, they'll be able to send a private message to the page, allowing them to contact you privately. As people may want to contact you to report problems, in most cases you'll want to have this enabled.

The *Tagging Ability* setting determines whether people can tag others in the photos you post on the page. In many cases, you'll want to uncheck this option, removing their ability to associate other people or pages with your pictures. You don't want them tagging your product with the name of a competitor, or associating parts of the photo with inappropriate tags.

As we discussed earlier in this chapter, notifications are important for knowing when someone has added something to your page. The *Notifications* section is used to control whether you're notified when someone has made a post, comment, or sent a message to your page. In choosing the available options, you should check the box(es) to have notifications sent to your email address, Facebook, or both.

The next two sections control who will see the page. By editing the *Country Restrictions* setting, you can control whether the page is visible or hidden from certain countries. In the field, you would type the names of the countries, and then click on the option to only show the page to people in those countries, or hide it from them. If left blank, it's visible to everyone.

If the page targets people over a certain age, then the *Age Restrictions* settings should also be configured. You might have content on the page that you don't want seen by people under a certain age, as in the case of a bar or club that doesn't allow minors. Once you select the minimum age that can see it, the page and its content won't be visible to anyone under that age.

The next two sections control what can be posted on the page. The *Page Moderation* section allows you to specify words that are blocked on the page. It keeps people from making posts or comments with certain words, preventing them from mentioning certain things. This would be useful if you didn't want people mentioning the names of your competition, or topics and people you have an issue with. The *Profanity Filter* also blocks certain words from being posted and prevents swearing on the page. It uses lists of words and phrases that have been reported to Facebook as inappropriate. You can choose to shut off the filter, limit profanity by choosing medium, or disallow any profanity by using the strong filter.

The *Similar Page Suggestions* setting can be useful in advertising your page to others. When someone likes a page similar to yours, your page may appear as a suggestion to the person on their Timeline. Since it's beneficial to you, it's a good idea to ensure the checkbox is checked.

The *Replies* setting allows people to reply to new comments made by others. While they can't reply to older ones, they can make a comment on new comments made by other people. This can help to generate some additional conversation, as people will be able to show their agreement or disagreement with people who have commented on your posts.

Vanity URLs

When you create a Facebook page, it's assigned a randomly generated numbers as part of its URL. While it works, it isn't easy to remember or type into the address bar of a browser. To make it easier for people to visit your page, you should create a vanity URL.

As we saw in Chapter 3, LinkedIn allows you to create a custom URL, so that people can visit your site using an address that's user friendly. Other sites also provide this ability. On Facebook, you can logon and visit www.facebook.com/username to access a wizard that takes you step-by-step through the process of creating a custom URL. To create a vanity URL for a page you've created, do the following:

1. Logon to Facebook. In the address bar of your browser, type "www.facebook. com/username" and press the *Enter* key on your keyboard.
2. In the *Each Page can have a username* section, select the page you're creating a URL for from the *Page name* drop-down list.
3. Click the *Check Availability* button.
4. Once you've selected a username that hasn't been taken, a screen similar to the one shown in Figure 11.9 will appear. If you decide to take the username, click the *Confirm* button.

In creating the name, don't make it too difficult to remember. You want it to be short, sweet, and memorable. As the warning in Figure 11.9 shows, you also can't transfer the username, or violate someone else's trademark. You also can't change it after setting it the first time, so you'll want to be careful what you choose.

Usernames for accounts

Facebook also allows you to create a username for your account, which creates a vanity URL to your Timeline, and also creates an email address for facebook.com that uses this name (i.e., *<username>*@facebook.com). As with pages, you can only do this once, so you should be careful what you change it to. This is created or modified by doing the following:

1. Click on the gear-shaped icon in the upper right-hand corner, and click on *Account Settings* when the menu appears.
2. Click on *General* in the left-hand pane of the page.
3. Click on the *Edit* link beside *Username*.

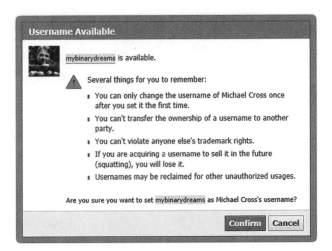

FIGURE 11.9

Creating a vanity URL in Facebook.

4. When the section expands, enter the name you want to use in the *Username* field.
5. Enter your password in the *Password* field.
6. Click *Save Changes*

Once you've completed the process, the email address that's created will appear in your Timeline, and you'll be able to direct people to your Timeline using the URL that's created.

Dialing it back and retaking control

Not everything works out the way you want or lasts as long as you hoped. You may be overwhelmed by the amount of work involved in maintaining a presence on too many sites, made mistakes that have created numerous problems, or found that a site no longer has the popularity it once had. Whatever the reason, you may want to take a step back and make changes to retake control of your social media presence on various sites.

By dialing back the number of accounts, sites, and work related to your social media, you can whittle it back to a manageable state. This may involve deactivating accounts that are no longer used, changing to more popular social networking sites, or taking steps to remove elements that are causing problems. In some cases, it may require adding people who can help maintain the site. As we'll see in the sections that follow, there are many options available for taking a floundering social media presence and getting it to the point where it can become more successful.

Reviewing social media

If you're not getting what you hoped out of the social media sites you're using, then it may be that you're using the wrong site. If you were hoping to find a relationship on Facebook, you might have done better using a dating site like eHarmony. If you were trying to reach people in China, you'd be better off using Sina Weibo (www. weibo.com) than Twitter. As we saw in Chapter 4, the demographics of people using different sites are not the same, meaning that if you're marketing to a specific age, gender, or race, the site might not be a favorite of your target audience.

The popularity of sites can fluctuate, making the most popular site today one of the least used later. Consider how Friendster (www.friendster.com) was the place to be, but declined in popularity as people joined MySpace (www.myspace.com), until Facebook became the social network of choice. To ensure you're using a site where your friends and customers are going, you need to stay aware of the site's popularity. To stay aware of the most popular social media, you can use sites like Alexa (www.alexa.com/topsites) to view a list of the top sites on the Web. By keeping up with the trends of sites being used, you may find an emerging social media site where you should consider having a presence.

Getting rid of accounts, pages, and sites

The interest people have in social media can also change. Many times you'll find that while a particular kind of social media was popular at first, enthusiasm in it dies over time. Employees may have created blogs, which were updated regularly with new content at first, but have had nothing new written in some time. You'll also find that some people have created accounts, only to check it out and decide it wasn't for them. Regardless of the situation, you need to review these sites and identify any that are no longer needed.

Any unused accounts or ones slotted for replacement should be deleted to prevent unauthorized users from logging into them. The same should be done with accounts belonging to employees that are no longer with your company. You should also delete any pages, blogs, or sites that are no longer being used. As we'll see in the next sections, there are different ways of getting rid of old accounts and pages. For example, on Facebook, you can permanently delete a page or unpublish it so that it's no longer visible to others. Regardless of which you choose, if you're not using it and won't in the foreseeable future, make it disappear.

Prior to shutting down accounts and sites, you should take the time to inform those using it. Even though a Twitter account hasn't had new tweets or a blog hasn't had recent posts, there may still be people following or subscribing to it. If they had interest before, they may have interest in new ones. Take the time to let people know about the new social media presence you're creating. Tweet a message about how a current account won't be used, but people can follow you at a new one. If you're leaving an account open to reserve the name, let people know it. While some may think it sad to see a farewell message (even if it's a temporary one), they'll appreciate knowing that they can follow you elsewhere.

In some cases, you can get people to visit your new site by redirecting them. In doing so, a person types the URL of the old site into their browser, but the browser sends them to your new site. There are a few ways of doing this. If a domain name is registered to a blog or site, you could contact your Internet Service Provider (or network administrator if it's an intranet site). The ISP or network administrator could make changes to DNS entries that are used to tell browsers and search engines how to find your site. Alternatively, if you have the ability to modify the HTML of a Web page, you could add JavaScript that sends visitors to another location. For example, if you added the following script to a page's HTML, the browser would read it when the page loads, and send the person to Google. If you changed www.google.com to the URL of your site, the browser would go to your site instead.

```
<script type = "text/javascript" >
 < !--
window.location = "http://www.google.com/"
//-- >
 < /script >
```

Deactivating a Facebook account

On Facebook, you have the option of deactivating an account that isn't being used anymore, so that it appears to be gone and won't appear in search results. If you're the sole admin of any pages, those pages will be unpublished so that others won't see them. What's nice about deactivating an account over deleting it is that you can simply logon to it to reactivate it.

If you're deactivating a business account, you should reset the password so that others won't be able to logon to the account and reactivate it. Since you don't want people to see any of the pages or content you've posted, the last thing you want is for this to happen. To deactivate an account, do the following:

1. On the upper right-hand corner of the page, click on the gear-shaped icon, and then click *Account Settings* on the menu that appears.
2. In the left pane of the page, click *Security*.
3. At the bottom of the page, click the *Deactivate your account* link.
4. When the new page appears, provide a reason for deactivating the account, and then click *Confirm*.

Deleting a Facebook account

If you're certain you'll never use the account again, you also have the option of permanently deleting it. In doing so, you won't be able to access it again and any content will be irrecoverable. Deleting the account is done by logging in and then going to www.facebook.com/help/delete_account, and then clicking the *Delete My Account* button. Before using this form, you should be certain you want to delete it rather than deactivating the account.

TOOLS & TIPS...

Make a Backup Before you Delete

When you delete an account, you lose everything you've posted, content you've uploaded, and information related to the account. Before taking this drastic step, you should archive the content as we discussed in Chapter 6. Sites like Facebook and Twitter provide features to save a copy of what you've posted, uploaded, and the data related to the account to your hard drive. This allows you to access it if you need it later for another site.

Of course, just because you've deleted it doesn't mean it's necessarily gone. As we mentioned, it may be some time before the account and content is actually removed, and no longer visible through search engines. Also, in deleting the account, it doesn't remove all of the content you don't want others to see. Someone will still be able to view things posted about you, photos others have uploaded, and content that's been downloaded and shared by others.

Deactivating a Twitter account

Unfortunately, when a Twitter account is deactivated, it doesn't simply prevent others from seeing it. The account is placed in a queue and deleted after 30 days. Because it will be permanently deleted, this is not something you want to do as a temporary measure, unless you keep careful track over the number of days since you took action to deactivate it. To deactivate a Twitter account, do the following:

1. Click on the gear-shaped icon in the upper right-hand corner of the page, and click on the *Settings* menu item.
2. Scroll down to the bottom of the page, and click on the *Deactivate my account* link.
3. When the confirmation page appears, click on the button to deactivate the account.

After you've deactivated the account, the content should disappear within a few minutes, but it's possible that some content may still be viewed for a few days. If you changed your mind within the 30 days, you could log back in and reactivate the account.

Closing a LinkedIn account

Accounts on LinkedIn can also be shut down if you no longer use them. When you shutdown the account, you'll lose your connections and any information you've added on your profile page. Before taking the following steps in closing the account, make sure you really don't want to use it anymore:

1. Hover your mouse over your name in the upper right-hand corner, and click *Settings* on the menu that appears.
2. When your account settings page appears, click on the *Account* tab near the bottom left of the page.
3. Click on the *Close your account* link.

4. When the page appears, provide information on why you're closing your account, and click through the wizard that takes you step-by-step in closing your account.

Deleting or unpublishing Facebook pages

Just as there are accounts you'll want to get rid of, you may have created pages that you no longer want to use. To delete pages you've created on Facebook, you can do the following:

1. Click on the *Admin Panel* button in the upper right-hand side of the page.
2. At the top of the page, click on the *Edit Page* button.
3. When the drop-down menu appears, click *Edit Settings*.
4. To unpublish the page so no one can see it:
    a. Click on the *Edit* link in the *Page Visibility* section.
    b. Click on the *Unpublish Page* checkbox so it appears checked.
    c. Click *Save Changes*.
5. To delete the page:
    a. Click on the *Edit* link in the *Remove Page* section.
    b. Click on the *Permanently delete* link.
    c. When the dialog box appears asking you to confirm the deletion, click the *Delete* button to permanently remove it.

Friends versus followers

When you add someone as a friend, they generally get more access to view your content. Even if a person is added to the Restricted list, he or she will have the added benefit of seeing your new public posts in their newsfeed. If you want to allow people to follow new public posts in their newsfeed, you don't have to add them as a friend. You can simply enable followers.

Followers only see public content, and aren't added as friends. When they visit your page, they will see a button entitled *Follow*. By clicking it, any content you post as public will display in their newsfeed. To turn on the feature of allowing followers:

1. Click on the gear-shaped icon in the upper right corner of the page, and click *Account Settings* on the menu that appears.
2. In the left-hand pane of the page, click *Followers*.
3. In the *Turn On Follow* section, click on the checkbox so it appears checked.

After turning on Followers, you will have a number of other settings appear. The first of these is *Follower Comments*, which controls who will be able to comment on public posts you make. To modify this setting, you would click on the Edit link. When the area expands, click on the button and choose who will be able to post on your public posts: Everyone, Friends-of-Friends, or just Friends.

The *Follower notifications* setting is used to control when someone comments on a public post you make. To modify this setting, you would click on the Edit link. When the area expands, click on the button and choose when you'll be notified about people following and sharing your content. You can turn on notifications for Everyone, Friends-of-Friends, or Everybody.

Additional settings for changing your username, which we discussed in the previous section, and linking Facebook and Twitter (which we discussed in Chapter 5) will also appear. Once the feature is activated, you'll also see a preview of a "Follow" button that can be added to other sites. Using the code in the box, you could copy it into a Web page, so that people on other sites can follow you on Facebook.

Removing friends and who you're following

It's wise to occasionally review the people you've added as friends. While adding them may have been a good idea at the time, the people you previously accepted as friends may not be the ones you want viewing your posts now. As we've seen in Chapter 9, many sites provide the ability to block users or limit what's visible to them. Occasionally though, you'll want to purge the friends you've added over the years to get your list down to a manageable size.

There are many reasons to delete a person you've added as a friend. Real-life friends who have fallen out of favor, past relationships you don't want to keep in contact with, and former coworkers and bosses are all candidates for removal. To unfriend someone on Facebook, follow these steps:

1. In the upper right-hand corner of the page, click on your name. When your Timeline appears, click on the *Friends* link near your profile picture.
2. Scroll down to the person you want to remove, and click on the drop-down list beside the picture. On the menu that appears, click *Unfriend*.

At times, you'll also want to trim down the number of people you follow on Twitter. The posts of those you follow will appear in your newfeed. After awhile, you'll find you aren't getting much from what they have to say, and their tweets appear like noise overshadowing useful content. As we'll see in the next chapter, tweets from certain people can also be blocked, but you may also want to simply stop following a person or group. To stop following people in Twitter, do the following:

1. On the top navigation bar, click on the *Me* link.
2. In the left pane of the page, click *Following*.
3. Scroll through the list until you find the person you want to stop following, and click the *Following* button beside their name.

Additional administrators

Sometimes, the workload of managing a page or blog can become overwhelming for a single person. Fortunately, some sites allow you to add additional people to administer the page, which can give them a high level of control over your page or blog. Before giving away the keys to the kingdom, you should identify how administrative access is given. For personal use, you'll want to limit this access to people you trust, and who will be efficient at moderating the page and/or contributing content. For businesses, you'll need to decide whether the Social Media Officer grants this access, or if it's controlled through a procedure or process.

Adding and removing administrators on a Facebook page

Facebook allows you to add extra admins to a page, so they can assist with managing the page. A person can be given one of several roles, each with a different level of access. Because of this, you wouldn't want to give a person more access than they need, or assign an untrustworthy person any access. Aside from the lowest level, a person in an admin role could create ads with a campaign budget that you'd be responsible paying for. The available roles you can assign a person are:

- *Insights Analyst*, which lets the person view Insights
- *Advertiser*, which lets them create ads and view Insights
- *Moderator*, which gives the previous access, plus lets them to send messages as the page, respond to comments, and delete them
- *Content Creator*, which gives the previous access, plus the ability to create posts as the page, edit the page, and add apps
- *Manager*, which allows them to do all of the above, plus manage admin roles

    To add an extra admin to a page in Facebook, you would do the following:

1. At the top of the page, click on the *Edit Page* button.
2. When the drop-down menu appears, click *Manage Admin Roles*.
3. In the field on the right-hand side, enter the name or email address of the person to add.
4. Click on the role beneath the name, and select the role you'd like to assign to the person from the drop-down list.

    There may be times when an admin you've added hasn't worked out, and you want to remove them from their previous role. To remove an existing page admin, you would go to this same page and click the "X" next to the person's name that you want to remove.

Adding and removing roles on a WordPress blog

WordPress also allows you to add people to assist with your blog. There are several different roles that can be given to a person:

- *Contributor*, who can edit posts but not publish them
- *Author*, who can edit, publish, and delete their own posts and also upload images and files
- *Editor*, who has the access mention previously, but can perform these actions on any post or page. This person can also moderate comments and manage categories, tags, and links
- *Administrator*, who has full control over the blog. Due to the high level of access, there should only be one person in this role.

To add a new person to a role, you would do the following:

1. After logging into your WordPress blog, hover over your name in the upper left-hand corner, and click *Dashboard* on the menu that appears.
2. On the left pane, click *Users*.
3. When the *Users* page appears, click *Invite New*.
4. Enter the usernames and email addresses of the person to add, and select the role you want to assign them from the drop-down menu.

To delete a person's access in a role, you would go to the *Users* page, and click on the checkbox beside their name so it appears checked. At the bottom of the page, you would select *Remove* from the drop-down list, and then click the *Apply* button.

Ongoing training

This may be the end of the book, but it shouldn't be the end of your learning about social media. Because there's significant benefit and risk in using social media, there is a significant need for training and guidance. New sites emerge, gain popularity, and become a forum for engaging in conversation. As new security settings are introduced, you need to be aware of them to set them properly. Employees need to be updated in how to use it in a way that represents your organization. Everyone needs to understand how to use it in an effective and secure manner.

For businesses, you may have trainers on staff who can help teach users how to properly use the company's social media and protect themselves while using it at home. As we discussed earlier in this chapter, your governance committee can be helpful in identifying topics that should be included in a training plan. Any plan you create should include laws and regulations related to your business, issues like defamation and properly netiquette when dealing with people online, and using security tools like antivirus/anti-malware software to safeguard personal devices and home computers.

To enhance your skills, there are also resources on the Internet that can help you use social media. Depending on your position in a company, you should look at organizations related to your industry or occupation to find information on social media specifically related to your job. For example, if you were a records manager, you should investigate the Association for Information and Image Management (www.aiim.org) and review their information on using social media. If you're looking for general information, use the help features on the social media sites you use to get instructions on using the tools and features of the site. Whatever you do, don't stop learning.

Bibliography

Bearstone, J. (2012, July 12). *@MrJeb Twitter Account*. Retrieved July 14, 2013, from Twitter: <https://twitter.com/MrJeb/status/223396325633425409>.

Bercovici, J. (2010, December 9). *Who coined 'social media'? Web pioneers compete for credit.* Retrieved March 11, 2013, from Forbes: <http://www.forbes.com/sites/jeffbercovici/2010/12/09/who-coined-social-media-web-pioneers-compete-for-credit/>.

Brenner, J. (2013, February 14). *Pew Internet: Social networking (full detail).* Retrieved March 10, 2012, from Pew Internet & American Life Project: <http://pewinternet.org/Commentary/2012/March/Pew-Internet-Social-Networking-full-detail.aspx>.

Cisco Visual Networking Index: Global mobile data traffic forecast update, *2012–2017.* (2013, February 6). Retrieved March 10, 2013, from Cisco: <http://www.cisco.com/en/US/solutions/collateral/ns341/ns525/ns537/ns705/ns827/white_paper_c11-520862.html>.

Clifford, S. (2009, April 15). *Video prank at Domino's taints brand.* Retrieved July 25, 2013, from New York Times: <http://www.nytimes.com/2009/04/16/business/media/16dominos.html?_r=0>.

Cummings, G. (2012, July 12). *@grahamcummings7 Twitter account.* Retrieved July 14, 2013, from Twitter: <https://twitter.com/grahamcummings7/status/223377691284471808>.

Harvard Business Review Analytic Services. (2010). The new conversation: Taking social media from talk to action. *Harvard Business Review.* <http://www.sas.com/resources/whitepaper/wp_23348.pdf>.

Kaplan, A. M., & Haenlein, (2010).M. (2010). Users of the world, unite! The challenges and opportunities of social media. *Business Horizons, 53*(1), 59–68.

Laningham, S. (2006, August 22). *Developerworks interviews: Tim Berners-Lee.* Retrieved March 11, 2013, from IBM: <http://www.ibm.com/developerworks/podcast/dwi/cm-int082206txt.html>.

Mobile Spurs Digital Coupon User Growth. (2013, January 13). Retrieved March 10, 2013, from eMarketer: <http://www.emarketer.com/Article/Mobile-Spurs-Digital-Coupon-User-Growth/1009639#VtDzxL6QcVIG76xo.99>.

Rao, L. (2010, March 2). *Toyota turns to Twitter to repair its image.* Retrieved July 25, 2013, from Techcrunch: <http://techcrunch.com/2010/03/02/toyota-turns-to-twitter-to-repair-its-image/>.

Stelzner, M. A. (2012). *2012 Social media marketing industry report.* Social Media Examiner.

Index

Note: Page numbers followed by *"b," "f," and "t"* refer to boxes, figures, and tables, respectively.

A

Abbreviations, 107–108
Acceptable Use Policy (AUP), 222
Accountability, 288–289
Account protection, with two-step verification
    process, 267–268
Acronyms, 107–108
Active sessions listing, in Facebook, 189
Additional administrators, 315–317
Adobe Photoshop, 28
Advertising
    opportunity in social media, 23
    on YouTube and Twitter, 98
Airwatch, 158
Albine, 50–51
AMBER Alert notification, 105
American Academy of Matrimonial Lawyers
    (AAML) report, 2010, 130
America Online (AOL), 14–15
Amy's Baking Company's Facebook page, 102*f*,
    103*f*
Android, 158
Anonymity of internet, 172
Antidiscrimination, 223–224
Antiharassment, 223–224
Anti-phishing protection, in browsers, 184–186
Antivirus software, 87–88
Apple iPhone, 182
Application Programming Interfaces (APIs), 147
Approved representatives, 92
Apps, in Facebook
    blocking of, 245
    privacy controlling of, 242–243
    unblocking of, 245
Archive/archiving
    content, 143–144
    Facebook, 145–146
    Twitter, 146
Assembly Bill 1844, California, 50
Audiences
    identification in social media site, 78–80
    younger, 79–80
Avast free antivirus software, 215
AVG Free Anti-Virus, 215

B

Backdoors, 213
Backupify online service, 147

Backup process
    for cell phone or tablet, 156
    definition of, 144
    of lost data, 152–156
        tools and tips to secure, 155*b*
        by using windows backup, 153–155
        web-based solutions, 155–156
    tools and tips for, 145*b*
Bad campaigning, of social media, 99–100
Bad passwords, 263–264
Baiting technique, 212
Basic information, on Facebook, 270–271
Being bold *vs* being overlooked, 97
Bing, 27, 61
Bitly, 88
Blackberry Enterprise Server, 150
Blacklisting users, on WordPress, 241
Blocked social media sites, 119*t*
Blocking apps, in Facebook, 245
    unblocking apps, 245
Blocking chat, in Facebook, 169–170
Blocking users, 238–241
    on Facebook, 238–240
        blocking invites, 239–240
        unblocking of users, 239
    on Twitter, 240
    on YouTube, 240–241
Blogging, 4–5
Blogs, 3
    definition of, 4
    using of tools on, 300
Bogus job offers, on Twitter and LinkedIn, 162
Bookmark, meaning of, 3–4
Boston Marathon bombing (2013), 135
Bots, 210–211
Brand/Branding, 82–85
    building of recognition, importance of, 24
    designing of documents by companies for,
        25
    feature of, 24
    inconsistency on internet in, 25
    meaning of, 24
    yourself for employment, 53–55
Brand hijacking, 195
Brandjacking
    definition of, 258
    as part of attack, 258–259
Bring Your Own Device (BOYD)
    advantages of, 157

Bring Your Own Device (BOYD) (*Continued*)
 agreement with employees to use personal
   devices at work, 158
 disadvantages of, 157–158
 meaning of, 157
British Telecommunications, 3
Browser
 blocking of sites through, 237
 hijacking, 212–213
Bulletin Board System (BBS), 14

C

Campaigning, for promotion of social media, 98–99
Candidate screening, 47–51
Carbonite site, 155–156
Celebrite's, 205
Cell phone backup, 156
Censorship
 by country, 119–120
 definition of, 119
 limitation must be impose by social media sites,
   119
 on your account pages and blogs, 120–121
Centralized corporate accounts and email, 90–91
Centralizing responsibility, for social media, 92
Chat rooms, 168–170
Chief Digital Officer, 14
Chrome, 88
Cingular Wireless, 3
Citidel ransomware, 211
Classified information, 139
CoasterVille game, 23
Code of conduct and ethics, 226–227
Collaboration project, classification of, 3–4
Collaboration sites, 3
Collaborative projects, 3
Collective intelligence, definition of, 41–42
Combat game, 7–8
Command-and-control (C&C) center, 210–211
Communications, 2
 benefits of content communities, 6
 strategy on internet, 4–5
Computer Fraud and Abuse Act (CFAA) of 1986,
   186–187
Confidentiality, 224–225
Consumer reporting agency, 50
Consumer's Online Brand Related Activity
   (COBRA), 35–36
Contact information, on Facebook, 269–270
Content communities, 3
 benefit to business from, 5
 communication benefits of, 6
 definition of, 5

features of, 5
 necessary to review site terms of service, 6
Content management
 definition of, 110–111
 tools for, 111
 usage of life cycle data in social media,
   110–111
Content security, 277–282
 block people to write on timelines, 279–281
 preapproving or turning off comments, 278–279
 seeing through other eyes, 281–282
Contest arrangement, in sites, 122
Context phishing, 181
Continuity planning, 294
Converse sneakers, 35*f*
Cookies, deletion from Internet Explorer, 107
Corporate espionage, 142
Corporate goals, setting up for social media, 86
Corporate social network, 81
Country, social media sites blocked by, 119*t*
Cracker, 186
Creation, 110
Crisis management, 293–294
Cross-posting, in sites, 114
Crowdsourcing, 41–42
Customers, engagement in social media, 27–30
Cyber-activism, 182
Cyberbullying
 definition of, 166–167
 post of abusive comments in social networking
   sites, 166
Cybercrime
 definition of, 161
 targets of, 161
Cybersex, 167–175
Cybersquatting, 258
Cyberstalking/cyberstalkers
 definition of, 164
 social media as a tool for, 164
 steps in protection from, 165–166

D

Daily Motion, 5
Dark side, of social media, 161
Data, in social media
 loss of, 148
 permanence of, 134
Daytum, 28
Defaced sites, 188–189
Defamation
 definition of, 202
 impact on businesses, 202
 in social media, 202

Defensive profiles, to prevent impersonation, 259–260
Deleted/deletion
    of cookies from Internet Explorer, 107
    of Facebook account, 312
    of unused accounts/pages/sites, 311–314
Delicious site, 3–4, 4f
Dephi Forums, 168
Dialing of account numbers, 310–317
Digital forensics, 203
Digital forensic software, 204–205
Digital information, 144
Digital Media Manager, 291–292
Digital Millennium Copyright Act (DMCA), 199–200
Directories browsing, in social media sites, 122
Discrimination, 223
    in social media, 201
    in workplaces between employees, 201–202
Disney, 3
Distributed Denial of Service (DDoS), 228
Divorce cases and social media, 129–130
Downloadr, 147
Download Your Information (DYI) tool, 146
Doxxing 101 technique, 275
Doxxing technique, 273–275
Dumpster diving, 180

E

eDiscovery (Electronic discovery), 143–144
Editing, 110
eHarmony, hacking of passwords, 64
Electronic word of mouth (eWOM), 36–38
Email accounts for social media, tools and tips for, 63b
Email address, 60–61, 63, 82, 206
Embarrassing content, in social media, 134
Employees, social media use to find, 45–47, 66–68
Employment and social media, 45
    branding yourself for employment, 53–55
    current employee's password, 50–51
    getting referrals through social networking sites, 52–53
    prohibition on employers to disclose login credentials, 50
    screening of candidates, 47–51
EnCase, 204
Enterprise Content Management (ECM), 225
Environmental Protection Agency's (EPA), 143
Erasing of data tools, 150
European Organization for Nuclear Research (CERN), 3

European Union, privacy laws to protect citizens, 81
Everquest, 7
Exchangable Image File (EXIF) data, 250
Explicit content
    on social media sites, 173–174
    of yourself or loved ones, 174–175
Exploit, 213–214
    distribution, 210–216

F

Facebook, 1–2, 6, 7f, 15, 21–23, 26, 29f, 111
    account protection with two-step verification process, 267–268
    accounts linkage with Twitter, 116, 117f
    addition and removal of administrators on, 316
    audience visits in, 78
    average users of, 37
    blocking apps in, 245
    blocking chat in, 169–170
    blocking of users in, 238–240
    comments on posts, 39
    controlling of exposure to search in, 277
    creation of pages, 306–310
    deactivation of account, steps in, 312
    deleting of account, 312
    deleting/unpublishing pages of, 314
    downloading of your content in
        steps in, 145
        tools and tips for, 146b
    getting people know about your job search, 59
    graph search, 276–277
    information people post about themselves in, 229t
    insights, 301
    listing of friends, 230–232
        creation of new lists, 231
        restricted list, 231–232
    location information removal from, 247–248
    Norton Safe Web for, 185f
    notification settings, 296f
    noting of questions in, 178
    page settings, 307f
    partnership with Skype, 168–169
    posts removal from, 132–133
    privacy controlling apps on, 242–243
    provision for follow conversations and view information, 85
    removal of photos and tags from, 132
        steps for, 132
    reporting of fake accounts on, 261
    restrictions on people to see your posts in, 232–234
        limitations on past posts, 233–234

Facebook (*Continued*)
  restrictions to see your friends and whom we
    follow, 234
  searching of people through email address, 206
  security issues, 34*f*
  security settings page in, steps to activate, 163–
    164, 189–190, 307–309
  update status profile in, 33
Fair information practice principles (FIPs), in US,
  198–199
Fake
  accounts, 257–262
  photos and videos, 172–173
  sites
    identification of, 182–184
    for purposes other than phishing, 182–183
False information, 135–139
  about yourself in internet, 137
  promotion of brand or product through, 138
Fear of Missing Out (FOMO)
  impact on businesses, 30
  meaning of, 29
  problem on real personal life, 30
  in social media, 29
Federal Bureau of Investigation (FBI), 162
Federal Credit Reporting Act (FCRA), 50–51
Federal Trade Commission (FTC), 50
Firefox, 184–185
FlickR, 5
FlicrEdit, 147
Forensics, 203–207
Forgot my Password option, in Facebook, 190
Foursquare, 111
Foursquare application site, 24
Friends
  removal of, 315
  vs followers, 314–315
Frostbox site, 147

G

Gapminder, 28
Gap tweet, 31*f*
Geotags/geotagging, 249
Global positioning system (GPS), 150, 176–177,
  245, 249
Good passwords, 264–265
Google, 27, 61
  removal of content from, 200
Google + , 6, 27, 111
Google Alerts, 83
Google analytics tool, 301
Google App, 187
Google Chrome, 184–186

Google Public Data, 28
Governance of social media, 289–291

H

Hacked/hacking
  accounts, 186–191
  of passwords, 64
  of Sarah Palin email account during US
    presidential election of 2008, 140
  working of accounts which are, 187–188
Hacker, 186
Hacking 101, 64–65, 266–267
Harassment, 202–203, 223
Hard disks wiping, 150
Harvard Business Review Analytics Services
  survey, 10, 13–14
Hash, 64–65
Hashtags, 38, 99
  McDonalds campaign, 99–100
  monitoring of, 299–300
Hazard, of social networking, 67
Health Information Technology for Economic and
  Clinical Health Act (HITECH), 93
Health Insurance Portability and Accountability Act
  (HIPPA) of 1996, 93, 198
Hiding content, in Facebook account page, 133
Hiding events, 248–249
Hijacking, 298–299
Hit Man Scam, 162
Hoaxes, through social media, 104–106
Homemade pornography, 174
HootSuite tool, for content management, 111, 112*f*,
  286, 303*f*
Human Flesh Search Engine, 275–276
Humor, 121
Hypertext Transfer Protocol Secure (HTTPS),
  65–66, 163, 182

I

Industry information, in LinkedIn, 66*f*
Infographics, 28*f*
Information
  acquiring from social media sites, 206–207
  categorization of, 139
  security of, 140
Information leakage, 139–143
  clearity about private things, 139
  by giving more information, 140
  WikiLeaks *see* WikiLeaks
Instagram, 27
  audience visits in, 78
Instant Messaging (IM), 168, 176
Insurance, 203

Intellectual property, 200, 225
International Telecommunication Union report
    (2013), 122
Internet, 161
    addition of social media content to web page,
        117–118
    representation of yourself in, identification of,
        91–92
    users in world, 123*f*
    users of social networking sites, 11*f*
    vs intranet, 80–82
Internet Crime Report (2012), 162, 168
Internet Explorer, 88, 184–185
    deletion of cookies from, 107
    SmartScreen Filter feature in, 185
Internet Service Providers (ISPs), 6, 14–15, 165, 189
Intranet, 25, 75, 80–82
IOS, 158
IP address, 172, 205
IPod, 5–6
ITunes site, 5–6

J

Jammers, 152
Jobvite survey, on referral candidates, 53

L

Lack of control, in use of social media, 287–288
Library of Congress, archiving of tweets on Twitter,
    143
Likes, on Facebook, 271–273
    tracking of, 298–299
LinkedIn, 1–2, 6, 15, 27, 111, 114–115
    account protection with two-step verification
        process, 267–268
    additional information can be added, 59–61
    bogus job offers on, 162
    closing down of account, 313–314
    creation of custom URL on, 58–59
    endorsements and recommendations in, 56–58, 57*f*
    features of, 55–56
    getting people know about your job search, 59
    goldmine for social engineers, 179
    hacking of passwords, 64
    job opportunities in, 56
    limitations on personal information, 59–66
    linking of Twitter to, 114–115
    method of searching for job in, 56
    Pew Internet & American Life Project (2012), 55
    public profiles, 61–63
    requirements for logging, 63
    search, 57*f*
    securing of other settings in account, 65–66

Linking, of content in different sites, 113–118
Location awareness, 245–251
Location-based social networks, 247
Location information, in LinkedIn, 66*f*
Location information removal
    from Facebook, 247–248
    from Twitter, 248
Locking down personal information, 269–273
Lookout Security and Antivirus, 150–151, 152*f*,
    156, 215
Loss of data/equipment, 148–158

M

#MAKEITCOUNT media campaign, 98
Malicious code/malcode, 210
Malicious software, 210–211
Malware, 184–185, 210–216
Malwarebytes, 211–212
Malware Domain List, 89
Marketing to customers, methods of, 22–26
Massively multiplayer online role playing games, 7
McAfee SiteAdvisor, 89
#McDStories campaign, 100*f*
Microblogging, 4–5, 275–276
Microblogs, 4
Microsoft, 42
Microsoft Exchange Server, 150
Microsoft SharePoint, 8, 42, 75, 80–81
Misrepresenting, in internet
    creation of false impression of anonymity, 137
    your business, 137–138
Missing person Tweet, 104*f*
Mistakes
    avoidance in social networking sites, steps
        acronyms and abbreviations in messaging,
            107–108
        netiquette network, 108–109
        oops factors, 106–107
        trolls and flamers people, avoidance of,
            109–110
    during responding to people, 39–41
Mixi, 111
Mobile device management (MDM) software, 158
Mobile device, methods of jamming, 152
MobileIron, 158
Mobile social media, 11–12
Mobile Spy, 176–177
Mobile tagging, 12
Monitoring, 110
    hashtags, 299–300
    social media
        conversation in, 83–85, 294–303
        of multiple sites, 302–303

Monitoring tools, for online safety, 176–177
Moonlighting, 225–226
MoSCoW principle, 74
Mozilla Firefox, 25
Multisite third-party tools, 147–148
MySpace, 6, 15, 22–23, 111

N

Name information, in LinkedIn, 66*f*
National White Collar Crime Center, 162
Netflix tweet, on service outage, 5*f*
Netiquette network
    definition of, 108–109
    rules of, 108–109
Netvibes, 302*f*
Nike's advertising, 98
Noncompete agreements, 226
Noncompliance, with record management
    regulations, 195
Noncorporate devices, 157–158
Nondisclosure agreements, 224
Nonsolicitation agreements, 226
Nonwork computers, 87–88
Norton 360, 214
Norton Anti-virus, 214
Norton Family, 176
Norton Internet Security, 214
Norton Mobile Security, 214
Norton Safe Web, 89–90, 184, 214
Notification settings
    on Facebook, 296*f*
    on Twitter, 297–298

O

Ongoing training, 317
Online game worlds, 7–8
Online safety, teaching of children and teenagers
    about, 175
Online scams, 162
Online social behavior, 219–220
OpenNet Initiative, 119
Opera browser, 184–185
Organization, in social media
    inappropriate use impact on, 144
    need of, 74–75
    people must read policies of, 221–222
    place in, 73–78
    training and policy for employees,
      94–95
    usage in, 75–77
Outdated content, 111–113, 208–209
Overlooked, being, 97, 100–103

P

Packet sniffer, 190
Parental control systems, 176, 238
Passwords, 63–65, 262–268
    bad, 263–264
    checker on Microsoft's safety and security center
      site, 265*f*
    good, 264–265
    hacking of LinkedIn accounts, 64
    procedure for change in LinkedIn accounts,
      63–64
    protection of, tool and tips for, 190*b*
    verification of reset, 267
Payment Card Industry Data Security Standard
    (PCI DSS), 199
Payment Card Industry Security Standards Council
    (PCI SSC), 199
People for the Ethical Treatment of Animals
    (PETA), 99–100
Personal data/equipment, 156–158
Personal profile customization, in LinkedIn, 62*f*
Phishing, 180–181
Phishing filter, 185
Pinboard, 41
Pinterest, 27
    audience visits in, 78
    login through Facebook and Twitter account, 262
Playstation 3 game system, 7–8
Podcasting, 22–23
Podcasts
    definition of, 5–6
    origin of, 5–6
Police use, of social media, 207–210
    defending yourself online, 208
    IACP survey in 2012, 207
    incriminating yourself, 207–208
    outdated content use, 208–209
    use directly to solve crimes, 209–210
Policy(ies)
    definition of, 217
    social media, 217
      acceptable use policy (AUP) *see* Acceptable
        Use Policy (AUP)
      addressing of online social behavior, 219
      enforcement of, 220–221
      impact on existing policies, 222–227
      methods of creation, 218–220
      personal use address, 220
      pros and cons of, 217–218
      reporting of policy violation, 227–228
      users must read the policies, 221–222
Preapproving comments, 278–279

Predators, 175–177
Preexisting accounts, 92
Privacy, 50, 229–230
    checking of apps before installation, 244
        removing apps, 244–245
    checking of site risk, 235–238
        blocking of sites through browser, 237
        parental control software, 238
    concerns in social media, 93–94, 229
    controlling apps, 241–245
        on Facebook, 242–243
    definition of, 92
    of personal and sensitive information, 268
        locking down of personal information, 269–273
    of photos, 249–251
    policies, 197
    protection by legislation, 92–93
    risk of posted personal information on social
        networking sites, 229
    settings in Facebook, 273
    vs safety, 176
Privacyfix
    on chrome browser, 236*f*
    healthbar, 237*f*
Privacy Score tool, 235, 236*f*
Promotion, of social media
    advertisement on sites, 121
    arrangement of contest in sites, 122
    browsing of directories, 122
    through posters in stores, 122–123
Protection yourself
    from social media frauds, 188
    from viruses and malware, 214–215
Protocol, 182
Public domain, 6
Public embarrassment, 128–134
Public sites, 42
Publishing, 110
PyCon hashtag, 227

Q

Questions noting, in Facebook, 178

R

Rainbow tables, 64–65
Ransomware, 211–212
Records retention, 225
Recycling equipment, 149–150
Reddit site, 3–4, 186–187
RedTube, 129
Referrals for job, 52–53
Removal, 110

Reporting
    of fake accounts on Facebook, 261
    inappropriate profiles on LinkedIn, 262
Reporting abuse, 133–134
    methods of, 133–134
Reset passwords verification, 267
Restoration, of lost data, 152–156
Restricted list, in Facebook, 231–232
Restriction, on Facebook posts, 232–234
Retaking control of account, 310–317
Retention content, 143–144
Retrieval of deleted data, wiping of hard disks, 150
Reverse lookups, 206
Reveton, 211
Rich Bride, Poor Bride TV show, 33–34
Right decisions, on use of social media, 85–91
Right to Financial Privacy Act (RFPA), 93
Risk management, 193–196
    laws and regulations for, 196–203
        Digital Millennium Copyright Act (DMCA)
            see Digital Millennium Copyright Act
            (DMCA)
        fair information practice principles, in US,
            198–199
        Health Insurance Portability and
            Accountability Act (HIPPA) of 1996
            see Health Insurance Portability and
            Accountability Act (HIPPA) of 1996
        non-deletion of messages, 205–206
        PCI DS Standard, 199
        privacy policies and terms of service, 197
        Sarbanes-Oxley Act of 2002 *see* Sarbanes–
            Oxley Act of 2002
Risk register, 221*t*
Risk revisited, sources of, 195–196
Risks assessment, steps in, 193–194
Risks, of social media, 127–128, 195
    backups of data, 157
    divorce cases, 129–130
    on posting of contents, 129–131
    sources of, 127–128
        removal of photos and tags from Facebook, 132
        videos removal from YouTube, 131–132
        videos removal from YouTube, 131–132
Romance scams, 168

S

Sandboxing technique, 184–185
SANS Investigative Forensic Toolkit (SIFT), 204
Sarbanes–Oxley (SOX) Act of 2002, 143–144,
    197–198, 220–221
Sarcasm, 121

Scams
bogus job offers on Twitter and LinkedIn, 162
financial motivation behind, 162
grandparent, 162
online, 162
romance, 168
Scareware, 211–212
Scheduling content, 112*f*
Scream TV, 138
Search engines, 27
Secondary employment, organization policies for, 225–226
Second Life, 15
Second Life site, 8
Secure browsing, 163–164
Security, 64–65
of accounts through passwords, 262–268
employees using social media in workplace and its impact on, 67
in Facebook account
issues in, 34*f*
rule in, 49
issue in using social media sites, 17–18
modification of setting in LinkedIn account, 65–66
social media accounts
reviews, 254–255
strategies for protection of, 255–257
tracking of, 254
trade-off of, 253
Self-censorship, 120
Selling equipment, 149–150
Senate Bill 1349, California, 50
Server(s), 6
act as command-and-control (C&C) center, 210–211
corporate network, 42, 48
network web, 65–66, 163
Sexting, 172
Sexual harassment, 223–224
SharePoint 2010, 80–81, 81*f*
Sharing information, 30–34
authenticity of information, 106
restriction on public for, 32–33
Shoulder surfing, 177
Site policies, of social media, 129
Sites, fall under multiple classifications, 8
Skype, 168–169
SmartScreen Filter, 185
Social authority
factors determine, 26
importance in organization, 27
meaning of, 26

Social bookmarking sites, 3–4, 4*f*, 41
Social engineering
associated with conversation, 178
creation of fake sites, 181–186
definition of, 177
methods to use, 177
scams, 177–178
Social media, 285
business of sites, 9*f*
campaigns, 306
categories of, 3
considerations for setting up of, 71–72
dealing with, tools and tips for, 287
definition of, 1–2
features of, 1–2, 11
generation of information through user or brand, 1–2
governance, 289
impact on marketing of brand/ideas, 22–23
implementation of
bringing of key people together, 86–87
remembering technology in equation, 87–91
setting up of corporate goals, 86
opportunities for, 21–22
problems faced by, 16–17
reasons for using, 72–73
information collection, requirements for, 72–73
requirement of successful strategy, conditions for, 14
review of, 289
sites used by small businesses, 10*f*
treatment as cutting edge, 13–16
use by employees, 66–68
use to find employment, 51–59
value of, 8–13
Social Media Marketing Industry Report (2012), 11
Social Media Officer, 14, 91–92, 221*t*, 255, 286, 291
Social media users, 1
Social networking sites, 3
benefits to business, 6–7
definition of, 6
history of, 14–16
impacts of sharing of information on, 18
information people post about themselves in, 229*t*
McKinsey Global Institute study in 2012, 1
security issues with, 17–18
SocialSafe insights, 148*f*, 304*f*
Social security number, 102–103, 162, 179
Social world, 8
SOTI system, 158

SPAM messages, 63, 89–90, 113
Spear phishing, 181
SplashData, 178–179
SQL Server., 153
Stale content, 111–113, 303–304
Stolen phone/tablet, lost, 150–152
Strangers are friends, in social networking sites, 140
Symantec Mobile Management, 158
System restore, use on Windows machine, 211–212

T

Tablet backup, 156
Tagging, 280
    controlling of, 280–281
Tags, 3–4
Terms of service, in social media, 197
Timelines
    hiding of sections in, 281
    stop people to post on, 279–281
TinyURL, 88
Topsy, 84*f*
Tracking
    of dislikes, 299
    of likes on Facebook, 298–299
    of recent login history, 189
Trademark infringement, 200–201
Traditional media, 2
Trending, 112–113
Trojans, 210
Trusted contacts, 190
Tumblr, 5, 27
    audience visits in, 78
Turning off comments, 278–279
TweetDeck, 300
Tweets/tweeting, 26
    false claim during Hurricane Sandy, 136*f*
    gap, 31*f*
    meaning of, 4
    protection of, 234–235
    social-media related, 38
    Twitter application for, 12
Twitter, 1–2, 8, 22–23, 26, 111
    account linkage
        with Facebook, 115–116
        with LinkedIn, 114–115
    account protection with two-step verification process, 267–268
    advanced search feature option in, 85
    audience visits in, 78
    Bill Gates account, 260*f*
    blocking of users in, 240
    bogus job offers on, 162

    deactivation of account, 313
    feed widget, 118*f*
    getting people know about your job search, 59
    location information removal from, 248
    methods of searching in, 85
    service of URL, 88
    trending topics in, 113
    uploading of mature or adult content, 173–174

U

Uniform Resource Locators (URLs), 163
    examination of suspicious, 89–90
    meaning of, 88
    shortened services of, 88, 183–184
United Nations Office on Drugs and Crime (UNODC), 201
United States Federal Trade Commission, 198–199
Untagging, 132
Unused accounts, 311
Upset customer, methods to deal with, 40–41
Urban legends, through social media, 104–106
URLVoid, 89
USA PATRIOT Act of 2001, 186
Usenet, 15
User-generated content, 34
Username for accounts, 309–310

V

Vanity URLs, 309, 310*f*
Video blogging, 5–6
Virtual game worlds, 3, 7
Virtual social worlds, 3, 7
Virtual worlds, 7–8
    benefits of, 8
Viruses, 210–216
Visual.ly tool, 28
Visual Trace Route Tool, 206

W

Web 2.0, concept of, 16
Web-based solutions, for storing data, 155–156
Weblog, 4
Web parts, 80–81
Whaling, 181
Whistle-blowing site, 141
Whopper Sacrifice media campaign, 98–99
Wi-Fi connections, 65–66, 150
Wiki
    importance of, 3
    meaning of, 3
    origin of, 3
WikiLeaks, 140–142
Wikipedia, 3, 16–17, 41–42

Wikitorial, 17
Windows backup, 153–155
WordPress, 85, 111, 241, 301*f*
   addition and removal roles on, 316–317
Workplace, use of social media
   bogged down of network performance, 69
   impact on employees productivity, 68
   security of network, risks on, 68–69
World of Warcraft, 7
World Wide Web, 15–16
Worms, 210

X
X-box game system, 7–8

Y
Yammer site, 42, 81–82, 82*f*
Younger audiences, 79–80
YouTube, 2, 5, 22–23, 27, 129
   videos removal from, 131–132

Z
Zip code field, in LinkedIn, 65